W9-BSD-252

The Catholic Tradition

REV. CHARLES J. DOLLEN
DR. JAMES K. McGOWAN
DR. JAMES J. MEGIVERN
EDITORS

The Catholic Tradition

Mass & the Sacraments

Volume 2

A Consortium Book

Copyright ©1979 McGrath Publishing Company
All rights reserved. No portion of this book may be reproduced without
permission in writing from the publisher.
Manufactured in the United States of America

Library of Congress Card Catalog Number: 79-1977
ISBN: 0-8434-0739-5
ISBN: 0-8434-0725-5 series

The publisher gratefully acknowledges permission to quote from the
following copyrighted sources. In cases where those properties contain
scholarly apparatus such as footnotes, such footnotes have been omitted
in the interest of the general reader.

THE AMERICA PRESS
> Selection from *Mediator Dei*, Encyclical Letter of Pope Pius XII,
> edited by Gerald Ellard, S.J., 1954.

ANDREWS AND McMEEL, INC.
> Pages 107–151 from *The Eucharist* by Edward Schillebeeckx, O.P.,
> translated by N. D. Smith. Copyright © 1968 Sheed and Ward, Inc.
> Reprinted by permission of Andrews and McMeel, Inc.

FORDHAM UNIVERSITY PRESS
> "The Poem of the Liturgy" reprinted by permission of the publisher from
> *The Love of Learning and the Desire for God* by Jean Leclercq, O.S.B.
> (New York: Fordham University Press, 1977), copyright © 1974 by
> Fordham University Press, pp. 287–308.

VERLAG HERDER KG
> Selections from *Penance and the Anointing of the Sick* by Bernard
> Poschmann, translated and revised by Francis Courtney, S.J., © 1964.
> Reprinted by permission of Herder KG.

THE LITURGICAL CONFERENCE
> Pages 46–82 from *Dry Bones* by Robert Hovda, copyright © 1973.
> Reprinted by permission of The Liturgical Conference.

THE LITURGICAL PRESS
> Selection from *Public Worship* by Josef A. Jungmann, S.J., translated
> by Clifford Howell, S.J., 1957; "Sign in the Liturgy" from *Theological
> Dimensions of the Liturgy* by Cyprian Vagaggini, O.S.B., translated by
> Leonard J. Doyle. Copyright ©1959 by The Order of St. Benedict, Inc.
> Reprinted by permission of The Liturgical Press.

MACMILLAN PUBLISHING CO., INC.
Selection from *The Dynamics of Liturgy* by Hans A. Reinhold. Copyright © 1938, 1941, 1943, 1950, 1961 by Hans A. Reinhold. Reprinted with permission of Macmillan Publishing Co., Inc.

FREDERICK R. McMANUS
Chapter 1 from *Sacramental Liturgy* by Frederick R. McManus. Copyright © 1967 by Herder and Herder, Inc. Reprinted by permission of Frederick R. McManus.

THE MISSIONARY SOCIETY OF ST. PAUL THE APOSTLE IN THE STATE OF NEW YORK
Pages 21-32 by Yves Congar from *The Sacraments in General*, Volume 31 of *Concilium*, edited by Edward Schillebeeckx, copyright 1968 by Paulist Fathers, Inc. and Stichting Concilium. Reprinted by permission of Paulist Press.

THE SEABURY PRESS
Pages 38-54 from *Sacramental Reconciliation* by Jean-Marie Tillard, edited by Edward Schillebeeckx, copyright © 1971. Reprinted by permission of The Seabury Press.

SHEED & WARD LTD.
Selections from *A Sacramental Spirituality* by Bernard Häring. Copyright © 1965 Burns & Oates Ltd. and Sheed & Ward, Inc.

UNIVERSITY OF NOTRE DAME PRESS
Chapters 5 and 6 from *Liturgical Piety* by Louis Bouyer, copyright © 1955. Reprinted by permission of University of Notre Dame Press.

Table of Contents

THE CATHOLIC TRADITION: Mass and the Sacraments

Hans Anscar Reinhold
1897-1968

Hans Reinhold was born in Hamburg, Germany, and studied at the Universities of Freiburg, Innsbruck, Münster, and the Pontifical Institute of Archaeology in Rome. He was wounded as an artilleryman in the First World War, and entered the Benedictine monastery of Maria Laach for a while thereafter. But he left there and was ordained a priest for the diocese of Osnabrück in 1925. He came under the influence of Guardini, Herwegen, and Casel, among others, who created in him an awareness of the potential and importance of the liturgy. Assigned to an apostolate to German seamen in Bremerhaven and Hamburg, he began some liturgical experimentation, such as dialogue Mass, Mass facing the people, night celebration of the Easter Vigil, which were startling novelties at the time.

Soon after Hitler came to power, Reinhold's outspoken criticism of the Nazis endangered his life; one day he evaded the Gestapo by bicycling into Holland and from there making his way to England. That was in 1935, and the next year he came to the United States to work for the placement of German Catholic refugees. His reputation for liturgical novelty, however, made him suspect in ecclesiastical circles, but he was finally incardinated into the Archdiocese of Seattle, where he founded a seamen's club, served as a curate, and was pastor at Sunnyside, Washington, from 1944 to 1956.

Reinhold took a leave of absence due to failing health and mounting tension with his bishop. His forthright style and outspokenness caused more alienation than he seemed to realize. Unwanted by many who were threatened by his critical approach, Reinhold was received by Bishop John Wright in Pittsburgh, whom he thanked for this kindness in the book excerpted here.

Reinhold's stimulating writings, especially in Orate Fratres *(later* Worship*), his frequent lectures around the country, and his annual paper at the Liturgical Week sponsored by the Liturgical Conference gave his ideas considerable exposure, gaining a following as well as provoking an opposition for him. He was beyond doubt a major catalyst in the pre-Vatican II controversies about liturgical ideals. Although he lived to see many of his ideas adopted in the conciliar reform, the advance of Parkinson's disease disabled him so that he was unable to take much part in the renewal.*

Pope John XXIII was elected in 1958 and opened Vatican II in 1962. It was in those preparatory years, when few knew for sure what direction the Church was about to take, that Reinhold brought out three little books, climaxing his career, summarizing his insights, contributing his important part to what was to follow. In 1958 came The American Parish and the Roman Liturgy; *1960 produced* Bringing the Mass to the Poeple; *and in 1961* The Dynamics of the Liturgy *made its appearance. Some of the material of this third book had appeared as early as 1938. It consists of eight chapters bringing together much of Reinhold's best work. The following selection consists of the first and most of the second chapter. In "The Beginnings of the Liturgical Movement" we have the account of the origins of renewal as viewed by one of the pioneer participants, while in "The Work of the People" we find his understanding of what the liturgy is and why it is therefore deserving of the effort toward restoration to which Father Reinhold devoted himself more than anything else in his adult life.*

THE DYNAMICS OF LITURGY

THE BEGINNINGS OF THE LITURGICAL MOVEMENT

THE CLOISTER AND SOCIETY

On an afternoon in 1913 the abbot of Maria Laach, in the Eifel Mountains near the Rhine, received four or five young men in one of the parlors of the eight-hundred-year-old monastery. They had asked for an interview because they wanted advice on their spiritual lives. One of them was Paul Simon, another was Professor Hermann Platz of Bonn University, a third was Father Kerkhey who later became preacher at Münster Cathedral and confessor of the whole city, and there was also young Dr. Heinrich Brüning.

Abbot Stotzingen with his customary friendliness asked them to state their problems. He was not a little surprised when he heard what these young laymen and future priests wanted from him. He told that he had a man in his monastery who might be able to help them—a young and very learned monk by the name of Dom Ildefonse Herwegen, who had often talked to him about his problems and who, strangely enough, as far as the abbot could remember, had not only touched upon the same matters but had even used the same terms.

So Dom Herwegen was called, and the young monk and these men of the world found themselves in perfect agreement. Thus began a revival that seized first the intelligentsia of Germany, then spread to the young clergy, invaded parishes and organizations, overcame the prejudices of religious superiors, and is now the consolation of millions.

The case was very simple, and now it seems incomprehensible that anyone could have looked on these endeavors as revolutionary. These men wanted nothing but their legitimate share in the liturgical life of the Church. They wanted to know what "it was all about." They felt the existence of a gap between their personal piety and the official worship on the altar that no one had been able to bridge. They had been sitting patiently through their Sunday Masses, saying their rosaries, singing popular hymns, or listening to the concert-like performance of a first- or second-rate choir. Some of them had even handled a missal in the vernacular—but they could not make head or tail of it even when they were initiated into such subtleties as the "ordo" and even when they did not fail to keep up with the priest.

What had all this to do with their personal happiness, their approach to Almighty God, their sanctification? Were these all dead formulas, relics of antiquity and the Middle Ages, jealously preserved by clerics who did not know themselves why they adhered to such petrified and circumstantial rites in our fast-living and subjectivist times? Or was there any meaning in this odd assortment of anthems, lessons, gospels, and prayers? Could they be used to deepen personal prayer? Could they be resuscitated by the individual and by a community, a community of men and women, children and old people, laborers and students who were not antiquarians and esthetes? Could all this become daily bread for the ordinary Catholic, or was it to be caviar for an élite? Must there continue always to be a clerical track for expresses to heaven while lay people rode slow trains freighted with popular devotions that had little in common with the things behind the altar rail but some general ideas and good intentions? Or was not the Church's prayer and sacrifice really the prayer and sacrifice of the whole Church, that is, all the faithful?

The outcome of this meeting was an invitation to these men and their friends to come back to Maria Laach for Holy Week, 1914. This was the first "Liturgical Week," which developed so amazingly into one of the permanent institutions of German Catholicism and bore such tremendous fruit.

World War I interrupted this new movement. But no sooner was it over than the first of a series of publications appeared. Romano Guardini opened the series, "Ecclesia Orans," with his now famous booklet *The Spirit of the Liturgy.*

For me, when I read this book, the restrictions and commandments that had seemed to be the essence of Catholicism, and that I had defended in fierce and dull despair, vanished before the vision of Christ's Mystical Body and the incredible

4

beauty of His Mystical Life among us through his sacraments and mysteries. For thousands of my Catholic fellow countrymen this book opened a new approach to Catholicism and gave them a deeper understanding and love of our holy Faith. We could hardly wait for the following volumes of the "Ecclesia Orans," Dom Hammenstede's *Liturgy as Experience,* and Dom Casel's two revolutionizing little booklets on the Mass as "Mysterion" and the real meaning of the Holy Canon.

At the same time the best speakers of the abbey, including Abbot Herwegen, who had meanwhile succeeded Abbot Stotzingen, traveled over Germany and spoke to large and small audiences, inviting them to their monastery. They met the leaders of the Catholic youth and intelligentsia, and addressed priests in retreats and conferences. At the same time scientific series devoted to liturgical sources, liturgics, and historical research were initiated under the leadership of Abbot Herwegen, and the cooperation of the best German and foreign historians was enlisted.

The Liturgical Weeks were soon followed by retreats based on the liturgy and on a piety of definitely objective and sacramental character. This example was imitated by other abbeys and religious societies, and finally three great agencies accomplished what a small community of monks could not, a nation-wide popularization. These three agencies were the Akademikerverband, a national union of Catholic university graduates in all professions; the huge Catholic youth organizations with their millions of members; and the Popular Apostolate for Liturgical Revival at Klosterneuburg near Vienna. They embraced the ideas of Maria Laach with profound enthusiasm, and within about fifteen years piety and devotion had been relinked to the "official" worship of the Church and its sacramental and biblical character in a degree that may have been realized only in some golden age of liturgy.

There was a period at the beginning of this liturgical movement when everyone was in such high spirits, especially the young clergy and students, that those who, with however little justification, claimed to stand for sound "tradition" had need to warn against exaggeration. I remember times when young people, in their joy at discovering the superior evangelical beauty of the liturgical "world," wanted to abolish altogether such popular substitutes as the Stations and the Rosary. But this purist fervor was never very widespread and never deserved those bitter attacks launched against a "new heresy" by narrow and overanxious "guardians of the Faith."

In spite of my own enthusiasm for the Church's prayer, I was very skeptical when I arrived at Maria Laach in 1920. One of the novices showed me the crypt of the glorious old Romanesque abbey church and pointed out that the lay brothers and novices had their community Mass there every morning, at which they recited the Gloria and Credo in common with the celebrant, replied in unison to his acclamations, and took part in an Offertory procession, bringing their own altar bread to the altar rail—thus reviving a custom that died out only a few centuries ago and that is now replaced by the certainly more prosaic money collection at the Offertory.

Since I was on my way back from Rome, I was not shocked at the fact that the altar was facing the people, because I had seen this in all the major churches in Rome and I thought this was much more sensible than for the priests to turn their back to those with whom they were acting the *Sacrum Mysterium* of Our Lord's Sacrifice. I thought, however, that at the abbey they were too romantic, just "crazy about vestments and all the external paraphernalia"—an attitude I had acknowledged with an indulgent smile in certain high Anglican communities who built themselves cozy little monasteries in Italian Romanesque and established themselves like Sicilian *curati.*

But I had been rash. The next morning at Mass I discovered that this was really the form that enabled me as a layman truly to share in the Church's sacrifice. This form flowed quite naturally from the real meaning of the Mass; it was almost suggested by its ceremonies and texts. The amazing thing was only this—why on earth had it not been thought of before? The atmosphere was normal and manly, and the gray-bearded old lay brothers were just as happy and at home in "their" Mass as the fervent young students fresh from the universities.

Two little incidents show that things did not always go so smoothly as might have been expected. Wild rumors had been spread throughout Germany, especially among the clergy. These monks of Maria Laach had invented a new liturgy, had disregarded

6

our good old (and comfortable) traditions, were advocating a lay priesthood that would destroy the respect for the priesthood proper and that almost smacked of Luther's doctrine of a universal priesthood.

One beautiful afternoon the seven mighty bells of our old minister rang, and a limousine drove up to the gatès. In it was the Cardinal Archbishop of Cologne. Apparently "Headquarters" had asked him to look into the matter and to find out what sort of *Mysteria* the monks and their guests were performing. Well, the result of this visit was that next morning a certain member of the Sacred College had tears in his eyes and that a year or so later he stood behind a portable altar in his own huge cathedral saying the *missa recitata* with the whole congregation. And from then on, at all the annual Catholic congresses in Germany, with their ten thousands of faithful attending, the Nuncios have said the Mass facing the congregation, and very often reciting the appropriate prayers with all those present.

As a natural consequence of this return to Bible and liturgy, very soon the popular substitutes and the hitherto extraliturgical practices and devotions became more imbued with liturgical and biblical spirit, and much of the sentimental and pseudo-baroque trash of the late nineteenth century dropped out. Once familiar with the central mystery of the Church, the faithful soon demanded more of the true bread of Christ. Baptisms, which hitherto had appeared to be a legal performance in a corner of the church, with much mumbling, salt, and other strange practices, regained in its performance its old majestic beauty, and many dioceses gave as many texts as possible in the vernacular. This happened, *mutatis mutandis,* with Extreme Unction, Matrimony, and Holy Orders. People no longer liked fifteen-minute Masses, and rushing through other ceremonies. And the clergy were glad to see their flock participate in the most vital and essential things of Catholic life. The heart of the faithful in their religious life began to beat in rhythm with the Church, or, as Guardini has put it, the Church awoke in the souls of the faithful.

The hierarchy hesitated only a short time to acknowledge this popular movement inaugurated by monks. Of course, exaggeration made some bishops cautious, and there was opposition from the older generation among people and clergy who had heard wild stories about self-appointed reformers and innovators. Some people tried to construe an incompatibility between extra-liturgical, so-called popular devotions and liturgical prayer, fearing from their own legalistic attitude toward liturgy that a cold and soulless piety might destroy what they thought to be the real food for Catholic souls. But this never happened. From time to time, certain ascetic schools have objected to the "free and easy" ascetism built on this less methodical and less technical attitude toward sanctification and have uttered grumbling warnings. But they underestimated the sound religious schooling of the leaders, who had an older tradition to defend than these men of the *Devotio Moderna* and the nineteenth century.

Those hard-working men, Abbot Herwegen, Dom Hammenstede, and Dom Casel with their confrères, and with the assistance of other orders, priests and laymen, threw open the doors of the sanctuary to God's people, a chosen generation, a kingly priesthood, a holy nation to offer up spiritual sacrifices.

CHAPTER 2

THE WORK OF THE PEOPLE

A SOCIAL LEAVEN?

Catholics and Protestant Christians outside the Anglo-Saxon orbit often blame us English-speaking Catholics for being "activists." The classical case was the heresy of "Americanism" at the turn of the century. It is a common assumption of the more profound Christian critics in Latin, Slavic, and Teutonic countries of the old Continent, and perhaps also in Latin America and Asia, that Catholicism in the Anglo-Saxon countries (not to speak of Protestantism) has lost an element of Christianity which is best expressed by the word "contemplative" although this term is as unfit to cover the whole complex as any other would be. There is much more involved than just contemplation itself.

It is the whole mood of cultural and civilizational optimism to which objection is taken. To these observers our "version" of Christ's religion, has all but—the cross. To them we, especially we in America, seem to fall into the ancient trap of millenarianism, confusing Jesus' message of spiritual redemption with earthly prosperity, and seeing in His life, since He rose from the dead, a rewarding "success story," while forgetting that His resurrection was, though a historical fact, in a new "aion" not accessible to mortal man in his life.

Our critics feel that the optimism with which we aggressively tackle the world to make it over is shallow and is the result of another shortcoming: a disregard for truth, for doctrine, for clarity. In their eyes we are so eager to go out and get going that we lose sight of the primacy of the "logos" over the "ethos" (to quote Guardini). And the result? The paradoxes of life, the intellectual mystery surrounding all matters of faith, are ignored, soft-pedaled: the "obscure light" becomes a very trite, banal, and obvious thing, as it were a neon tube substituting for the sun.

Anglo-Saxon Christianity, even in its Catholic form, appears to all the rest of the world as entirely too practical, too efficient, too ethical a thing to be commendable. It is too fond of immediate results, of statistics, of building programs and pat answers, and too easily satisfied with solutions. Our critics fear that in centuries to come so much of the practical, Protestant ethos will have been assimilated that we will become a "do-gooding," charitable service organization, with a dogma and liturgy on a level with the weird ritual of Masons and Shriners and a moral code like a libertine perversion of Methodism or Lutheranism.

Reinhold Niebuhr once stated that we live in a country where churches become sects and sects churches. By this he meant, if I understood him rightly, that even the majesty and universality of the Catholic Church are hard to assert in our climate: for the smallest group of crackpots and fanatics not only (and justly) finds the right to speak and teach, but because the majesty of tradition, of an integrated structure of doctrine, of well defined laws and discipline, of cultural accomplishment count for nothing in the face of zeal and aggressiveness is accepted without credentials as an equal, or worse, as a foreign, strange, and dangerous "sect."

How long will Catholics be able to maintain their claim in this climate? Are the devices now used, often borrowed from others, like the publicity we so generously achieve, sufficient? Are we really made for competition in an atmosphere of Bible-quoting puritanism? Is the claim of having answers others do not have sufficient? These are questions that worry the responsible leaders.

After this introduction one might come to the conclusion: If all this be so, if we need something to offset our alleged activism, our optimism so purely spiritual, then, as a part of a whole, our liturgical movement is one of the best antidotes. For what could be more antiutilitarian than to express worship of God in solemnity? What could heal us more than Pelagian self-perfection, trust in human activity and achievement, than the freely given graces of the sacraments?

Yet more: Why bring in sociological references which will only make it appear as if even the liturgy is being used to bolster activism? Let us restore the liturgy in its fullness to the people, as outlined by our Holy Father, and social action will flow from it quite naturally—as someone has said not long ago. If activism is our peculiar danger (and Guardini's words, written back in 1918, show that it is a very real danger even to our critics in Europe), is it wise to provide it with another source?

I think that chance must be taken. It would be utterly unrealistic not to do so. We all know of daily communicants who fail to be a witness in their circles and whose only mark of lived religion seems to be their daily Holy Communion and what it involves. They are in good faith. They are earnest. They make great sacrifices by going to Communion and by "staying in the state of grace" week after week, year after year. One cannot track down the workings of grace and their nearness to God; their transformation into members of Christ cannot be registered under microscopes or with chemico-electric waves on charts. Something is bound to happen to them and to those with whom they live, on which their daily divine repast has had a determining influence. But still: the quietism latent in their attitude, unknown to themselves, frustrates the fullest effectiveness of the Holy Eucharist. In a bold image: it is like high-octane gas in a broken-down one-cylinder motor.

After all, grace presupposes and perfects nature. Which means, reversed, that we are obliged to "work on nature" and do what we can to give grace a broader, deeper, and more sensitive surface to tackle. And this involves not only, as activism wants us to believe, the ennobling of will and emotions, but also the broadening and deepening of our natural knowledge. Thomas à Kempis' statement that it is better to have contrition than to be able to define it is only good as far as it goes: to have contrition plus the most profound knowledge of true contrition is better still! There is an objective scale of values in the realm of being that many spiritual writers disregard for the sake of pouring comfort into the hearts of those whose invincible ignorance needs comforting.

If then there are sociological and social implications in our sacramental system as embodied in our liturgy, we should make much of them! The bride-and-groom relationship of the soul and Jesus in Communion, or the aspect of divine visitation in the Holy Eucharist, are certainly sublime ideals for any soul, and highly commendable. But that is not all there is to it! The Lord's Supper is also, even primarily, a banquet and a sacrifice. That the altar rail is full of people like myself is not just accidental, but part and parcel of the visible sign, signifying a reality of this sacrament. The poor at my side must be an alarm to me. If the colored parishioners are discriminated against, the sacrament must inflame me. The beauty of the liturgy and its order must be a thorn in my side if at the same time the socio-economic order of my country is a mockery of the Gospel and if Christ's friends, the poor, are ignored while the well washed, well dressed, well housed and respectable are given practical preference as the "good" Catholics.

Justice and charity cannot be excluded: the liturgy carried out to perfection, not only exteriorly, but even with the knowledge and spiritual disposition striven after by the best liturgists, will be a tinkling cymbal in the ears of God unless the ones who celebrate it continue to glorify the same Lord in the economic, social, political, and cultural fields.

These implications simply don't take care of themselves. The sacraments challenge our whole nature: body, will, reason. If we were Quakers we might be satisfied with God in our hearts only and exclusively—although *they* aren't, as their good deeds show. But since we are members of that Mystical Body which prolongs the Incarnation, the state of the body social is a liturgical concern.

11

So in the name of Baptism and Confirmation, of Penance, of Eucharist and Holy Orders, of Matrimony and of the Unction for eternal glory, in the name of their garb of prayers, rites, and readings, we who claim to live by them must be found in the forefront of those who work for a new society built according to the justice and charity of Christ.

Of course, no confusion of function is intended: housing, care of health, interracial justice, the living wage and family subsidies are not topics for Liturgical Weeks. Nor is it a directly liturgical concern to decide whether "free enterprise" can exist the Roepke-Hayek-Mises way, or whether a society compounded of social and individual ownership is the solution for our complex social age. These are questions for the Social Action movement, to be solved according to the progressively developed teaching of papal encyclicals. But a disinterested liturgical movement, or even a mildly concerned one, would be as worthy of suspicion as the one castigated in *Mediator Dei* as archaic. One ought not to demand more participation for the people, more ways for the laity to share in the conscious celebration of Christ's mysteries, unless it makes us better Christians. And this means that we have a concern, or rather, an anxiety in our heart, to see all realms of life permeated by the Savior's Spirit.

Whether the New-Deal-like legislation of the past or another method to establish the brotherhood of man is right is subject to debate. But to withdraw into a fools' paradise fenced in by rubrics, and to tend vestments and rites, to give blessings to things of the earth without making them serve the just and right way, cannot be debated: it is wrong.

Dom Virgil Michel and the movement inspired by his leadership saw this from the beginning, and the movement never lost itself in romantic dreams of sacral empires, of societies made up of sacred estates, of crowns and coronations. It looked forward, well knowing that Utopia would never become real and that the kingdom of Christ fully realized is an event, not of the year A.D. 2000 or 3000, but of the post-parousia. As in the lives of the saints, it is not the achievements but the heroic degree of virtue with which we strive that constitutes our task.

Between shallow activism and naive optimism, this-worldly and natural, on the one hand, and, on the other, awareness of our duty to lay down our lives for justice and charity's sake in order to implement what we do in sacred signs, there is a world of difference. The same men and women who beg for more vernacular, who strive for sanctity through a more intense living in the sacramental world of the liturgy and through their ascetic efforts, must be the ones who not only give alms—person to person or in drives—but who help unions, sit on employers' councils and housing committees, in interracial groups and Catholic Action centers, who campaign for medical services for the strata that cannot afford them, who oppose demagoguery and injustice to the freedoms needed by man, and make the cause of enslaved nations a matter of their own heart. It is not much use to shout about the "collective tendencies" in industrial society if we don't want to pay the price for a more individualistic form, which is a lower standard of living. That means that we must not be content with consecrating individuals; we must now tackle whole groups and promote the concept of justice that necessarily accompanies this new situation.

A refusal to do so would amount to setting the clock back. A Christian who looks forward to the parousia cannot act thus.

THUNDERSTORM RELIGION

We hear a great deal about the shrinking of the religious sphere in human lives. I am not talking about our fellow Christians whose entire religious practice consists in appearing in church to be "hatched, matched, and dispatched." The Church has always had them with her, like the physically poor. Nor do I allude to that ever-growing number of men and women, young and old, who seem to have been born without a *potentia obedientialis*, in plain English, without an organ for religion. They are often nice and decent people, yet they seem to be incarnate ghosts of an order different from our own. They give you a blank stare when you indicate that faith and religious practice mean more to you than just a lovable or detestable whim of your mind.

I am talking about sincerely practicing Catholics and other religious people who believe in God and a supernatural end and aim of our lives. Even their religion has shrunk extensively, and in a dozen different ways.

Their prayer life, once rich and all-embracing, is now reduced to a set of half a dozen formulas. They can't speak to God unless they recite and repeat Our Fathers and Hail Marys. God is the "great bureaucrat" to whom you submit your applications, which appear the more urgent the longer they are. You must see forms stabilized by tradition and custom. You don't sing hymns and psalms to God, nor do you use the language of your own heart. We have become religiously inarticulate.

Still another shrinkage and impoverishment can be observed: the language of most of our devotions has become poor because of overstatement, superlatives, and the tendency to be effusive and gushy. Its province has narrow boundaries of feeling, narrower boundaries of reason, and no cosmic character at all. Most of our devotions speak the language and think the thoughts of the eighteenth century. Almost all of our hymns are on the sentimental side.

A more serious shrinkage is that of dogmatic consciousness. We live on a few crumbs from the table of tradition and revelation. Moralism and pragmatism have overtaken us, in spite of a certain counteremphasis by men like Karl Adam, de Lubac, Guardini, and Rahner. Those aspects of our sacraments that fit into this picture of moralism and pragmatism, symptoms of a bourgeois mind, are the only ones we appreciate. The loftier ones, born from a rich and full appreciation of the whole sacramental system, are gone to live a paper life in dogma books.

Naturally this has happened to our liturgy too. Most of the *Pontificale* and *Rituale*, the *Graduale* and *Vesperale* is never done or sung. All we have is some field baggage in a knapsack, while the trunks are locked in a dusty attic. We go up there once in a while to look at them. We point to these hidden and forgotten treasures for apologetic reasons, but we don't *use* them. A half-hour for Mass, which is no longer a solemn rite of celebration but either a show or a commodity for our subjective complement or a means of acquiring something for ourselves, together with some abbreviated daily prayers, a few concentrated attacks on ourselves in missions, retreats, parades, novenas, and mammoth congresses—these are our modern substitutes for the rich, organic life that embraced and carried our ancestors to eternal glory.

Why is this so? Because we are disoriented. Religion has unwittingly been dislocated. It is not so much bad will, lack of interest, or intentional disregard. It began long ago. The sphere of the supernatural has been shriveling in our minds and, since acting always follows being, it shrank in our practical lives too. The materialist says that religion is only a childish attempt to explain and endure nature. According to him science has done away with its necessity. Man understand now that a thunderstorm is a purely natural thing, a discharge of electricity, aero-physics, and what not, and not a grandiose manifestation of God's anger. A flash of lightning neither hits arbitrarily nor is it a moral weapon of God's justice. We don't yet know the complicated formula for every individual flash but we know the general theory.

What seemed to be a very moody thing, the weather, is something that ultimately is governed by iron laws and hard facts: the stars, air, electricity, pressures, the sun, and a thousand other factors determine it with iron necessity. It only seems to be whimsical. It really is very reasonable, and if we knew all its components and were able to weigh and measure them, we could predict the weather for July 4, 1972. God is not constantly meddling with it, they say. He will not change it because the sodality has a picnic, or the parish has a procession, or Hitler needs it for a show or a battle. To our fathers nature was not only a revelation of God's wisdom, beauty, power, goodness, and justice, but it shared His supernatural, superrational "mysteriosity" in some way. Then came the age of science, and the "mystery" began its retreat. Everything became an object of chemistry, physics, astronomy, and mathematics. Now we can make gold out of iron, at least theoretically, without being suspected of having the devil as our partner.

Psychoanalysis did the rest. Even the functions of dreams have been recognized. Of course, a great deal of misinterpretation has occurred. Freud was wrong in many things, but on the whole his thesis has been accepted even by Christian psychology.

Thus "secularism" has superseded what I should like to call good old thunderstorm religion. We seem to need God for only so few things nowadays, the things we can't cope with ourselves: moral failure, metaphysical blues, and cultural hangovers. The more we know, the less we seem to need Him. Thus our religious consciousness and practice, our popular piety and pulpit theology, lag sadly behind our times. Everywhere we seem to be on the defensive, losing ground not only in public but also in the souls of our faithful. We retreat further and further, become more and more minimalistic in every respect, hoping secretly that this will blow over as did Nero's persecution, the migration of nations, the Dark Ages, heresies, and revolutions. We seem to say: "Let us just sit tight, and through sheer force of numbers, through tradition and inertia, we shall simply outlive them. They are dying out anyhow, through birth control, at a faster rate than we. We still have some brakes to rely on that they do not have. The siege will be over someday." I don't say that this is a conscious strategic plan of action, but it seems to be a subconscious certainty: it happened before. "The gates of hell, and so on . . ." Some of us meet the situation differently by resentment and escape: science is no good, overrated, uncertain, contradictory. We are romantics and medievalists. The golden age once was; it will come again. Nicolai Berdyaev and others sell us this theory, thinking, of course, of the great features of that era: its art, its philosophy, its saints, and its "world conception," closed, rational, secure, well integrated in faith and God. But although they call it "new," it is all an attempt to set the clock back because we are late.

We do not want it. It would be distrust in the power of the Kingdom of God. It would be a sin against the Spirit. Science has brought us truths, and even purely natural truth makes us free. Christ consecrated the universe through His advent. This world consecration has to go on. We cannot lay down our tools and weapons because we are tired of the breath-taking advance of progress, because of the tragic and sanguinary failures it constantly suffers, or because we have lost our orientation and have reduced religion to a commodity serving those aspects of life that progress *as yet* does not satisfy. Mere "salvation religion" degenerates into its own shadow of being an escape. Religion's consecratory and sacerdotal aspect has to be reinstated to disprove agnosticism and materialism. Present-day Catholicism is awakening, but is not yet really alive to its task. The Popes have indicated the general direction, but the Church responds only slowly. The liturgical movement is its most profound and radical response. It involves a fundamental change and frees us from our present negative attitude, our minimalism in doctrine, our insincere, halfhearted attitude toward true progress, our *ressentiment*, our lack of rational orientation. If we are not able to warm the new, cold, immense universe science has discovered with our faith and charity, we shall have failed our times. A brave, new faith and charity are necessary, built on the original mysteries of Christ.

THE DEXTERITY OF MISSING THE POINT

It is hard to remember the many witty and trenchant remarks of Chesterton, but I seem to recollect his saying somewhere: "It is remarkable how some people have an unfailing ability to miss the point." He may have said this in a mood of exasperation while he tried to make a point with some dissident brother on a matter of Catholic doctrine. But you don't have to be a heretic to have this ability—there are plenty of people among our own who are endowed with this striking and bewildering talent. Nobody defending the basic or even marginal aspects of the liturgical movement can long remain unaware of this.

There is the good man who inveighs against altars facing the people. As I understand it, taught by those who are experts in rubrical matters, the problem is simple. The general rubrics of the missal consider such an altar as one of the two possibilities. Historically, at least in Rome whence we received our own liturgy, this position seems to be older than our present custom, but neither could be called the "correct" one in an exclusive way; for there are good reasons and established tradition for each. It is obviously the right of the local ordinary to decide which is more appropriate in our day and will serve the people and the liturgy best.

But there seemingly is no end to fighting the altar facing the people with arguments such as: the Holy See frowns on the practice (which would, incidentally, put the Holy Father under the embarrassing obligation of frowning for hours every time he descends to one of his basilicas to sing Holy Mass). Or the other one, that you need permission from Rome. Or the one that it detracts from the celebrant's devotion (which presupposes that the average priest regards the Mass as his private and intimate devotion).

The weightiest argument is always that of *"admiratio populi"* (astonishment of the faithful), understood as if you should always leave the churchgoing public with the comfortable idea that there is no better way of doing things than the way they are being done. But there is also a good *"admiratio populi,"* created by the proper authority as was the case when Pope Pius X advanced the age of first Communion, and when Pius XII gave us psalms we could understand, the power to confirm in emergencies, the new Holy Week, and other things that made people reflect and ask questions. The argument for or against, in the matter of the altar facing the people, is solely one of expediency and proper procedure. All others bark up the wrong tree.

The vernacular movement runs into the same sort of argumentation. Answered a hundred times, someone who has never heard the argument will parade the same old hobbyhorse as others before him. Among them is sure to be the one that goes something like this: "It is painful to listen to the average priest's hasty pronunciation, and luckily most of them whisper so they do not disturb the devotion of the attendants. Now just imagine some priest bellowing the English text from the altar, possibly with a French or German accent or a juicy Irish brogue."

Then there is what the later Father Gosling called the argument *"ex tourismo,"* in other words: When you go to China you will hear the familiar (*sic!*) Latin and feel at home at once (probably because you understand about as much of it as of Chinese). Or, to mention the other horn of the dilemma: What will the English-speaking priest do when he travels in Iraq or Sicily? Although we never dreamed of suggesting that Rome forbid the use of Latin missals, but only that the mother tongue be permitted for those parts of the Mass that are meant for the congregation at parish Mass and in parishes only, the opponents always assume that the vernacularists want to pour out the baby with the bath. A Latin missal will come into its own in such a case: the traveling priest will use it for his private Mass. Seems sensible and simple to me.

Hans Anscar Reinhold

Hardly has this been explained, then out come all the other reasons: the everlasting claim that the Mass is a mystery and therefore demands a dead, mysterious language. Why this should apply to collect, gospel, and epistle I for one cannot see. Then comes the claim that Latin is a necessary safeguard of unity. That the use of Latin in the liturgy is "a manifest and beautiful sign of unity . . . in a considerable portion of the Church" is clear enough, and has been explicitly stated by the Holy Father (*Mediator Dei*, n. 60). But it is equally clear that the Eucharist, the sacraments, and the Creed, not even mentioning the Holy See itself, are the really necessary and effective symbols of unity. Else, what about the Catholics of Greek, Old Slavonic, and other rites? Some insist that Latin in itself is sacred, more musical, and better adapted to worship than any modern language. This is very much a matter of personal opinion and would hardly stand close scrutiny. Or do we really claim that the Lord's Prayer in English is not as sacred as in a foreign and obsolete tongue?

It would be a waste of time to continue. When Rome changed from Greek to Latin, it changed from the language of the few to the language of the many, in other words, to vernacular. Since the Holy See has officially declared that a partial use of the mother tongue in the liturgy is beneficial, there is only one *problem* involved: the problem of making the change in the right fashion: and it is on this score that we can have sensible arguments and exciting ones. We should argue about the amount of vernacular, the quality of the translation, the way to prepare the people for a change, the replacing of spurious and obsolete reasons for Latin in our catechisms with more adequate ones (for example, tradition), the best manner of making our wishes known to our hierarchy, and the mode of transition.

The problem, as I see it, is big enough without sham arguments. The departure from a tradition of sixteen hundred years and the thorny question of making the right change at the right time and in the right way constitute formidable tasks: granted. But I personally feel that the reasons for the change and against all-Latin are more urgent and that Rome knows well enough how to make changes prudently. But I am willing to discuss the merits of true arguments. What bothers me is the dexterity with which so many miss the point and drag in unreasonable reasons.

This same attitude comes to mind every time I instruct a convert concerning the Holy Eucharist. There are, thank God, always those who scrutinize what they are being offered and who want reasons. Their argument is then: "Father, Jesus said in Matthew, 'All of you drink of this,' and in Mark it says, 'they all drank of it,' and St. Paul (1 Cor. 11:25) definitely states that this 'cup is the new covenant in my blood; do this. . . .' " (The text of our missal follows the explicit command of St. Matthew: "Take and drink ye all of it.")

Father Yves Congar, O.P., in his great work *True and False Reform in the Church*, says that the use of the chalice for the people "was not a question of dogma, and the Holy See will end by allowing the use of the chalice." And yet, when you look at the average catechism, this point of discipline and expediency is made a point of dogma. The use of the chalice was never "abolished" by any decree. Like all such changes, it came about as gradually as a geological change. Reasons were many, among them a shift of dogmatic emphasis, but this was hardly the most powerful driving force. And yet it would seem that way, when you read our ordinary means of instruction. If you say that the *reason* for giving Communion under one species only is that Christ is present, whole and entire, under the species of bread, you will once in a while get the puzzled question: "Then why did Jesus institute two species and add the command to drink?" The answer that two species were needed for the Sacrifice but not for Communion is a reasonable one and will be accepted; but is it the best we can do?

The true reasons, the historical ones, were those of convenience and reverence (difficulty in administering the sacrament to large crowds, fear of spilling the sacred species, and some others). These reasons could never have prevailed had not the dogmatic emphasis on the background truth—as developed during the age of scholasticism—conditioned the minds for a change. When rebellious minds like Hus, Wycliffe, Luther, Zwingli, and Calvin linked this question with heresy and schism, what Father Congar calls the "rightist" and the "Spanish" attitude prevailed, and the Church protected the recent tradition as legitimate.

Moreover, the partial theology that concerns itself largely with the Real Presence, an emphasis thrust on the Church by heresies, is not the complete approach to this mystery. Eucharist as banquet, as sacrifice, as the center of the Mystical Body, is much wider and larger, and in this wider and larger view the real proportions are restored.

No loyal Catholic will doubt the power of the Church to rule and govern. If the Church saw fit to withhold one species of the Blessed Sacrament for valid reasons (as she previously had substituted the less onerous baptism by pouring for the fuller rite of immersion), a loyal son of the Church accepts this disciplinary change. But it is an unenlightened and poor conception of loyalty to use dogmatic arguments to justify what may be temporary. Once a thing is dogmatically established, no Pope or general council can restore the initial state. Could Pius X have restored the true conception of the Holy Eucharist if infrequent Communion had been based on dogmatic reasons instead of discipline?

The Church is not a fossil, but a living organism. Nor is she a skeleton, but a Body with a skeleton, if one may use this image. She lives, and a living organism adapts itself. Should the Holy See judge that the twentieth century Catholic needs an even fuller Eucharist and would be more deeply immersed in Eucharistic spirit by partaking of both species of the sacred banquet, an appeal to the wrong reasons now would make it practically impossible to adjust the sacramental practice to the potential demands of sacramental completeness. It is perhaps beside the point that under each of the species we have the complete Christ— a truth no Christian doubts: the point may be the completeness of signification.

A concatenation of historical causes in which dogmatic links provided firm support brought about this change. We should defend the right of the Church to adapt discipline to successive ages, but if we try to prove too much we do harm. Therefore we should leave the dogmatic justification in right proportion. Otherwise we are not only right for the wrong reasons, but commit the Apostolic See to positions only the Pope and a general council can take up. We should not forget that perfectly orthodox Catholics in union with Rome to this day give both species and that any Latin Catholics may go to Holy Communion in such churches; that the chalice in some instances was given to the people as late as the late fifteenth century; that the Council of Trent even allowed reintroduction of this use in Austria and other countries for a time; and that the rubric, prescribing the chalice of ablution for the laity—though now out of use and obsolete—is still in our books.

To be sure the issues mentioned above—the vernacular, the altar facing the people, and the very remote and in-actual question of the two species—are brought in for arguing the point that many people attack issues for the wrong reasons. The liturgical movement in America has made none of these issues it own. The last one has not even been mentioned, nor, to be truthful, even been thought of. I could have brought up popular participation in high Mass or dialogue Mass just as well. But I felt these three instances were more illuminating than any others, and apt illustrations of "dexterity in missing the point."

Pope Pius XII
1876-1958

Eugenio Pacelli was born in 1876, the son of the dean of the Vatican lawyers. He was ordained in 1899, and taught in the Roman Seminary until entering the papal secretariat of state at the call of Cardinal Gasparri. His task during World War I was the supervision of prisoner exchange and care of the wounded. In 1917 he was sent as papal nuncio to Bavaria and remained in Munich despite the turmoil in which his life was threatened. After concluding a Concordat with Bavaria in 1925, he was sent to Berlin, but upon Cardinal Gasparri's death in 1929, Pacelli was recalled to Rome to succeed him as secretary of state. He traveled to South America in 1934 and North America in 1936, and in the conclave of 1939 was elected pope on the first ballot.

As Pope Pius XII, Pacelli put his impress upon two decades of Catholic life. An aristocrat, an intellectual, a man of vast interests and many talents, he led the Church through difficult days. He surpassed all his predecessors in both the volume and scope of his teaching, giving nearly 1,000 allocutions on a broad array of topics. But his place in Catholic history will probably hinge, more than anything else, on his three greatest encyclical letters: on the Bible (Divino Afflante Spiritu, 1943), on the Church (Mystici Corporis, 1943), and on the Liturgy (Mediator Dei, 1947). In all three he manifested his awareness of what was happening in the Church and managed to promote all three movements, which were viewed by many with more than a little suspicion at the time.

It has become commonplace to refer to Mediator Dei *as the "Magna Charta" of the liturgical movement. As is evident from the earlier authors represented in this volume, that movement began outside of official circles in response to felt needs within the Christian community. For long it was actively opposed or ignored by many bishops and others in influential positions. The great significance of the encyclical was that it for the first time presented an official statement of the theology of the liturgy, tying it directly to those principles set forth in* Mystici Corporis. *In the eyes of many the liturgy had been reduced to rubrics and rituals. This papal teaching made it impossible to maintain such reductionism for the future.*

Mediator Dei *condemns various extremes and aberrations, but its real importance lies in the positive principles set forth. It is a careful study of the true nature of the Christian liturgy and how it is meant to enrich the lives of those who participate in it. It is just as critical of those who are indifferent to the liturgy as it is of those who go to extremes.*

The document has six main sections. 1) The Introduction puts the stamp of approval on all that is best in the liturgical movement, emphasizing the theological dimensions that makes the liturgy the chief activity of the Church in its union with Christ. 2) The Nature, Origin and Development of the liturgy are then dealt with, especially its "incarnational" quality, combining internal dispositions and external rites, personal prayer and public worship, engaging the body and elevating the soul. 3) The Mass is placed in the center as the apex of Christian life and worship, and from this perspective the need for full, intelligent participation is readily derived. The need for total renewal was inherent in the logic here embraced. 4) The Divine Office is explained as the prayer of the Church, and 5) the Liturgical Year is viewed as a present reliving of the mysteries of Christ. 6) Pastoral suggestions of a practical nature round out this unusual and important document that was to be so influential in carrying the liturgical movement into its next stages on the road to Vatican II.

MEDIATOR DEI

INTRODUCTION

Mediator between God and men and High Priest who has gone before us into heaven, Jesus the Son of God quite clearly had one aim in view when He undertook the mission of mercy which was to endow mankind with the rich blessings of supernatural grace. Sin had disturbed the right relationship between man and his Creator; the Son of God would restore it. The children of Adam were wretched heirs to the infection of original sin; He would bring them back to their heavenly Father, the primal source and final destiny of all things. For this reason He was not content, while He dwelt with us on earth, merely to give notice that redemption had begun, and to proclaim the long-awaited Kingdom of God, but gave Himself besides in prayer and sacrifice to the task of saving souls, even to the point of offering Himself, as He hung from the cross, a Victim unspotted unto God, to purify our conscience of dead works, to serve the living God. Thus happily were all men summoned back from the byways leading them down to ruin and disaster, to be set squarely once again upon the path that leads to God. Thanks to the shedding of the blood of the Immaculate Lamb, now each might set about the personal task of achieving his own sanctification, so rendering to God the glory due to Him.

2. But what is more, the divine Redeemer has so willed it that the priestly life begun with the supplication and sacrifice of His mortal body should continue without intermission down the ages in His Mystical Body which is the Church. That is why He established a visible priesthood to offer everywhere the clean oblation which would enable men from East to West, freed from the shackles of sin, to offer God that unconstrained and voluntary homage which their conscience dictates.

3. In obedience, therefore, to her Founder's behest, the Church prolongs the priestly mission of Jesus Christ mainly by means of the sacred liturgy. She does this in the first place at the altar, where constantly the sacrifice of the cross is represented and, with a single difference in the manner of its offering, renewed. She does it next by means of the sacraments, those special channels through which men are made partakers in the supernatural life. She does it, finally, by offering to God, all Good and Great, the daily tribute of her prayer of praise. "What a spectacle for heaven and earth," observes Our predecessor of happy memory, Pius XI, " is not the Church at prayer! For centuries without interruption, from midnight to midnight, the divine psalmody of the inspired canticles is repeated on earth; there is no hour of the day that is not hallowed by its special liturgy; there is no stage of human life that has not its part in the thanksgiving, praise, supplication and reparation of this common prayer of the Mystical Body of Christ which is His Church!"

4. You are of course familiar with the fact, Venerable Brethren, that a remarkably widespread revival of scholarly interest in the sacred liturgy took place towards the end of the last century and has continued through the early years of this one. The movement owed its rise to commendable private initiative and more particularly to the zealous and persistent labor of several monasteries within the distinguished Order of Saint Benedict. Thus there developed in this field among many European nations, and in lands beyond the seas as well, a rivalry as welcome as it was productive of results. Indeed, the salutary fruits of this rivalry among the scholars were plain for all to see, both in the sphere of the sacred sciences, where the liturgical rites of the Western and Eastern Church were made the object of extensive research and profound study, and in the spiritual life of considerable numbers of individual Christians.

5. The majestic ceremonies of the sacrifice of the altar became better known, understood and appreciated. With more widespread and more frequent reception of the sacraments, the worship of the Eucharist came to be regarded for what it really is: the fountain-head of genuine Christian devotion. Bolder relief was given likewise to the fact that all the faithful

make up a single and very compact body with Christ for its Head, and that the Christian community is in duty bound to participate in the liturgical rites according to their station.

6. You are surely well aware that this Apostolic See has always made careful provision for the schooling of the people committed to its charge in the correct spirit and practice of the liturgy; and that it has been no less careful to insist that the sacred rites should be performed with due external dignity. In this connection We ourselves, in the course of our traditional address to the Lenten preachers of this gracious city of Rome in 1943, urged them warmly to exhort their respective hearers to more faithful participation in the Eucharistic sacrifice. Only a short while previously, with the design of rendering the prayers of the liturgy more correctly understood and their truth and unction more easy to perceive, We arranged to have the Book of Psalms, which forms such an important part of these prayers in the Catholic Church, translated once more into Latin from their original text.

7. But while We derive no little satisfaction from the wholesome results of the movement just described, duty obliges Us to give serious attention to this "revival" as it is advocated in some quarters, and to take proper steps to preserve it at the outset from excess or outright perversion.

8. Indeed, though We are sorely grieved to note, on the one hand, that there are places where the spirit, understanding or practice of the sacred liturgy is defective, or all but inexistent, We observe with considerable anxiety and some misgiving, that elsewhere certain enthusiasts, over eager in their search for novelty, are straying beyond the path of sound doctrine and prudence. Not seldom, in fact, they interlard their plans and hopes for a revival of the sacred liturgy with principles which compromise this holiest of causes in theory or practice, and sometimes even taint it with errors touching Catholic faith and ascetical doctrine.

9. Yet the integrity of faith and morals ought to be the special criterion of this sacred science, which must conform exactly to what the Church out of the abundance of her wisdom teaches and prescribes. It is, consequently, Our prerogative to commend and approve whatever is done properly, and to

check or censure any aberration from the path of truth and rectitude.

10. Let not the apathetic or half-hearted imagine, however, that We agree with them when We reprove the erring and restrain the overbold. No more must the imprudent think that We are commending them when We correct the faults of those who are negligent and sluggish.

11. If in this encyclical letter We treat chiefly of the Latin liturgy, it is not because We esteem less highly the venerable liturgies of the Eastern Church, whose ancient and honorable ritual traditions are just as dear to Us. The reason lies rather in a special situation prevailing in the Western Church, of sufficient importance, it would seem to require this exercise of Our authority.

12. With docile hearts, then, let all Christians hearken to the voice of their Common Father, who would have them, each and every one, intimately united with him as they approach the altar of God, professing the same faith, obedient to the same law, sharing in the same Sacrifice with a single intention and one sole desire. This is a duty imposed, of course, by the honor due to God. But the needs of our day and age demand it as well. After a long and cruel war which has rent whole peoples asunder with its rivalry and slaughter, men of good will are spending themselves in the effort to find the best possible way to restore peace to the world. It is, notwithstanding, success than that fervent religious spirit and zeal by which Christians must be formed and guided; in this way their common and whole-hearted acceptance of the same truth, along with their united obedience and loyalty to their appointed pastors, while rendering to God the worship due to Him, makes of them one brotherhood: "for we, being many, are one body: all that partake of one bread."

PART I

THE NATURE, SOURCE AND DEVELOPMENT OF THE LITURGY

A. THE LITURGY IS PUBLIC WORSHIP

13. It is unquestionably the fundamental duty of man to orientate his person and his life towards God. "For He it is to whom we must first be bound, as to an unfailing principle; to whom even our free choice must be directed as to an ultimate objective. It is He, too, whom we lose when carelessly we sin. It is He whom we must recover by our faith and trust." But man turns properly to God when he acknowledges His supreme majesty and supreme authority; when he accepts divinely revealed truths with a submissive mind; when he scrupulously obeys divine law, centering in God his every act and aspiration; when he accords, in short, due worship to the One True God by practicing the virtue of religion.

14. This duty is incumbent, first of all, on men as individuals. But it also binds the whole community of human beings, grouped together by mutual social ties: mankind, too, depends on the sovereign authority of God.

15. It should be noted, moreover, that men are bound by this obligation in a special way in virtue of the fact that God has raised them to the supernatural order.

16. Thus we observe that when God institutes the Old Law, He makes provision besides for sacred rites, and determines in exact detail the rules to be observed by His people in rendering Him the worship He ordains. To this end He established various kinds of sacrifice and designated the ceremonies with which they were to be offered to Him. His enactments on all matters relating to the Ark of the Covenant, the Temple and the holy days are minute and clear. He established a sacerdotal tribe with its high priest, selected and described the vestments with which the sacred ministers were to be clothed, and every function in any way pertaining to divine worship. Yet this was nothing more than a faint foreshadowing of the worship which the High Priest of the New Testament was to render to the Father in heaven.

17. No sooner, in fact, "is the Word made flesh" than He shows Himself to the world vested with a priestly office, making to the Eternal Father an act of submission which will continue uninterruptedly as long as He lives: "When He cometh into the world He saith ... 'behold I come ... to do Thy will'." This act He was to consummate admirably in the bloody Sacrifice of the Cross: "In the which will we are sanctified by the oblation of the Body of Jesus Christ once." He plans His active life among men with no other purpose in view. As a child He is presented to the Lord in the Temple. To the Temple He returns as a grown boy, and often afterwards to instruct the people and to pray. He fasts for forty days before beginning His public ministry. His counsel and example summon all to prayer, daily and at night as well. As Teacher of the truth He "enlighteneth every man" to the end that mortals may duly acknowledge the immortal God, "not withdrawing unto perdition, but faithful to the saving of the soul." As Shepherd He watches over His flock, leads it to life-giving pasture, lays down a law that none shall wander from His side, off the straight path He has pointed out, and that all shall lead holy lives imbued with His spirit and moved by His active aid. At the Last Supper He celebrates a new Pasch with solemn rite and ceremonial, and provides for its continuance through the divine institution of the Eucharist. On the morrow, lifted up between heaven and earth, He offers the saving sacrifice of His life, and pours forth, as it were, from His pierced Heart the sacraments destined to impart the treasures of redemption to the souls of men. All this He does with but a single aim: the glory of His Father and man's ever greater sanctification.

18. But it is His will, besides, that the worship He instituted and practiced during His life on earth shall continue ever afterwards without any intermission. For he has not left mankind an orphan. He still offers us the support of His powerful, unfailing intercession, acting as our "advocate with the Father." He aids us likewise through His Church, where He is present indefectibly as the ages run their course: through the Church which He constituted "the pillar of truth" and dispenser of grace, and which by His sacrifice on the cross, He founded, consecrated and confirmed forever.

19. The Church has, therefore, in common with the Word Incarnate the aim, the obligation and the function of teaching all men the truth, of governing and directing them aright, of offering to God the pleasing and acceptable sacrifice; in this way the Church re-establishes between the Creator and His creatures that unity and harmony to which the Apostle of the Gentiles alludes in these words: "Now, therefore, you are no more strangers and foreigners; but you are fellow citizens with the saints and domestics of God, built upon the foundation of the apostles and prophets, Jesus Christ Himself being the chief corner-stone; in whom all the building, being framed together, groweth up into a holy temple in the Lord, in whom you also are built together into a habitation of God in the Spirit." Thus the society founded by the divine Redeemer, whether in her doctrine and government, or in the sacrifice and sacraments instituted by Him or finally, in the ministry, which He has confided to her charge with the outpouring of His prayer and the shedding of His blood, has no other goal or purpose than to increase ever in strength and unity.

20. This result is, in fact, achieved when Christ lives and thrives, as it were, in the hearts of men, and when men's hearts in turn are fashioned and expanded as though by Christ. This makes it possible for the sacred temple, where the Divine Majesty receives the acceptable worship which His law prescribes, to increase and prosper day by day in this land of exile on earth. Along with the Church, therefore, her Divine Founder is present at every liturgical function: Christ is present at the august sacrifice of the altar both in the person of His minister and above all under the eucharistic species. He is present in the sacraments, infusing into them the power which makes them ready instruments of sanctification. He is present, finally, in the prayer of praise and petition we direct to God, as it is written: "Where there are two or three gathered together in My Name, there am I in the midst of them." The sacred liturgy is, consequently, the public worship which our Redeemer as Head of the Church renders to the Father, as well as the worship which the community of the faithful renders to its Founder, and through Him to the heavenly Father. It is, in short, the

worship rendered by the Mystical Body of Christ in the entirety of its Head and members.

21. Liturgical practice begins with the very founding of the Church. The first Christians, in fact, "were persevering in the doctrine of the apostles and in the communication of the breaking of bread and in prayers." Whenever their pastors can summon a little group of the faithful together, they set up an altar on which they proceed to offer the sacrifice, and around which are ranged all the other ties appropriate for the saving of souls and for the honor due to God. Among these latter rites, the first place is reserved for the sacraments, namely, the seven principal founts of salvation. There follows the celebration of the divine praises in which the faithful also join, obeying the behest of the Apostle Paul, "In all wisdom, teaching and admonishing one another in psalms, hymns and spiritual canticles, singing in grace in your hearts to God." Next comes the reading of the Law, the prophets, the gospel and the apostolic epistles; and last of all the homily or sermon in which the official head of the congregation recalls and explains the practical bearing of the commandments of the divine Master and the chief events of His life, combining instruction with appropriate exhortation and illustration for the benefit of all his listeners.

22. As circumstances and the needs of Christians warrant, public worship is organized, developed and enriched by new rites, ceremonies and regulations, always with the single end in view, "that we may use these external signs to keep us alert, learn from them what distance we have come along the road, and by them be heartened to go on further with more eager step; for the effect will be more precious the warmer the affection which precedes it." Here then is a better and more suitable way to raise the heart to God. Thenceforth the priesthood of Jesus Christ is a living and continuous reality through all the ages to the end of time, since the liturgy is nothing more nor less than the exercise of this priestly function. Like her divine Head, the Church is forever present in the midst of her children. She aids and exhorts them to holiness, so that they may one day return to the Father in heaven clothed in that beauteous raiment of the supernatural. To all who are born to

life on earth she gives a second, supernatural kind of birth. She arms them with the Holy Spirit for the struggle against the implacable enemy. She gathers all Christians about her altars, inviting and urging them repeatedly to take part in the celebration of the Mass, feeding them with the Bread of Angels to make them ever stronger. She purifies and consoles the hearts that sin has wounded and soiled. Solemnly she consecrates those whom God has called to the priestly ministry. She fortifies with new gifts of grace the chaste nuptials of those who are destined to found and bring up a Christian family. When at last she has soothed and refreshed the closing hours of this earthly life by holy Viaticum and extreme unction, with the utmost affection she accompanies the mortal remains of her children to the grave, lays them reverently to rest, and confides them to the protection of the cross, against the day when they will triumph over death and rise again. She has a further solemn blessing and invocation for those of her children who dedicate themselves to the service of God in the life of religious perfection. Finally, she extends to the souls in purgatory, who implore her intercession and her prayers, the helping hand which may lead them happily at last to eternal blessedness in heaven.

B. THE LITURGY IS EXTERIOR AND INTERIOR WORSHIP

23. The worship rendered by the Church to God must be, in its entirety, interior as well as exterior. It is exterior because the nature of man as a composite of body and soul requires it to be so. Likewise, because divine Providence has disposed that "while we recognize God visibly, we may be drawn by Him to love of things unseen." Every impulse of the human heart, besides, expresses itself naturally through the senses; and the worship of God, being the concern not merely of individuals but of the whole community of mankind, must therefore be social as well. This obviously it cannot be unless religious activity is also organized and manifested outwardly. Exterior worship, finally, reveals and emphasizes the unity of the Mystical Body, feeds new fuel to its holy zeal, fortifies its energy, intensifies its action day by day: "for although the ceremonies themselves can claim no perfection or sanctity in their own right, they are, nevertheless, the outward acts of religion, de-

signed to rouse the heart, like signals of a sort, to veneration of the sacred realities, and to raise the mind to meditation on the supernatural. They serve to foster piety, to kindle the flame of charity, to increase our faith and deepen our devotion. They provide instruction for simple folk, decoration for divine worship, continuity of religious practice. They make it possible to tell genuine Christians from their false or heretical counterparts."

24. But the chief element of divine worship must be interior. For we must always live in Christ and give ourselves to Him completely, so that in Him, with Him and through Him the heavenly Father may be duly glorified. The sacred liturgy requires, however, that both of these elements be intimately linked with each other. This recommendation the liturgy itself is careful to repeat, as often as it prescribes an exterior act of worship. Thus we are urged, when there is question of fasting, for example, "to give interior effect to our outward observance." Otherwise religion clearly amounts to mere formalism, without meaning and without content. You recall, Venerable Brethren, how the divine Master expels from the sacred temple, as unworthy to worship there, people who pretend to honor God with nothing but neat and well-turned phrases, like actors in a theatre, and think themselves perfectly capable of working out their eternal salvation without plucking their inveterate vices from their hearts. It is, therefore, the keen desire of the Church that all of the faithful kneel at the feet of the Redeemer to tell Him how much they venerate and love Him. She wants them present in crowds—like the children whose joyous cries accompanied His entry into Jerusalem—to sing their hymns and chant their song of praise and thanksgiving to Him who is King of Kings and Source of every blessing. She would have them move their lips in prayer, sometimes in petition, sometimes in joy and gratitude, and in this way experience His merciful aid and power like the apostles at the lakeside of Tiberias, or abandon themselves totally, like Peter on Mount Tabor, to mystic union with the eternal God in contemplation.

25. It is an error, consequently, and a mistake to think of the sacred liturgy as merely the outward or visible part of divine worship or as an ornamental ceremonial. No less erroneous is the notion that it consists solely in a list of laws and

prescriptions according to which the ecclesiastical hierarchy orders the sacred rites to be performed.

26. It should be clear to all, then, that God cannot be honored worthily unless the mind and heart turn to Him in quest of the perfect life, and that the worship rendered to God by the Church in union with her divine Head is the most efficacious means of achieving sanctity.

27. This efficacy, where there is question of the eucharistic sacrifice and the sacraments, derives first of all and principally from the act itself (*ex opere operato*). But if one considers the part which the Immaculate Spouse of Jesus Christ takes in the action, embellishing the sacrifice and sacraments with prayer and sacred ceremonies, or if one refers to the "sacramentals" and the other rites instituted by the hierarchy of the Church, then its effectiveness is due rather to the action of the Church (*ex opere operantis Ecclesiae*), inasmuch as she is holy and acts always in closest union with her Head.

28. In this connection, Venerable Brethren, We desire to direct your attention to certain recent theories touching a so-called "objective" piety. While these theories attempt, it is true, to throw light on the mystery of the Mystical Body, on the effective reality of sanctifying grace, on the action of God in the sacraments and in the Mass, it is nonethless apparent that they tend to belittle, or pass over in silence, what they call "subjective," or "personal" piety.

29. It is an unquestionable fact that the work of our redemption is continued, and that its fruits are imparted to us, during the celebration of the liturgy, notably in the august sacrifice of the altar. Christ acts each day to save us, in the sacraments and in His holy sacrifice. By means of them He is constantly atoning for the sins of mankind, constantly consecrating it to God. Sacraments and sacrifice do, then, possess that "objective" power to make us really and personally sharers in the divine life of Jesus Christ. Not from any ability of our own, but by the power of God, are they endowed with the capacity to unite the piety of members with that of the Head, and to make this, in a sense, the action of the whole community. From these profound considerations some are led to conclude that all Christian piety must be centered in the mystery of the

Mystical Body of Christ, with no regard for what is "personal" or "subjective," as they would have it. As a result they feel that all other religious exercises not directly connected with the sacred liturgy, and performed outside public worship, should be omitted.

30. But though the principles set forth above are excellent, it must be plain to everyone that the conclusions drawn from them respecting two sorts of piety are false, insidious and quite pernicious.

31. Very truly, the sacraments and the sacrifice of the altar, being Christ's own actions, must be held to be capable in themselves of conveying and dispensing grace from the divine Head to the members of the Mystical Body. But if they are to produce their proper effect, it is absolutely necessary that our hearts be properly disposed to receive them. Hence the warning of Paul the Apostle with reference to holy communion, "But let a man first prove himself; and then let him eat of this bread and drink of the chalice." This explains why the Church in a brief and significant phrase calls the various acts of mortification, especially those practised during the season of Lent, "the Christian army's defenses." They represent, in fact, the personal effort and activity of members who desire, as grace urges and aids them, to join forces with their Captain—"that we may discover . . . in our Captain," to borrow St. Augustine's words, "the fountain of grace itself." But observe that these members are alive, endowed and equipped with an intelligence and will of their own. It follows that they are strictly required to put their own lips to the fountain, imbibe and absorb for themselves the life-giving water, and rid themselves personally of anything that might hinder its nutritive effect in their souls. Emphatically, therefore, the work of redemption, which in itself is independent of our will, requires a serious interior effort on our part if we are to achieve eternal salvation.

32. If the private and interior devotion of individuals were to neglect the august sacrifice of the altar and the sacraments, and to withdraw them from the stream of vital energy that flows from Head to members, it would indeed be sterile, and deserve to be condemned. But when devotional exercises, and pious practices in general, not strictly connected with the

sacred liturgy, confine themselves to merely human acts, with
the express purpose of directing these latter to the Father in
heaven, of rousing people to repentance and holy fear of God,
of weaning them from the seductions of the world and its vice,
and leading them back to the difficult path of perfection, then
certainly such practices are not only highly praiseworthy but
absolutely indispensable, because they expose the dangers
threatening the spiritual life; because they promote the ac-
quisition of virtue; and because they increase the fervor and
generosity with which we are bound to dedicate all that we are
and all that we have to service of Jesus Christ. Genuine and real
piety, which the Angelic Doctor calls "devotion," and which is
the principal act of the virtue of religion—that act which correctly relates and fitly directs men to God; and by which they
freely and spontaneously give themselves to the worship of
God in its fullest sense—piety of this authentic sort needs meditation on the supernatural realities and spiritual exercises, if
it is to be nurtured, stimulated and sustained, and if it is to
prompt us to lead a more perfect life. For the Christian religion,
practiced as it should be, demands that the will especially be
consecrated to God and exert its influence on all the other
spiritual faculties. But every act of the will presupposes an act
of the intelligence, and before one can express the desire and
the intention of offering oneself in sacrifice to the eternal
Godhead, a knowledge of the facts and truths which make
religion a duty of submission to our Creator; and, finally, the
inexhaustible treasures of love with which God yearns to enrich
us, as well as the necessity of supernatural grace for the achievement of our destiny, and that special path marked out for us
by divine Providence in virtue of the fact that we have been
united, one and all, like members of body, to Jesus Christ the
Head. But further, since our hearts, disturbed as they are at
times by the lower appetites, do not always respond to motives
of love, it is also extremely helpful to let consideration and
contemplation of the justice of God provoke us on occasion to
salutary fear, and guide us thence to Christian humility, repentance and amendment.

33. But it will not do to possess these facts and truths
after the fashion of an abstract memory lesson or lifeless com-

mentary. They must lead to practical results. They must impel us to subject our senses and their faculties to reason, as illuminated by the Catholic faith. They must help to cleanse and purify the heart, uniting it to Christ more intimately every day, growing ever more to His likeness, and drawing from Him the divine inspiration and strength of which it stands in need. They must serve as increasingly effective incentives to action: urging men to produce good fruit, to perform their individual duties faithfully, to give themselves eagerly to the regular practice of their religion and the energetic exercise of virtue. "You are Christ's, and Christ is God's." Let everything, therefore, have its proper place and arrangement; let everything be "theocentric," so to speak, if we really wish to direct everything to the glory of God through the life and power which flow from the divine Head into our hearts: "Having therefore, brethren, a confidence in the entering into the holies by the blood of Christ, a new and living way which He both dedicated for us through the veil, that is to say, His flesh, and a high priest over the house of God; let us draw near with a true heart, in fulness of faith, having our hearts sprinkled from an evil conscience and our bodies washed with clean water, let us hold fast the confession of our hope without wavering . . . and let us consider one another, to provoke unto charity and to good works."

34. Here is the source of the harmony and equilibrium which prevails among the members of the Mystical Body of Jesus Christ. When the Church teaches us our Catholic faith and exhorts us to obey the commandments of Christ, she is paving a way for her priestly, sanctifying action in its highest sense; she disposes us likewise for more serious meditation on the life of the divine Redeemer and guides us to profounder knowledge of the mysteries of faith where we may draw the supernatural sustenance, strength and vitality that enable us to progress safely, through Christ, towards a more perfect life. Not only through her ministers but with the help of the faithful individually, who have imbibed in this fashion the spirit of Christ, the Church endeavors to permeate with this same spirit the life and labors of men—their private and family life, their social, even economic and political life—that all who are called

God's children may reach more readily the end He has proposed for them.

35. Such action on the part of individual Christians, then, along with the ascetic effort prompting them to purify their hearts, actually stimulates in the faithful those energies which enable them to participate in the august sacrifice of the altar with better dispositions. They now can receive the sacraments with more abundant fruit, and come from the celebration of the sacred rites more eager, more firmly resolved to pray and deny themselves like Christians, to answer the inspirations and invitation of divine grace and to imitate daily more closely the virtues of our Redeemer. And all of this not simply for their own advantage, but for that of the whole Church, where whatever good is accomplished proceeds from the power of her Head and redounds to the advancement of all her members.

36. In the spiritual life, consequently, there can be no opposition between the action of God, who pours forth His grace into men's hearts so that the work of the redemption may always abide, and the tireless collaboration of man, who must not render vain the gift of God. No more can the efficacy of the external administration of the sacraments, which comes from the rite itself (*ex opere operato*), be opposed to the meritorious action of their ministers or recipients, which we call the agent's action (*opus operantis*). Similarly, no conflict exists between public prayer and prayers in private, between morality and contemplation, between the ascetical life and devotion to the liturgy. Finally, there is no opposition between the jurisdiction and teaching office of the ecclesiastical hierarchy, and the specifically priestly power exercised in the sacred ministry.

37. Considering their special designation to perform the liturgical functions of the holy sacrifice and divine office, the Church has serious reason for prescribing that the ministers she assigns to the service of the sanctuary and members of religious institutes betake themselves at stated times to mental prayer, to examination of conscience, and to various other spiritual exercises. Unquestionably, liturgical prayer, being the public supplication of the illustrious Spouse of Jesus Christ, is superior in excellence to private prayers. But this superior

worth does not at all imply contrast or incompatibility between these two kinds of prayer. For both merge harmoniously in the single spirit which animates them, "Christ is all and in all." Both tend to the same objective: until Christ be formed in us.

C. THE LITURGY UNDER THE HIERARCHY OF THE CHURCH

38. For a better and more accurate understanding of the sacred liturgy another of its characteristic features, no less important, needs to be considered.

39. The Church is a society, and as such requires an authority and hierarchy of her own. Though it is true that all the members of the Mystical Body partake of the same blessings and pursue the same objective, they do not all enjoy the same powers, nor are they all qualified to perform the same acts. The divine Redeemer has willed, as a matter of fact, that His Kingdom should be built and solidly supported, as it were, on a holy order, which resembles in some sort the heavenly hierarchy.

40. Only to the apostles, and thenceforth to those on whom their successors have imposed hands, is granted the power of the priesthood, in virtue of which they represent the person of Jesus Christ before their people, acting at the same time as representatives of their people before God. This priesthood is not transmitted by heredity or human descent. It does not emanate from the Christian community. It is not a delegation from the people. Prior to acting as representative of the community before the throne of God, the priest is the ambassador of the divine Redeemer. He is God's vice-gerent in the midst of his flock precisely because Jesus Christ is Head of that body of which Christians are the members. The power entrusted to him, therefore, bears no natural resemblance to anything human. It is entirely supernatural. It comes from God. "As the Father hath sent me, I also send you . . . he that heareth you heareth me . . . go ye into the whole world and preach the gospel to every creature; he that believeth and is baptized shall be saved."

41. That is why the visible, external priesthood of Jesus Christ is not handed down indiscriminately to all members of

the Church in general, but is conferred on designated men, through what may be called the spiritual generation of holy orders.

42. This latter, one of the seven sacraments, not only imparts the grace appropriate to the function and state of life, but imparts an indelible "character" besides, indicating the sacred ministers' conformity to Jesus Christ the Priest and qualifying them to perform those official acts of religion by which men are sanctified and God is duly glorified in keeping with the divine laws and regulations.

43. In the same way, actually, that baptism is the distinctive mark of all Christians, and serves to differentiate them from those who have not been cleansed in this purifying stream and consequently are not members of Christ, the sacrament of holy orders sets the priest apart from the rest of the faithful who have not received this consecration. For they alone, in answer to an inward supernatural call, have entered the august ministry, where they are assigned to service in the sanctuary and become, as it were, the instruments God uses to communicate supernatural life from on high to the Mystical Body of Jesus Christ. Add to this, as We have noted above, the fact that they alone have been marked with the indelible sign "conforming" them to Christ the Priest, and that their hands alone have been consecrated "in order that whatever they bless may be blessed, whatever they consecrate may become sacred and holy, in the name of our Lord Jesus Christ." Let all, then, who would live in Christ flock to their priests. By them they will be supplied with the comforts and food of the spiritual life. From them they will procure the medicine of salvation assuring their cure and happy recovery from the fatal sickness of their sins. The priest, finally, will bless their homes, consecrate their families and help them, as they breathe their last, across the threshold of eternal happiness.

44. Since, therefore, it is the priest chiefly who performs the sacred liturgy in the name of the Church, its organization, regulation and details cannot but be subject to Church authority. This conclusion, based on the nature of Christian worship itself, is further confirmed by the testimony of history.

45. Additional proof of this indefeasible right of the ecclesiastical hierarchy lies in the circumstances that the sacred liturgy is intimately bound up with doctrinal propositions which the Church proposes to be perfectly true and certain, and must as a consequence conform to the decrees respecting Catholic faith issued by the supreme teaching authority of the Church with a view to safeguarding the integrity of the religion revealed by God.

46. On this subject We judge it Our duty to rectify an attitude with which you are doubtless familiar, Venerable Brethren. We refer to the error and fallacious reasoning of those who have claimed that the sacred liturgy is a kind of proving ground for the truths to be held of faith, meaning by this that the Church is obliged to declare such a doctrine sound when it is found to have produced fruits of piety and sanctity through the sacred rites of the liturgy, and to reject it otherwise. Hence the epigram, *"Lex orandi, lex credendi"*—the law for prayer is the law for faith.

47. But this is not what the Church teaches and enjoins. The worship she offers to God, all good and great, is a continuous profession of Catholic faith and a continuous exercise of hope and charity, as Augustine puts it tersely. "God is to be worshipped," he says, "by faith, hope and charity." In the sacred liturgy we profess the Catholic faith explicitly and openly, not only by the celebration of the mysteries, and by offering the holy sacrifice and administering the sacraments, but also by saying or singing the credo or Symbol of the faith— it is indeed the sign and badge, as it were, of the Christian— along with other texts, and likewise by the reading of holy scripture, written under the inspiration of the Holy Ghost. The entire liturgy, therefore, has the Catholic faith for its content, inasmuch as it bears public witness to the faith of the Church.

48. For this reason, whenever there was question of defining a truth revealed by God, the Sovereign Pontiff and the Councils in their recourse to the "theological sources," as they are called, have not seldom drawn many an argument from this sacred science of the liturgy. For an example in point, Our predecessor of immortal memory, Pius IX, so argued when he

proclaimed the Immaculate Conception of the Virgin Mary. Similarly during the discussion of a doubtful or controversial truth, the Church and the Holy Fathers have not failed to look to the age-old and age-honored sacred rites for enlightenment. Hence the well-known and venerable maxim, *"Legem credendi lex statuat supplicandi"*—let the rule for prayer determine the rule of belief. The sacred liturgy, consequently, does not decide or determine independently and of itself what is of Catholic faith. More properly, since the liturgy is also a profession of eternal truths, and subject, as such, to the supreme teaching authority of the Church, it can supply proofs and testimony, quite clearly of no little value, towards the determination of a particular point of Christian doctrine. But if one desires to differentiate and describe the relationship between faith and the sacred liturgy in absolute and general terms, it is perfectly correct to say, *"lex credendi legem statuat supplicandi"*—let the rule of belief determine the rule of prayer. The same holds true for the other theological virtues also, *"In . . . fide, spe, caritate continuato desiderio semper oramus"*— we pray always, with constant yearning in faith, hope and charity.

D. PROGRESS AND DEVELOPMENT OF THE LITURGY

49. From time immemorial the ecclesiastical hierarchy has exercised this right in matters liturgical. It has organized and regulated divine worship, enriching it constantly with new splendor and beauty, to the glory of God and the spiritual profit of Christians. What is more, it has not been slow—keeping the substance of the Mass and sacraments carefully intact—to modify what it deemed not altogether fitting, and to add what appeared more likely to increase the honor paid to Jesus Christ and the august Trinity, and to instruct and stimulate the Christian people to greater advantage.

50. The sacred liturgy does, in fact, include divine as well as human elements. The former, instituted as they have been by God, cannot be changed in any way by men. But the human components admit of various modifications, as the needs of the age, circumstance and the good of souls may require, and as the ecclesiastical hierarchy, under guidance of the Holy

Spirit, may have authorized. This will explain the marvellous variety of Eastern and Western rites. Here is the reason for the gradual addition, through successive development, of particular religious customs and practices of piety only faintly discernible in earlier times. Hence likewise it happens from time to time that certain devotions long since forgotten are revived and practiced anew. All these developments attest the abiding life of the immaculate Spouse of Jesus Christ through these many centuries. They are the sacred language she uses, as the ages run their course, to profess to her divine Spouse her own faith along with that of the nations committed to her charge, and her own unfailing love. They furnish proof, besides, of the wisdom of the teaching method she employs to arouse and nourish constantly the "Christian instinct."

51. Several causes, really, have been instrumental in the progress and development of the sacred liturgy during the long and glorious life of the Church.

52. Thus, for example, as Catholic doctrine on the Incarnate Word of God, the eucharistic sacrament and sacrifice and Mary the Virgin Mother of God came to be determined with greater certitude and clarity, new ritual forms were introduced through which the acts of the liturgy proceeded to reproduce this brighter light issuing from the decrees of the teaching authority of the Church, and to reflect it, in a sense, so that it might reach the minds and hearts of Christ's people more readily.

53. The subsequent advances in ecclesiastical discipline for the administering of the sacraments, that of penance for example; the institution and later suppression of the catechumenate; and again, the practice of eucharistic communion under a single species, adopted in the Latin Church; these developments were assuredly responsible in no little measure for the modification of the ancient ritual in the course of time, and for the gradual introduction of new rites considered more in accord with prevailing discipline in these matters.

54. Just as notable a contribution to this progressive transformation was made by devotional trends and practices not directly related to the sacred liturgy, which began to appear, by God's wonderful design, in later periods, and grew to be so

popular. We may instance the spread and ever mounting ardor of devotion to the Blessed Eucharist, devotion to the most bitter passion of our Redeemer, devotion to the most Sacred Heart of Jesus, to the Virgin Mother of God and to her most chaste spouse.

55. Other manifestations of piety have also played their circumstantial part in this same liturgical development. Among them may be cited the public pilgrimages to the tombs of the martyrs prompted by motives of devotion, the special periods of fasting instituted for the same reason, and lastly, in this gracious city of Rome, the penitential recitation of the litanies during the "station" processions, in which even the Sovereign Pontiff frequently joined.

56. It is likewise easy to understand that the progress of the fine arts, those of architecture, painting and music above all, has exerted considerable influence on the choice and disposition of the various external features of the sacred liturgy.

57. The Church has further used her right of control over liturgical observance to protect the purity of divine worship against abuse from dangerous and imprudent innovations introduced by private individuals and particular churches. Thus it came about—during the 16th centruy, when usages and customs of this sort had become increasingly prevalent and exaggerated, and when private initiative in matters liturgical threatened to compromise the integrity of faith and devotion, to the great advantage of heretics and further spread of their errors—that in the year 1588, Our predecessor Sixtus V of immortal memory established the Sacred Congregation of Rites, charged with the prohibition of any spurious innovation. This body fulfils even today the official function of supervision and legislation with regard to all matters touching the sacred liturgy.

E. ITS DEVELOPMENT MAY NOT BE LEFT TO PRIVATE JUDGMENT

58. It follows from this that the Sovereign Pontiff alone enjoys the right to recognize and establish any practice touching the worship of God, to introduce and approve new rites, as also to modify those he judges to require modification. Bishops,

for their part, have the right and duty carefully to watch over the exact observance of the prescriptions of the sacred canons respecting divine worship. Private individuals, therefore, even though they be clerics, may not be left to decide for themselves in these holy and venerable matters, involving as they do the religious life of Christian society along with the exercise of the priesthood of Jesus Christ and worship of God; concerned as they are with the honor due to the Blessed Trinity, the Word Incarnate and His august mother and the other saints, and with the salvation of souls as well. For the same reason no private person has any authority to regulate external practices of this kind, which are intimately bound up with Church discipline and with the order, unity and concord of the Mystical Body and frequently even with the integrity of Catholic faith itself.

59. The Church is without question a living organism, and as an organism, in respect of the sacred liturgy also, she grows, matures, develops, adapts and accommodates herself to temporal needs and circumstances, provided only that the integrity of her doctrine be safeguarded. This notwithstanding, the temerity and daring of those who introduce novel liturgical practices, or call for the revival of obsolete rites out of harmony with prevailing laws and rubrics, deserve severe reproof. It has pained Us grievously to note, Venerable Brethren, that such innovations are actually being introduced, not merely in minor details but in matters of major importance as well. We instance, in point of fact, those who make use of the vernacular in the celebration of the august eucharistic sacrifice; those who transfer certain feast-days—which have been appointed and established after mature deliberation—to other dates; those, finally, who delete from the prayer-books approved for public use the sacred texts of the Old Testament, deeming them little suited and inopportune for modern times.

60. The use of the Latin language, customary in a considerable portion of the Church, is a manifest and beautiful sign of unity, as well as an effective antidote for any corruption of doctrinal truth. In spite of this, the use of the mother tongue in connection with several of the rites may be of much advantage to the people. But the Apostolic See alone is empowered

to grant this permission. It is forbidden, therefore, to take any action whatever of this nature without having requested and obtained such consent, since the sacred liturgy, as We have said, is entirely subject to the discretion and approval of the Holy See.

61. The same reasoning holds in the case of some persons who are bent on the restoration of all the ancient rites and ceremonies indiscriminately. The liturgy of the early ages is most certainly worthy of all veneration. But ancient usage must not be esteemed more suitable and proper, either in its own right or in its significance for later times and new situations, on the simple ground that it carries the savor and aroma of antiquity. The more recent liturgical rites likewise deserve reverence and respect. They, too, owe their inspiration to the Holy Spirit, who assists the Church in every age even to the consummation of the world. They are equally the resources used by the majestic Spouse of Jesus Christ to promote and procure the sanctity of man.

62. Assuredly it is a wise and most laudable thing to return in spirit and affection to the sources of the sacred liturgy. For research in this field of study, by tracing it back to its origins, contributes valuable assistance towards a more thorough and careful investigation of the significance of feast-days, and of the meaning of the texts and sacred ceremonies employed on their occasion. But it is neither wise nor laudable to reduce everything to antiquity by every possible device. Thus, to cite some instances, one would be straying from the straight path were he to wish the altar restored to its primitive table-form; were he to want black excluded as a color for the liturgical vestments; were he to forbid the use of sacred images and statues in Churches; were he to order the crucifix so designed that the divine Redeemer's body shows no trace of His cruel sufferings; and lastly were he to disdain and reject polyphonic music or singing in parts, even where it conforms to regulations issued by the Holy See.

63. Clearly no sincere Catholic can refuse to accept the formulation of Christian doctrine more recently elaborated and proclaimed as dogmas by the Church, under the inspiration and guidance of the Holy Spirit with abundant fruit for souls,

because it pleases him to hark back to the old formulas. No more can any Catholic in his right senses repudiate existing legislation of the Church to revert to prescriptions based on the earliest sources of canon law. Just as obviously unwise and mistaken is the zeal of one who in matters liturgical would go back to the rites and usage of antiquity, discarding the new patterns introduced by disposition of divine Providence to meet the changes of circumstances and situation.

64. This way of acting bids fair to revive the exaggerated and senseless antiquarianism to which the illegal Council of Pistoia gave rise. It likewise attempts to reinstate a series of errors which were responsible for the calling of that meeting as well as for those resulting from it, with grievous harm to souls, and which the Church, the ever watchful guardian of the "deposit of faith" committed to her charge by her divine Founder, had every right and reason to condemn. For perverse designs and ventures of this sort tend to paralyze and weaken that process of sanctification by which the sacred liturgy directs the sons of adoption to their Heavenly Father for their souls' salvation.

65. In every measure taken, then, let proper contact with the ecclesiastical hierarchy be maintained. Let no one arrogate to himself the right to make regulations and impose them on others at will. Only the Sovereign Pontiff, as the successor of Saint Peter, charged by the divine Redeemer with the feeding of His entire flock, and with him, in obedience to the Apostolic See, the bishops "whom the Holy Ghost has placed . . . to rule the Church of God," have the right and the duty to govern the Christian people. Consequently, Venerable Brethren, whenever you assert your authority—even on occasion with wholesome severity—you are not merely acquitting yourselves of your duty; you are defending the very will of the Founder of the Church.

Bernard Poschmann
1878-1955

Bernard Poschmann taught at Braunsberg, Breslau, Münster, and Königstein. He established himself as an international authority on the history of the sacrament of penance. The fact that he provided such solid scholarship at the middle of our century indicates his importance. He was one of the pioneers who, in the tradition of men like Louis Duchesne, recognized the great need for substantial historical groundwork if any true renewal were to take place.

Catholic theology in the first half of our century was often criticized for its comparative lack of concern with history. So often its focus on the content of traditional statements resulted in those statements being viewed in a vacuum. But text without context is incomplete, and it is the function of the historian to recreate the context insofar as possible for any historical document or development.

Penance was one of the areas in which considerable conflict and controversy took place between Catholic and Protestant theologians after the Reformation. The introduction of the "confessional box" after the Council of Trent led to an emphasis on "private confession" that became one of the hallmarks of Catholic piety, and naturally the impression was left that this was something that had been part of Catholic life and practice since apostolic times. Polemics regularly cause havoc with history, leading people to assume that the piety of one age must be defended as having been the piety of all earlier ages. It is thus in a special way the role of the Church historian to serve truth by exposing unwarranted assumptions, confident that in doing so, all will ultimately benefit.

Poschmann applied his meticulous scholarship to this realm of penance and produced the most comprehensive account of its history ever attempted. The German original appeared in 1951, and the first English edition came out in 1964, at the very time when Vatican II had accepted the need for liturgical reform. The impact of the book on subsequent thinking is obvious, although the author did not live to see it.

The book is divided according to the four historical periods of development in the Church: 1) from the New Testament to the 6th century; 2) the early middle ages; 3) from Scholasticism to the Council of Trent; and 4) Trent and post-Tridentine teaching. Twenty-five pages on indulgences and twenty-five pages on the Anointing of the Sick round out the book.

The selection that follows consists of two excerpts, one from the first period and the other from the second period. The former reviews the data from the New Testament and the Post-Apostolic Age. It illustrates Poschmann's talent for recovering the essentials. There have been such broad variations in penitential practice over the ages that it is refreshing to see the New Testament origins brought into focus: "Every sin calls for penance; but no sin, not even the gravest, is excluded from forgiveness, provided that sincere penance is performed."

The second excerpt is even more illuminating, since it deals with the single most striking change in the history of penance, giving the setting in which this change took place: "The Rise of Private Penance." In balanced fashion the role of monasticism is acknowledged without being exaggerated. As evident, it was scholarship such as this that provided the groundwork for renewal by pointing out what was essential in practices of Christian piety and what were modifications induced by the conditions of a certain age. Poschmann's example has served to direct others into similar fruitful paths of understanding and insight.

PENANCE AND THE
ANOINTING OF THE SICK

CHAPTER I

EARLY CHRISTIAN PENANCE

I. THE NEW TESTAMENT

1. The Gospels

Penance and the forgiveness of sins are at the very centre of the preaching of Jesus. He entered on his messianic work with the appeal "repent and believe the Gospel" (Mk. 1:15) and he took leave of his disciples with the charge that "penance and the remission of sins should be preached in his name to all nations" (Lk. 24:47). The divine willingness to forgive the repentant knows no bounds (Lk. 15:20ff.). Faith and baptism do away with all sins (Mk. 16:16). All this is universally acknowledged as the clear teaching of the Gospel.

Not even those who fall away by sinning afresh after baptism are excluded from pardon. Jesus does indeed insist on a wholehearted, irrevocable renunciation of evil on the part of sinners. They are now confronted with a sole alternative: either with Christ or against him (Lk. 9:62; 14:25). A merely passing conversion is of no avail (Mt. 13:3ff.). The state of the recidivist is far worse than it was before his conversion (Mt. 12:43ff.). Yet all this leaves untouched the possibility of a new conversion; for such is the weakness of man that a relapse can always occur, even where at first the will was most determined. Forgiveness is excluded only when a sinner impenitently hardens his heart against God, thus committing "the sin against the Holy Ghost" (Mt. 12:31f. and par.). The idea, very prevalent among Protestant theologians, that Jesus did not envisage the possibility of a further repentance after baptism is untenable. Against it is the immensity of the divine mercy on which Jesus laid such emphasis in his preaching, and also his attitude to the sinfulness with which he had to reckon everywhere, even among his closest followers (Mt. 6:12; 7:11). Not even the infidelity and apostasy of his disciples were in his sight an impediment to their restoration to grace and to their vocation to leadership in the kingdom of God. Moreover, if the Father in heaven will forgive our sins in the same measure as we are ready to grant repeated forgiveness to our brethren (Mt. 18:22, 35), then repeated acts of divine forgiveness are obviously presupposed.

Forgiveness, however, is not a matter which is concluded simply between God and man: it comes through the mediation of the Church, of which a Christian has become a member by baptism, and which by his sin he has dishonoured and defiled. Jesus expressly grants to the Church disciplinary power over believers who fall into sin (Mt. 18:15-17). After a fruitless private admonition "in the sight of four eyes", or before two witnesses, the sinner is to be denounced to the Church, and, if he will not listen to this highest tribunal, he is to be treated "as the heathen and the publican". This means that in accordance with Jewish usage (cf. Jn. 9:22; 12:42; 16:1) he is to be excommunicated. Then, in confirmation of this ecclesiastical authority, the word of power is directed to the disciples in their capacity as the authoritative representatives of the Church: "Amen I say to you, whatsoever ye shall bind upon earth shall be bound in heaven; and whatsoever ye shall loose upon earth shall be loosed in heaven" (Mt. 18:18). "Binding" and "loosing" are rabbinical expressions; they signify in the first place "to forbid" and "to permit", but they also have the secondary meaning "to impose the ban" and "to lift the ban". As our text is dealing with a case of punishment only this second meaning comes into question. When, therefore, the disciples "bind", they exclude the guilty not only from the fellowship of the earthly Church, but also from the Kingdom of Heaven. "Loosing", on the other hand, has indirectly the sense of "forgiveness of sins", inasmuch as by the lifting or non-imposition of the penalty sin has no further consequences for men.

In non-metaphorical language forgiveness of sins is announced as an apostolic power in Jn. 20:21-23. Here the risen Saviour passes on to his disciples the mission which he himself has received from the Father. The structure of the sentence is very similar to that in the Matthaean passage. "Forgive" and "retain" are parallel to "bind" and "loose". In both places no limits are assigned to the plenitude of power which is conveyed: no sins are excluded from its scope. In both texts the objective efficacy for the hereafter of the act of forgiveness is vividly expressed by the use of perfect passive verbal forms. We may leave on one side the question whether the disciples, as fully empowered by God, thereby grant pardon directly in his name; or whether, in the first place, as the representatives of the Church, they only grant forgiveness on her part, which then has forgiveness from God as its certain result. The biblical texts allow both interpretations. In any case Jesus has given power to the disciples to forgive sins with effect for the hereafter.

2. St. Paul

Penance plays an important part in the epistles of St. Paul, even though he only occasionally uses the word μετάνοια. Like Jesus he insists on a thoroughgoing conversion (1 Cor. 5:7f.; Rom 6:2-12; 8:5-13; Gal. 2:19f.). Yet for him sin remains a frightening power, even in the lives of the baptized. Confronted by it neither he nor the faithful can feel secure (1 Cor. 4:4; 9:27; Phil. 2:12). Constantly and insistently he warns them against it (Rom. 6:12f.; 13:14; 1 Cor. 6:18f.; Col. 3:10; Eph. 4:24 etc.). And it is not only with the danger of sinning that he has to reckon. His catalogues of sins (Gal. 5:19ff.; 1 Cor. 6:9f.; Eph. 5:3ff.; Col. 3:5) are manifestly conditioned by actual moral failings of believers. On a number of occasions he expressly reproves concrete lapses in the communities, such as dissensions, uncharitableness (1 Cor. 3:3ff.; 11:18ff.), idleness (2 Thess. 3:6ff.), and other "impure adulterous and wanton living" (2 Cor. 12:21). Yet not even such backsliding Christians are lost. "For the grief that is according to God worketh repentance without regret, unto salvation" (2 Cor. 7:10). Christ, seated at the right hand of God and pleading for us, gives us assurance of forgiveness (Rom. 8:34). For this reason all the Apostle's warnings to sinning believers are aimed at moving them to repentance. The theory of sinlessness finds no support in St. Paul. In addition to sincere conversion, penance also includes expiation. Judgement awaits sin, and judgement can only be averted if the sinner is chastised here on earth either by his own hand or by God (1 Cor. 11:31f.). The "destruction of the flesh" is the way by which the "spirit may find salvation in the day of the Lord" (1 Cor. 5:5). Penance is "sorrow that is according to God"; its fruits are goodness of will, holy fear, expiation, obedience (2 Cor. 7:10f.; cf. 2:9). Fundamentally sin, and consequently penance, is something which concerns the Church too. She is responsible for the holiness of her members. Fraternal charity imposes the duty of admonishing one who errs (Gal. 6:1f.; 2 Tim. 4:2; 2:25), but where there is gross immorality severe proceedings must be taken against the offenders. The classical example is provided by the case of the incestuous man. Faced with this appalling crime, the community should have at once broken off all intercourse with the evildoer in obedience to an earlier instruction of the Apostle. This they had negligently omitted to do, and Paul now does it himself. Conscious of his union with them in spirit, he pronounces judgement along with them in the name of Jesus "to deliver up such a one to Satan for the destruction of the flesh, that his spirit may be saved in the day of the Lord" (5:3-5). The "delivering up to Satan", as the context indicates, as also does the traditional meaning of the term attested as early as Tertullian, is nothing else than excommunication. It implies, however, that the person excommunicated is subjected to Satan's dominion more completely than before, and is punished by him with bodily and spiritual afflictions. In 1 Tim. 1:20, Paul makes use of the same formula in excommunicating Hymenaeus and Alexander who have made shipwreck of their faith, "in order that they may be taught not to blaspheme". The same procedure is attested without the use of the formula in 2 Thess. 3:6, 14-16, except that in this less serious case the curative purpose and the maintenance of love are more emphasized. "And do not regard him as an enemy, but admonish him as a brother." Excommunication, or severance of relations with an evildoer, is simply the severest form of admonition. In Tit. 3:10 the charge "give a heretic one warning, then a second, and after that avoid his company" corresponds perfectly with the directions in St. Matthew's gospel, 18:15-17.

From what has been said it follows that the exclusion of the sinner does not imply his final condemnation; its chief purpose is to promote his salvation. The question then arises, whether his pardon is something to be hoped for only from God in "the day of the Lord", or whether the Church too grants her pardon and reconciliation. The traditional view, supported by all the Fathers (except Tertullian in his Montanist period), by the medieval theologians, and until recently by more modern exegetes, finds this question settled in 2 Cor. 2:5-11. In this text it sees attested the restoration of the incestuous man of 1 Cor. 5. Contemporary opinion is rather more inclined to take the line that in 2 Cor. there is question of an altogether different case, one involving a personal affront of the Apostle. Even so, the text retains its importance as evidence for ecclesiastical forgiveness. Paul, desirous of maintaining his authority, has required the community to assert itself against the offender. Now that satisfaction has been made him, he finds that "this punishment inflicted on him by so many" is sufficient, and that it is time "to pardon and comfort him" and to "assure him of love", "lest he be overwhelmed by excess of grief" (2:7-8). This can only mean that the faithful have broken off intercourse with him. The punishment has now served its purpose, which was to make him see reason and bring him to repentance. A prolongation of the excommunication could only have harmful effects on his state of soul, with the result that he would be "overreached by Satan" (2:11). For this reason the penitent must be restored to grace. To use a later terminology, reconciliation must follow excommunication. The procedure employed here as a matter of course, so to speak, is also obviously applicable to other similar cases (1 Cor. 5:5; 2 Thess. 3:14ff.; 1 Tim. 1:20). It is also presupposed in 2 Cor. 12:21, where the Apostle expresses the hope that on his next visit he will not have "to mourn" over those guilty of unchastity who have not yet done their penance. He expects, therefore, that by that time these sinners will once more have set right their relationship to the community.

Ecclesiastical forgiveness is, therefore, attested by Paul. However, he provides no direct answer to the final and most important problem of the relationship of ecclesiastical to divine forgiveness. Nevertheless, he makes it quite clear that he attaches supratemporal consequences to the Church's measures in regard to a sinner. The excommunication of the incestuous man is a judgement which the community pronounces over him "in the name of Jesus" (1 Cor. 5:4). The effect of the judgement, "handing over to Satan", essentially exceeds the power of any human sentence. The same, then, must also hold good for the act of reconciliation with or reincorporation into the Church. If the Church is not just an external association, but, as the Apostle teaches, the body of Christ, the living instrument of his grace, the indispensably necessary society of salvation, then it follows that expulsion from the Church, if deserved, and, conversely, readmission to it are of decisive insignificance. This conclusion is further justified by the fact that it is in harmony with the Gospel proclamation (Mt. 18:18; Jn. 20:23), and also with the claims of the Church which will soon be unmistakably manifest.

3. The Epistle to the Hebrews

This epistle only calls for special consideration in so far as a few texts in it have been made to serve as the principal proof for the "baptism theory". It is supposed that they absolutely exclude the possibility of penance to those who have lapsed from the faith. In fact, however, this interpretation is untenable.

In Heb 6:4—6 we read: "For it is impossible to renew again unto repentance those who have once been enlightened, and have tasted the heavenly gift . . . and then have fallen away; since they crucify again for themselves the Son of God, and make him a mockery." A careful exegesis, which takes account of the context, makes it clear that the author has no intention of rejecting as useless any eventual repentance on the part of an apostate. What he does say is that those people who have thrown away the blessings of salvation, and who make a mockery of the grace of the redemption, are impossible to convert once more. It is a question of the possibility of conversion, and not of whether the penance of the apostate is still of any profit to him if he is converted. It is a bad misunderstanding to confuse these two questions. All the text says is that those who have apostatized with full deliberation are in a state of obduracy, and normally indisposed for penance.

No less mistaken is the exposition of another passage, 10:26 ff., in a sense which excludes the possibility of penance for Christians. "For if we sin willingly after having received knowledge of the truth, there remaineth no further sacrifice for sin; but only a terrible expectation of judgment . . ." Almost always the phrase οὐκέτι περὶ ἁμαρτιῶν, ἀπολείπεται θυσία is understood to mean that for deliberate sinners" there is no question of a new sacrifice of Christ, which would make possible a renewal of forgiveness. In reality what we have is an allusion to the Old Testament law (Num 15:22—31), according to which unpremeditated offences are to be expiated by sin-offerings, whereas anyone who sins deliberately "with upraised hand" is a "blasphemer against the Lord", and must be ruthlessly exterminated. Now the author of the Epistle finds the condition of such a "deliberate sin" verified, if anywhere at all, in the apostate Christian who has "trodden under foot the Son of God . . . and has insulted the Spirit of grace" (10:29). Such a one is inevitably liable to judgment; but this is not because the sacrifice of Christ can be of no avail to him a second time, but by reason of his state of soul which is closed against the operation of grace. No "sin-offering" can help him. Judgment is the unavoidable consequence of fully deliberate separation from Christ. The problem of the dogmatic possibility of a renewed reception into grace, which was raised by the Novatianists and by modern historians of dogma, is very far from the mind of the author of the Epistle. Chapter 12, v. 17 expresses the same idea as 10:26f., but makes use of a different scriptural argument. For those who are tempted to fall away the terrifying example is adduced of Esau, who sold his birthright for a single dish and then "afterwards, when he wished to inherit the blessing, he was rejected: μετανοίας γὰρ τόπον οὐχ εὗρεν, καίπερ μετὰ δακρύων ἐκζητήσας αὐτήν". This text can indeed be lined up in favour of the theory of a single baptismal repentance if τόπος μετανοίας is understood in its obvious sense of the possibility of doing penance. However, that cannot be the meaning of the expression here. There is not a word in Scripture of any fervent striving after penance in the sense of conversion on Esau's part. What it does relate is simply his attempt to secure the reversal of what had been done. Consequently μετάνοια must also be here understood in this sense, and translated with more recent authors: "found no possibility of reversing what had been done". This text, also, then, is not concerned with the dogmatic possibility of penance.

From all this it follows that the sin which the Epistle to the Hebrews declares unforgivable is none other than deliberate renunciation of Christ, that is the sin against the Holy Ghost. By reason of the sacrifice of our High Priest which is forever efficacious, a Christian finds forgiveness for all other sins in the measure that he strives after it by repentance. He "who has been tried in every way, like ourselves" has "compassion on our infirmities", and so, we can "go, therefore, with confidence to the throne of grace, that we may obtain mercy, and find grace" (4:15, 16; cf. 5:2; 7:24f.).

4. The Catholic Epistles and the Apocalypse

In general we find confirmed in the writings of the original Apostles the conclusions we have drawn from Paul. Indeed, James and John provide a valuable supplement to them. The campaign against the sins of Christians is very wide in its scope. The tension between the ideal of sinlessness and the reality of life is very clearly revealed. Christians are "begotten by God through the word of truth" (Jas. 1:18). Their business is to be "perfect and entire, failing in nothing" (1:4). Even more pointedly, John says "Whosoever is born of God committeth not sin: for his seed abideth in him, and he cannot sin, because he is born of God ..." (1 Jn. 3:9f.; cf. 2:8-11 etc.). In contrast to these texts, there is not merely the complaint that many Christians are unfaithful to their obligations, but the fact of a general sinfulness is established. James recognizes that "in many things we all offend" (3:2). He campaigns against a sham Christianity that consists of words instead of deeds (1:22f.; 2:14f.). For John, in his war with heretical teachers, who do not admit Christ to be the Son of God, and who therefore deny sin and the need of forgiveness, the recognition of the universality of sin is an essential point of the faith. "If we say that we have no sin, we deceive ourselves, and the truth is not in us" (1 Jn. 1:8).

Thus sin is universal, but divine forgiveness is also universal if there is sincere repentance. Even the gravest sinner can count on forgiveness (Jas. 1:21; 5:19f.). The deferment of the *Parousia* is only to be explained by the patience of the Lord who is "not willing that any should perish, but that all should return to penance" (2 Pet. 3:9). John gives the reason for the mercy which is denied to none: "But if any man sin, we have an advocate with the Father, Jesus Christ the just. And he is the propitiation for our sins, and not for ours only, but also for those of the whole world" (1 Jn. 2:1f.). The universality of forgiveness is not prejudiced by the distinction, so important for the later history of penance, between the "sin unto death" and the "sin not unto death", of which pair only the latter can be the object of efficacious prayer (1 Jn. 5:16). The distinction does not signify the opposition between mortal sins and venial sins in the sense of later theology, according to which mortal sin destroys the life of grace, and venial sin does not. John concedes that "life" is also lost through the "sin not unto death", just as, according to him, it is restored through intercessory prayer. He has another kind of opposition in mind: the "sin unto death" has for its consequence final death, the "second death" (Apoc. 2:11) or "eternal death" (*Barn.* 20, 1). Its distinctive sign is not the special gravity of the offence, but the fundamental falling away from Christ that is manifested in it, which makes men "children of the devil" (1 Jn. 3:10). In other words, like the "unforgivable sin" of the Epistle to the Hebrews, it coincides with the "sin against the Holy Ghost" (Mt. 12:31).

If intercessory prayer is recommended as a means for securing forgiveness, this is because, in accordance with Pauline teaching, the sin of an individual affects the whole community. The sinner's own penitential zeal is obviously presupposed along with the intercessory prayer. In any case John promises that the prayer will certainly be heard (1 Jn. 5:14f.). Even more explicitly James does the same in the classical text on the anointing of the sick (5:14-16) when he ends the directive for the presbyters with the charge: "Confess, therefore, your sins one to another, and pray for one another, that you may be saved. For the continual prayer of a just man availeth much." Prayer is the connatural way in which penance and the assistance given in it by others first manifests itself. As a further way of doing penance James recommends mercy (2:13) and the conversion of a sinner (5:19f.).

In contrast to Paul the emphasis on confession is new, both in James and also in 1 Jn. 1:9. In the context of the Johannine text the "confession of sins" is contrasted with the false self-righteousness of the heretical teachers who say that they "have no sin" (1:8). Confession is, therefore, a contrite consciousness of guilt, linked to a desire and prayer for forgiveness. It cannot be deduced from the text whether, in addition to interior confession to God, John also has in mind an external acknowledgement before others, such as the rulers of the church or the community, particularly in the form of a detailed confession of individual sins. Comparison with Jas. 5:16 seems to indicate some kind of public confession. It is evident from the *Didache* (ch. 14) that some form of outward confession of sins was practised by the early Christians. However, when John, in 1 Jn. 1:9, makes confession of a prerequisite for the remission of sins, he certainly does not envisage the outward form as the essential element of this confession.

The Apocalypse provides an instructive supplement to the apostolic teaching on penance. In the introductory letters the moral condition of the Church is depicted in a few bold strokes. Those who have been censured are required in the plainest terms to do penance. For less serious failings, even for those which of their nature lead to spiritual ruin, such as negligence and tepidity, all that is required is repentance and emendation (2:5; 3:1-5, 15-19). But the bishops must not tolerate grave sins, such as idolatry and unchastity, in their churches. They will be severely judged if they do not take action against these offenders, *i.e.* if the do not expel them from the community (2:2; 2:14-16; 2:20). However, even the worst evildoers, such as the woman Jezebel, are not thereby delivered up to final perdition. On the contrary, God subjects them to affliction in order even now to induce them to repent, and to give them an opportunity of salvation, notwithstanding their obduracy hitherto. Here we have a practical commentary on the concept of "the sin unto death".

If we now summarize the results of our examination of the apostolic writings it is evident that much is lacking for a complete picture of primitive penitential doctrine and practice. Nevertheless, the main outlines have become clear. Every sin calls for penance; but no sin, not even the gravest, is excluded from forgiveness, provided that sincere penance is performed. Prayer and works of mercy are means for obtaining the remission of sins. Personal prayer receives efficacious support from the intercession of the faithful as its counterpart. Joined to prayer is confession of sins. Where the sins are grave, the rulers of the Church are obliged to admonish the guilty, and, if this proves fruitless, to exclude them from the community. If the excommunicated person is converted the Church grants him her forgiveness, and this is a guarantee of "forgiveness in heaven" also, in accordance with the promise of the Lord.

II. THE POST-APOSTOLIC AGE

1. General Evidence for Penance

The writings of the post-Apostolic age (up to the second half of the second century) likewise provide only scanty material for a knowledge of the nature of penance. Hermas treats *ex professo* of penance, but only from the point of view of its necessity. Apart from him all we have are occasional observations which throw light on this or that point. They are, however, amply sufficient to confirm the basic conclusions which we have derived from the New Testament. But they leave us in the dark in regard to the detailed administrations of the penitential procedure. There was as yet no uniformity in practice. It was left to the bishop to determine the form in which the Gospel principles should be carried out, and to hold a just balance between severity in the imposition of penance and the divine readiness to grant forgiveness. It was only gradually that forms of administration became fixed. Common problems contributed to the process of unification; thus the rise of heresies like Montanism and Novatianism, or mass apostasy during persecutions, called for a uniform regulation of penance sanctioned by conciliar decisions.

Witnesses from the earliest period are in agreement first of all that even for baptized Christians penance is still available. The modern theory of a sole baptismal penance has no advocate among them. They all lay emphasis on the absolute character of the baptismal obligation, and make profession of the Christian ideal of holiness. Yet, in extolling this ideal, none of them closes his eyes to the fact that sin is to be found even among Christians, and not merely in the form of minor failings, but gross crimes also such as unchastity, adultery, hatred and abominable arrogance. The so-called *Second Epistle of Clement* (14, 1), the oldest surviving Christian homily, does not shrink from applying the prophetical image of the "den of thieves" (Jer. 1:11; Mt. 21:13) to the Church on earth, in reference to its sinful members. Nevertheless, it is consistently taught that, thanks to the precious blood of Christ, there remains a possibility of penance and salvation for all. Just as a potter can refashion a vessel that breaks in his hands while being shaped, as long as he has not thrown it into the furnace, so a man who is still living and has time for repentance is capable of being refashioned by God (2 *Clem.* 8, 1-3). The apocryphal *Epistola Apostolorum* provides an illustration of the same truth in an exposition of the parable of the wise and foolish virgins. All its instructions are more or less direct admonitions to do penance while there is yet time.

Turning to the content of penance, we find that, as we would expect, its first requirement is conversion, or a break with sin, and obedience to the law of God (1 *Clem.* 56, 1; 2 *Clem.* 8, 4, etc.). In addition, the sinner must also seek to appease God by special penitential exercises. First among these comes prayer. According to the *Didache* (8, 2f.) Christians say the Our Father three times daily, and in the fifth petition implore forgiveness for their sins. The *First Epistle of Clement* (ch. 40) and St. Justin (*Dial.* 90, 141) speak of weeping and prostrations at prayer. Having regard to later penitential practice as evidenced by Tertullian, we take these to be not just a metaphorical expression but real actions connected with prayer and deriving from Jewish tradition. Fasting and almsdeeds are joined to prayer. Almsgiving is a "ransom for sins" (*Did.* 4, 6; *Barn.* 19, 10). In the *Didache* (7, 1) and Justin (*Apol.* 1, 61), fasting is required before baptism and for this reason it will also have its place in penance. For an appreciation of it, *Second Clement* 16, 14 is instructive: "Almsgiving is good as penance for sin; fasting is better than prayer, and almsgiving better than both. 'But charity covereth a multitude of sins' (1 Pet. 4:8), and prayer from a good conscience purifies from death." But the penitential works are by no means a material equivalent of guilt. Rather it is "repentance from an upright heart which is true compensation" (ἀντιμισθία [ibid. 9:7f.]). Great importance is attached to confession of sins. As in John, this is to be understood first of all as confession to God, inasmuch as the sinner, instead of remaining obdurate in his own perverted will, humbly acknowledges his guilt and professes his readiness to do penance (1 *Clem.* 51, 3). Thus "confession" is just the same thing as doing penance, and corresponds to the term ἐξομόλογησις which is found later in Tertullian. On the other hand, it also approximates to the meaning of "praise", which it has in Scripture, and which is still prevalent in early-Christian literature. Penance is indeed true praise of God, not with the lips, but in mind and deed (2 *Clem.* 3, 4). Inasmuch as it is manifested externally, confession before God becomes also confession before men. But besides this indirect mode, formal, external confession was also practised. The evidence for this is clear from two passages of the *Didache*: "In the assembly (ἐν ἐκκλησια) confess your sins and go not to the prayer with an evil conscience" (4, 17), and similarly 14, 1: "But on the Lord's Day come together, break bread and give thanks, after you have first confessed your sins, that thereby your sacrifices may be pure." On the question of the interpretation of this confession, it is to be observed that in both texts it serves as a preparation for the prayer. It is required as a condition of God's propitious acceptance of the prayer, and is, so to speak, an essential element in it. In accordance with 1 Cor. 11:28 it is clearly most appropriate before the celebration of the eucharist, because communal liturgical prayer also calls for a preliminary purification of conscience. It is a public self-accusation before God couched in a general form, without mention of particular sins, a general prayer for forgiveness in the style of the later *Confiteor*. The designation of this kind of general self-accusation as a "confession of sins" was customary both in Judaism (cf. Lev. 16:21) and throughout Christian antiquity. Detailed confession by all the assembled faithful in the course of the liturgy would hardly have been practicable, even in a community of only moderate size. Most decisive, however, is the consideration that the idea of a Sunday confession of this kind, which supposedly would suffice to allow access to the eucharist to everyone, including those guilty of mortal sin, lies altogether beyond the horizon of early-Christian penitential procedure, as known from other sources. On the other hand, a confession in the sense of a contrite prayer for forgiveness, such as is found for example in the Our Father, is in perfect harmony with early Church practice.

The ecclesiastical aspect of penance appears first in the concern common to all for the salvation of sinners (cf. 1 *Clem.* 2, 4, 6). Fraternal correction, no less than its counterpart, intercession, is an elementary obligation of Charity (*Did.* 15, 3; Ignatius, *Eph.* 10, 1; 1 *Clem.* 56, 2; 2 *Clem.* 15, 2; 17, 2; *Ep. Apost.* Ae 148, 1ff.; 150, 4). In principle this obligation is incumbent on all, yet first of all it devolves upon the rulers of the Church, who in virtue of their office are responsible for ecclesiastical discipline. Excommunication of obstinate sinners is required, and imposed as a normal procedure (*Did.* 4, 3; 15, 3; Ignatius, *Smyrn.* 4, 1: 7, 2; *Eph.* 7, 1; Polycarp, *Phil.* 6, 11; 11, 2; *Barn.* 19, 4; 2 *Clem.* 17, 3, 5). Its effect is that all intercourse is broken off with the offender "until he does penance" (*Did.* 15, 3). There is no irrevocable exclusion of sinners. Conformably with 2 Thess. 3:15 they are not to be treated as enemies but rather to be recalled as *passibilia membra* (Polycarp, *Phil.* 11, 4). Prayer is offered for them even during the period of their exclusion (Ignatius, *Smyrn,* 4, 1).

Naturally resort was had to the penal measures only where the sins were grave. Venial or "indeliberate" sins were healed by contrite confession and prayer (1 *Clem.* 2, 3; *Did.* 4, 14; 14, 1). Mortal sin, on the other hand, has to be expiated by appropriate penance. For this reason, a sinner, even when prepared to do penance, continued to be excluded from the eucharist until he had made full satisfaction. This principle, for which there is clear evidence later, was also applied in the early-Christian period, as is shown by the solemn invitation at the end of the eucharistic prayer in the *Didache*: "Εἴ τις ἅγιός ἐστιν, ἐρχέσθω· εἴ τις οὐχ ἔστι, μετανοείτω" (10, 6). He who is holy, that is, free from sin, so that the offering is not defiled (14, 1) or profaned (14, 2) by him, may draw near; he who is not so should do penance. the word μετανοείτω cannot refer to the confession of sins before the breaking of bread, which was mentioned in 14, 1-3. For that confession is made by all without exception, and, besides, it has already been made before the celebration of the eucharist. On the other hand, the word is quite naturally explained as a warning against an unworthy communion, and is thus in harmony with the Pauline directive and with what was soon to become general practice. Even without ecclesiastical condemnation the sinner must "judge" himself (1 Cor. 11:31), and, accepting the disgrace which it involved, separate himself from the communal Christian celebration until he has "purged" his sin. Whether the cooperation of the Church was also enlisted in a penance of this kind which had been undertaken on one's own initiative cannot be clearly established from the text, but from the nature of the case it is likely. The need to seek counsel on the amount of penance that was requisite and to obtain a share in the intercessory prayers of the community on which such great store was set, would of themselves have induced a sincerely penitent Christian to confess his sin. In addition, his protracted abstention from the eucharist would be bound to give the Church authorities an occasion for addressing and admonishing him. At the very least we can say that the prescriptions of the *Didache* leave plenty of room for a sacramental procedure envisaged in the sense of Mt. 18:18.

The act of ecclesiastical forgiveness coincides with readmission to communion with the Church. Once the sinner has done the required penance, the Church, as has been shown, refrains from further punishment and thereby assures him of forgiveness. Pardon, just as punishment, belongs to the judicial office of the rulers of the Church. That is why Polycarp warns the presbyters to be impartial, mild in judgement and ready to "forgive", as "they also hoped to receive forgiveness from the Lord" (*Phil.* 6, 1f.). The forgiveness here invisaged is, as indeed constantly in other authors too, in the first place simply an ecclesiastical forgiveness. Nevertheless we find confirmation of our conclusion from Paul. Given the universal recognition of the significance of the Church as the community of salvation, readmission into the Church is also a guarantee of God's forgiveness. Thus Ignatius, *Philad.* 3, 2: "All who are of God and of Jesus Christ are with the bishop; and all who do penance and come into the unity of the Church, these also will be of God"; similarly, 1 *Clem.* 57, 2: "It is better to be a little one and to be found inside Christ's flock, than to be held in high repute, but to be excluded from its hope."

V. THE RISE OF PRIVATE PENANCE

At the close of Christian antiquity canonical penance had come to a dead end in its development. The increasing rigidity of its forms had gradually conducted it to the utopian objective of obliging all the faithful sooner or later to a kind of monastic renunciation of the world. The result of such an excessive demand was that ecclesiastical penance ceased to play any practical part in life, and was almost exclusively regarded simply as a means of preparation for death. Precisely in the years when sins importuned men most strongly there was no sacramental remedy at their disposal. No amount of pastoral care by way of preaching, personal admonition or penal measures could make up for the privation of the sacrament. In the absence of a penitential institution which was obligatory on all and repeatedly available to all, the great mass of men in that age of brutalized morals put off not only the *accipere paenitentiam*, but also the *agere paenitentiam*. The situation is illustrated by a brief remark of the monk Jonas in the *Life of Columban* (c. 11) stating that on the arrival of the great missionary in Gaul, about 590, *paenitentiae medicamenta et mortificationis amor vix vel paucis in illis reperiebatur locis* (*PL* 87, 1018f.).

An effective reform of ecclesiastical penance was only possible if there was a retreat from the rigid principle which forbade its repetition. This was the chief cause of the whole peculiar development. We have already heard that Chrysostom was accused by his enemies of having acted contrary to the principle. It remains an open question to what extent the reproach was justified. Undoubtedly it is a possibility not to be ruled out that the great bishop set aside the law which was not founded on the doctrine of faith, and which was such a grave handicap in pastoral care, and that he granted repeated forgiveness in a private mode of procedure. However, this is the sole evidence that exists. In the continental Western Church two full centuries elapsed before this new procedure was mentioned for the first time, and, significantly, once again in the form of a sharp condemnation. The well known canon II of the Third Synod of Toledo (589) rejects as an *execrabilis praesumptio* the practice that *per quasdam Hispaniarum ecclesias non secundum*

66

canonem, sed foedissime pro suis peccatis homines agere paenitentiam, ut quotiescumque peccare libuerit, totiens a presbytero reconciliari expostulent. The observance of the canonical form, including excommunication, the penitential dress, the status of a penitent, the penitential blessing and reconciliation, is most emphatically enjoined. It is, however, noteworthy that the "abuse" had already gained ground in all the churches of Spain. Now, at the very time that the sixty-four bishops and the seven episcopal delegates delivered their verdict on it, private penance began its triumphant migration to the European mainland. Its home were the Celtic churches in Britain and Ireland. Our first task, then, is to describe Celtic penance, and to give an account of its transplanting on to the Continent.

1. Penance in the Celtic and Anglo-Saxon Churches

Because of its isolation the Celtic Church occupied a special place apart in questions of worship and discipline, and for centuries remained fixed in its usages which differed from those of the rest of the Church. Also peculiar to it was the fact that it had no knowledge of the institution of a public ecclesiastical penance which could not be repeated, and which involved canonical obligations. It had not shared in the faulty development which has been described, nor blocked the way for itself for an effective practice of penance. Penance is here private in character. Its "reception" consists in confession, in the acceptance of the satisfaction fixed by the priest, and finally in reconciliation. It has no defamatory or juridical consequences, and is available to all at any time. The sources for Celtic penitential practice date from the sixth century. In essentials they consist of the penitential books, native to the islands, which provide precisely determined penances for all offences, whether grave or slight in character (Tariff penance). Casuistical in form, they were for the use of confessors. In contrast to the canonical decisions of councils and popes their authority is purely private, and they carry weight only in virtue of the prestige of their authors, rather like the so-called "canonical letters" of the ancient Eastern Church. The oldest comprehensive collection is the Irish *Penitential of Finnian* dating from the sixth century, of which the prescriptions passed in large part into the later penitential books. Among these are the *Penitential of Cummean*, and the *Penitential of Columban*, named after the famous missionary. Best known, however, is the Anglo-Saxon *Penitential of Theodore* named after the Greek Theodore († 690) who as archbishop of Canterbury exercised a strong influence on the penitential discipline, with the result that his pronouncements, mingled with decisions deriving from other sources, were propagated in a number of collections. The author of the penitential, who in the preface describes himself as the *discipulus Umbrensium*, intends to give a critical and ordered compilation of the prescriptions of Theodore. The origin of the work is not to be put before the middle of the eighth century. Essentially more imperfect are two other Anglo-Saxon penitential books which also erroneously bear the names of famous men. These are the *Penitential of Bede* († 735) and the *Penitential of Egbert*, Archbishop of York († 767); both are jumbled compilations from older collections dating from about the year 800. It is significant that the Anglo-Saxon Church took over the arrangement of penance from the Celtic Church, even though the latter had for long sharply separated itself from the Germanic conquerors. The *Penitential of Theodore* is the very first to express the difference between the arrangement of penance which is observed in Rome and that "in this province". *Reconciliatio in hac provincia publice statuta non est, quia et publica paenitentia non est* (I, c. 12).

Among the penitential prescriptions fasting joined with fervent prayer occupies the most prominent place, so that in the penitential books *paenitere* simply means "to fast". It admits of different degrees, both in regard to abstinence from certain foods and drinks and also in the restriction of eating and drinking to a small amount. Thus there is fasting "on bread and water", and abstinence from flesh meat, from solid food and from wine; there are stricter fasts on certain days of the week (*feriae legitimae*) or times of the year (the three *quadragesimae* [the forty days before Easter, and those before Christmas and after Pentecost. Cf. *Pen.* II, xiv, 1. Tr.]. For the shedding of blood and sins of unchastity abstention from marital intercourse and renunciation of weapons were normally required, and for certain specially heinous sins exile (*peregrinatio perennis*) was also imposed in addition to other penitential works. Naturally almsgiving is not forgotten. The duration of these penances is graded according to the gravity of the sins, and varies in the different books. In Theodore penances are generally greater than in the Celtic collections and in Bede and Egbert; these two are clearly seeking to mitigate the harshness of the Theodorean discipline. Starting from sentences of life-long penance for certain specific crimes, we find others of fifteen, twelve, ten or seven years downwards to one year; and for lighter sins of forty, twenty, seven days or one day (*e.g.* for drunkenness, seven days; for immoderate eating, one day); and in the case of repeated offences each individual act is taken into account.

The value of the individual penitential acts is determined by the degree of self-denial which they entail. Consequently a longer penance can be replaced by a shorter one of a more intensive character. In this case the fasting is carried to the point of complete abstinence from food, and is combined with vigils, continuous recitation of psalms in a standing posture with arms outstretched, genuflexions and other similar complications. In this way, for example, a *triduanum, i.e.* a forced fast of this kind lasting for three days, is reckoned as the *arreum anni*, that is as the equivalent of a normal penance of one year. A substitution of this sort often proved necessary for the reason that, owing to the high scale of the tariff penance, the whole length of a man's life would not have sufficed for the fulfilment of a normal penitential burden. Redemptions represented a special kind of commutation. Their original purpose was to adapt penance to personal circumstances and needs. That was necessary in the first place for the sick, for whom there could no longer be any question of fasting. The most convenient substitute was almsgiving (cf. *Pen Cummeani* VIII, 21). The redemption was taken over from Celtic tribal law, and was the equivalent of the "wergeld" [O. Ir. éric. Tr.] by payment of which every offence could be expiated. Quite early, however, it came to be employed in other cases, and this obviously involved the danger of externalism and moral worthlessness.

The Synod of Cloveshoe (747) spoke out against the practice, characterising it as a "new invention" and as a "dangerous custom" (Mansi XII 403). Nevertheless it continued to develop. In the penitentials of Bede and Egbert the penances proper are already practically replaced by the redemptions which are immediately subjoined. Sufficient justification is now seen in the fact that the proper penance *ardua et difficilis est (Pen. Bedae* c. XI). The most dubious case was when a person paid money for others to take his place in the performance of penance. The principle of penance by proxy could have a certain justification when a person was hindered from performing it (cf. *Pen. Bedae* c. X, 8). In practice, however, its outcome is shown by the direction in the [spurious-Tr.] penitential canons of King Edgar dating from the second half of the tenth century, which indicates how a magnate could finish his seven-year penance in three days by means of an equivalent number of fasts by hired men (Mansi XVIII 525).

In evaluating the penitential books and their strange, even revolting, prescriptions, account has to be taken of the historical situation in which they had their origins. It was a matter of waging war on the savagery and vice of still half pagan children of nature, on bloodshed, drunkenness and all kinds of natural and unnatural forms of unchastity. The robust discipline, and what may be called its homely directness, with its drastic remedies and strenuous exercises was admirably adapted to the violence of instinct. The size and strict standardization of the punishments become intelligible to us when we remember that the penitential laws also represented secular penal law. The penitential books sought to meet the danger of penance becoming a mechanical business by laying the greatest emphasis on the truth that the performance of penance is only efficacious where there is sincere contrition and conversion. Constant prayer, in conjunction with tears and sighs, is for them indispensable, in the same way as in ancient Christian penitential practice. An unprejudiced judge must at any rate recognize the deep moral earnestness and the stern and unrelenting notion of atonement on which the system was based. In this respect the disappearance of publicity in the procedure had brought no change in its spirit of severity. The practice of redemptions was a concession to human weakness, and we may find its numbering and balancing of good works little to our taste; but underlying it there was a firm belief in the reality of the concepts of guilt and atonement. Precisely because for the men of that age these realities were indistinguishable from the concrete things of life they "reckoned" also with these, and this they did in the rough and ready way appropriate to their stage of cultural development. Contemporary critics should hesitate to bring forward the charge of laxity, all the more so when it is considered that what was demanded for a redemption goes far beyond what could be expected of modern man in the way of expiation.

Although in ancient Celtic penance great emphasis was laid on penitential works, yet the ecclesiastical and sacramental aspect of penance stands forth clearly. It is only efficacious through the ministry of the priest; as judge he has to adapt the punishment to the gravity of the guilt and to individual circumstances in the light of the penitential book. The phrase *iudice sacerdote* constantly recurs in the canons (*Finnian* 9, 23; *Cummean* III 3, 12; IV 4; V 2; VIII 2, 3, 20). In contrast to ancient ecclesiastical practice, priests appear from the outset as the ordinary ministers of the sacrament of penance alongside of the bishop (*Theodore* II 2, 15), and only in exceptional cases is a particularly grave sin reserved to the bishop (*Cummean* X 18; *Columban* B 25). The judical function of the priest presupposes confession, which makes known to him the state of soul of the sinner. In this system with its personal mode of procedure and its provision of a special punishment for every individual offence, confession is naturally more strongly emphasized as compared with the old canonical penance; although, precisely because it is so obvious a matter it is seldom mentioned in the penitential books. A novelty appears in that now even slighter sins in the greatest variety are submitted to confession. Here we have a link between this sacramental ecclesiastical penance which allows of repetition and the frequent confession which was practised in monasteries and pious lay circles with a view to spiritual therapy. As the care of souls among the Celts was largely in the hands of monks, the extension of monastic practice to the laity occurred quite naturally. Here and there the ancient penitentials reveal the connexion with monastic discipline quite clearly.

But it is wrong to exaggerate this connexion and to regard monastic confession as the primary source of the entire later institution of penance. Confession of grave sins was also of strict obligation in the ancient Church, and in regard to the other essential parts of the sacrament—contrition, satisfaction and reconciliation—Celtic penitential practice is also in complete harmony with that of the ancient Church. Further, exclusion from the eucharist until reconciliation is likewise required, as also are special penitential obligations, such as abstention from marital intercourse and renunciation of military service. In view of all this, the differences which we have described, however important in themselves, are only of an accidental character, and do not abolish the historic connexion of the new system with the old one. According to the *Penitential of Theodore* it is the same penance *in hac provincia*, except that it is differently organized than *apud Romanos*. The clear attestation of the act of reconciliation is of special significance; this had its place only in canonical penance, and not in "Monastic confession". In canons of all kinds, after the determination of the penance, the note is found, *et reconcilietur altario* or *recipiatur ad communionem (Finnian 6, 14, 35, 36; Columban B 3, 13, 15, 18, 25)*. Canon 14 of the first synod under St. Patrick has the formula *et postea resolvetur a sacerdote*, an undeniable reference to the power of the keys. Strictly speaking, after the disappearance of the excommunication which was linked with public penance, the concept of "reconciliation" is no longer quite appropriate. However, as the exclusion of a penitent from the eucharist was still kept up, the phrase *reconcilietur altario* could still be used in reference to the renewed concession of Communion. The very fact of the application of a concept which is no longer quite appropriate to a differently organized penitential institution is a clear proof of its connexion with canonical penance.

2. *The Transplanting of the Celtic Penitential System on the Continent*

Among the primitive people of the British Isles Christianity attained to an unexpectedly early flowering. Notwithstanding their wild and passionate character they were fundamentally unspoiled, and unlike the Germanic tribes on the Continent they were not exposed to the corrupting influence of a decadent ancient society. They were, therefore, in a position to employ some of their surplus energy in the service of other churches. It is impossible to overestimate the historic importance of the Irish and the Anglo-Saxons as new fertilizing agents on the widest scale of the religious and intellectual life of the West; thereby they made a decisive contribution to the establishment of medieval civilization. Great numbers of monks followed in the wake of Columban († 615), that ardent, eccentric and strongwilled pioneer of the missionary activity, and they became the apostles and teachers of the Continent which was then showing signs of the most serious religious decay. Naturally the immediate aim of their work of reformation was the awakening of the spirit of penance and, as was only to be expected, in this activity they retained the organization of penance which was native to them. Proof of this is seen in the *Penitential of Columban* which was entirely composed on Frankish soil, and which at least in regard to its nucleus is correctly named. Its whole content places it in the Celtic system of penance and we have, therefore, put it without hesitation in that category. Boudinhon says with justice: "The route taken by the tariff penance in Gaul and Germany is easy to follow: it is none other than that of the missionary monks."

Generally speaking, the introduction of the new penitential procedure passed off without friction and without opposition, in sharp contrast to the severe condemnation which the same innovation had encountered in the Third Synod of Toledo. There is nowhere mention of an alteration introduced by the Celtic missionaries. There is no reference at all to the *Penitential of Columban* even though many Gallic synods dealt with questions concerning penance. The interest of contemporaries was centred on the energy and emphasis with which the northern monks insisted on penance as the most elementary requirement of the Gospel, and not on the ecclesiastical form of penance. The first ecclesiastical document to adopt an attitude to the new procedure is canon 8 of the Synod of Chalon about the year 650: *De paenitentia vero, quae est medela animae, utilem hominibus esse censemus; et ut paenitentibus a sacer-*

dotibus data confessione indicatur paenitentia, universitas sacerdotum noscitur consentire. The declaration, as Loening and Hinschius have perceived, can only refer to a new institution. The obvious truth of the usefulness of penance does not need a synodal decree, but the new form of penance with its special characteristics does. The sense is that the faithful confess repeatedly to the priest, are instructed by him, and receive from him appropriate penances for individual sins; whereas formerly, apart from the penance received once only at the end of life, they were left to themselves to do personal works of penance. Yet the fact that the question was a subject of deliberation shows that even at Chalon certain scruples had been felt against the new practice. However, the synod adopted the opposite attitude to that of the fathers of Toledo half a century earlier and unanimously approved the new procedure. It is worth noting that amongst those who took part in the synod were men who were products of Columban's famous monastery at Luxeuil, such as St. Giles of Noyon, Donatus of Besancon and Chagnoald of Laon. In them the method of penance sanctioned by their master had its most effective advocates.

The best proof for the adoption of the tariff penance is provided by the Frankish penitential books which were already numerous in the second half of the eighth century. Thanks to the thorough research work which has been done, we now have a fairly clear view of their origin and interdependence. They derive from three sources: 1. Canonical material, chiefly taken from the collection of Dionysius which was received in Gaul, and from the ordinances of Gallo-Merovingian synods—*iudicia canonica*; 2. Celtic statutes—*iudicia Cummeani*; 3. Anglo-Saxon statutes—*iudicia Theodori*. As was to be expected, there has been a fusion of the penitential statutes used in Gaul with those brought with them by the missionaries. In connexion with this Fournier has established a very significant fact. This is the inclusion of a considerable number of texts from the *Penitential of Columban* among the *iudicia canonica*. This means that the decisions of the celebrated abbot of Luxeuil were from the first put on a level with the canonical norms. This is further confirmation that his practice was by no means regarded as something new in principle, but simply as the continuation and further development of the ancient procedure. The borrowings from Celtic and Anglo-Saxon penitentials are primarily to be attributed to the practice of the missionaries, who continued to make use of their native form of penance. These penitentials must have been welcome to the Frankish priests as a supplement to their scanty canonical decisions. Above all, however, they commended themselves by their greater mildness as compared with the canonical decrees. This appears not only in regard to the amount of penance, but still more in reference to the redemptions, particularly as set forth in the penitentials of Bede and Egbert which from the turn of the eighth century had a wide circulation in the Frankish kingdom.

Naturally the penitentials were very convenient in practice, but their indiscriminate use necessarily led to confusion in the administration of penance and to a serious relaxation of ecclesiastical discipline. A reaction against this made itself felt in the so-called Carolingian reform. The reforming synods of Tours, Chalon and Rheims which were held in the year 813 expressly decreed that the penitential books should be repudiated, and that a return should be made to the ancient canonical procedure. With a view to implementing the decrees a series of new penitential ordinances was drawn up which substantially were restricted to a systematic compilation of the *sententiae patrum,* and of canons and decretals. Circumstances were, however, stronger than the will to reform. The penitential books proved indispensable to the average clergy. Consequently the Synod of Tours (Canon 22) in its verdict allowed from the outset the retention of a single authorized book chosen from them all, and Halitgar appended a proper penitential as the sixth book to his collection of canons, giving as a reason: *simplicioribus qui maiora non valent capere, poterit prodesse.* However, the ancient penitential books also continued in existence and were augmented by new ones. As late as the opening of the eleventh century the *Decretum Burchardi* provides in the *Corrector* a new and very extensive penitential containing extracts from earlier books. It was not until the great reform of Gregory VII that the penitential books were effectively withdrawn from circulation.

Public penance, of which the voluntary reception was already in the sixth century a rare event, had practically disappeared by about the year 800, to judge from the complaints of the reforming synods. These insist on its reintroduction, with the sanctions of the civil power when occasion demands (*e.g.* in regard to *incestuosi et parricidae*). Here public penance is from the first restricted to public sinners. The reformers are no longer aware that in the past it was required for all mortal sins, and do not even suspect that private penance even for secret sins was first introduced through the despised penitential books in contravention of the ancient canonical ordinance. In reality the axiom which they proclaimed: public penance for public sins, private penance for secret sins, is an important innovation in the development of the administration of penance. Henceforth public and private penance go forward together with equality of right. In principle they are equivalent, both in their effect and in their demands. For this reason the leaders of the reform require that in private penance the same punishments shall apply as in public penance. Admittedly care had to be taken here to preserve secrecy, although on this point there was no scrupulosity. In any case the redemptions provided a convenient means of sparing a secret sinner embarrassing penitential exercises.

In public penance the form of administration was the old canonical rite, but now further developed. The imposition of hands at the commencement of penance was linked with the distribution of ashes, and followed by the expulsion of the penitents from the church. Specially noteworthy is the prescription which already occurs in the *Gelasian Sacramentary* (at the beginning of the eighth century) and in a great variety of later *ordines* that the penitent is to be kept in confinement from the beginning of his penance on Ash Wednesday until Maundy Thursday, the ancient date for reconciliation. The detailed observance of the regulation will have varied according to local circumstances. The essential point was the detection and punishment of the criminals, and the control of their penance in custody, whether in the bishop's residence or in their own dwelling-place. Only criminal cases such as murder, incest, adultery and perjury were involved. The Carolingian reform took stringent measures to enforce the law in this respect. On Maundy Thursday the penitents were again brought before the bishop by their "deans", and he then decided whether they should be admitted to reconciliation or continue to do penance during Lent of the next year. The reason for this was that often, in fact in the majority of cases, in view of the gravity of the crimes penance during one Lent was insufficient. In the *Gelasian Sacramentary* a more elaborate arrangement of the rite of reconciliation is already visible. The penitent lies prostrate on the ground in the presence of the congregation, the deacon presents him to the bishop and begs for his readmission, whereupon the bishop pronounces over him the prayers of reconciliation. From the ninth century a further development appears, corresponding to the rite of expulsion on Ash Wednesday; this is the solemn readmission of the penitents into the church, a ceremony which gives vivid and moving expression both to the original meaning of reconciliation and to its immediate effect.

The earliest information on the arrangement of private penance is found in the penitential books of the eighth century which were composed in Frankish lands. Appended to these was an instruction for the reception of confessions. About the turn of the ninth century there were already formal *ordines* for confession with directions for the conduct of the penitent and the confessor, along with rubrics and formulae, after the manner of other church functions which were regulated by their corresponding *ordines*. We will examine these more closely in the next section.

Louis Bouyer
1913-

Père Bouyer has been one of the most prolific and scholarly contributors to the Catholic renewal over the past three decades. As a young man he entered the Lutheran ministry, and the development of this thought that led to his becoming a Catholic is set forth in his Spirit and Forms of Protestantism *(1956). He has always had a great interest in the early Church, in the Bible, the liturgy, monasticism, and spirituality in general. Among his works are biographies of St. Anthony, Cardinal Newman, Erasmus, Philip Neri, and Dom Lambert Beauduin. As a priest of the French Oratory he has taught for many years at the Institut Catholique in Paris and at the University of Notre Dame in Indiana.*

Bouyer's monumental work on the Eucharist *(1966) is a striking example of how liturgical studies had progressed since the time of Dom Guéranger. With a much firmer grasp on the patristic material Bouyer was able to show the rich roots of the Christian eucharist in the Jewish liturgy and the traditional forms of table blessings. He also delineated more clearly the problems found in medieval trends with a silent canon, a substitute piety, and an off-center theology. On the other hand, he was convinced that "the work of the great scholars . . . of the 17th century·is far from being appreciated even yet as it ought to be."*

In The Decomposition of Catholicism *(1969) Bouyer used biting satire to reveal his intense anger at some of the doings of both right-wing and left-wing extremists in the post-Vatican II Church. He felt that both lacked any true sense of the meaning of tradition, and that the future was bleak unless that sense was recovered. His scathing criticism touches on so many areas that few escape his wrath, but in the end he acknowledges that this is not the whole picture and that the possiblity of recovery exists if Catholics will plunge their roots into the liturgy "in all its human and sacral fullness, together with the living interpretation of God's Word, which alone can give this culture to us and make it what it should be."*

These later works of Père Bouyer are mentioned in order to illustrate the way in which his earlier promise has borne fruit. The book by which he first became something of a "household word" was his 1955 Liturgical Piety, *which is excerpted here. It would be difficult to calculate its precise influence, but it was a major factor in bringing a generation of American Catholics to their first awareness of the solidity of the roots of the early Liturgical Movement. The rich combination of Biblical and liturgical, of patristics and spirituality, was still a relative novelty at the time of its appearance. The intervening years have served to help all to appreciate how much of a contribution Bouyer really made.*

The following selection contains two of the 19 chapters of Liturgical Piety: *the fifth, which sketches the highlights in the history of the continental Liturgical Movement, (and which serves as an interesting complement to the account given by H. A. Reinhold that is also in this volume.) And the sixth, which reviews "The Catholic Tradition concerning the Shape of the Eucharist". Here, a decade before the reform of Vatican II, he was already warning about the double danger that threatens all reforms: "false traditionalism" on the one extreme, and "rash modernism" on the other. Few contemporaries have had as much of substance to offer in this entire realm as Père Louis Bouyer.*

LITURGICAL PIETY

CHAPTER FIVE

CONTEMPORARY MOVEMENTS: SOLESMES, BELGIUM, GERMANY, FRANCE SINCE THE LAST WAR

From what has been said, in the last chapter especially, some readers might conclude that Dom Guéranger has been given the part of the villain all through our story. Nothing could be further from the truth. We are forced to point out his greatest mistakes in order ourselves to avoid their inevitable and disastrous consequences. But doing so must not blind us to the fact that there is no achievement whatever in the contemporary liturgical movement which did not originate in some way with Dom Guéranger. The very least that we can say in his praise is that he brought the liturgy back to life as something to be lived and loved for its own sake. This new life, as he understood it, had a galvanic quality, in both senses of the word; for while it implied a measure of artifice, it had also a thrilling power to arouse the interest and to stir the mind and heart of a good many men of his time. His love of the liturgy, like so many passionate loves, embraced something that often was more chimerical than real, but nevertheless this love was on fire with a burning passion, and so was capable of communicating itself to others. And we must also praise, not so much the intrinsic beauty with which the liturgy was performed at Solesmes and its dependent monasteries—since this beauty attracted the few but repelled the many, and among them some of the best men of the period—as the deep reverence that always pervaded it. This characteristic, along with others that might also be mentioned, sufficed to indicate to some lofty souls and deep minds what treasures of religious thought and sentiment—of piety in the best sense of the word—were hidden in the Roman Liturgy, and what a complete expression of human needs and aspirations could be found in it.

After his time, it was slowly discovered that the "Roman Liturgy" in the form that Dom Guéranger had tried to make supreme and exclusive was not, in fact, the Roman Liturgy at its best. It was rather a late embodiment of that liturgy, an embodiment produced by many conflicting forces, and the very Popes who had canonized the liturgical books of Pius V had never intended the liturgy they prescribed to remain unchanged. Even before this discovery of the true nature of the "Roman" liturgy, people began to feel that the setting which Guéranger had worked so hard to provide for the liturgy was not, perhaps, so much in tune with its enduring mentality as he had innocently imagined. Even in the recent, post-tridentine form in which it is embodied in the books of Pius V, the Roman Liturgy everywhere implicitly protests against the attempt to make of it an impersonal ceremonial in which none of the people take part, designed merely to provide a few spiritual dilettantes with an exquisite but highly sophisticated kind of nourishment.

But all these criticisms were made by Dom Guéranger's own disciples sooner than by anybody else; and the best way to provide a balance for the criticisms we ourselves have made of his work is to realize that his followers were only able to go deeper and further than he himself into the true nature of the liturgy because he had already given them so much of positive value.

In my opinion, the decisive turning point for the Liturgical Movement came in 1909, when, at a Catholic Conference held at Malines in Belgium, Dom Lambert Beauduin, a monk of Mont César, proposed what was to become the basis of the Belgian liturgical renewal.

In the years preceding this conference, Saint Pius X had paved the way for such a revival. By his proposed reformation of the Roman Breviary (which was carried out two years after the conference), by his strenuous efforts to make Holy Communion once again a normal and regular practice in the Christian daily life, by the motives for the fostering of the chant emphasized in the *Motu Proprio* on Sacred Music, the Pope had led the way toward a rediscovery of the liturgy as true prayer. And he had, by the same means, led the way toward a new realization of the fundamental principle that the liturgy is something which we are not meant merely to see or to hear, but in which we are, above all, to take part, as in the traditional and collective glorification of God, bringing before Him the whole individual man in the whole Christian community.

But to gather up all these lines of rediscovery, to apply all these implications of the work of Pius X to actual personal and pastoral practice required the soul of a contemplative and a priest. The task called for a man imbued with the perception and the love of the Church as a living mystery, a man also to whom liturgical life should be life itself, and who would be inspired with an intense desire to make it possible for all his brethren in Christ to enjoy the same experience. This man, this priest, was found in the person of Dom Lambert Beauduin. In him we should revere one of the most simple and unpretentious yet one of the greatest figures of the Church in the twentieth century. His great mind, possessed both of clarity and depth, his open heart, his intense devotion to Our Lord and His Church, his acute perception of the needs of both the faithful and the clergy, make this humble monk able to lead some of the most courageous and providential enterprises of the Church in our times, enterprises whose lasting value cannot yet be ascertained.

We should never forget that Dom Beauduin, before he became a Benedictine at Mont César, had been a secular priest of the diocese of Liège. He had worked there for eight years in an extremely active ministry, especially among working men, as one of those "Chaplains of Workmen" appointed in this diocese to forward the practical application of the great Encyclical of Pope Leo XIII, *Rerum Novarum*. But Dom Beauduin was attracted to the cloister by the need he felt for a more deeply founded piety. And, as a monk, he was called to teach theology to the younger monks. Thus were providentially combined in this priest of wide experience, zeal for the souls of modern men, desire for a true and deep kind of piety, and interest in a better understanding of Christian dogma.

All these qualifications caused Dom Lambert to realize, first of all, that the liturgy itself, properly understood, is the fundamental catechesis of Christian doctrine, and that its presentation is the means most capable of stimulating and feeding the highest and purest spiritual life. And he also realized that the liturgy itself, thus understood, is meant to be the well-spring of spiritual vitality and to provide the framework for Christian living, not only for individuals, not only for some Christians, but for the whole Christian people in the Church. As he says in his little book: *La Piété de l'Eglise* (first published in 1914) he often thought that great marvels could be accomplished by the clergy in reinvigorating Christian life in their parishes if only they worked to have their people find in their parish church the house of God and the gate of heaven; in their parish priest, the man who offers, blesses, leads, teaches and baptizes; in the parish Mass, the great weekly meeting of the Christian people in which, by the action of the visible priesthood, men united in bonds of brotherhood are to be transformed into the whole Christ! What pains priests take, he often thought,—this priest who had been active for so many years in so many kinds of social work—what labors they undergo to organize so many works that are certainly useful, but of secondary importance! But what would be the effects if priests took the same pains to promote the rediscovery of essentials through a rediscovery of the liturgy, if they labored to have the liturgy understood and practised by the whole Christian people as its collective and personal life of prayer and worship in Christ and the Church? One sentence in the *Motu Proprio* of Pius X could sum up this program and express its ideal aim, and to this sentence Dom Lambert referred again and again: "Our deepest wish is that the true Christian spirit should once again flourish in every way and establish itself among the faithful; and to that end it is necessary first of all to provide for the sanctity and dignity of the temple where the faithful meet together precisely in order to find that spirit at its primary and indispensable source, that is . . . the active participation in the most holy and sacred mysteries and in the solemn and common prayer of the Church." No man of the time was so well prepared as Dom Lambert to listen to the words of the Blessed Pope, and no one else was so ready as he to proclaim these words so forcefully.

In the Catholic Conference previously mentioned at Malines in 1909, where the Belgian Liturgical Movement actually began, Dom Lambert's aims and his practical program met with the complete approval of Cardinal Mercier, one of the most eminent prelates of modern times, and of Godefroy Kurth, a famous layman and historian. These desiderata were, therefore, formulated under Dom Lambert's direction:

1) That the Roman missal should be translated, and its use promoted widely among the faithful as their chief devotional book, to popularize at least the complete text of Sunday Mass and Vespers.

2) That an effort should be made to have all piety grow more "liturgical," especially by means of the recitation of Compline as evening prayer, by attendance at the parochial Mass and Vespers, and by teaching the people to find in their participation in the prayers of the Mass the best preparation for receiving Holy Communion and the best way of making their thanksgiving afterward. All this should be accompanied by the attempt to restore earlier liturgical traditions in Christian homes.

3) That Gregorian chant should be fostered, according to the Pope's desires.

4) That the choir members in each parish should be encouraged to make annual retreats in some center of liturgical life such as a Benedictine abbey.

In the years following the Conference at Malines, Dom Lambert and his brethren at Mont César were the leading and principal workers in carrying out this program. But, as Dom Olivier Rousseau emphasizes, Dom Lambert himself soon came to widen the scope of the last point and thus to transform it. For he came to find his foremost liturgical apostolate in winning not so much lay people who were choir members, but first of all the priests themselves, especially the parish priests. Here is shown most clearly the perceptive genius of this great Benedictine. He himself, led by the teaching of the Pope and by his own Christian and priestly experience, had come to rediscover the liturgy as the prayer and worship of the Christian people. In the same way, he now realized that since the liturgy is the pastoral work *par excellence,* the pastors must be the first to be convinced of its value; they must be encouraged not only to promote the liturgy for the sake of their parishioners, but, first of all, to find in it for themselves the true source of their spiritual life and apostolate.

But we must add that however important was this vision of Dom Lambert's, it would probably have produced no fruit if he had not also possessed in abundance the practical insight into men's minds and the sympathetic fraternal affection required to help his brethren in the priesthood to make for themselves and for their people the discovery of the liturgy that he had already made for himself.

We do not need to go thoroughly here into the history of the review *Questions liturgiques et paroissiales* and of the *"Semaines liturgiques,"* the two main organs through which the liturgical movement was soon to become the focus of the life of the Church in Belgium. But we must point out some of the characteristics of the work which Dom Beauduin accomplished through these means and many others.

The most striking characteristic is what we might call its realism, taking the word in its best sense and referring it to two complementary aspects of the work of restoring the liturgy. In the first place, Dom Lambert and his followers have always kept in mind the actual people whom they were addressing, both priests and lay people, and the actual parishes of these priests and people, each with its own problems. So Dom Lambert and his followers spared no pains to make everything that they proposed quite clear to priests and people, in a patient and prudent, but decidedly progressive fashion. They also tried in every way to arouse the interest of their audience, and to establish and develop the natural connection between whatever was already in the minds of their readers and what the liturgy had to offer them. And by this we mean not only the way in which the liturgy could answer needs of which priests and people were already aware, but the way in which it could correct, purify and enrich their whole view of religion and of the Christian life.

The Belgian liturgical movement has also showed this character of true realism in a second way: by always going to work with the actual liturgy of the Church of today. Dom Lambert was far too learned to imagine that the Roman Missal as it now stands is in a state of perfection that has never been surpassed or that never could be surpassed. But he deliberately refrained from any attempt to confuse liturgical renewal with liturgical reformation, either by going back to more ancient rites

86

and usages or by undertaking new and unprecedented experiments. With a wisdom which we cannot esteem too highly, he always held to a principle which could be expressed in this way: the liturgy belongs to the Church; let us, then, take it just as the Church of today has treasured it for us and as she offers it to us; let us try to know it, to understand it, to carry it out *as it is,* as perfectly as we can. Let this work suffice for us now; when we have done our best to accomplish it, then will be the time to see whether there is also something further to be attempted.

This wisdom proceeded, of course, from Dom Lambert's own personal experience. The life of a Benedictine had shown this young and active priest, in search of a source of a more intense and effective spirituality than that he already possessed, that we have a forgotten treasure in the actual liturgy of today, the liturgy of the modern Roman Missal and Breviary. Nobody would ever dream how much a man could rediscover in it and could strive to carry out in his own life and priestly ministry. For anyone, then, to allow himself to wander about in dreamy fields of anticipation of future reforms or restoration of practices of the past before he had attempted fully to make use of what exists in the present,—this would be to give in to the most foolish kind of temptation.

Here, then, is the clue to the great importance of the Belgian movement,—that it never got lost in archeologism or antiquarianism, and it was never tempted to wander off into innovations of doubtful value. This movement consisted in the pure and strong rediscovery of living tradition as it is: not a thing of the past, but the actual reality of the Church of today to be lived by the people of today, a reality so continually overflowing with riches as yet unknown as to render foolish any wish to look for something different until this reality as it is has been once more fully explored and put to use. We have now in the liturgy of the Church, treasures that we do not make use of because we do not know of their existence. Let us come to know them. What could be more matter-of-fact, more simple, and more healthful than this modest program?

This was the first foundation of all Dom Lambert's work; and it is wonderful to see how his wide and deep knowledge of history, and his piety that was so soundly doctrinal, springing as it did from the highest sources of tradition, contributed so much to a real understanding of the rites and prayers of the Church and to their appreciation. We would admire him even more greatly, if we were to follow all his activities for the purpose of restoring a vital practice by priests and people, and observe the balance of true learning, a most personal piety, pastoral experience and love of souls shown throughout all his work.

This true realism of the Belgian liturgical movement was ruled and inspired by a wide and deep devotion of the Church, the actual hierarchical and collective Church of today, acknowledged and loved as the living body of Christ. This *ecclesiastical* characteristic of all Dom Lambert's work, and, in particular, the completely revitalized understanding of the sense of that word "ecclesiastical" which his work brings about, is, perhaps, the true reason for its astonishing success. But also, in close connection with this rediscovery of the Church in and through the rediscovery of the liturgy, we must realize the importance of Dom Lambert's understanding of the nature of the priesthood and of its unique role in the Church and in the liturgical renewal. For this understanding is the key to the practical method used by Dom Beauduin in going about the work of renewal, as it is also the key to that pastoral character which is an essential quality of the liturgical movement. We must always remember that Dom Beauduin himself did not go to the monastery in order to escape from the priestly responsibilities he had already assumed, but rather to be more capable of being faithful to them. So he was able to explain vividly to his fellow priests how the two purposes a priest should have in studying the liturgy are actually one: how will the liturgy enable me to live as God wants me to live; how will it enable me to have my people live that same life, the life of Christ in them? So also Dom Lambert was able to understand so well and to make others understand the two-fold aspect of the liturgy, that since it is, as we have said, the possession of the Church, it is both the possession of the whole Christian people in its vital unity and the most important reality at the basis of every Christian's most personal life.

The perfection of this synthesis, so completely and spontaneously achieved by Dom Lambert, may perhaps be described best by saying that it shows us how to appreciate that word, Catholic; and no better priase can be given that great priest and religious than to say that in all his work he shows himself to be *homo Catholicus* par excellence.

In connection with the Belgian liturgical movement, we must mention the new missals that were produced with complete translations and sound explanations. Such missals were proposed first of all at Malines, and became the main instrument of the movement. And the movement itself was largely responsible for their astonishingly quick and widespread diffusion. In this field, we need only mention the names of Dom Fernand Cabrol, Abbot of Farnborough, and Dom Gaspar Lefebvre, the famous monk of Bruges.

Another great characteristic of the Belgian liturgical movement was that it was not the work of a party or of specialists, nor was it a kind of separate activity in the Church. From the first everyone understood it to be a general renewal of Christian teaching and life, both indvidual and collective, a renewal of the Church itself through the renewal of its parochial life. And so the whole movement had the same outstandingly Catholic quality as Dom Lambert, its chief inspirer.

After the first World War, while the Liturgical Movement in Belgium was once more beginning to develop and to attain its full success, two new advances were taking place in Germany. But we must admit that the first beginnings of the German movement (as described so well in the long introduction by Count Robert d'Harcourt to the French edition of Guardini's *Spirit of the Liturgy*), did not possess that complete and healthy balance which was so distinctive a quality of the Belgian movement. The movement in Germany, as it was connected with the monasteries of Beuron and especially with that of Maria Laach, was at first rather the concern of the few, of an intellectual élite, than of the whole Christian people. In this it held closely to the primitive Solesmian tradition. But it soon began to depart from that tradition inasmuch as the deep historical and theological culture of men like Abbot Herwegen and Dom Casel differed from the amateurish kind of scholarship of Dom Guéranger.

What has been said in a previous chapter about these men is enough to show how greatly they contributed to a complete renewal of our fundamental conceptions of liturgical questions. Especially in the field of theology, the work of Dom Casel was to strengthen and deepen that comprehension, so vital to Dom Beauduin, of the liturgy as not a detail, however important, but the center and, in a way, the whole of the life of the Church and of all Christianity.

But we can only realize the full importance of the German contribution, when we perceive that the work of the somewhat aristocratic and high-brow school of Maria-Laach was complemented by the more popular work of the school of Klosterneuburg, in Austria, under the leadership of Pius Parsch. This afterwards became the widespread work of many parish priests and religious in Germany and Austria, including such pastors as Pinsk in Berlin and such Jesuits as Jungmann of Innsbruck. Thus a movement sprang up in Germany which closely resembled that of Belgium in its practical inspiration and undertakings, while being able to make full use of the vast stores of scholarship and speculative thought, as well as of the intense and magnificent piety of Maria-Laach.

A most important new development of the modern liturgical movement which was due primarily to the Augustinian canons of Klosterneuburg, and especially among them, Pius Parsch, consisted in the explicit promotion of a biblical movement in conjunction with the liturgical movment itself. The review *Bibel und Liturgie,* which was distinguished by the same remarkable psychological and pedagogical tactfulness as animated Dom Beauduin's work, initiated the task of showing how a living understanding of the Roman Liturgy could be effectively deepened and enriched by a wider knowledge of the Bible.

The advance caused by this development cannot be too greatly emphasized. First, it enabled men to grasp the full significance of the liturgy itself by uniting it once more with its chief source, this source also now being valued in its fullness. At the same time, the liturgical movement came in this way at last to promote that direct and abundant use of God's Word in all forms of Christian spirituality which for so long had been rendered suspect in the eyes of Catholics rather than effectively promoted by the sixteenth century reformers. This particular effect of the Biblical movement was accomplished by giving the Bible that living commentary without which it cannot be properly understood. For it is in the liturgy that the Church best prepares us to understand God's Word, both by means of the light thrown on the texts of Holy Scripture by one another as they are placed together in the liturgy, and also by the way in which the liturgy itself handles the inspired themes which make up the unity of Revelation itself.

This widening of the scope of the liturgical movement is a fact of the very greatest significance in the history of its development, for the importance of this biblical renewal inside the liturgical movement goes far beyond the sphere of practical methods, and involves theological implications of the greatest value. From what has been said in a previous chapter, we can see how close is the interrelation between Revelation and the liturgy, or, more exacly, between the Divine Word and the congregational worship of the Church. To realize this interrelation and to grasp its full significance will prove to be one of the decisive factors in our attaining a true and renewed understanding of the nature of the Church itself. And such an understanding is certainly the supreme aim of the whole liturgical movement. Thus we are led to believe that it was the work of divine providence to bring together in a harmonious balance the work of the two great liturgical centers in Germany, Maria Laach and Klosterneuburg, for it is only in and through each other that the Mystery of Christian worship and the living Word of God can both be rightly understood in the living Church.

And we may hope that this synthesis will, in a few years, become the outstanding characteristic of a third phase of the movement, a phase which is now beginning in France,—if this phase develops as it should.

It is only since the second world war that France has become at last the theatre of new developments in the liturgical renewal. Long before, of course, the Abbey of Solesmes, and, in spite all its defects, Dom Guéranger's work, *l'Année Liturgique,* had already exercised a wide influence in France. The great school of Catholic literature which includes Péguy and Claudel had educated many minds and given them a new perception of

Catholic teaching and practice. None of this, however, had really won the clergy or affected to any great extent the rank and file of ordinary Catholics.

But, in the years immediately after the war, a new beginning was made, inspired by some French Dominicans and a few secular priests. From the outset, these men were eager to profit by all the experience of their Belgian and German confreres. On the other hand, the fact that they began their work in the milieux already prepared by Catholic Action, especially by the various Catholic Youth Movements, established it firmly in contemporary life. We must note the fact that the French movement gained its first adherents from among those men who were, at the same time, beginning suddenly to realize the necessity for a true home missionary effort in the great de-christianized centres of industry. As a result of all these factors, the French movement, like the Belgian, was from the start directly pastoral in its orientation. But it is important to remark that the French movement did not so explicitly identify its pastoral purpose with a parochial one as had the Belgian movement. We may even ask ourselves whether some men in this French movement were not perhaps too quick to admit that the parish could not be made once more the actual center of Christian worship. And along with this tendency went another to give precedence to missionary work among modern pagans rather than to the work of helping faithful Christians in the Church to rediscover their own treasures.

These various factors could lead, and sometimes have led to some neglect of the traditional aspect of the liturgy, and to an interest perhaps not perfectly balanced in making or re-making the liturgy. The creation and overwhelming success of what have been called "para-liturgies" are proofs of what we have just been saying. Composed first to be a means of education, a transitional device preparing the way for an understanding of the liturgy itself, these "para-liturgies" have often become ends in themselves. Some people, that is, have been tempted to find in these para-liturgies, not a means toward taking part in the real liturgy, but rather a "liturgy of the future" which will more or less replace or refashion the official liturgy itself.

It cannot be denied that there are grave dangers threatening such a mode of thought. In their generous desire to meet today's unbelievers on their own ground, are not some Christians unconsciously inclined rather to canonize modern ideologies than to communicate the Christian faith?

But it is precisely here that we can see clearly the vast import of the connection so recently reestablished between biblical and liturgical renewal,—and also the great importance of the Patristic revival which provides the living link between the Bible and the liturgy, and which is so conspicuous a work of the Church in France today. For the most effective counterbalance to those dubious missionary efforts which tend to bring the spirit of the modern pagan world into the Church rather than effectively to christianize that world, will certainly be the new discovery of the Word of God, set down in the Bible but only to be truly understood in Catholic communion with the Fathers and in the midst of the liturgical assembly of the Church of today and of all ages.

The problem that now besets us is, of course, that of reconciling permanence with adaptation in the tradition of the Church and especially in its liturgical tradition. There is no longer any question of considering the liturgy as something set once for all in the forms now established, something that can never be altered in any way. But the only alternative to a deadly anarchy must be sought in a revival of tradition itself which will have the combined strength and suppleness of a truly living organism. And nothing will prove more effective for such a purpose than a return to the sources of tradition, a return entirely free of all archeologism.

One of the most reassuring phenomenon now visible in the midst of a confusion which might otherwise seem disquieting is a new development, daily more clearly discernible, in the various "para-liturgies" themselves. Sometimes in the recent past they have exhibited a tendency to lay aside the traditional liturgy and to try hastily to embody modern ideals more or less foreign to the spirit of the Church and of the revelation that has been entrusted to her. But now we see an exactly contrary tendency. "Para-liturgies" are tending more and more to take the form of meetings for reading the Bible and for prayer, and this reading and prayer is determined by the great themes of the Christian mystery as laid out in the authentic tradition of the liturgy itself. So we are beginning to find once more a spontaneous and vital atmosphere similar to that in which the liturgy was developed in the great creative period of its history. Nothing could be more conducive to a true rediscovery and revitalization of the liturgy, a renewal which would give back to the liturgy all that richness and fullness of life which it once possessed and which, through the Middle Ages, was increasingly lost.

The recent restoration of the Easter Vigil and its immense success in France,—greater, perhaps, than in any other country,—is a striking proof of what can be accomplished through a return to authentic tradition. But, in order to promote this return, nothing is now more urgent than a careful consideration of what the liturgy is in its permanent essence and in the laws of its vital development. The task we must now undertake before proceeding any further, therefore, is that of laying out the way by which to approach such a consideration, using the light of the Encyclical *Mediator Dei* and taking advantage of all the recent work of research and of the accumulated experience of the past which we have just been reviewing.

CHAPTER SIX

THE CATHOLIC TRADITION CONCERNING THE SHAPE OF THE EUCHARIST

In approaching the reform of the liturgy, we must, first of all, keep in mind the danger of either a false traditionalism, on the one hand, or a rash modernism, on the other. The spirit of false traditionalism would reduce the liturgy to a sort of framework to be accepted purely on authority, a completely stylized, purely external routine—in other words, something virtually dead. Rash modernism, at the other extreme, would, by reaction, awaken in the people the desire for a "new" liturgy—a so-called "living" liturgy—and then satisfy that desire with "paraliturgies" which spring full-fledged from their sponsors' minds, regard having been paid, not to tradition, but only, under the pretext of meeting the needs of the present, to expediency or even to momentary fashion.

Louis Bouyer

Both these results, let us not forget, have much the same source. To attain them together, therefore, it is only necessary that we continue to leave the liturgy of the Church untouched, even if this means its gradual disappearance as a living thing, while in its place the newly made "paraliturgies" may prosper freely if they but stop short of using for themselves the official title of the liturgy.

Priests will continue to say the Breviary in their spare time; they will say Mass and administer Baptism at record speed, without changing a single word to be sure, but also without taking the trouble to make the people understand what is going on, much less to take part in it. On some special occasions, a solemn or pontifical Mass will be correctly performed as a distinctive pageant of Catholic loyalty. And at the same time, the people will continue to be fed with pious devices of all kinds, with individual exercises of devotion, more or less spiritual practices, revelations to nuns, and so on. Or, in some modern quarters, mass religious meetings will take place on the pattern of contemporary pagan worship of the nation, of man's work, of earthly ideals, only "christianized" by their mode of expression. . . . And everybody will be happy, living and letting others live. . . .

But if the Church were ever to acquiesce in such a state of things, she would abandon her most sacred duty and practically give up everything for which she was designed by her divine Founder.

Here, then, we come to the necessity for a rediscovery in the field of the liturgy itself, which is its principal locus, of what tradition truly is, and what are its authentic relations both to authority and to individual initiative and personal needs. For tradition is not a dead thing to be accepted blindly only under the external pressure of authority. Nor, in order to bring it to life again, should tradition by any subterfuge be taken away from the regulation of authority and developed by anybody in his own irresponsible way.

The true idea of tradition held by the Council of Trent in entrusting the Holy See with a much needed reform of liturgical books, was equally opposed to both mistakes. The Council of Trent was far from allowing any individual the freedom to make up a liturgy or paraliturgy of his own which would usurp the place of the Church's one whole liturgy. But it was far from any desire to impose any prefabricated and immovable liturgy on the Church. The authority of the Council and its appeal to the authority of the Holy See itself was to be understood as the safeguard at once of the genuine authenticity and of the continual adaptability of tradition. And this has always been the case with authority and always will be in the Catholic Church.

Therefore—as was still clearly understood by all the canonists who wrote on the liturgy during the seventeenth and eighteenth centuries, from a private author like Lebrun to a great Pontiff, who was at the same time a canonist of genius, like Benedict XIV—the authority attached to the liturgy is not dependent completely and solely on that of the actual Popes or Bishops who have canonized such and such books with their rubrics, or who have guaranteed such and such answers of any commission, from the Sacred Congregation of Rites down to the commission appointed for the reformation of the Parisian liturgy by Hardouin de Perefixe. No, the authority attached to the liturgy was for these men fundamentally that of tradition itself. And it was only as the guarantor of tradition under both its aspects of permanence and of living adaptability that the authority of Popes and Bishops gave their sanction to the liturgy.

More exactly—as can be seen in the statements of the Council of Trent and in the detailed formulations of the various Pontifical Bulls canonizing the Missal and Breviary of Pius V, and, finally, in the Encyclical *Mediator Dei,*—in the field of liturgy as in every other, the living authority of the Holy See itself and of all the Bishops, at Trent and elsewhere, intervenes precisely in order to *canonize what it considers to be the most perfect vehicle available in our age for the maintenance of the tradition which through Christian antiquity has come down from the Apostles themselves.*

This definition seems to give a clue of paramount importance to the understanding of the liturgy as a living thing, along the lines of the forceful formulations of *Mediator Dei.*

Just because the liturgy is in no way merely a detail of discipline to be changed at will either by authority with no precedent to guide it, or by individuals deferring to their own irresponsible hobbies, just because the liturgy is the living heart of the Catholic tradition, that is, because it embodies the ultimate revelation of the eternal Word of God to His People, while it includes the act of redemption and new creation realized by that selfsame Word,—the liturgy shows the distinctive features of the Catholic tradition in its most solemn form.

The Catholic tradition is not a thing of the past, fixed once for all in detailed written form, never to change or progress. Neither is it a changeable thing to be remodelled at will either by individuals or by an authority which, if it did such a thing, would be as unfettered and irresponsible as an individual. This tradition is, rather, a living pattern given once for all in its essentials by Christ and His apostles. And this pattern has to be lived out through all the ages, not by individuals separately, but by a living community, grounded on Christ and His Apostles through being always in communion and one with the successors of the Apostles and the vicars of Christ.

In this living communion, the Popes and the Bishops are not to do everything while the rest are to accept their governance in a purely passive way. Nor are individuals allowed to do as they like. Still less is the authority meant to be all-powerful in some field isolated from real life, while the individuals are left alone to do everything or nothing in all other fields of activity.

Rather, we may apply here most effectively Newman's fruitful statement about the two component parts of tradition in the Church and their mutual and necessary interplay. As he says, there is only one tradition, which is that of the whole body, head and members; but this tradition takes two complementary forms which are never to be confounded, which can never be reduced to one, and which are never to be separated from each other.

What may be called the episcopal tradition is the whole body of decisions which have arisen from the extraordinary magisterium of the Church. Only this form of tradition may be considered to be properly and strictly authoritative. But it must never be seen as separated from, let alone as opposed to, what Newman calls prophetic tradition, that is, as Newman uses the word according to St. Paul's phrase, *"the mind of the Spirit*, the thoughts, the principles which are like the breathing of the Church, the way in which habitually and, as it were, unconsciously, she looks at things, rather than any set of dogmas, static and systematic." This prophetic tradition is maintained throughout the whole body of the Church, not only passively but also actively, always of course in conjunction with those who are at its head. It expresses itself in countless ways; and the records of these ways are kept for us by history, or, more exactly, by all the documents and monuments on which the study of history must be built. But the great point is that this tradition cannot be recognized in these records except by those who are living in the Church, who are breathing with her breath, who are living in her life and praying her prayer. And the episcopal tradition itself is, as it were, plunged in that prophetic tradition, always leading it, but also founded on it, in order to guarantee it at every step, to be able to distinguish its main stream from divergent backwaters; making solemn and definite pronouncements which are never meant to take the place of the continuous life and light of the "prophetic" tradition, which is far too rich ever to be fully defined, but rather to preserve it both from stultification and from alteration.

Now we can see how the individual in the Church is meant to respond to the stimulation given by authority, especially in the field of the liturgy. He is not meant to answer by a strictly correct but purely passive and external adherence to the material injunctions of authority. He is, rather, to make an ever-renewed effort to know, to understand in a living way, to keep faithfully, by adapting it to new needs, "the faith once given to the saints," not as a naked and abstract idea but as a living body. Knowledge of the past, then, and personal understanding of the actual present are not to be renounced for the sake of a dead acceptance of authority; rather they are to be used to promote a filial obedience to authority, to illuminate and vivify what is received from authority. In so doing, far from ever coming into conflict with authority, we shall be preparing the way for it. We shall at once help to develop the seed which the preacher is to sow and make ready for it not a hard rock, but fertile ground. We shall provide authority with a living material which it can correct and perfect by its paternal injunctions, not with a dead carcass which it could galvanize into action artifically and from the outside.

Having reached this point, we are now faced with the task of trying to encourage this attitude which we have progressively been defining. We propose to do so by three consecutive steps. First, we shall attempt to disengage from history some of the essential features of what has happily been called the permanent shape of the liturgy. Then, we shall try to develop the deep theological significance of this shape. And, finally, we shall propose some means whereby this ever constant wealth of Christian tradition may be applied to the present situation and its needs. But from everything that has been said so far, we must realize that the important point for us is not so much any particular detail of our own tentative work, but rather the promotion of that true spirit of living and faithful orthodoxy in regard to the liturgy which we have been at such great pains to define.

We shall now try to find out from tradition, then, what we called the permanent shape of the liturgy. But we must be careful not to confuse this research with a search for any abstract or purely logical scheme, still less for an abstract formula or concept from which to deduce the whole of Christian worship. Precisely because the liturgy is so living a thing, no development along a straight line, no exact concept of reason can be the clue to it. Of course, from what has already been said on the "Qehal Yahweh" and on the brotherly meal of those who are expecting the consolation of Israel, it has already been made sufficiently clear that the core of the Christian liturgy is to be found in the Eucharistic *synaxis*, in the Mass. But the Mass as found in liturgical tradition is not to be reduced to any single idea, not even to any single trend of thought. It is an action which possesses in itself, certainly, the perfect unity of a great living thing; but this unity is one of elements which are very complex because they are very rich; it should not be allowed to disappear in a confused mixture of these elements; we should rather learn to see these elements in their unity, each and all taking value and depth of meaning from their mutual interaction.

From this point of view, we may welcome, at least as a great incentive to our research, the summary of the question proposed by a Swedish scholar, Yngve Brilioth, in his book *Eucharistic Faith and Practice.* He insists precisely on the fact that, without doing violence to the texts, it is impossible for us to reduce any of the great historical forms of the Eucharistic liturgy to one single element, or to one single set of elements in logical combination. He even goes so far as to say, what seems to us to be simple common sense, that any period in the history of the Church in which a tendency arises to make such a simplification and logical ordering of the Eucharist is shown by this very fact to be a period of decay, preparing only for further corruption.

In the traditional shape of the Christian liturgy, as Brilioth believes, there are to be found at least four irreducible elements. And to these must be added what is not properly another element, but a deeper and almost indefinable reality which permeates all four elements but to each its own individuality. These four elements are: communion, sacrifice, eucharist properly speaking (that is, thanksgiving) and memorial. The further reality, which cannot be separated from these four elements which it is to animate, is the Mystery. We shall soon try to state just what is to be understood by each of these words. But let us first consider their necessary connection with one another. When these four elements are combined in proper proportions and are wide open to the illumination given them by the Mystery—without losing their own individuality—then we have the full Catholic tradition in all its wealth and purity. But when a given age overemphasizes one of these elements so that the others are partly lost sight of, or so that they are subordinated to it, then the fullness of tradition is lost, the spirit of the authentic liturgy is endangered as well as that of authentic Christianity, and one may look for the appearance of all kinds of errors, in doctrine as well as in practice. Let us, then, take each of these five terms and try to understand them.

Communion, as the word is used here, is not to be understood in its modern usage, that is, as the reception of the Sacrament by an individual believer. Rather it is to be understood, as χοιωωνία was always used by the Fathers, to mean "communion with" other people in a common partaking of the same gifts. This use of the word combines the two different meanings of the Latin phrase "communio sanctorum," and explains each by the other: that is, "communio sanctorum" taking *sanctorum* in the masculine) as meaning the communion among the saints, which is brought about through "communio sanctorum" (taking *sanctorum* in the neuter), that is, communion *in* the holy things. Thus, the element of "Communion" means that the Eucharist is a meal, a community meal, in which all the participants are brought together to have a common share in common goods, these common goods being first of all the bread and wine of a real human meal, whatever their deeper significance. And to describe this element, we have the Apostle's sentence: "Because the bread is one, we though many, are one body, all of us who partake of the one bread."

Sacrifice, then, is to be understood as the actual sacrifice which the Church has always intended to offer when it is assembled to celebrate the Eucharist. It is striking to find that Brilioth, a Protestant author, emphasizes the fact that in the most primitive and basic usage of all the ancient liturgies, the terminology of sacrifice is directly applied to what the Church does when she meets for the Eucharist.

The use of these sacrificial terms did not arise, as might be supposed, from an idea of the Cross as being in some way represented in the Mass. Far from it,—historical evidence leads us rather to the supposition that the terminology of sacrifice came to be applied to the Cross by the Church because the Cross was felt to be at the heart of the sacrifice which is offered by the Church in the Eucharistic celebration. We may note, as a fact in support of this interpretation, that, in the New Testament, it is practically only in the Epistle to the Hebrews that we find a sacrificial explanation of the Cross, and this explanation is given by reference to the liturgy of the Old Covenant taken as an allegory of the New. We may also note that the earliest Christian ecclesiastical writers habitually use all the notions of sacrifice in direct reference to the Christian liturgy. It seems to be true that the continuity from the "Qehal Yahweh" to the Christian *synaxis* which we ourselves brought out earlier in this book, was so well understood from the very beginnings of Christianity that the whole sacrificial terminology of the Old Testament was applied without any intermediate stage to the liturgy of the New Testament. This fact can be seen most strikingly in the Apostolic Fathers, no less in the writings of St. Clement or St. Ignatius than in the Epistle of Barnabas, famous for its radical idea that the ritual of the Old Testament had never had any other meaning than to be an allegory of the New.

But just here, of course, the question arises: what, then, according to that primitive view, is properly sacrificial in the Christian *synaxis* (the Christian assembly)? We must answer that, from the ways in which the first Christian authors, beginning with St. Paul, express themselves, everything in the Christian *synaxis* is sacrificial. The distinctive feature of the New Testament, as these men understood it in the light of the 31st chapter of Jeremias, is precisely that its sacrifice is now no more confined to any special rite, but is the whole of the Christian life inasmuch as it is a life in the *agape*, the divine Love. This is, of course, to say that the meal which expresses and, as it were, incorporates that *agape*, is itself and in all its details sacrificial in the highest sense. Thus, not only are the eating and drinking in this meal sacrificial, but so, too, is the sanctifying prayer which is said over the food; and when we understand it in this way, this prayer becomes the perfect form of that sacrifice of pure lips which the teaching of the Prophets had already so strikingly outlined. But, since the Christians have partaken in the meal of *agape*, the whole Christian life of each individual is now imbued with that sacrificial virtue. So we must realize that St. Paul is not using a figure of speech when he speaks in sacrificial terms of the offerings made by the Corinthians for the poor of Jerusalem, or when he speaks of the oblation that he himself is making of his own life and his labors for the benefit of souls, as he concludes with: "I rejoice now in the sufferings I bear for your sake; and what is lacking of the sufferings of Christ I fill up in my flesh for his body, which is the Church" (Col. 1:24). One of the most perfect expressions of this synthesizing view of the Eucharist and the Christian life is that given by St. Augustine in the *City of God*: "Tota redempta civitas est unum sacrificium quo seipsam offert Deo Patri"; "The whole city of the redeemed is one sacrifice through which it offers itself to God the Father." And this is the "unceasing oblation" properly speaking which was foreseen by the Prophet Malachias whose words are so often quoted by the Fathers, since they understood this oblation to be realized in the Christian dispensation.

Thirdly, then, the Eucharist is the *thanksgiving* which finds its central expression in the great prayer always said by the president of the *synaxis*. It is a thanksgiving to God for all His gifts, including in one view the whole of creation and redemption but always taking as a starting point the bread and wine, typical of all created things, and the consuming of which is the actual occasion both of the meal itself and of the celebration attached to it. But this element of thanksgiving, the jubilant acknowledgment that everything is a grace, and that the grace of God is marvelous, is also as it were a general atmosphere which pervades the whole Eucharistic service. This thanksgiving finds another expression that, in its own way, is also essential, in the "sacrifice of praise" which is the purpose of almost all the psalmody that from the first inhered in the celebration of the Eucharist. In conjunction with the Christian sacrifice, this element of thanksgiving is, in a still deeper sense, a new attitude of man, as he stands before God in the Church, an attitude which springs from the exultant faith which receives and drinks in the divine *agape* as it flows from its source in the Holy Spirit. The keynote of the thanksgiving here is, therefore, the *Alleluja,*—what we might call a contemplative prayer which penetrates the whole of life, but penetrates it with the contemplation, not of a sublime and lofty abstraction, but of the divine condescension of the living God.

For the fourth element in the Eucharist is what we have called the *Memorial.* This is, of course, first of all the Memorial of the Cross as the great saving act through which the divine *agape* overflowed into this our world, a memorial, effected through the *anamnesis* made over the bread and the chalice, of the broken Body and of the Blood that was shed. But the Eucharist is also the Memorial of everything that led up to the Cross throughout all history, not only from the Birth of Christ, but from the sacrifice of Abel, the offering of Abraham and the sacrifice of Melchisedech, through the whole sacred history of the People of God. And it is also the Memorial of everything that has resulted from the lifegiving Passion of Christ, that is, His resurrection, His glorification (which includes the outpouring of the Spirit, the building up of the Church and, finally, the consummation of everything in the divine *agape*). In this way,

103

we can understand the apparent strangeness of some ancient liturgies which make the *anamnesis* not only of Christ's sitting at the right hand of the Father, but also of His coming again to judge the living and the dead, just as St. Paul speaks of us as already risen again and seated in heaven with Our Lord.

But this is not enough. The whole Eucharistic celebration is also a memorial. And here we must keep in mind a most important point, which we have touched on already and to which we shall again return, namely, that there is an inseparable connection between the two parts of the Christian *synaxis*, that is, between the Bible readings and the meal. For the readings lead up to the meal. They recall to memory God's action of entering into human history, redeeming it and fulfilling it from within; while the meal itself commemorates the climax of this process in the Cross of Christ. And the meal needs the readings to point out to us the way to see it aright, not as a separate event of today, but understandable only in reference to a decisive action accomplished once and for all in the past. Such a consideration will bring us in due time to see that the whole Mass is a single liturgy of the Word, Who began by speaking to man; Who continued speaking to him more and more intimately; Who finally spoke to him most directly as the Word-made-flesh; and Who now speaks from the very heart of man himself to God the Father through the Spirit.

Having thus paved the way by what has been said so far, we are now prepared to understand the decisive importance of the Mystery as synthesizing and elevating all the preceding aspects. If each of the constitutive elements of the Mass which we have examined is better described than defined, how much more difficult is it to give any definition of what the Mystery is! Following still Brilioth's lines of thought, but using now our own words, we may say that the Mystery embodies the Church's three-fold conviction when she celebrates the Eucharist. She believes that Christ is present in an ineffable way in the celebration; she believes that what she does today, He Himself is doing and through her; she believes that this action of today, which is His as it is hers, is, finally, the one saving action of God in Christ throughout history. That is to say, that the Mass is the Cross, but the Cross always seen in the whole perspective of which we spoke when we were discussing the Memorial.

We shall need to examine other definitions of the Mystery; but we may well keep the above as a particularly plain definition carrying with it no serious difficulties, a definition which, from the outset, gives a whole view of the idea, even if it does not go as deeply into it as we shall wish to go later on. The Mystery, then, is not a fifth element of the Mass to be added to the four others; it is rather a new depth in each of them, through which all are brought together into a single living unity, entirely supernatural. In his exposition, Brilioth warns us of the grave danger of trying to make of the Mystery, not that ineffable quality common to the four elements of the Christian Eucharist, but a distinct element added to them, and an element which, because of its intrinsic importance, may easily tend to absorb all the others. We may, of course, notice here some influence on the author of Protestant prejudice. But we may well ask ourselves also whether there is not a good deal of truth in his warning. In some forms of modern Catholicism, certainly, the overemphasis on the Real Presence (which, in a way, corresponds to the first aspect of the Mystery as described above) has eclipsed people's appreciation of the Eucharist as communion, sacrifice, thanksgiving and memorial, and has also degraded rather than exalted the Christian apprehension of the Mystery itself. As Brilioth sees it, the true balance would emphasize equally the fact that the holy things, the partaking of which makes us one, are nothing else but Christ Himself; that the substance of all Christian sacrifice is the one sacrifice of the Cross; that the Christian thanksgiving is Christ's own, our thanksgiving making us all acknowledge His God and Father as our God and our Father; and, finally, that everything that is "announced" to us in the liturgy is announced, not only as part of the past, but as the one great reality of the present also, as well as of all the future.

Clearly, this balanced view of the celebration of the Eucharist can enable us to grasp fully the idea of the real presence of Christ in His Church. We are not, in a word, to focus our contemplation on the sacramental bread and wine alone, but on two other realities as well. If there is a necessity, first of all, to consider the presence of Christ as victim in the eucharistic elements, we must not for that reason neglect His presence as high priest in the whole hierarchy. Christ will be present in the elements only because He is present in the man who is to preside over the *synaxis* and to say the thanksgiving in Christ's own name, this presence being brought about through the apostolic succession. And, thirdly, Christ is to be present in the whole body of the Church, for the Church enjoys the Eucharistic presence only to be made one, *in* Christ and *with* Christ, through the Eucharistic celebration, and especially through the consummation in the holy meal. When these three realities of the divine presence are not seen in their right interrelation, they are seen falsely and misconceived—just as, according to Brilioth, the whole celebration is not understood unless it is understood in all its constituent parts and their unity.

Now, as we said above, in the final stages of such a disintegration, there tends to be a retrogression from true religion to magic. Brilioth himself explains this by his insistence on the idea that the Mystery, though from many points of view the most characteristically Christian quality in the Eucharist, making Christ all in all as it does, yet from another point of view may be regarded as that quality of the Eucharist which links it up with natural religion, and, more particularly, within the Greco-Roman world contemporary with primitive Christianity, those religions which were precisely called "mystery religions."

This idea of a similarity between the Eucharist and the pagan "mystery-religions" certainly poses a question of great importance, which is difficult to treat but which we cannot evade, if we are trying to understand fully the Christian tradition of liturgy. In discussions of this similarity, the so-called "mystery religions" are seen to bear an analogy to the Christian religion in so far as they involved a δρώμενον, that is to say, a ritual enactment of the death and return to life of a god, this enactment being carried out in such a way as to make the "mystes," or initiates, partakers of the life of that god, becoming in some way identified with him. Even if we thus put the case in terms as plain as possible, and make no attempt to force analogies into close similarities, we still cannot but be struck by the resemblance of the δρώμενον with the Christian mystery. It is true also that this resemblance belongs only to the Mystery proper. The religions of the Roman empire had no interest in a Memorial of anything; they had no interest in history as such, but rather in a myth, that is, in a symbolic picture of events always recurring in a cycle—in this case, the cycle of the seasons—; for the mystery gods were above all gods of nature, with its perpetual recurrence of death followed by a return to life. Nor did these religions have any element of thanksgiving,—this idea, as we shall see later, being purely Jewish in its origins and Christian in its developments. These religions must undoubtedly have had a certain contemplative aspect, but this was simply the contemplation of the unchanging cosmos, not at all of an intervention of God in the world once for all, to make an irreversible change in it.

Certainly in these religions there was some kind of sacrifice, but merely in the ancient sense in which all natural and pagan religion was sacrificial; they knew nothing of that transformation of the idea of Sacrifice which the prophets had prepared, and which is shown so conspicuously in the primitive Church. These religions may, perhaps, have achieved some limited Communion between fellow initiates, but here it is well to remember the distinction made by Bergson between the closed communions of the old religions, and the communion inaugurated by the Christian *agape* which is radically new because open to everyone.

It is the Mystery, then, which fully seems to afford the only line of continuity between these mystery religions and Christianity. To see how far one can go with this idea, we shall now consider one of the most important books of the last generation on the origin and development of the Christian Eucharist, Lietzmann's *Messe und Herrenmahl.* We might say that Brilioth wrote his book simply to answer Lietzmann's. But he attempted to do so by holding in the main to Lietzmann's idea of the Mystery, and trying to complete it by showing how, in authentic Christianity, the Mystery is inseparable from the four fundamental elements which he himself emphasized so strongly.

Are we, then, to follow Brilioth in his acceptance of this major point in the thesis of Lietzmann and many other modern scholars, that is, that the Christian Mystery as such and the pagan mysteries must be considered to be at least analogous to each other? In order to answer this very important question, we must begin by considering Lietzmann's ideas more fully.

Lietzmann holds that we find in the Catholic Eucharist not so much a tension between irreducible elements, as in Brilioth's conception of it, but rather an inner opposition between two conflicting factors. Only one of these factors is Christian, coming from Our Lord through the primitive Christian community. The other factor is foreign both to Christianity and to Judaism; it was an import from Greco-Romanism, borrowed from the mystery religions by St. Paul. If we may put it in such a way, there are not one but two, Christian eucharists and these two are irreconcilable. One of them comes straight down to us from the community meals of the disciples before the Passion, meals in which they had Our Lord in their midst. This form is eucharistic properly speaking, because it is full to overflowing with exultant faith in Christ's presence, but it has no connection with the Lord's last supper on Maundy Thursday nor with the Cross. And we must add that, even if it is full of the conviction that the Lord is invisibly present with His own, yet there is nothing to focus that presence on the elements of the meal, which are not necessarily even bread and wine. The Lord is present, yes, but not as the spiritual food of His disciples. He is present as an invisible guest who is still taking part in the community meal, and so bringing to it an inexhaustible source of gladness. It is in just this way that the word of the Apocalypse is fulfilled: "Behold, I stand at the door and knock; if any man listens to my voice and opens the door to me, I will come in to him and will sup with him and he with me."

In Lietzmann's theory, the other eucharist comes completely from St. Paul. This eucharist beholds a radical transformation of the primitive community meal which the Apostle attempted to introduce for the sake of converts from paganism, especially those at Corinth. It imposes a completely new meaning on that meal, one that goes hand in hand with an interpretation of our Lord's death which is also purely Pauline,—both interpretations coming from the same source, the pagan mysteries. The emphasis is no longer on the resurrection but on the death of our Lord: "For as often as you shall eat this bread and drink this cup, you proclaim the death of the Lord, until he comes." St. Paul, in other words, has interpreted the Cross as a life-giving mystery concentrated on the ritual reenactment of a God's death, and so he implies that the Cross is to be understood as the δ ρώμενον in the pagan mysteries. From this fact also would be derived the idea of the localization of the presence of the Lord in the bread and wine, since these are seen as the supernatural means of union between men and the saving death of Christ, through an identification of the believer with his God—this idea itself being as congenial to the pagan mysteries as it was foreign to the thought of Judaism.

Later on we shall see how every line of this theory poses more problems than it pretends to solve, attributing to the pagan mysteries a great many purely Jewish or Christian ideas simply in order to enable these mysteries to be able to give us an explanation of Christianity itself. But now let us only ask what should be our opinion of this distinction between a primitive Jewish and a completely remodelled Pauline Eucharist?

Oscar Cullman, one of the greatest contemporary scholars of the New Testament, stresses very strongly a point which Lietzmann entirely neglects. And it is precisely from the neglect of this particular point that the possibility can arise of making such a sharp distinction and opposition between the two supposed types of eucharist. Lietzmann takes as alternative possibilities for the origin of the eucharist, the meal that the disciples took with Christ on the eve of His death, and the meals they took with Christ before His Passion. But what he does not see is that the Lord's supper on Maundy Thursday, the meals taken with Him in the past and the meals of the primitive Church were all in continuity, *through the meals after the resurrection,* in which He had appeared to His disciples as the Conqueror of death. No ground of opposition, therefore, can be found between them. And we must also add the fact that Lietzmann completely misunderstands the relationship between the Cross and the eucharistic joy as it was understood in primitive Christianity, because he is interpreting this relationship from the viewpoint of modern sentimental forms of piety wholly foreign to the ancient Church. Certainly, there never was any opposition in the minds of primitive Christians between the eucharistic joy which springs from the resurrection, and a fancied sad and gloomy piety concentrating on the Cross. From the very first, Christians saw the Cross as illuminated by the resurrection; the resurrection was not to them the reversal, but, so to speak, the natural product of the Cross. Thus, the whole construction of Lietzmann falls to pieces.

But to say this is not enough. Why did Lietzmann conceive the idea that there must have been two origins for the Christian Eucharist? Because to him, as to all the scholars of the "liberal" school at the end of the last century, it was unthinkable that Jesus on the first Maundy Thursday evening should have created a sacramental religion and told His disciples, "Do this in remembrance of Me." According to these scholars, the idea that Christ gave the command to continue the rite He had made up was absolutely out of the question, not only for Him but for the whole primitive Church, since it did not believe that it would continue for many years, let alone centuries, but rather that it would soon be met by the Parousia.

Whatever our opinions may be on this last point, however, we have still to make it clear that Lietzmann's whole argument derives from a radical misconstruction of the sentence: "Do this in remembrance of Me." The reasoning we have just set forth puts the emphasis on the "do this" as if Jesus was seen as really creating a new rite and imposing it on a community still entirely in the future. But, following Gregory Dix, in the work already cited, *The Shape of the Liturgy,* we must frankly say that such a notion is completely mistaken. Recent scholarship shows with perfect clarity that, far from creating a new rite, Jesus was only performing once again a thoroughly traditional rite of Judaism, while infusing into it a new meaning and a new reality. This fact, as we shall see, makes wholly useless the supposition of any fundamental influence of paganism on the Christian Mystery, and forces us to conceive that Mystery and the liturgy of which it is the living heart along purely Jewish lines.

Josef Andreas Jungmann
1889-1974

Josef Jungmann was born in Austria in 1889 and joined the Jesuits in 1917. He joined the faculty of the University of Innsbruck in 1930 and spent most of his career there, except for the interruption of World War II. It was precisely during those years of "exile" from 1939 to 1945, which Jungmann spent first in Vienna, then in the small Danube village of Hainstetten, that he produced his masterpiece, Missarum Sollemnia, *translated into English as* The Mass of the Roman Rite. *It came out in German in 1948, in a two-volume English edition in 1951, and in a one-volume abridgement in 1958. It would be difficult indeed to assess its overall impact, for there was simply nothing comparable to it in illuminating how the Mass had developed historically. It can safely be said that there could have been no sensible reform proposed by Vatican II without the groundwork done by Father Jungmann.*

His interests and contributions, however, were not confined to the liturgy. He was also much involved in the renewal of catechetics. In fact, many date the beginning of the modern catechetical revival from the appearance of his book of 1936, advocating the return to the "kerygma," the core preaching of the New Testament. His work was characterized throughout his career by a deep pastoral concern; he labored ceaselessly to improve and revivify the teaching, the preaching, and the worship of the Church.

The selection given here is taken from a work which he put together in 1955 at the behest of the publishers of Civilta Cattolica *in Rome. They asked him to survey the entire liturgy in a relatively short book. So, as he says in the preface, "I have taken the opportunity of summarising and setting in order the most important elements of the lectures I have been wont to deliver to young theological students during the past three decades." When translated into English in 1957, this book was entitled* Public Worship. *The first two chapters are reproduced here, since they present a fine picture of just how things stood in Catholic liturgy in the mid-1950s, as viewed by the best-informed liturgists of the day. A few years later his life's work was to pay off beyond his dreams with the reform of Vatican II. In that process everyone involved recognized Josef Jungmann as having made a greater contribution than any other single individual.*

PUBLIC WORSHIP

BASIC CONCEPTS

The Church has a twofold duty to perform on earth: she must concern herself with men, and proclaim to them the good tidings about the way of salvation opened to us by Christ; but also, and in company with those whom she has filled with faith, she must concern herself with God in order to render to him glory. She must bring the faithful together, that they may be 'built up on him, stones that live and breathe, into a spiritual fabric; to be a holy priesthood, able to offer up that spiritual sacrifice which God accepts through Jesus Christ' (1 Peter ii, 5), and that they may 'proclaim the exploits of the God who called them out of darkness into his wonderful light' (*ibid.*, 11, 9).

The Christian is not meant to be a solitary pilgrim through the darkness of this world, and only in the next to join in for the first time with the songs of praise of the heavenly armies; even here below on earth he is to associate with his fellows as the 'holy people of God' and begin the praise of his Creator.

This is what happens in the Christian public worship, in the Liturgy. The word 'liturgy' comes from the Greek λειτουργία, which itself is derived from λίιτον ('pertaining to the people'— λαος), and ἔργον—meaning 'work' or 'service'. It is thus 'public work' or 'service in the interest of the people'. The Greeks called it a 'liturgy' if a man undertook the equipment of a warship, or the costs of a public entertainment. Later on the meaning of the word was restricted to matters connected with worship. In this sense it is used many times in the Greek versions of the Bible, and from there it has passed into the vocabulary of the Church.

In the Church's parlance, therefore, liturgy means 'divine service in the interests of the people'—that is, briefly, 'the divine worship of the Church.' It is, in consequence, public worship—

worship which is done for or by the community; thus it is something different from private prayer said by an individual. But because there are various intermediate steps, we shall have to define our concept of liturgy much more accurately.

Formerly the definition of liturgy used to be restriced to whatever the priest does according to the regulations in the liturgical books. That is, however, too narrow; for, as we shall see later, what is done by the Christian people also belongs in the liturgy. Moreover it is not essential to liturgy that there should be precise regulations and fixed prayer texts. If that were so, then the divine service conducted by the apostles and the bishops of the first few centuries of the Christian era would not have been liturgy; and in considering the history of our subject we would have to leave out of account precisely the period in which the decisive development of liturgy took place.

Whenever the Church, as 'the people of God', comes before God in prayer we have liturgy. This is verified in perfect form when on Sundays the parishioners gather about their pastor to celebrate the Holy Sacrifice with him, as the Church prescribes; or when he sings Vespers with them; or even when a choir of clerics sings Vespers.

It is liturgy also when the appointed representative of the Church performs all by himself an official act of divine worship, baptises, blesses, or celebrates Mass, even if no one else be present—because even in these circumstances the Church is active as the people of God. It was also liturgy when in early times the priest conducted divine service in any way that seemed best to him (because there were no precise regulations), in so far as he was in communion with the bishop and, through him, with the Chief Shepherd of the Church, and was prepared to conform to whatever laws there were at the time.

It may perhaps seem doubtful whether the administration of sacraments should be included in the concept of liturgy thus defined, since the sacraments are directed towards man rather than towards God. But they are rightly included as liturgy since their very administration and reception are a profession of the faith, and because they have the characteristics of worship by reason of the purpose for which they are designed. It is also divine worship—and thus liturgy in the broader sense of 'diocesan liturgy'—if the pastor and his people hold evening devotions, so long as these are in a form approved by the bishop by inclusion, for example, in an official Manual of Prayers or Hymnal.

On the other hand it is not liturgy—though it is a truly valuable form of prayer—if the father of a family says night prayers in common with his wife and children. Even if these prayers should have a liturgical form such as Compline it is still not liturgy because it is not the prayer of the hierarchically constituted and led people of God.

If we thus bring the people of God, the Church, into such prominence in the essential concept of liturgy we are faced with a question. In what sense, we must ask, is the congregation active in the liturgy in addition to the hierarchical representative of the Church? Above all, in what sense is Christ himself, the Head of the Church, thus active? Christ is not merely the founder of the liturgy in that he instituted the sacraments; he is for ever and ever the principal agent in them. The Encyclical *Mediator Dei* of Pius XII says of the liturgy: 'It is the entire public worship of the Mystical Body of Jesus Christ, Head and members.' Without Christ the Church would be but an earthly association of men. It is only through him that we have access to the Father (Rom. v, 2; Eph. ii, 18); it is only because of our union with him that our prayers and sacrifices have any value. 'He lives on still to make intercession on our behalf' (Heb. vii, 25). In every sacramental act it is he who, properly speaking, is the true agent; it is ultimately he who baptises or consecrates. The earthly liturgy is but the visible manifestation of his activity.

It is worth noting that in the New Testament the word commonly used at that time for 'priest' (ἱερεύς) is predicated in the first instance of Christ Himself (Heb. v, sqq.), and secondarily of all those who are united with him, that is, of the redeemed people (1 Peter ii, 5, 9; Apoc. i, 6; v, 10). It was only later on that it became customary to apply the word in a special way to those who had been ordained by the laying on of hands, and to give the name of 'priest' to those who used to be called 'presbyters', using it primarily for them. The fact is that Christ is the High Priest (properly so-called) of our liturgy.

But also the Christian people have a much more important position in the liturgy than was allotted to the people in the ancient pagan cults, or—for that matter—to the people in the Old Testament. In heathendom the people were not generally considered to have any part at all in the sacrifices and prayers of their priests. Nor was any space provided for the people in the temples. The interior of these pagan temples consisted of nothing but a dark room wherein the idol was placed. All the splendour and magnificence of the temple, with its colonnades, its friezes and its sculptures, was displayed on the exterior. By contrast the Christian divine worship is arranged, as regards its essential features, as an assembly of the Christian people. And Christian architecture is conceived in terms of providing an interior space for the accommodation of the Christian people, the Church (ἐκκλησία). It is from them that the building derives its name and is simply called *ecclesia*, church. The material structure is, in a sense, but a shelter for the spiritual temple of which St. Paul said to the Christians: 'It is a holy thing, this temple of God, which is nothing other than yourselves' (1 Cor. iii, 17). The faithful, by virtue of their baptism, have a share in the priesthood of Christ, though, of course, not in the same way as the ordained clergy. Even the holiest action of the Christian liturgy, the offering of the sacrifice, is attributed in the Canon of the Mass to the people (*sed et plebs tua sancta*). That is why the concordant voice of the people, their communal praying and singing, have always exercised an influence in determining the form of the prayers and chants. In the liturgy the people ought not always to be there merely as dumb spectators, but should be active participants, as the Popes since Pius X have repeatedly emphasised.

Because the Christian liturgy is in a special sense communal or social worship its exterior form is of considerable importance. In private prayer the form is entirely secondary—it may even be altogether formless; what matters most there is warmth of the heart, interior self-dedication to God. But for liturgy external forms are necessary. A community cannot be active except in a social way, in forms which express visibly or audibly the things which are the concern of all. Therefore in the course of the centuries there have been evolved for the liturgy all manner of varied forms, prayer-texts, melodies, ceremonies, vestments and—above all—church buildings with all that piety and artistry have been able to devise therein.

Exterior form pertains so intimately to the essence of liturgy that—and this is its danger—it is always liturgy when its externals are there, even if interior participation be completely lacking, even if it be a sinful priest who performs them. It is just the same with the sacraments: they are validly administered provided that he who is their minister, even if he be interiorly hardened in sin, truly does that which the Church intends to be done in the sacrament. Of course liturgy is as it should be only if its externals are accompanied by the right interior dispositions so that God is worshipped 'in spirit and in truth.'

Because liturgy is the expression of social worship it must necessarily be objective, must be valid for all. Private prayer may and should take into account the needs and circumstances of the individual suppliant. As prayer of petition it will sometimes halt before some shrine that appeals to the heart; it will seek protection and help from some heavenly patron who inspires confidence, without going any further. But in liturgical prayer there must be expressed more clearly that which is of the very nature of prayer in its full sense, that law of prayer which holds good for all. And this law requires that liturgical worship, though it may well turn in hymn or prayer to any of the blessed in heaven, cannot rest there but finally completes its true course. Ultimately it always turns to God himself, to him who is the beginning and the end of all things. Indeed precisely because it is the prayer of a community it seeks to display the right order of divine things and the way of salvation by which all of us must travel.

The Christian cosmos must be reflected in the Christian liturgy: God as our final end, Christ as our mediator, the saints as our friends and intercessors, the Church as the community of the redeemed, and the temporal world with all its dangers as the stage of our testing. The prayer of the liturgy will, then, often be a cry for help and a petition for God's grace, but above all it must be adoration, a bowing down before the Divine Majesty. It must, in short, be cult—the worship of God.

The communal and objective character of the liturgy, coupled with the holiness of its purpose, naturally gives rise to a desire to clothe it with the noblest possible forms. Liturgy has to be beautiful. Religion has always been the mother of the arts.

But ever since the Son of God became man and rose from the dead in his glorified Body, material creation is invited in a new way to take part in glorifying God. And so the most precious of its treasures are assembled as a setting for the praise of God in the liturgy: gold and silver and marble and jewels and light and incense and colour and sound are all called into service, and the artistic powers of men have been at work to mould them into the loveliest and noblest of forms.

To us it has long been self-evident that within the house of God all the arts should find a place. Nevertheless some limitations are needed in the matter. Christian antiquity strove for a long time to prevent the inclusion in divine worship of music—that is, of genuinely artistic singing. Even as late as the Council of Trent there was much difference of opinion as to whether polyphonic singing ought to be allowed in church. When Romanesque architecture was in full flower St. Bernard arose to stigmatise this earthly splendour as unbecoming to the house of God. And later still St. Francis of Assissi, of set purpose, gave an example of the utmost poverty in the churches of his order.

Admittedly the arts do also constitute a danger for the liturgy. The social prayer of the people, for instance, finds expression in song; next this song is refined to a higher artistic standard within the competence only of skilled singers—and the people become condemned to silence. Then comes the final step when the singing is yet further elaborated till it becomes concert music, retaining indeed the religious texts, but utterly worldly in its spirit and ministering only to aesthetic tastes. Or take the Mass vestments of the priest: they become ornamented with fine embroidery. But to display the beauty of the patterns to the best advantage it becomes important to avoid creases. So the chasuble is made of stiff material and then, to give freedom to the arms, parts of it have to be cut away. And so arises a shape having very little resemblance to an enveloping garment. The altar, which is essentially a table, is equipped with an ornamental centre-piece displaying, for example, a picture of the saint here venerated. From this centre-piece of Romanesque art there develops the gothic folding tryptich; and from this in turn grows the colossal reredos of the baroque period, by which the essential features of the altar are disguised rather than emphasised.

Josef Andreas Jungmann

In art there seems to be a kind of centrifugal force, a tendency to break loose from the holy foundation of humble divine worship and to become an end in itself. It is necessary, therefore, constantly to return to the living principles for its proper use. The increasing attention paid to simple unison singing by the people, whether in the form of Gregorian Chant or in vernacular hymns, is thus a very welcome feature of the contemporary liturgical movement. And we should not find it a matter for unmixed regret that the prevailing poverty of these days has necessitated the choice of simple forms in church building and ornamentation, since through these the essential basic thoughts are more clearly expressed and can be more easily understood.

There is another sphere in which intelligibility of form raises serious questions, namely, in the words of the liturgy. Liturgical formulation has, of its very nature, a tendency to assume a character independent of time and respectfully hesitant ever to touch sacred things; this is manifested in the retention of prescribed forms. It is a phenomenon which keeps re-appearing to a greater or lesser extent in all religions and in all cults, and is the reason why dead languages come to be used in worship in various parts of the world. In Catholic worship there is the added consideration of supra-national unity which can be manifested not least in the identical way of celebrating the sacred mysteries in the same language everywhere.

On the other hand the intelligent participation of the faithful is a requirement which springs from the very nature of Christian liturgy. To satisfy this requirement it is not, indeed, necessary that everything must be intelligible word by word. And besides, it is possible to provide a substitute for the audible words of the priest by reading to the people simultaneously in translation, or letting them follow a translation for themselves. But reflection on the very nature of Christian liturgy is bound to give rise to the desire that some place should be found within it for the living speech of the people. It is at all times the responsibility of Authority within the Church to decide how the balance between these two opposing interests can best be sought.

CHAPTER TWO

HISTORY

Christ our Lord once compared the Kingdom of Heaven to a mustard seed which, small though it be, grows up into a tree greater than all garden shrubs. This parable of his may truthfully be applied also to the Church's liturgy. Our Lord gave to his Church for her function of divine worship only what we might call a sacramental seed and a few directives. It was the task of the Church to foster the growth of what had been given her, making use of human resources and the help from above which would never fail her. And she has in fact developed it until it has assumed the rich and manifold forms of today—forms which often seem to us far from clear and give the impression of being strange because they originated in cultures now remote. We may think they are rigid and immutable, as if they had always been like that and were now fixed for all time. And yet in truth they all grew up little by little from particular circumstances. So our study of Christian worship ought to begin with a glance through history, in order that we may review, at least in broad outline, the way in which its forms have come to be as they are now.

The study of liturgical history began in earnest only some three centuries ago. Since the end of the nineteenth century it has advanced enormously. A great many of the sources of knowledge concerning the earliest period of liturgical history—sources which obviously are of the greatest importance—have become available only in our day. In previous centuries scholars knew indeed of a number of statements concerning arrangements for divine worship to be found here and there in the writings of the Fathers, especially of Tertullian, Cyprian, Ambrose and Augustine. But apart from a few writings about Baptism they knew of no explicit descriptions of ancient Christian liturgy apart from that of the Sunday service in the first Apology of Justin Martyr († ca. 165) and the liturgical text of the so-called Apostolic Constitution. This latter, though not held to be genuinely apostolic, was certainly thought to be very old indeed, whereas in fact it only goes back to the end of the fourth century. From about the same date there were also 'the Mystagogical Catecheses usually ascribed to St. Cyril of Jerusalem († 386); these contain, amongst other things, a detailed description of the Mass liturgy. During the past eighty years, however, these scanty sources have been augmented by a number of others. The most important of them are:

The Didache, or 'Teaching of the Twelve Apostles', dating from the beginning of the second century, and containing prayers having reference to the Eucharist.

The 'Apostolic Tradition', was written about the year 215 A.D. by Hyppolytus of Rome. Later on he set himself up as an anti-Pope, but in due course was reconciled to the Church and died a martyr. His work contains the full text for the celebration of the Mass, for the conferring of Holy Orders, and for various blessings; also exact information about the requirements and conditions for the reception of Baptism, and about the procedure in its administration.

The Euchologion of Serapion, Bishop of Thmuis in Egypt († *ca.* 360), which consists principally of Mass prayers.

An account of a pilgrimage by a nun called Aetheria. She came from Gaul, visited the Holy Land about the year 400 A.D., and has given us a vivid account of divine worship in Jerusalem, especially of the celebration of Easter.

The Catecheses of Bishop Theodore of Mopsuestia († 428) which, in their final chapters, deal with Baptism and the celebration of the Eucharist.

The *Testamentum Domini*, of Syrian origin, dating from 5th-6th century, containing the texts of various prayers.

Besides all these there are sundry valuable fragments on papyrus. The most famous one is the Papyrus of Dêr-Balyzeh, from the sixth century. It was discovered in the ruins of a Coptic monastery and consists mainly of Mass prayers.

It should be clear that with the help of all these discoveries we are able today to obtain a much clearer picture of the beginnings and early development of our liturgy than was possible a century ago.

Further, many medieval sources have been more exactly established by carefully planned collection and comparison of manuscripts, while others have become available for the first time. But reference will be made to them in due course.

THE CATHOLIC TRADITION: Mass and the Sacraments

I. *Primitive Times*

It is not self-evident that Christianity from its very beginning was associated with any richness of liturgical life. The teaching of Jesus, as we meet it in the Gospels, was concerned above all to lead individual men to an interior piety, and to make them independent of external circumstances. It was neither on Mount Garizim nor in Jerusalem that the perfect divine service would be found. The Father was seeking adorers who would worship him in spirit and in truth (John iv, 21 sqq.). And Stephen died as a martyr because he called in question both the Law and the Temple and proclaimed a spiritual worship of God (Acts vii, 48 sqq.).

On the other hand, with the foundation of a visible Church there would be associated a communal worship, a liturgy cast in external forms. From the very beginning the kernel of it was in the visible signs of the sacraments, above all, of Baptism and the Eucharist. It was through the sacramental rite of Baptism that men entered the Church, and in the sacramental rite of the Eucharist. It was through the sacramental rite of Baptism that men entered the Church, and in the sacramental rite of the Eucharist and the life of the Church was concentrated. The people were vividly conscious of the fact that through both of these they entered into personal union with Christ who had died and risen again. The times for their celebration were carefully chosen precisely in order that this might be evident: the Eucharist, even in apostolic times, was celebrated on Sunday (Acts xx, 7), the memorial day of the Resurrection, and it has remained connected with Sunday ever since. Baptism, as early as the second century, was connected with the first of all Sundays, Easter Sunday.

From the earliest times it was considered of great importance that all should be present at the Eucharistic celebration. Bishop Ignatius of Antioch († *ca.* 110) writes in his Letter to the Ephesians (xx, 2): all should come together 'in the one faith and in the one Christ' in order that, together with their bishop and his clergy, they might 'break the one Bread which is the food of immortality'.

Justin Martyr, about the year 150 A.D., describes in his first Apology (ch. 67) how on Sunday all those who dwelt in the city or the country came together; and how, after readings from Holy Scripture, the bishop spoke a Prayer of Thanksgiving over bread and wine. Now at that time it was precisely this coming together which brought upon the Christians not only vicious calumnies but also, in some cases, bloody persecution. For it was not so much their beliefs as their particular manner of worship which aroused the suspicions of the heathen.

As regards any special place of assembly there are, at most, mere hints. The Christians did not consider it important that they should possess temples, as did the pagans, and as the Jews used to do. No emphasis was laid on the question of a place, and that for reasons carefully considered. The right place was held to be wherever a community of the faithful came together. For this community was itself a living temple. And thus we find that at first Christian worship was carried out in private houses; the Acts of the Apostles and the Epistles provide us with many instances of this. Archaeological researches have long established the fact that in Rome many of the churches still bear the names of those Christians who possessed at some particular spot a house which they put at the disposal of the Christian community: some examples are San Clemente, Santa Pudenziana, Santa Caecilia.

Some excavations in Mesopotamia in 1932 uncovered the ruins of such a dwelling house. It used to be the church of the Roman garrison Dura-Europos, and was destroyed and buried by desert sand since the year 265 A.D. From an inscription we learn that the original dwelling house was made into a church in the year 232 A.D. chiefly by the removal of a wall from one place, and thus an assembly hall was provided.

2. *The Heritage from the Synagogue*

Although the kernel of Christian liturgy is derived from the prescriptions of our Lord quite independently, its developments show signs of influences from the surrounding world. Elements from the religious life of the Jews and from Greek and Roman civilisations of that time have contributed to the building up of the forms of Christian liturgy.

It is but natural that the religious traditions of the Old Testament revelation should continue to be effective in Christendom so far as they had not been abrogated by new institutions. With the other books of the Old Testament the Church took over the

123

Book of Psalms, if not primarily as a prayer book, at least as a lectionary. She took over in addition something of the Jewish calendar: Easter remained the chief feast, even though it was given a new meaning. Pentecost remained also as a day of importance. As the Jewish calendar remained in force for both of these it followed that all the feasts of the Easter Cycle were 'movable feasts' within the Roman Julian calendar. There remained also the division of time into weeks of seven days, and the designation of the days in numerical order as is still customary today in liturgical language (*feria* II, III, etc.—and it is similar in Portuguese). Moreover the designation of the Sabbath (Saturday) goes back to Jewish—in fact to general semitic—usage, and at the time when Christianity began it was current also in the hellenistic world.

As we shall see later, the Christian celebration of the Eucharist derived certain usages from the Sabbath meal which began and ended in the same way as the paschal mean (and thus also as the Last Supper of our Lord). Some traditions of Synagogue worship survived also in the Church; in particular there was the manner of singing the psalms, according to which the people used to answer or 'respond' to a solo singer (this is known as 'responsorial singing'). There was the manner, too, in which prayers were begun and terminated; they were opened with an invitation to pray, and concluded with a reference to God's eternity (*per omnia saecula saeculorum*). The preliminary greeting of the people and their answer to it are even today couched in Hebraic terms, and the assenting *Amen* of the people, (as also *Alleluia* and a few other expressions) has retained even the Hebraic-Aramaic language.

Finally we can trace even the original arrangement of the canonical Hours to the customs of pious Jews in the time of Christ. There were three Hours during the day—corresponding to Terce, Sext and None; there were evening prayer and morning prayer and also an Hour during the night (what we now call Vespers, Lauds and Matins respectively) all sanctified by prayer.

The same tradition is responsible for that arrangement of the Christian liturgy according to which the Office of the day may start with the evening before, thus introducing some feast days with 'First Vespers'.

And although the idea of Sunday has its own special origin quite distinct from the idea of the Sabbath, yet the Synagogue service of the Sabbath morning with its readings from the Law and the Prophets has been continued by the Church in her Sunday service. The Syriac liturgies have even retained a reading from the Law (Pentateuch) and one from the Prophets, merely adding New Testament readings to these, though indeed the choice of the readings has been altered.

3. *The Influence of Antiquity*

The Christian liturgy has been influenced by the pagan culture of the Roman Empire—not in so far as it was pagan, but in so far as it was the national or supra-national hellenistic mode of life in those days. The aspects of this culture which had less effects than any others were those concerned with religion and philosophy. This is true especially for the first centuries which were a time of strife. In so far as there was any effect at all, it was to make Christianity and its liturgy lay emphasis on the opposite ideas. In pagan worship, more even than in that of the Jews, much importance was attached to externals, to the material element. A sacrifice had to be performed exactly according to the prescribed rite, and its value was estimated in terms of the number and costliness of the sacrificial gifts. In contrast with this Christianity emphasised the interior element, the spiritual sacrifice, the λογική θυσία, of which later Greek philosophy had spoken.

On the other hand there arose a Gnosis which desired even to outdo Christianity in emphasising the spiritual. Gnosticism tried to combine with the concepts of Christianity some lines of thought taken from ancienct philosophical systems and from oriental religions, and thus to develop a sort of 'enlightened Christianity'. Its chief tenet was that all material things are evil, and only spiritual things are good. In order to counter this tendency, the Catholic liturgy, especially since the third century, began more and more to stress the material and external element—the very gifts of bread and wine—and to give them greater prominence. The Offertory of the Mass underwent development. In the first centuries the altar had been a simple wooden table; now it became a fixture in the church building and was made

125

the focus of attention, whereas formerly this had been the cathe-
dra (or throne) of the bishop, or the bishop himself.

In other respects too the influence of the ancient culture
made itself felt, especially since the time of Constantine when
the Church was given her freedom and hordes of people joined
her ranks. Now that the Emperor, hitherto the persecutor of the
Church, had suddenly become her protector it is not surprising
that the Church's liturgy took on a certain splendour. Enormous
church buildings were erected; for these all the riches of the
upper classes became available, and they were given the name of
Basilica. ('Basilica' originally meant 'Imperial Building, Palace',
and then more generally 'Hall'). The palace of the Emperor with
its throne-room and mosaic decorations became the model for
the new church buildings. The basilica which was built by the
Emperor himself over the tomb of St. Peter was but the most
famous of many examples. We should note with admiration that
the basilica style which now developed, in spite of the richness
of its interior decorations, did not succumb to the temptation
of worldliness.

Something of the same kind happened in the realm of music.
At every pagan festivity, even at a ceremonial banquet, there
used to be music. The Church began now to permit the assistance
of a choir of skilled singers. From the middle of the fourth century the so-called 'antiphonal singing' spread from Antioch to
other ecclesiastical centres, but for hundreds of years to come no
musical instruments were allowed. The chief reason was that certain musical instruments were too closely identified with the
worship of pagan gods (for instance, the lyre with the cult of
Apollo); but it was also a matter of principle, for it was considered
that only the human voice was really fitted for the expression
of the heart's adoration.

On the other hand those features of civil and national life
in the Greek and Roman world which had some influence from
the beginning in the shaping of the liturgy were now able to
produce their effects all the more easily. It was always taken for
granted that the language of the liturgy should be the language
of the people, so long as this was itself a language of culture.
And yet the usages of the common people were not without effect on the style of the language. The oldest liturgical text which

we have in Greek—the Euchologion of Serapion—shows an involved and ornate manner of addressing God with many attributes and in the rhetorical periods of the Greeks. But the Latin texts from the very beginning display the concise, prosaic and juridical style of the Romans. The love for descriptions of nature, characteristic of the later classical period, often appears in the forms of liturgical prayer of thanksgiving (eucharistic prayers) as they do in the simple painting in the catacombs.

Social customs of the civil life of those days were also incorporated into the liturgy. For example, reception into some community used to be ratified by a kiss. And so, when a neophyte had been confirmed by the bishop, he received in like manner this kiss of greeting. And when he entered the assembly of the faithful, they, too, gave him a kiss. When the priest goes up to the altar for the first time, and when he finally leaves it, he kisses it, just as in those early days members of a family used to kiss the table when they came to a meal, or the threshold of a temple before they entered it. When those who had assembled for the liturgy were to be dismissed, they were told so in the words *Ite missa est*, which was the same as or similar to the formulae in use to signify the end of a trial in the courts, or of an audience with an important person. According to a law of conservatism, which has a particularly strong influence in the sphere of religion, these and other formulae which originated in the civil customs of early days have been preserved more or less unchanged until now.

With certain moderate changes the liturgy has preserved also the form of dress which used to be worn on formal occasions in the later days of the Roman empire. The tunic, fastened with a girdle, remains with us as the alb; the old neck-cloth as the amice. It is from the Roman outer garment, the *paenula*, which replaced the *toga*, that our chasuble is derived. As a sign of high rank the Romans of the upper classes used to carry the *mappula*, an ornate form of what used to be a handkerchief. That survives in our maniple. It is probable that our stole, formerly the *orarium*, has a similar origin.

Constantine saw to it that within the odor of precedence among the Roman civil officials, a fitting position should be given to the clerics, especially to bishops, and above all to the

Bishop of Rome. Not only the maniple and stole, but also the pallium and buskins appear to derive from this.

For the same reason the formal court ceremonial of the Imperial Household had an important influence on the liturgy, especially in pontifical functions. Much of this had been taken over by Rome from oriental courts. Anyone who entered the presence of a prince had to salute him with a *prostratio* (προςκύνησις), throwing himself upon the ground. When such a prince walked abroad he was accompanied by two servants who supported him on the left and right as he walked so as to save him from exhaustion (*sustentatio*). According to old Roman custom a consul had the right when he appeared in public to have fire carried in front of him—a torch or a brazier constantly fed with sweet-smelling spices. These signs of honour were now adopted for bishops. Even today one genuflects when greeting a bishop; in many countries it is still the custom during liturgical functions that any lesser cleric, when passing in front of a bishop, should make a genuflection. At a Pontifical Mass the bishop has at his side not only the deacon and subdeacon, but also two special deacons who accompany him step by step; according to earlier custom they had to support him as he walked. Furthermore, lights and incense, which have so many liturgical uses, have their origin in this same court ceremonial. They entered the Roman liturgy first of all as signs of honour to the Pope: as he went in procession to a stational service he was preceded by seven acolytes who carried lighted candles on torch-holders, and by a thurifer swinging his censer. It was not until later that the altar was incensed, and not until after the first millennium that the candles were placed on the altar during divine service, so that these honours have now become most fittingly transferred to the altar and to the Sacrament of the Altar.

Finally there are some elements from pagan worship which have found a place in the Christian liturgy. Naturally these have been drawn only from the periphery of pagan religious usage, and are either forms which appear in every kind of religion or else could be given a Christian meaning. One of these is the adoption at prayer of a position facing the east, the region of the rising sun. Such a position was given also to religious buildings. This 'orientation' was an old tradition among the people of Mediterranean countries and was much used in sun-worship, a religion which flourished even in Rome at the end of pagan times. The Christians retain this usage, but in doing so they had in their minds the thought of Christ whom they named the 'True Sun' and who had called himself 'The Light of the World'. Churches also were built so that they faced towards the east. At the beginning, however, there was a certain hesitation as to whether the facade ought to be facing east (as in the case with many of the old churches in Rome) or whether the apse should look towards the east (as became the general custom later on). What helped the latter view to prevail was the consideration that in this manner those who were at prayer would be able to face eastwards while at the same time looking at the altar.

Those rites which, for the individual, are milestones on the path of life have also retained certain ancient customs. A special significance was attached in pre-Christian cults to the presentation of milk and honey. In Christian antiquity, for several hundreds of years, it was the custom to give milk and honey to those who had just been baptised. And even in the later middle ages we find that various Mass-books give a formula for the blessing of milk and honey on what were formerly baptismal days.

In some places, especially in ancient Greece, the crowning of the bride and bridegroom was a feature of the marriage rite. In the Byzantine liturgy bride and bridegroom are even today crowned in this manner at their wedding; in the course of the ceremony they interchange crowns. The wedding ceremony itself is frequently called 'Crowning' ($\sigma\tau\epsilon\phi\acute{a}\nu\omega\sigma\iota\varsigma$). Nowadays the bride usually carries a wreath.

When someone was buried, or if a remembrance day was held, there followed, according to ancient Roman custom, a meal called the *refrigerium* at which an empty place, and even a portion of the food, was set aside for the dead person. At least until the time of St. Augustine the Christians retained this custom; but a number of abuses crept in, and finally it was superseded by the Requiem Mass and sometimes by almsgiving.

Custom used to regulate also the selection of certain days for remembrance of the dead. These were, besides the burial day itself, the third, seventh (in some places the ninth) and the thirtieth day (in some places the fortieth). Particular importance was attributed to these days in reference to the soul's judgment by God, in consequence of ideas then current according to which the soul was only gradually released from the body. The Fathers of the Church fought in vain against the observance of these days. They had to satisfy themselves finally with the thought that these periods of time all had some significance in Holy Scripture: the Lord himself rose again on the third day, the patriarch Jacob was mourned for seven days—and so on. So, besides the Masses for the day of burial and for the anniversary, we still find in the Roman Missal special Masses for the third, seventh and thirtieth days; in the East the third, ninth and fortieth days are observed in like manner.

Pre-Christian antiquity has left some traces also in the Christian calendar of feasts. The feast of St. Peter's Chair on February 22nd is based on an old Roman remembrance feast of the dead called *caristia* or *cara cognatio*, which was celebrated about that time and lasted for several days. It seems that at the corresponding feast held by the Christian community the chair of St. Peter originally took the place of the dead person's chair mentioned above.

The Rogation procession on St. Mark's Day has nothing to do with the feast of the Evangelist. It is the continuance of an old Roman prayer-procession called the *Robigalia*; and in Rome the Christian procession used to take practically the same route as that previously followed by the pagan procession. Much the same may be said also of the Candlemas procession on February 2nd.

As we shall see later, the two great feasts of Christmas and Epiphany took the place of pre-Christian festivals in honour of the winter solstice.

Have the pagan mystery-cults had any effect on the Christian liturgy? A number of writers on the comparative history of religions are firmly convinced that they did. For these mystery-cults were flourishing at the time of Christ; they involved rites somewhat reminiscent of the sacraments; they had mysterious rites of initiation, and an annually recurrent festival in which the fate of some god (Dionysius, Persephone) was dramatically re-enacted and lived over again by the initiates.

But closer examination has shown that in apostolic times, when Baptism and the Eucharist were thoroughly established in the Church, there was no contact whatever between Christianity and the mystery-cults; the word *mysterium* is indeed found in the New Testament, but at that time its meaning had nothing to do with worship. The apologists of the second and third centuries knew about the mystery-cults, but were vigorously opposed to them and cried to their devotees: 'Come to us! We have the true mysteries!' For they were fully aware of the fundamental distinction that existed between them and which, in the last analysis, goes back to this: that the mystery-cults were based on ancient fertility-rites that were concerned only with the annual decay and resurgence of nature, whereas the Christian eucharistic mysteries were concerned with the historical fact that the God-man died and rose again, once and for all. Only during the last phase of these mystery-cults, when paganism was dying out, were a few expressions and forms taken from them and introduced into Christian vocabulary. The newly baptised were called 'the Initiates', and their instructors were called 'Mystagogues'. The language of Pseudo-Dionysius (*ca.* 500) is saturated with the terminology of the mysteries.

A relationship with them which touches the liturgy may well be the ancient Christian 'discipline of the secret' which appeared in the third century and reached its height in the fourth. The *disciplina arcani* required that certain of the sacred rites and formulae, especially the Creed, the Lord's Prayer and the words of consecration, should be kept hidden from those who were not baptised. In consequence these might never be put in writing but might be communicated only by word of mouth. This is the reason why even today the *Pater noster* is said aloud during the Mass, because at that point only the baptised might be present, while at other times only the opening and concluding words might be uttered audibly.

4. *The final period of Christian antiquity*

The Church made every effort to accommodate her divine services to the Christian people and their traditions; and this was very necessary. For, apart from works of charity, divine service was practically the only form of pastoral care for many centuries. There were no such things as Christian schools, or catechism classes for baptised children; nor were there any Christian confraternities or any kind of youth-apostolate. Preaching was usually reserved to the bishop, and could not possibly reach all. But the divine service on Sunday was there for everybody.

By the end of primitive Christian times the Sunday service had taken a form in which not only its language and ritual actions were intelligible to all, but which was thoroughly effective in drawing all the people into it. It was hardly possible to be there as a mere inactive spectator. All understood the *Dominus vobiscum* and *Sursum corda* as addressed to themselves. All, with loud voices, gave the answers, so that St. Jerome was able to report that in the Roman basilicas the *Amen* of the people resounded like heavenly thunder. The readings, which were given not only at Mass on Sundays but also had a place daily in the morning and evening services (Lauds and Vespers), were actually still addressed to the assembled faithful and familiarised them with the scriptures. The responsorial psalm-singing, which usually followed the readings, was so arranged that the congregation had to reply to the cantor by singing repeatedly a short verse known as the responsory. In the Offertory procession each one brought up his gift; and the Communion, at least in the West, was for a very long time the affair of the whole people.

From the fourth century monasticism began to flourish in the Church. This led to new enrichment of the liturgy. The canonical Hours made their appearance. It is true, as we have already remarked, that at this time it was already customary, in cities which had a bishop, for the clergy to hold a daily morning and evening service made up of scripture readings and psalm singing for those of the people who desired to come. But the monks went further than this. They observed also the ancient hours of prayer, the third, sixth and ninth hours, as well as the midnight prayer—all held in common in the same way as the Lauds and Vespers of episcopal cities.

In general it is legitimate to speak of a uniformed development of the liturgy throughout the whole of Christendom until about the fourth century. This does not mean that there arose a fixed order of things laid down by a central authority in terms of rubrics and prayer-texts to which all had to conform; it means rather that a definite framework, actually used by all, grew up through tradition and custom. About 215 Hyppolytus of Rome in his 'Apostolic Tradition' wrote down the texts for the most important liturgical functions of the bishop, but then he expressly remarked: 'It is by no means necessary that he should say precisely those same words which we have written down here.' It was still the function of the celebrant to select the wording of the prayers he proposed to use. It is this uniformity in broad outlines coupled with freedom in details which explains the use of the liturgical texts of Hyppolytus later on in distant lands such as Egypt and Syria.

But now there took place a very remarkable change. Communities of increasing size, and large churches, brought with them a necessity for stricter regulation. So in the centres of ecclesiastical authority liturgical texts were gradually prescribed. It is significant that in an edition of the work of Hyppolytus which was widely circulated in Egypt the sentence quoted above was altered by the deletion of the word 'not'; so that now it ran: 'It is very necessary that he should say precisely those same words which we have written down here.'

These new regulations were promulgated chiefly by Synods, ultimately by those that took place in the leading cities. So, in the Greek Orient, the three patriarchates of Alexandria, Antioch and Byzantium gradually became independent liturgical regions; there grew up an Egyptian liturgy (later differentiated into Coptic and Ethiopian), a West Syrian liturgy (which in due course became the Jacobite and Maronite liturgies), and finally a Byzantine liturgy which drew the whole of Asia Minor into its sphere of influence and now embraces the entire territory of the eastern Slavic peoples.

This was the original Greek-speaking liturgical group, though from it there later split off the Egyptians and Syrians (apart from the border-lands) who returned to their national tongues and became monophysites. Besides this Greek-speaking group there was also, before the fourth century, another group which spoke Syriac; it is that usually known to us as the East Syrian liturgical group and which later fell into Nestorianism. But also, since the strengthening of the Latin elements in Rome and North Africa, there was a Latin-speaking group. Within this group itself we must make a further distinction between the Romano-Africa liturgy and the Gallic; and this latter has to be subdivided into old Spanish, Irish-Celtic, Gallican and Milanese liturgies, each of them with its own repertoire of liturgical texts.

From this point onwards we shall, in the main, be concerned only with the line of development of the Roman liturgy, for this—apart from a few exceptional instances—became the liturgy of the western Church as a whole.

Originally the Roman order of celebration of divine worship was limited to Rome and its immediate environs. A letter has survived from the year 416, written by Bishop Decentius of Gubbio to Pope Innocent I, asking advice on sundry liturgical questions. This shows us that in many important points the liturgical practice of Gubbio was quite different from that of Rome, even though this small town in the Apennines was not very far away from Rome.

Rome was, however, the See of the Pope. And so from Rome decisions were sought in many questions of church discipline. Also Rome had early developed a particularly rich liturgical life, and had laid down clear rules about it. As early as the fifth and sixth centuries there were already in Rome twenty-five titular churches (what we would call parish churches), and also a still greater number of basilicas erected over the tombs of martyrs; all of these had their regular divine services.

It was a great honour for the individual churches when, on a prescribed day, the Pope himself with all his court went there to conduct the service. This was known as 'holding a station'. From all over the city people converged upon that church, and each time there was held a celebration which varied in its degree of splendour—for in the confused political circumstances of those days the Pope was both the true Lord or Ruler of Rome and the firm support for its inhabitants.

It was for these 'stational services' of the Pope that, since the fifth century, the liturgical texts were written down; for the most part they were those which we still have in our missals. The Roman practice was to have new formulations of the prayers which the celebrant had to speak on the different occasions throughout the year; in the East this was done only for the readings and the chants. In Rome there was for each occasion a special text for the prayer which followed the *Kyrie eleison*, for the prayer over the gifts (what we call the Secret), for the Preface and for the Post-Communion. Only the chief part of the Canon remained unchanged. The texts of all these prayers were no longer improvised but were written out beforehand and then preserved. The formulae which belonged together were collected into a *libellus*, that they might be used again. Finally all these *libelli* were themselves incorporated into one book, so that there emerged a *liber sacramentorum* or *sacramentarium* which held all the texts which the priest would need throughout the entire year.

There are three Roman sacramentaries of this type which are known to us: the Leonine, Gelasian and Gregorian Sacramentaries. Only the third of these has a real right to its name: it is the official edition of the sacramentary compiled by Pope Gregory the Great († 604). The Leonine Sacramentary was but a private collection, and the Gelasian is not really a Roman document but was put together somewhere in Gaul from Roman material.

About the same time or a little later, detailed collections were made in Rome also for the readings. These indicated what scripture passages were to be read on the respective Sundays and feast days (Lectionaries, Evangelaries). Much the same obtained for the changing chants which were collected together in Antiphonaries and Responsorials. Finally for any solemn celebration, such as the Pope's Stational Service, and for other more complicated and less frequent occasions, it becomes necessary to put down in writing the order of the ceremonies. This was done in the so-called Roman *Ordines*.

5. *The Middle Ages*

By the seventh century the development of the Roman liturgy, by that time written down in books, was in all essentials complete. The next few centuries were in Rome a period of intellectual stagnation. From the eight century the cultural leadership of the West passed over to an ever-increasing degree to the Frankish kingdom ruled by the powerful Carolingian Emperors. This is referred to as the Carolingian Renaissance. There was an intellectual revival having its effect on every sphere of life—on politics, monasticism, art, learning, calligraphy and—by no means least—the liturgy.

In Gaul, or, more precisely, in the Merovingian kingdom of the Franks, divine service had been conducted for many generations in the forms of the Gallican liturgy. There were many varieties of this liturgy: individual monasteries and episcopal sees composed their own liturgical texts which they exchanged with each other and developed further. The Celtic temperament with its taste for variety was continually producing new forms which were often rather dubious departures from tradition. There was no particular centre, such as the see of a Patriarch, which could concern itself with ensuring order and a certain degree of uniformity. And so, even from the beginning of the seventh century, the thoughts of many and, later on, especially of the Carolingian rulers, turned to Rome which had a definite and well-ordered liturgy all written down in books.

It was not Rome which imposed its liturgy on the Frankish kindgom. It did, of course, give its liturgy to its monks who had been at work since 596 founding Christianity among the Anglo-Saxons. But it was the Frankish prelates and princes who, of their own accord, worked for the introduction of Roman liturgy into their own lands. Many of them made pilgrimages to Rome where they took the greatest interest in getting to know about Roman ceremonies, in acquiring Roman liturgical books and in persuading Roman cantors to come back with them to teach Roman chants. In Carolingian scriptoria monks devoted themselves eagerly to the task of copying our Roman liturgical texts. A climax in this evolution came in 785/86 when Charlemagne received a copy of the Gregorian Sacramentary from the Pope and placed it in the library of his court at Aachen, so that bishops might make copies of it and introduce it into their churches.

But it would have been very unnatural if the entire Gallican tradition of liturgical customs which had been in use throughout the country for centuries had been jettisoned in its entirety. Nor did that in fact come to pass. But the Roman liturgy did induce very important changes in the Frankish realms: additions to pray and enrichments of rites—for example, the introduction of incense, and the 'handing over of instruments' in ordinations. The net result was that the old Roman forms were given a new stamp in the spirit of local traditions.

Josef Andreas Jungmann

It was a hard and fast principle of Roman liturgy that prayers of the priest should always be addressed to God the Father, and should end with the formula 'Through our Lord Jesus Christ thy Son. . .'. This directing of prayers to God through Christ was the ancient Christian style of liturgical prayer. Only from the fourth century was there, in some countries, any change from this usage. It came about because the Arians were denying the true divinity of Christ and were saying that the Son was not of the same substance as the Father, but was only a creature and thus subordinate to the Father. And in support of this they appealed to the usage observed throughout the whole Catholic Church of directing prayer through Christ to God the Father. This, they said, shows that Christ is subordinate to the Father. Of course they were given the correct answer: this subordination is true only as regards the humanity of Christ in virtue of which he is our Mediator and High Priest; it does not apply to his Godhead. But that did not prevent a certain confusion from arising in the minds of the faithful; and so the bishops, particularly of those countries in which the controversy was raging with especial fury, found a way out by discontinuing the use of the formula 'Through our Lord Jesus Christ . . .'.

That had happened in Spain where there was great hostility between the Catholics and the Visigoths who were masters of the country and until 589 were Arians. It happened also in Gaul. In fact the Roman Church was almost alone in preserving the ancient custom untouched. But now that Roman liturgy began to take root in Frankish soil, the new style of praying was to some extent applied to it. There were inserted not only many new prayers which were addressed to Christ himself, but even some of the old Roman formulae (for instance, most of the Advent prayers) were changed by the omission of *Per Dominum nostrum* . . . and the substitution for it of *Qui vivis et regnas* . . . as a termination.

That might seem to be a thing of very small account. But it was in fact a manifestation of a very deep-seated change which, though it altered the liturgy only a little, penetrated all the more completely throughout the piety of the Christian people. Though no point of the Christian faith was in any way shaken by it, the people shifted the emphasis of their thought and devotion; attention became fixed less on Christ as High Priest and Mediator and much more on his divine dignity. What stood in the foreground was no longer the paschal mystery: the Risen Lord as Shepherd of the faithful and Head of the Mystical Body; rather was it the Christmas mystery (or, more precisely, that of the Epiphany): the Son of God who has entered this world and whom we approach in fealty.

This development of the Roman liturgy on Frankish soil is of such great importance because of what happened later. About the end of the tenth century the Roman liturgy which had thus been shaped in a new mould began to flow back into Rome, and there it submerged the more ancient and indigenous tradition. Rome, and Italy as a whole, were at that time in a state of decadence which affected also its liturgical life. Resources were not then available for producing new copies of the old liturgical books. And so no one raised any objections when monks coming from Cluny, or prelates accompanying the German Emperor on pilgrimage to Rome, brought with them their own liturgical books and introduced these into the abbeys and basilicas of Italy and even of Rome itself. In fact Pope Gregory V, in return for certain privileges, in the year 998 imposed on the Abbey of Reichenau (which then had a famous scriptorium) the duty of supplying some liturgical books.

So the liturgy which from this time onwards was used in Rome was not really the old Roman liturgy, but Roman-Frankish. And this Romano-Frankish liturgy soon came to predominate throughout the whole of the West. For it was introduced, in place of the former (and related) old Spanish liturgy, as part of the reorganisation of church life which took place in Spain as that country was gradually freed from the domination of the Moors. It was introduced also in Ireland. Only Milan has retained till today its own ancient traditional liturgy.

However, we must not imagine that there was now a strict uniformity in the celebration of divine worship throughout the West. For the foreign elements that were added to the old Roman tradition were not everywhere fixed in writing, but were often determined by local usage. Also at some places within the wide territories of the Carolingian domains different editions or interpretations had been laid down, and these tended to spread to other places. Only some of the chief centres, and above all both new and old religious orders, took measures to lay down definite rules for the new modifications (for example, the prayers and ceremonies of the Offertory and Communion). That is why we have even now within the Roman liturgy such variations as the Dominican liturgy, the Carthusian liturgy, and so on.

But even among all the differences which still existed, especially in northern lands, there was a certain unity of spirit which made itself felt in these innovations. It expressed itself most clearly in Gothic art and architecture, in the desire to present the supernatural to the senses, and to impart the sense of the supernatural in all sorts of ways by a varied exuberance of paintings and statues. This spirit is also discernible in the liturgy. It shows itself in a tendency to dissolve the old order of things, which laid emphasis on the community, in favour of the individual. Formerly, at High Mass, when the lector read out the scriptures or the schola sang the chants, the celebrant just listened to them. But now he was expected to read the texts himself; so these were incorporated into the 'Missal' which thus came into being as a compendium of all the texts. The priest carried on as if no lector and no schola were there, just as he would in private Mass; and private Masses assumed an ever-increasing importance.

On the other hand, those features of the liturgy which appealed to the senses were more and more cultivated: the singing, for instance, began to be accompanied by the organ. Then experiments were made with harmonised singing. The colour of the Mass vestments assumed an added importance. The 'Canon of colours' was evolved—rubrics which laid down that the colour of the vestents must suit the feast of the day—red for a martyr's day, purple for a penitential day, and so on. The churches should contain the largest possible number of objects which could help the mind to 'see the heavenly'. And they wanted, too, to see the Holiest of all: about the year 1200 there was introduced the custom of holding up the Sacred Host at the Consecration in order that the people might see and adore it. Also apart from the Mass people wanted to see the Blessed Sacrament; monstrances were invented in which it was exposed for adoration. The fear of *Corpus Christi*, with its solemn procession, belongs to this period of development.

The delight in novelty and variety could now easily degenerate into indiscretion wherever there was no strong spirit of discipline. In the liturgical life of the later Middle Ages, and in the liturgical books dating from that time, there do, in fact, occur a number of examples which belong to the category of abuses, even of superstitions.

6. *Modern times*

In that state of affairs it is not surprising that the 'Reformers' were able to find a good deal of material in the sphere of divine worship as subject-matter for their complaints against the Church. The great reforming Council of Trent, therefore, had to take action in this domain. Its most important task was to purge the liturgical books of questionable accretions. This was greatly facilitated by the invention of printing. For printing made it possible to distribute everywhere rigidly uniform texts. By wish of the Council subsequent Popes energetically applied themselves to this task, and produced new and revised editions of the liturgical books: the Roman Breviary in 1568, the Roman Missal in 1570, the Roman Pontifical in 1596. This last contains the liturgical formulae for pontifical functions, and was supplemented in 1600 by the Ceremonial of Bishops which regulates their performance. Finally, in 1614, came the Roman Ritual for the administration of the sacraments.

The Missal, Breviary and Pontifical in the forms issued by Rome were prescribed for the whole of the western Church. Exceptions were made only for certain episcopal sees and religious orders which had possessed their own well-ordered liturgical books for at least two centuries. This applied to nearly all the old religious orders and to not a few bishoprics. Even so, in the course of the next few centuries, most of these bishoprics and some of the religious orders adopted of their own accord the liturgical books emanating from Rome. Only Lyons in France and Braga in Portugal have held firmly to their own traditions until now; and there are still special rites for Carthusians, called Carmelites and Dominicans.

In 1588 Pope Sixtus V founded the Sacred Congregation of Rites whose task it became to see that the reforms were carried out, and to decide, by their decrees, any disputed points that might arise.

By these means a clear and stable order was created for the liturgical life of western Christianity. In the succeeding centuries nothing of any great importance was changed. There were, indeed, some new feasts introduced, especially a great many feasts of saints; and both church architecture and church music made great strides during the baroque period. But the substance of the texts and ceremonies handed down were not touched. This carried with it a certain danger of fossilisation, all the more dangerous because of the fact that the surrounding world, and with it the Christian people, have themselves changed so much. Between the ancient forms of the service and the people's mode of thought, between the altar and the people, there developed a cleft which grew ever greater. Since the early Middle Ages there had grown up an elaborate liturgy carried out by a clergy which was both numerous and well grounded in the Latin traditions. But it became to an ever-increasing degree an exclusively clerical liturgy. Partly it was performed without the people sharing in it in any way—as happened in the many collegiate churches, which had no functions other than the carrying out of divine worship, until their secularisation. Partly also it had become more and more alien to the people—even to the educated—in proportion as the Latin culture of the Middle Ages died out. The cultivation of all kinds of devotions which appeal to the people's feelings was able to produce only a partial substitute for it.

Towards the end of the eighteenth century those concerned with pastoral theology realised that some remedy must be found. But their leaders were themselves too much infected with the rationalism of the 'Period of Enlightenment' to be able to discover the right path. At the Synod of Pistoia (1786) a great many defects were explicitly enumerated, but the remedies then proposed were so out of keeping with Catholic tradition that a number of propositions of this Synod had to be condemned by Pius VI.

The nineteenth century saw a renewal of scholastic theology, and with it, a great upsurge of historical research. Deep study of the writings of the Fathers, and the opening of the catacombs (John Baptist de Rossi, † 1894) gave a new insight into the ways of living and of thinking of the ancient Church. Abbot Prosper Guéranger of Solesmes († 1876) brought about a renewal of Gregorian chant. He was also a pioneer in drawing general attention to the beauty of the forms and texts that have been preserved in the Roman liturgy; he achieved this by writings, especially his great work on the Church's Year. Then decisive steps were taken by Pius X, the great pastor who occupied the papal throne. By his decree on Frequent and Daily Communion (1905) he led the Church back to the authentic fount of religious revival.

In 1909, there appeared, first of all in Belgium, the 'Liturgical Movement' which soon spread to other countries. Its purpose was to make the Christian people more familiar with the liturgy, above all with the Mass. The first means taken to achieve this end was the dissemination of liturgical texts, especially the Missal, in the people's own tongue. But soon it was felt that the mere silent and simultaneous reading of liturgical texts was not enough. The active participation of the faithful in the liturgy, of which Pius X had spoken, was the next objective. It was at this point that the language difficulty became apparent, as also the great tension which existed between the age-old forms of the liturgy and the understanding of the people. There arose problems that could be solved only by the highest authority in the Church.

For those rites assembled in the Ritual which concern the Christian people with special intimacy (such as Baptism, Marriage and Funerals) the use of the people's own tongue is now allowed to a considerable degree in many countries. The bold reform of the liturgy of the Paschal Vigil—one of the most important celebrations in the whole Church's year—which was ordered in 1951 and extended to the rest of Holy Week in 1955, shows that the Supreme Authority in the Church is ready to carry through a revitalising of the forms and a renewal of the content of the liturgy when the needs of the faithful require it.

Cipriano Vagaggini
1909-

Vagaggini was born in Siena, Italy, and for many years taught at the international Benedictine school in Rome, Sant' Anselmo. He is himself a monk of the Benedictine Abbey of St. André in Belgium. As a peritus at Vatican II he was closely involved in the preparation of the Constitution on the Liturgy, *and subsequently served as a consultor to the Consilium for its implementation.*

Few of those involved in the major liturgical reform mandated by Vatican II were better prepared for that demanding task than Vagaggini. His monumental Theological Dimensions of the Liturgy *had already been circulated in its second Italian edition before part of it came out in English in 1959. It was greeted as a long-awaited synthesis that drew together in impressive fashion the manifold riches brought to light by the Liturgical Movement of the previous half-century. In this regard it anticipated many features that would come to characterize the Constitution. Most important was the insistence on the primacy of the theological, subordinating the juridical which had been far too prominent for far too long.*

The influence of this approach is clearly seen in article 16 of the conciliar Constitution: "The study of sacred liturgy is to be ranked among the compulsory and major courses in semi-

THE CATHOLIC TRADITION: Mass and the Sacraments

naries and religious houses of studies. In theological faculties it is to rank among the principal courses. It is to be taught under its theological, historical, spiritual, pastoral, and juridical aspects." At the time there was hardly a better model on hand than the work of Vagaggini.

That work has subsequently gone through several revisions, been translated into all the major languages, and been updated as the reforms advocated were implemented. In 1966 Vagaggini brought out another work, translated into English the following year as The Canon of the Mass and Liturgical Reform. *This presentation of his insights to the Church at large at the very time that the question of revising the most sacred part of the liturgy was highly appreciated. He helped many who had never realized it before to see why the Roman canon (untouchable to many) needed revision. At the same time he suggested and evaluated some possible solutions.*

His Theological Dimensions, *however, is undoubtedly the work by which he will continue to be know by posterity. The preconciliar English edition only offered the first two parts: 1) the Nature of the Liturgy, and 2) the Liturgy and the General Laws of the Divine Economy in the World. In 13 chapters a wealth of history and theology found expression with a clarity and profundity that made one quickly realize how unusual and important a book it was. In its complete form, first made available in English in the 1970s, it has nine more chapters divided into three more parts: 3) Liturgy and Bible, 4) Liturgy, Faith, and Theology, and 5) Liturgy and Life. It is certainly a work that will continue to enrich all those seriously involved in liturgical instruction in the postconciliar Church.*

The brief selection that follows is taken from the second chapter of the first part, dealing with the basic notion of "sign," which is so crucial for a proper understanding of the sacramental life of the Christian Church. It has always been, and will without doubt continue to be, decisive for appreciating the "incarnational" mode in which God deals with His people through His Word made Flesh.

THEOLOGICAL DIMENSIONS

CHAPTER 2

THE LITURGY AS A COMPLEXUS OF SIGNS

3. Sign in the Liturgy

T he use of signs in the Catholic liturgy constitutes a part of the general phenomenon of recourse to symbolism in religions. These signs always have a religious value: they are sacred signs; they concern the relations between God and man, and more precisely the relations between God and man in the Christian and Catholic regime.

It must be observed also that everything in the liturgy involves recourse to signs: the whole liturgy and each of its parts has the value of sign; of every rite we may say, "One thing is seen and another understood." Further, we must know how to interpret these signs, and not fall back into the arbitrary and naive explanations of an Amalarius or a Durandus.

How to Interpret the Liturgical Signs

The first observation to be made is that the liturgical signs are never purely and simply natural signs. They are always, at least to some extent, free signs, whose meaning has been determined by the free will of Christ or of the Church. In fact, the liturgical signs signify supernatural realities which surpass absolutely the order of nature; no sensible thing can be the natural sign of such realities.

The immersion in water and the emersion from water may well signify naturally a disappearance and a reappearance, but they are not the *natural* sign of participation in the death and Resurrection of Christ. A kiss is not the natural sign of fraternal love in Christ. A bow is not the natural sign of worship rendered to God in Christ.

If the liturgical signs, then, are not natural but free signs, their meaning depends on the will of the one who has instituted them. To interpret them correctly, we must know what was the intention of Christ or of the Church. There is no other way.

One man or a group of men as private persons have not the power to create liturgical signs or to establish their meaning. And this holds not only when there is question of the Mass and the sacraments in their substance, but also when there is question of the secondary rites of the sacraments, when there is question of the sacramentals and of all the rest. In the former case, the only competent one is Christ, for the sacrments were instituted by Him. In the latter case the only competent one is the Church, for the liturgy as worship is an action of the Church, and therefore the signs in which worship is expressed depend on the Church and not on individuals.

But the fact remains that Christ and the Church have taken account of natural connections in the choice of the liturgical signs, and that often they have simply taken up pre-existing symbols, to give them a larger and more elevated signification.

If Christ chose water to signify the purification from sin and the birth to a new life, this was obviously because of its natural symbolism and because of the use which had been made of it in Judaism, for example by St. John the Baptist. Similarly, if Christ chose bread and wine to signify His body and blood given as food, this was because of their natural signification and at the same time because of the use which had been made of them by the Jews in feastday meals, especially in the Paschal supper. As for the laying-on of hands and the anointings, they were known and practiced in Judaism.

If we pass on to the liturgical signs adopted by the ancient Church, we find that almost all of them were already used, whether in religious or in profane context, by Semitic and Greco-Roman society. In the same way, the liturgical signs instituted by the Church in the Middle Ages are inspired by the customs of the court of Byzantium or of the Germanic courts.

These observations lead us to posit as a principle that the meaning of the liturgical signs depends essentially on the free will of Christ or of the Church.

The intention of Christ relative to the liturgical signs He instituted is known to us by revelation, interpreted according to the general laws of exegesis and of theology.

146

As to the intention of the Church, it is most often made known to us by the texts which accompany the rites and reveal their meaning.

Thus, the symbolism (*mysterium*) of mixing water with the wine in the chalice at the offertory is established by the accompanying prayer: "Grant that through the mystery (*mysterium*) of this water and this wine we may become sharers of His divinity who was pleased to become a partaker of our humanity." The significance of the incensation of the altar is explained by the prayer which accompanies it: "May my prayer, O Lord, arise as incense in Your sight."

The meaning of the Palm Sunday procession used to be clearly explained by the fifth prayer of the blessing: ". . . that the devoted hearts of Your faithful may understand to their benefit the mystery alluded to in the act of the multitude (*quid mystice designet in facto*) who today, inspired by a heavenly illumination, went out to meet the Savior and strewed His path with branches of palm and olive. The palm branches signify His triumph over the prince of death, while the sprigs of olive proclaim in a way the coming of Him in whom there is spiritual unction. . . . And we, in fervent faith retaining both the ceremony and its signification (*factum et significatum retinentes*) . . ."

But in many cases it is hard for us today to see the exact meaning of the rites. This happens sometimes because they are not accompanied by an explanatory text; for example, the drawing with ashes of a great cross on the floor of the nave in the rite of consecration of a church. In other cases it happens because they are so reduced or effaced that a person can scarcely see them as symbols; for example, the gesture of the priest in raising his hand slightly when he gives absolution is much less expressive than the ancient laying-on of hands.

This leads us to enunciate a second principle of the interpretation of liturgical signs: in order to know the exact meaning which the Church has chosen to give them, it is indispensable to study the origin and the development of the rites.

This study is long and difficult, to be sure; but only by devoting ourselves to it, less for itself, however, than for its results, will we attain to a real understanding of the liturgy.

It is the only means of avoiding the fanciful interpretations indulged in by too many medieval liturgists, beginning with Amalarius of Metz. Their fault lay in proposing personal opinions instead of reporting the mind of the Church. By the reaction they aroused, their exaggerations were the principal cause of the disrepute into which even the authentic liturgical symbolism fell, beginning with the Renaissance. We cannot truthfully say that this medieval allegorism has left no traces in certain books of devotion.

Classification of Liturgical Signs

To go over the individual signs used in the liturgy, explaining their meaning and efficacy, would be the task of a complete and detailed study. Here we must confine ourselves to the general outlook and attempt a classification of the signs. It seems that we may divide them into four principal groups.

Speech as sign

Speech is the most important of the signs employed by the liturgy, both in the elements originating with Christ and in those which come from the Church.

In the essential parts of the Mass and the sacraments, speech is the "form" which determines the meaning of the "matter": it is the words of baptism which give to the fact of being immersed in water and of coming out of the water the meaning of a participation in Christ's death and Resurrection. In every sacrament it is by speech that the material element becomes the sign of the supernatural reality in which the sacrament consists; and both together constitute, inseparably, the one sacramental sign. As early a writer as St. Augustine set down, à propos of baptism, a formula which has become famous: "Take away the words and what is the water but just water? Add the words to the element and you have a sacrament (accedit verbum ad elementum et fit sacramentum), which itself is like a visible word."

We need only think of the place held by the sacramental economy in the present phase of the history of salvation to grasp the importance of the role played by speech as sign in the fulfilment of this history. St. Thomas was not going too far when he compared the dignity of the word in the sacraments to the dignity of the Word in the Incarnation, and considered the sacrament as a sort of word made flesh: "It is common to all the sacraments to consist in words and corporeal things, just as in Christ, the Author of the sacraments, the Word is made flesh. And just as the flesh of Christ is sanctified and has the power of sanctifying by the Word which is united to it, so also the sacramental elements are sanctified and have the power of sanctifying by the words which are pronounced over them."

Just as the incarnate Word is the substantial and personal manifestation in the world of God's intentions with regard to men, so in the sacraments, through which Christ's action is prolonged, the word is the sensible manifestation of God's intentions. In both cases God communicates through signs, He has recourse to the economy of the *sacramentum.* The sign which is speech is therefore extremely important in the liturgy as sanctification of the Church. And since they are the instrument of Christ's action, the words of the sacraments, in that which is essential in them, have necessarily been instituted by Him.

Speech also takes first place among the signs in the liturgy instituted by the Church. Better than any other sign it incarnates and expresses the Church's reply to the divine work of sanctification. It incarnates and expresses the spiritual and interior worship of the Church, whether in prayer under all its forms or, more remotely, in preaching, which is a sign and an instrument used by the Church to prepare the faithful for receiving grace and participating in worship. Speech as sign also has a leading part to play in the sacramentals. These are constructed in the likeness of the sacraments, and it is thanks to the words that the material elements in the sacramentals become the sign of the invisible realities which God at the Church's behest grants to those who use these sacramentals with the right dispositions.

Thus we see that among the sacred signs of the liturgy (*signa rei sacrae, sacramenta*) speech occupies first place, though in intimate union with the signs which are gestures and elements. God has willed that speech be the means of exchange

149

between Himself and men in the Christian economy. This is the proof of the social and communitarian character of that economy, and at the same time of its agreement with the deepest tendencies of man, for whom speech is the most natural way of expressing his thoughts and feelings.

Let us add that when the liturgy makes use of metaphor and extensive imagery in its language, as it very frequently does, speech becomes a sort of sign in the second degree: a sign as vehicle of other signs.

Gesture as sign

If gesture plays a relatively small part in the liturgy of praise, it does play a larger part in the sacrificial and sacramental liturgy. Gesture involves the body. Sometimes the body expresses the disposition of the soul, as in bowing, extending the hands, striking the breast. Sometimes it permits action on an external thing, as in blessings, anointings, insufflations. And sometimes the body itself is to be sanctified, or else it is to be touched as a means of reaching the soul, as in the baptismal immersion or the laying-on of hands. Almost always, in the last two cases, the gesture is accompanied by words. The words specify the meaning of the gesture, but the gesture gives weight to the words. A rite in which gestures are absent or reduced to a minimum seems tenuous and unsubstantial to us. Compare, for example, matrimony and holy orders, from this point of view, or penance and extreme unction.

Things as signs

Thinks, like gestures, play a greater part in the sacrificial and sacramental liturgy than in the liturgy of praise. Things were created by God for the service of man, and it is normal that man use them for his worship. He thereby makes them attain their last end, for they have been ordained to man only in as much as he is ordained to God. That is why, in using these subjects, the liturgy often recalls that they are the creatures of God: *hanc creaturam aquae* . . . .

The things used as signs by the liturgy fall into two groups: the natural elements, such as bread and wine, water, oil, chrism, salt, ashes, incense, light, palms; and objects which result from

150

man's work, such as the altar, the cross, the sacred vestments; to this second group belong the signs which depend on sacred art.

Person as sign

The simple fact of the faithful being gathered in a church for a liturgical celebration has the value of sign. It is the visible expression of the invisible relations between God and mankind called together and assembled by Christ. It is not just any meeting, but the *ecclesia* of God in Christ, fulfilment of the "Qahal Yahweh" of the Old Testament and at the same time a sign and sketch of the gathering of the elect for the heavenly liturgy.

With still more reason, the ministers of the liturgy have the value of sign. Under various titles, they are the delegates and the representatives of Christ. This is what St. Ignatius of Antioch recalled in his letter to the Magnesians: ". . . Be zealous to do all things in the peace of God, the bishop presiding in the place of God and the priests in the place of the Apostolic college, and my beloved deacons being entrusted with the ministry of Jesus Christ . . . who came forth from one Father, existed in the unity of one Father and returned to Him."

Such are the signs employed by the liturgy. It must be remarked that in most cases these signs are not employed in isolation, independently of one another. The liturgy is not a collection of signs in juxtaposition, but a complexus of celebrations, functions or rites. In each of these functions the liturgy has recourse to many signs, to signs of several categories and often of all categories. For a valid exegesis, therefore, it will not be enough to look for what such and such a sign signifies in itself. We must look for what it signifies in the general context of the function in which it is used. And above all we must find out what this function signifies when taken as a whole.

The Role of Art in the Liturgy

The question of the use of signs in the liturgy is the proper heading under which to study the principles that explain and determine the Church's recourse to art in her worship.

Art is a sensible quality, which of itself has the value of sign, and which can embellish the other liturgical signs, speech as well as gestures or things. By giving an artistic character to the signs it uses, the liturgy reinforces them, since it confers on them that power of expression or of impression which art alone possesses.

All the arts are drawn upon for their contribution to the liturgy, but the first place goes to those that reinforce the sign which is speech: rhetoric, poetry and especially song. Song, the ideal means of forming or expressing a communitarian spirit, is the art form best suited to the liturgy. As for instrumental music, it may be considered here as a development of song, which has, however, more or less freed itself from song.

Signs have the right of admission into the liturgy only in so far as they are signs, that is to say, in as much as they represent the invisible realities which the Church wants to express through them. In the same way, it is not because of any value of its own that art is entitled to admission into the liturgy, but in so far as it can serve the liturgy's particular end, in so far as it can help the Church express her worship or sanctify the faithful.

In order to determine precisely the conditions under which this collaboration of art and liturgy can take place, it would be necessary to analyze the nature of art in general (and also of each one of the arts, in particular of song, architecture and painting), then find out in what religious or sacred art consists essentially, and finally show the possible relations between the proper end of art and the proper end of the liturgy, thus being enabled to give a definition of liturgical art. But such an inquiry would lead us far afield, so controversial are the notions of art and sacred art. We shall limit ourselves to a few remarks.

Art and esthetic pleasure

Art must be defined in relation to the beautiful. And the beautiful can be defined only in relation to that enjoyment which it causes in us, called esthetic pleasure. Hence art can be defined as the aptitude for perceiving and expressing sensibly in things the quality which makes them a source of esthetic pleasure.

It remains to define esthetic pleasure, which is something easier to experience than to translate into concepts. In terms of Aristotelian-Thomistic psychology, it is the enjoyment of the faculties of knowledge—especially of sight, hearing and imagination—conformably to their natural inclination and to the acquired dispositions of the subject.

This enjoyment has the particular characteristic of being disinterested. That is to say, its cause—and its goal—is not the physical possession of its object, but only its contemplative possession. And it is a source of peace because it gratifies fully the faculties of knowledge.

Beauty is not in things considered in themselves, but in things considered in relation to the faculties of knowledge. Thus art involves an objective aspect and a subjective aspect. For if the faculties are the same, essentially, in all men, the innate or acquired dispositions which help determine them vary considerably from one epoch to another, from one society to another, from one individual to another; and in one individual they are easily modified by various influences. That is why taste, which is the aptitude to experience an esthetic pleasure in the presence of certain things, may vary and hence may be formed by an appropriate education.

The esthetic perception, involving a certain accord between the object and the dispositions of the subject, is an instinctive or intuitive type of perception. It is not analytic but synthetic. It cannot be communicated directly, therefore, like a science, but only indirectly. One must seek to induce in the listener or the spectator the dispositions which were those of the artist, in such a way that the same object will awaken in him the same esthetic perception.

The intrinsic end of art (the end of the work, as the scholastics say) is therefore simply to actuate the cognitive faculties in such a way as to bring about esthetic enjoyment in the subject, and nothing else. And this enjoyment is morally indifferent, as is scientific knowledge or technical knowledge. It becomes good or bad action according to whether the further end for which it is sought (the end of the agent) is good or bad.

Thus an object or an action morally bad can be truly artistic, if it is presented in such a way as to stimulate esthetic pleasure. By the same token, it is not enough that an object or an action be morally good, or that the artist have a morally right intention, in order that the result be esthetic!

Still, because he who makes a work of art and he who admires it are men and not only artists, it is their duty to consider their act not in itself but in terms of man's last end. Art is indeed a good for man, but a particular good and not the total good. To act in an ordered way, therefore, man must subordinate his esthetic pleasure to his total good, that is, to the moral good. As far as the end of the agent is concerned, art can and must be qualified in moral terms.

Art and religion

It is here that the possibility of a religious art comes in, a sacred art; that is to say, an art which, while remaining faithful to its own requirements, subordinates itself to a specifically religious end.

The end of religion is to produce in man that substantially interior attitude which is made up of admiration, submission, faith, hope and love towards God. Art subordinates itself to this end when the esthetic enjoyment which is its own end is not only juxtaposed but really ordained to the religious end.

No one would think of denying the possibility of the harmonious collaboration between art and religion. It is sufficiently proved by achievements such as Gregorian chant, the painting of Fra Angelico, the sculptures of the portals of the cathedral of Chartres, the ancient Christian basilical architecture. But how is this collaboration to be explained?

Most of the schools of spirituality have exercises of psychological preparation for meditation and prayer. Some of these devices are of a simply physical or psychic nature, and have the aim of creating a state of recollection by acting on the senses and through them on the whole person.

St. Ignatius, for example, advises one to close the window and to stand in the dark or with a dim light for meditating; to say certain prayers by pronouncing the words slowly to the rhythm of inhalation and exhalation; to take certain bodily attitudes, for example placing the hand to the breast, keeping the eyes fixed in one position or on some object.

This physical and psychic recollection is not yet prayer, but it is an effective preparation for prayer, it creates a climate in which prayer flows out more readily.

The esthetic experience can, in a certain measure and under certain conditions, play an analogous role. The reason for this is that esthetic pleasure, resulting from an accord between subject and object, involves an activity of the senses and of the intellect which is intuitive, synthetic, without effort and without investigation, quite different from their ordinary activity. The subject has the impression of going beyond the usual process of knowledge and of entering into immediate and profound contact with the real. He seems to be seeing things no longer from the outside but from the inside.

If this esthetic experience is accompanied by the required moral dispositions, it easily becomes a fertile ground for prayer. For prayer also, especially if it is contemplative, implies a certain surpassing of the usual activity of the senses and of the analytical and discursive activity of the intellect. Prayer also wants to be a direct contact with the object; it also wants to be an experience.

But, just as the spiritual authors recommend that the psychological means of preparation for prayer be used only with discretion, so also prudence must be advised in the recourse to the esthetic experience. This prudence is needed because of the danger of stopping at the esthetic pleasure instead of using it to rise up to God. The danger will be greater or lesser according to the subject's dispositions and his ability to control his senses. It will vary also according to the means employed by the artist: if they are not adequately spiritualized, they run the risk of riveting the attention on the sensible, that is, on the sign.

Art and liturgy

Religious art is not yet liturgical art. Liturgical art requires not only that the work be beautiful and the enjoyment which it arouses be directed to the religious attitude in general, but also that it serve to promote that particular type of religious attitude which is the liturgical attitude.

As will be seen in the following chapters, it is characteristic of the liturgy to be an action, a communitarian action of an assembly in which the members all have a role to play, an action centered on the Mass and the sacraments, finally an action whose whole meaning is to have the mystery of Christ relived by those who take part in it.

It is this particular form of religion which liturgical art must express and help establish. To produce an authentic work of liturgical art, therefore, the artist must not only be truly religious, but he must really have penetrated into the world of the liturgy.

Numerous practical consequences flow from these principles for all the arts which find a place in the liturgy, especially for the arts of singing and of instrumental music, for architecture and for painting.

On condition that these rules be observed, the liturgy opens the door wide to art. It has done so from the very beginning: at first to the arts of speech and of song; then, beginning with the third-fourth century, to architecture, to mosaics, to painting, to the arts of movement and to the lesser arts; finally, in more recent times, to sculpture and to polyphonic and instrumental music.

And because art and taste, involving a noteworthy subjective aspect, vary with times, places and people, the liturgy has admitted works of the most varied taste and style. And today it remains open to new quests. This is so much the more proper because there is evolution not only in the artistic sensibility but also in the religious sensibility, that is, the way in which man reacts, on the sensible level, in the presence of the religious phenomenon.

Let us note that here again there are dangers to be feared. Like sacred art in general, liturgical art runs the risk of forgetting its properly religious end and seeking "art for art's sake." Moreover, it is in danger of forgetting the requirements proper to the liturgy, especially its communitarian requirements.

Song, music and architecture have too often failed on this score.

Is it not a mistake to have given the liturgical chants a development and a perfection which have undoubtedly made them superlative works from the artistic point of view, but which have necessitated their being withdrawn from the people and entrusted to a schola?

Is it not a mistake to have built churches which are perhaps admirable and which give witness to a profound religious sense, but in which the people are so far removed from the altar that they can no longer see what is being done there?

Is it not a mistake to have raised up altars which do certainly constitute magnificent settings for the exposition of the Blessed Sacrament, but in which it is hard to recognize the Eucharistic table which the communicants should be surrounding?

It would be only too easy to multiply similar examples. All these deviations come from forgetfulness of the proper requirements of liturgical art. The liturgy makes use of art as a sign; and every sign is at the service of that which it is supposed to express and, in a certain measure, to make real. It is therefore a duty for the artist who wants to work in the liturgical field to become permeated with the realities which his art presumes to express, and to submit himself to their requirements.

Why This Regime of Signs?

Before inquiring what the liturgical signs signify, we must ask ourselves why the encounter between God and man takes place in a regime of signs, by means of signs. The modern man often fears that this introduction of signs between himself and God will impede the spontaneity and the sincerity of his religious life. God has asked us to adore Him in spirit and in truth, and to pray to Him in secret. Then why all these intermediaries and all this stage setting?

There is no doubt that God could have adopted a system in which religion would have been a purely interior and individual affair, without the mediation of things or of persons. Actually, God has chosen and imposed on those who want to come to Him another way, which is the way of the Incarnation: it is through men and sensible things that God communicates Himself to us and that we go to Him.

God communicates Himself to us and we go to Him by the Word made flesh, by the Church, spiritual and visible at the same time, which prolongs Him, by the liturgy whose visible signs signify, contain and give the invisible realities. We may apply to the present phase of history of salvation what Origen said of the story of Abraham: "Everything that is done, is done *in sacramentis.*"

Such is the regime God has established; and His decisions, in the last analysis, have no other reason than His free will; man can do nothing but ascertain them and conform to them.

In submitting the whole of His relations with man to the law of incarnation, God, moreover, is merely adapting Himself to the nature of His partner. For man is made of spirit and matter, and his spirit acquires knowledge only by means of the sensible, and expresses itself only by means of the sensible. To this incarnated spirit the way of incarnation and the regime of signs are perfectly suited.

The Fathers have often observed this in connection with the *sacramenta* in general and the sacraments in particular. Thus St. John Chrysostom remarks, "Since the Word says, 'This is My body,' let us assent and believe and consider Him in this sacrament with spiritual eyes. Actually what Christ has given us is not anything sensible. Rather, the realities given are wholly spiritual, though clothed in sensible things. The same holds for baptism: the gift is given through a sensible thing, water; the spiritual reality accomplished is birth and renewal. If you had been incorporeal, He would have given you bare, incorporeal gifts; but since the soul is united to the body, He offers you spiritual realities in sensible things."

This idea of the harmony of the sign with the nature of man can readily be particularized and probed if a person examines in what manner and with what effect the mind is instructed and expresses itself by means of the different liturgical signs and the different rites.

In ancient times, St. Augustine had already been struck by this power of sign and symbol over the human spirit: "All these things brought home to us in figures have the aim of feeding and somehow fanning the flame of love which, like a sort of specific gravity, carries us above or within ourselves until we come to rest. Thus proposed, these realities move and enkindle love more than if they were set forth in a starkly intellectual way and not as *sacramenta*. It is hard to say why this should be so. But it is certain that anything expressed by way of allegory is more moving, more pleasing and better heeded than if it were said outright in the most appropriate words. I think the soul is slower to catch fire as long as it is involved in mere earthly things; while if it is directed to bodily symbols (*similitudines*) and from the symbols to the spiritual realities expressed by them in figure, this very process enlivens it, enkindles it like a waving torch and draws it with more ardent love to its resting-place."

What Augustine had surmised with his usual perspicacity, the moderns have striven to describe in detail by means of psychological analysis, and this in the religious sphere as well as the profane. Among the Catholics, Romano Guardini has shown particular interest in this aspect of the liturgy. Among the Protestants a noteworthy work is that of Robert Will, *Le culte,* in three volumes, the second of which is devoted entirely to the phenomenology of worship. Through very attentive observation, Will seeks to understand the source of the psychological effectiveness of the signs and rites of worship.

Apart, of course, from certain defects congenital to the mentality of a Protestant when he speaks of Catholic worship, many of Will's observations on the psychological necessity and efficacy of the liturgy in its structure as a complexus of signs are quite justified; and some of his effective passages on this subject can, with a few changes, be fully approved by a Catholic.

Thus, for example, on the psychological necessity of a worship embodied in signs: "All worship demands expressive forms: images, sounds, words, gestures, rites, persons. These forms, interposed between God and the faithful, serve as commutators for the currents of life which connect the subjective pole to the objective pole or vice versa. They give concrete expression to the soul's aspirations and raise them up. In the other direction, they make concrete the graces descending from on high and channel them into souls. Thus phenomena in the sphere of worship, placing themselves at the service both of the religious subject and of the divine object, respond to a twofold necessity, the one being of the psychological order, the other of the metaphysical order. In other words, the nature of man demands phenomena and the essence of revelation also requires them."

Again: "The rites of worship appear, therefore, as means designed to preserve the objective values of religion, because they are considered as translating into phenomena the supersensible data of divine revelation. Without this translation into figures, religion, purely subjective, would run the risk of deteriorating into mystical states, cold ideologies or moralizations. . . . The religion which has no interest in worship wastes away in the rarefied atmosphere of an excessive spiritualism. . . . In short, there is no more justification for denying to transcendental inspiration a representation by figures perceptible to the senses than there is for denying such representation to the soul's aspiration. The translation of the transcendental realities into the sensible world is a postulate of the divine essence in communication with the world, as the concrete figuration of the data of religious consciousness is a postulate of human nature."

Or again this observation on private religious life and worship: "The worship-experience will be an empirical prolongation and a concrete enlargement of the religious experience. The encounter with God in worship will be the end result and the combination of all the experiences provided us by our previous contact with God, by our faith and by our prayer." "In short, worship, prolongation of the mediating action of Christ, is the religious symbol *par excellence*. Forming the bridge which leads from transcendence to immanence, it has the mission of helping the whole world to be penetrated with the divine presence."

Any Catholic will surely welcome these observations by a Protestant; for they prove how natural, effective and morally necessary it is, from the psychological viewpoint alone, that the encounter between God and man take place in a regime of signs. They show the irreplaceable role played by visible worship in assuring a just balance in the life of religion and in preventing religion from being transformed into a mere psychological experience, into a philosophy cut off from life or into an ethics without foundation.

If Protestantism has not been able to avoid these dangers, this is due in large part to its almost complete rejection of the incarnated forms of the Catholic liturgy. "It is a fact," writes Will, "that the Protestant churches, and especially reformed Puritanism, have tipped the balance of the two hemispheres— the external and the internal—in favor of the internal. The spiritual impoverishment resulting from this imbalance does not respond to the demands of our dualist nature or to the needs of popular piety or to the trends of our generation so eager for reality, objectivity and intense life."

Such observations, already recognized as accurate from the psychological viewpoint, acquire still more force if we add that this imbalance is contrary to the will of God manifested in Christ, and that it ignores not only the laws of psychology but also and above all the laws to which God has chosen to submit His relations with men: law of objectivity, law of incarnation, law of salvation in community.

Thus it is understandable that the discovery of the liturgy, even by men sensible especially to its psychological utility, as is the case today with many Protestants, carries with it in germ the recognition of values which, logically developed, might lead to the discovery of Catholicism.

If the regime of signs is in harmony with man's condition, material and spiritual at the same time, it is equally in harmony with his social character. Man is a social being, and the Christian is a member of that body which is the Church. The homage he must render God cannot be the homage of an isolated individual. The people of God must render God a collective worship, a liturgical worship, in the etymological sense of the term.

Now the sign is the means *par excellence* for communication among men, the instrument which assures the unity of the group as well as its distinction from other groups. At the same time it is the necessary point of departure for common action. No one could conceive of a community offering God an exclusively spiritual worship. In order to be common to all, worship must have recourse to the indispensable means of human communication, that is, to signs. It is only around signs that the gathering of the community will take place, and by means of signs that its worship will be expressed. Thus the fact that God has willed that men go to Him by using signs is explained by the prior fact that He has desired them to go to Him in a group, in community.

This communitarian and social character of the liturgy is rich in consequences, to which we shall have occasion to return. Let us point out at least, right now, that if the sign is made for the community, it must be within reach of their understanding, under pain of losing its psychological effectiveness. This simple observation, as we shall see later, is very helpful in solving the problems of the liturgical pastoral art.

Jean Leclercq
1911-

Jean Leclercq was born in Avesnes, France, in 1911 and entered the Benedictine Abbey of Clervaux in Luxembourg in 1928. He studied in both Rome and Paris, immersing himself especially in the medieval monastic heritage. In his "spiritual treasure-hunt" he was responsible for the discovery and publication of many manuscripts that have cumulatively thrown much new light on the so-called "Dark Ages," revealing the extent of the monastic contribution to the survival of Western culture.

The book from which the present selection is taken was the outgrowth of his lectures given at the Institute of Monastic Studies of Sant' Anselmo in Rome during 1955-1956. Through a mass of detail, in the style of the best historian, Leclercq penetrates to the heart of the monastic civilization he recreates. At that heart he finds the conflict between the "City" and the "Desert" stimulating the entire development. In this perspective one gains a new appreciation for the central place of the liturgy, for it is therein that the City and the Desert find their harmony.

The ten chapters of the book are divided into three parts: 1) The Formation of Monastic Culture, 2) the Sources of Monastic Culture, and 3) the Fruits of Monastic Culture. The selection reproduced here is chapter ten, "The Poem of the Liturgy." The reasons for including it will become obvious upon reading it. In the current efforts to reform the liturgy the influ-

ence of monasticism has sometimes been blamed for certain problems of the past. In acknowledging the grounds for such criticism, however, it would be unfortunate if the ledger were not balanced. The monastic contribution to the richness of the Western liturgical heritage is so overwhelming that it ordinarily would not require that special attention be drawn to it.

Dom Leclercq's observations, based on solid scholarship, provide food for thought in our era of reform. If, as he claims, "the liturgy is at once the mirror of a culture and its culmination," the seriousness and complexity of appropriate reform becomes all the more striking. Even though his reflections were written only a half-dozen years before Vatican II, he could not then have known how imminent liturgical reform was, so that his words take on an unusual relevance. It is such well-informed, thoughtful commentary as this which can best serve to set the tone for what the liturgy ought to become in its own way in each new era.

THE LOVE OF LEARNING AND
THE DESIRE FOR GOD

CHAPTER X

THE POEM OF THE LITURGY

T he sense of the majesty of the Lord was one of the
salient characteristics of the monks' religious reflection,
and it was expressed, even more than in their theological writings, in their liturgical production. The latter merits
consideration and should be reserved to the last because it is
linked with all other aspects of monastic life: with its practice,
since it is connected with one of its principal observances, that
is the celebration of the cult; and with its culture for which it
is both the stimulus and the outcome. There is no doubt but
that liturgy constitutes one of the sources of this culture: it is
partly through it and in it that the monks made contact with
the Scripture and the Fathers and were permeated by the great
traditional religious themes. But it was equally in the liturgy
that their culture found one of its chosen fields for expression:
for it, and in connection with it, they composed the greatest
number of texts. These have almost been forgotten by now with
the exception of a few masterpieces whose monastic origin is
mostly unknown because they have been absorbed into the
common treasury of Western liturgy. But these choice examples
are part of a very large collection, without which we could have
no complete idea of monastic literature.

Liturgy: Synthesis of the Arts

The word liturgy in this study is used in the broad sense to
mean all the activities involved in prayer. In the Middle Ages the
public celebration of the divine office represents their perfect
expression and synthesis. This cannot be said of every period,
since the first generations of monks had either privately or
together, recited the Psalms, and occasionally large numbers
participated; but in their life of retirement from the world, little

attention was given to the Church's public worship. St. Benedict, on this point as well as on others, stood for moderation: twelve Psalms a night, and the whole Psalter each week. He had enriched the monastic office with non-biblical texts which some churches were using in the celebration of the cult, like the hymns he called "Ambrosian." He had emphasized the great value of this common prayer, the details of which were almost entirely determined by St. Benedict in his *Rule*. Yet in his *Rule,* the divine office is not among the occupations requiring the most time. However, under the influence of circumstances he could not have foreseen, the role played by the liturgy in the monastic life tended to grow, and Benedict of Aniane ratified this evolution. From then on, the monks' life, in this respect, bore a great resemblance to that of canons who performed the services of the cult in the cathedral churches. From the ninth to the twelfth century, monastic liturgy continued to grow richer and developed to the point where, in certain localities, it accounted for almost the entire day. In this domain, beginning in particular with the middle of the tenth century, a difference in practice grew up and was maintained between the two regions whose predominating points of view are symbolized by the names of Gorze and Cluny. In the beginning, less time was allotted to the office. But monastic life everywhere remained marked by its great esteem for public worship. The monks' entire life was led under the sign of the liturgy, in rhythm with its hours, its seasons and its feasts; it was dominated by the desire to glorify God in everything, and first of all, by celebrating His mysteries.

The literary productions which resulted from this pre-occupation were extremely varied. For our purposes they can be grouped under three headings: those which treat of the liturgy, those which constitute texts for use in the cult itself and those which describe the characteristics which the liturgy conferred on the monks' religion.

The monks wrote little as to their attitude toward the liturgy: its importance was quite taken for granted and for men who were living constantly under its influence it hardly needed any commentary. Rather, it was the liturgy itself which formed the usual and ordinary commentary on Holy Scripture and the Fathers. This is true especially of Cluny where liturgy occupied such an important place. St. Odo in his *Conferences* and his poem on the *Occupation,* St. Odilo in his sermons, Peter the Venerable in his various writings do not explain the liturgy and they rarely mention it. No doubt texts were written that were intended for reading at Cluny: legends of the Saints, solemn sermons like those of Peter the Venerable on St. Marcellus or on the relics of a saint, or those of St. Bernard on St. Victor. Treatises on the *computus* were composed in which all the resources of arithmetic and astronomy were enlisted in calculating the dates of movable feasts. The liturgy was called upon to supply themes for sermons even when the latter consisted in the interpretation of Scripture; thus St. Bernard's sermons on the Psalm *Qui habitat* abound in allusions to Lent during which verses of this Psalm are often sung. Still it remains true that we possess few monastic writings on the liturgy, although some do exist; the most outstanding have been published, while others are as yet unpublished. In general—and here again we encounter one of the constants of monastic culture—the rites are sanctioned on historical grounds as in the "manual of liturgy" in which Walafrid Strabo made a study of the origins and growth of certain ecclesiastical observances. But these treatises, practical or scholarly in nature, are not eulogies of the divine office, its beauty or its pedagogical merit; nor are they exhortations to reserve a position of preference for it in religious life. Literary works of the latter type become necessary only in periods when the liturgical sense must be reanimated and the liturgy restored. The monks themselves are unanimously convinced of the primary importance which belongs by right to the activity in which they proclaim the glory of God. Belief in the Lord's majesty directs and dominates all their expository works, such as Rupert of Deutz' treatise *On the Divine Offices.* In its prologue he asserts very forcibly that:

> The rites which, following the yearly cycle, are performed at the divine office are symbols of the highest realities; they embrace the greatest sacraments and all the majesty of the heavenly mysteries. They were instituted for the glory of the head of the Church, Our Lord Jesus Christ, by men who understood all the sublimity of the mysteries of His Incarnation, His

Nativity, His Passion, His Resurrection and His Ascension and who had the ability to proclaim it in the spoken word, the written word, and in the rites. . . . But celebrating the rites without understanding them is like speaking without interpreting what is being said. The Apostle St. Paul counsels him who has the gift of speaking to pray that he may receive the ability to interpret what he says. Among the spiritual gifts with which the Holy Spirit enriches His Church, we should lovingly cultivate the one which consists in the power to understand what we say in prayer and in psalmody: this is no less than a manner of prophesying.

All the liturgical literature of the monks consisted in similarly commenting, "with the voice and the written word," the content of the rites. Rather than treatises on the rites, their commentary took the form of texts for use in conjunction with the celebration and which displayed its riches.

The liturgical texts consist of written formulas to be used in the various exercises of the cult. Before describing them we should recognize the fact that additional texts were constantly being composed. For the liturgy was not considered as a complete, and final whole to which nothing could be added. In this realm St. Benedict was an innovator since he had introduced into monastic liturgy the "Ambrosian hymns," amongst others. The tendency to embellish the divine service with new texts, and especially poetic texts, continued to manifest itself everywhere.

St. Notker and the Sequence

First of all, new offices had to be composed as new feasts were added to the Church's calendar. But above all, the texts already in existence soon became a subject for amplifications. The origin of this practice is well known, thanks to the account St. Notker of St. Gall gives of it in the preface to his collected sequences. He tells us how difficult it was to remember, so as to sing them correctly, "the very long melodies" which prolonged the final *a* of the *alleluia* at the Gradual. But one day around the year 860, a monk of Jumièges, fleeing before the Normans, arrived at St. Gall with an antiphonary in which each note of the Alleluia corresponded to a syllable, and all were in great admiration of this mnemonic device for preserving the melodies. Now, at St. Gall there was a real poet, Notker, and around him a whole school of disciples and successors to perfect the technique which had come to them from Jumièges. This was the origin of *prosae*.

Thereafter, these compositions never ceased being multiplied, amplified and diversified; *meters, versus, versiculi,* tropes, sequences, *prosulae,* motets, *organa,* each of these forms had its laws and its own history. Over the centuries all were transformed and corrupted: out of dialogued tropes grew the *ludi,* and the latter contributed, to a great extent, to the origin of liturgical drama. We need not describe here these different literary forms nor relate the evolution of each since this obviously could not be done in a few pages with the precision the subject demands. It is enough for us to record the fact that during the entire Middle Ages throughout the West, men continually composed literary texts that were intended to be sung in the divine service.

These texts form the largest part of the forty-two thousand pieces of verse mentioned in the *Repertorium hymnologium* by Ulysse Chevalier, and of the fifty-five volumes of the *Analecta Hymnica* published by Dreves and Blume. These are texts one seldom has occasion to read today; they were not written to be read but to be chanted in the divine office, but we would have only an inadequate idea of the life led by the monks and of their literary activity if we lost sight of the place these compositions held in their schedule and in their preoccupations.

For these texts were loved. Those who had a reason and the talent for doing so, loved to compose them.

> And all loved to sing
> The delightful kyrielles
> The sweet and lovely sequences
> With full voice and in rich tones.

It happened that certain communities would inaugurate a feast or add to its solemnity in order to have the joy of singing or reading beautiful texts. It has been remarked that "some feasts have a strictly literary origin. It is quite possible that the celebration of the feast of a certain saint may have been initiated

169

in a monastery because its library had a marvelous *Life* which had guaranteed him a local celebrity." At St. Bertin, in the eleventh century, St. Vincent was celebrated with only three lessons and three *responsoria*. But, one fine day, some brethren who had come from other parts brought along a greater number of *responsoria*. These were written down and delighted the monks and especially the young oblates. Hence, it was decided to adopt them; to carry this out, St. Vincent's feast became a twelve-lesson feast. "And," adds the chronicler, "the devotion of the brethren to God and the holy martyr increased from day to day."

No doubt many of these literary and musical compositions would no longer be to our taste, and to us their length might well seem tiresome. We wonder if they were equally so for the great many who sang, heard or copied them? They may very well correspond to a taste whose criteria are not ours and exemplify a different concept of time and a different internal rhythm. The verve of primitive, original and youthfully exuberant spirits is often combined in these authors with a curious need for purely conventional artifices. They are willing slaves of the *clausulae;* they overexaggerate the use of diminutives and superlatives, unusual words and Greek expressions. Mythological allusions betray the pedantry and preciosity of some of them. But side by side with these defects, this literature has real qualities which it has been claimed make it "often lofty and grand, with at times the majesty of a Romanesque cathedral." In these productions are to be found many examples of true poetry, more than they are sometimes believed to have. Literary historians—Léon Gauthier, Rémy de Gourmont, W. von den Steiner—are the ones who have brought this home to us. The *Alma Redemptoris mater,* the *Veni Creator* and other jewels of our present-day liturgy were born of the medieval monks' intensely felt need to versify for God.

Almost everything in this material, as the historians admit, is of monastic origin. It is true that some of the manuscripts in which these texts have been preserved have come from cathedrals; still it is true that almost all the known authors were monks. Their poems became the common fund of the universal liturgy but they had arisen in monastic milieus and expressed the aspirations of monks everywhere. St. Gall, Fleury, Monte Cassino, St. Martial of Limoges are only the most renowned of the abbeys to which we are indebted for them. For the list to be complete many other abbeys would have to be mentioned in the countries of the Empire as well as in England, France and Italy. This proliferation of texts whose purpose was to embellish other texts could, of course, give rise to dangers, and abuses did occur. The Cistercians inaugurated a reaction, almost a revolution, when they reinstated the pure and simple liturgy in which biblical texts play the predominant part. Still, not a few of their number prefer solemn masses to austere psalmody. The Order as a whole, finally, although tardily, like the others adopted the votive office of the Blessed Virgin. St. Bernard was to compose a hymn in honor of St. Malachy and—for the black monks, to be sure—an office in honor of St. Victor.

The fact, then, is that whereas the essential elements of the missal and even of the divine office had been settled before the monastic revival of the Carolingian period, it was during the great monastic centuries, from the ninth to the twelfth, that the minor texts were established, such as the formulas for the benedictions of the lessons, the absolutions, and all the accessory pieces which enriched the primary texts of the liturgy.

As for characteristics of these productions, they are precisely those which our knowledge of monastic culture would lead us to expect, and all the elements of this culture are present. The most important are highly traditional; meter alone was to evolve and take a new direction.

Sources of Inspiration

The tradition bases were primarily the Bible and the Fathers. If all these compositions are essentially poetic in character, they owe it to minds which had been fashioned by Holy Scripture. Their modes of expression are concrete and rich in images. The value of their words lies more in what they mean than in what they actually say: their evocative power is greater than their precision; each of them is like a note which awakens harmonics. All the delicacy of liturgical poetry comes from the free and harmonious use it makes of the sacred words: the groups of versicles, each of which, because of its origin and own particular meaning, has special significance and whose combination produces a more complex, and a newer whole; they are daring in juxtaposing two texts, one of which throws light upon the other, thereby forming, because it is so different, a contrast with it which makes each one's individual light more intense; their way of lending a wide range of different colors to the same unchanging texts by, for example, incorporating verses of the Psalms within the antiphons; the continual passage from fact to allegory, from event to idea; the alternation of formulas, each of which evokes a different reality, which complete each other within a whole that is richer still, as the facets of a diamond permit us to see all its fires asparkle. All this art—and how much it recalls Claudel and Péguy—belongs to the great traditional liturgy. This is the style in which the *responsoria* are generally composed. The antiphons and versicles composed for new offices and other developments added to the ancient forms, all derive from the same inspiration. Their authors know how to make use of the Old Testament as the liturgy had done in its great creative period; they introduced into the cult, with exquisite taste, all the imagery of the Canticle of Canticles which was so well suited to singing the joys of the Church, of Mary and of every Christian soul. At the height of the Middle Ages in the West, they were able to maintain in the cult the biblical spirit and a whole glowing play of oriental colors.

This biblical sense was authentic and vouched for by the tradition of the Fathers who had known how to make the sacred works sparkle with the same purity and the same freedom in the service of the Church's great dogmas. All the doctrinal advances of centuries during which incomparable doctors had sought to explain the faith or fight for its truth were reflected in the ancient liturgy, and in the writings of the Latin and Greek Fathers as well. Constant association with such teachers made it possible for the monks to safeguard the hierarchy of religious values. They knew enough not to allow devotions to triumph over *devotio*. The great realities of salvation remained the core of their piety, their thought, and the greater number of their texts. Their cult celebrated the mysteries of Redemption, the saints who had lived by them, and the Virgin

Mary in whom these mysteries found their perfect fulfillment. The result is triumphant devotion brimming with enthusiasm, animated with intense joy, and with the confidence of the children of God. This vigor, this joy and this craving for a life in God explain, and to some extent justify, the occasionally strained epithets and the preciosity of certain images. They had to sing, accentuate, proclaim and reiterate their happiness at what God was doing for man. "Joy," says Léon Gauthier, "is the 'dominant' in all that poetry: *Dominum veneremur, eia et eia, laudes persolvemus, canentes, eia.* This cry *eia* rings out a thousand times in each of our Troparies; it is, somehow, both their résumé and their essence." And this faith in the Redemption, this confidence in Christ's victory are the special mark of the religion of the patristic centuries and the writings which gave it expression. So long as it was maintained, contact with these sources prevented the liveliest imaginations from getting lost in pious fantasies. The piety expressed in these poems owes its vitality to doctrine. "Our monks," Léon Gauthier goes on to say, "are those rare theologians whose enthusiasm is not wanting in exactness." Furthermore, the same historian was able to distill from their poems what he describes as "an exposition of Catholic doctrine." Moreover, he has offered us nothing more than an outline; the tropes and sequences of the ninth to the twelfth centuries present on a great many points a reflection of doctrinal progress and their evidence is well worth compiling.

To be sure all excesses were not avoided. In this immense production, naivetés, lapses from good taste and gross exaggerations can be found. But, almost always, these have to do with the details of the mode of expression. On the whole, it can be maintained that the religious sense was unerring. It accorded less importance to intense feeling than to precise ideas. The emotions intervened only in the orchestration of the ideas; they were not the source from which the poetry sprang. This religion made no pretense of remaining an "interior religion." It engendered an uncontrollable need to speak of God and to God; for it is He, His grandeur and His mysteries that were sung, more often than man and his lowliness. Above all, the poets loved to exalt the royalty of Jesus Christ. A special type of trope called the *Regnum* commented, in a sort of royal litany of the Incarnate Word, on the words of the *Gloria: Quoniam tu solus altissimus, Iesu Christe.* This was at first done briefly in the form of a decade of profound and sonorous acclamations; then, on this theme which they knew was inexhaustible, they would yield to the universal tendency to protract, which often resulted in a real "debauchery of interior vocalisation." This trope almost always began with the words from which it took its name: *Regnum tuum solidum* . . . , and after the identical beginning, the theme was played upon with an endless number of variations. This trope, remarks Léon Gauthier "fills up our Troparies . . . There are as many as seventeen in a single Tropary." It can be said to have set the tone of monastic religion nurtured as it was on the religion of the Apostles and the Fathers.

In the interests of this biblical and patristic inspiration they marshalled all the resources of their literary culture. This culture had shaped and set free talents which could henceforth realize their full potential and fulfill their highest ambitions. Worship, since the time of St. Benedict, had been the culmination of their culture. Literary experience was necessary to understand and sing the Psalms and to take part in the reading of the offices. In the Carolingian era, culture had been still more explicitly oriented to divine worship; the revival of studies was intended to teach the monks and the clerics the right way to live, and at the same time how to speak well and write well in order to pray well: "For many desired to pray to God properly but prayed to Him poorly because of books full of mistakes." Consequently, in teaching grammar, they were very careful not to forget the liturgical texts: Abbo of Fleury, in his *Grammatical Questions,* takes examples from the *Te Deum* and the "Ambrosian hymns;" he explains at length an article of the Athanasian Creed, exactness in expression being important for doctrinal precision. And Conrad of Hirsau praised secular literature which through the beauty of its words and phrases, can become an ornament for the divine cult. "When you offer God your person and your possessions, everything that remains in you from your education is lawful if you order it, as you should, to the divine service." The composition of a new

office—like those of St. Philibert and St. Aycardus at Jumièges—
was a work of art with which they took great pains. The task
required the writing of a kind of long poem each division of
which had to be made to conform with the laws governing
meter. They preferred the expression not to be unworthy of the
beauty and truth of the mystery they were singing or the
examples they were extolling.

Thus, Peter the Venerable entirely recomposed a hymn to
St. Benedict because the one they had been singing at Cluny
seemed to him to run counter to metrical laws, and was, besides,
full of empty phrases: "You know how distasteful it is to me
to sing things in church which do not ring true, and how odious
I find melodious nonsense," the *canorae nugae* of which Horace
spoke. Talent, however, was not always able to live up to such
expectations, yet they always made every effort to use in the
divine cult everything they knew about literature.

Sacred Music

In any other type of literary production whatever, the
style itself was sufficient. But in composing for the liturgy, a
new and different element intervened: music. Actually almost
everything in the divine office was chanted; the text was obliged
to conform to the laws of a special rhythm which is not like
that of ordinary or even of artistic prose nor yet that of recited
poetry. Not that the divine office was a concert: it was not an
aesthetic activity. And many a monk would have subscribed to
the opinion of the anonymous author of the *Speculum virginum:*
it is better to sing in a hoarse voice than to be bored in choir.
But if the composer knew beforehand that his text was to be
chanted, and in what manner and at what moment in the liturgy, it was his duty to cast it in a literary form which made this
possible. Thus the Venerable Bede in his treatise on meter,
proposes a special rule for hymns to be sung by two alternating
choirs. Music theorists were then called upon to supplement
the work of the metrical experts. St. Odo of Cluny is only one
of the monks who had to study both literature and chant.

The monks did even this in their own way. For example,
neither arithmetic nor astronomy was studied for its own sake.
Through the *Computus*, those disciplines which served to

determine the dates of coming feasts became auxiliary sciences for the liturgy. In the same fashion the monks took an interest in "speculative music" insofar as it was necessary for the particular ends of monastic life. Guido of Arezzo, the greatest among them, said quite definitely, in proposing his new notation, that his intention was to do so "as a monk for monks": *me monachum monachis praestare.* And in order to give him a title, one of the plays on words the Middle Ages liked so well was used uniting his two functions as if they were indivisible: *musicus et monachus.* Many others were, like him, monk-musicians, and they were musicians because they were monks. Among their writings on music, there are good reasons for studying not only their theories on the modes and tones but what they have to say about their ideas on the liturgy and of monastic life. We can discern in the general intent of their study—and sometimes even in the prologues to their treatises—their awareness of the majesty of God. Their purpose is to help their brethren by means of ordered, unanimous song to join in the praise which the universe and the angels render to God, to sing in anticipation on earth the song they will continue in Heaven, and the means they worked out to attain this eschatological end are an outgrowth of Christian grammar. The task called for illustrating in melodies the words of God as transmitted by the traditional liturgy and the Bible even when the language these use is not that of the secular authors. Accents had to be found in which to express redeemed man's consent to the mysteries he is celebrating and whose benefits he receives. The few capitals from Cluny that have been preserved show, not the chimeras which St. Bernard deprecated, but the Christological symbols for the different tones of the chant. The third tone, for example, like compunction, moves the soul deeply and causes it, as it were, to experience Christ's Resurrection. It is hard to conceive vocal prayer more efficaciously transformed into mental prayer, in conformity with St. Benedict's desire.

The Cistercians had the same end in view as the earlier tradition, and used similar methods in prefacing their reformed antiphonary with a long explanatory introduction. In it, ideas on musical techniques were adapted to spiritual considerations. One of these concepts is explained by the theme of the "region of dissimilarity," so dear to St. Bernard: in this context, the *regio dissimilitudinis* is the confusion of poorly organized chant. The remedy is found in Scripture: the authority of the Psalter restores dignity to each note by suggesting the use of the ten-note scale. This biblical norm, unknown to pure musical science in combination with the laws established by Guido of Arezzo, was to make it possible for the Cistercians as well as all the other monk-musicians to achieve their ends: to add to the holy words of the Gospel the color and beauty of song.

The latter had extremely complex repercussions in the field of versification that have been analyzed in great detail by philologists. It will be sufficient, at this point, to state that from that time on, poetic compositions conformed to one or the other of two different techniques. One was in the classical poetic tradition based on the quantity of the syllables, long or short. This method of versification continued in use, as, in the twelfth century at the abbey of Tegernsee, Metellus was to compose poems in the Horatian meters in honor of St. Quirinus. We know even the copy of Horace which provided his inspiration for these *Odae Quirinales.* But most of the liturgical compositions were in a different style—that of syllabic poetry whose rhythm is determined by the stress of the accents. Each of these two techniques evolved, influenced in part by the pronunciation proper to the varying regions. No particular one grew into a set of laws fixed for all time and beyond the possibility of variation. Authors were not condemned to the pastiche, to the artificial imitation of verses which had themselves already been written in accordance with the dictates of an outdated phonetics. Each poet, provided he deserved the name, retained a certain liberty in regard to the disposition of his verbal material; medieval meter remained a living art form and an art practiced by the living.

This it is, no doubt, which accounts for the number and variety of liturgical poems. In this respect we can offer no more telling example than the "poetic school" of Nonantola of the eleventh and twelfth centuries. There, toward the middle of the eleventh century, we can follow a growing preference for the Leonine hexameter. This technique came to be widely used, but, at the same time, rhythmical pieces of various other structures were also being composed. And not one of these genres was limited in practice to a small number of formulas. They were, on the contrary, multiplied; there are twenty-three *benedictiones De sancta Maria* and as many as fifty-five *benedictiones* for Pentecost. A like profusion is seen in many other cases whether they concern *benedictiones* or other parts of the office. The present-day Roman liturgy has kept only fifteen or so of these *benedictiones,* but each of them is a little masterpiece. Their very existence presupposes an unlimited inspiration. Innumerable texts bear out this supposition although among them there are some texts which are less felicitous. But all testify to the fact that the milieus which produced them were animated by an intense vitality.

To these texts which were used in the conventual celebration of the liturgy may be added all those which fostered private devotion. These are not always easy to distinguish from the former since they often take the form of offices or liturgical prayers. And many of them eventually found a place in public worship, such as the *Rythmus de nomine Jesu* which so richly deserved it. Gilson remarked that one would have to have "a manuscript in place of a heart" not to recognize in this admirable poem a masterpiece inspired by St. Bernard's sermons. Its vast dissemination proves that it corresponded to the aspirations of many fervent souls who continued to copy it, to sing it and to transform it. For, in medieval times, texts like these are living texts. They are not confined within the perfection of an established critical edition *ne varietur.* Dom Wilmart has shown how the *Adoro te* had experienced similar vicissitudes. St. Bernard's ardent prose would undoubtedly inspire some talented unknown to write verses which in turn belong to anyone since they belong to all. Many other Pseudo-Bernards furnish proof that the great movement of piety given impetus by the Abbot of Clairvaux tended spontaneously to find expression in verse as if to complete and set off the great poem of the liturgy.

The Mystery of the Cult

The non-liturgical texts of the monks were not written for purposes of formal worship. But they would not be what they are if their authors had not lived in the light of the cult. Consequently we must now point out what monastic literature as a whole owes to the liturgy.

It is, to begin with, the general atmosphere this literature breathed, the atmosphere of Christian optimism, of faith in the Redemption which makes Christ's victory a constant and personal cause for hope. If each author, each reader, in a word, each monk, believes he can attain to a certain experience of God, it is because he knows that this union between himself and the Lord is realized primarily in the mystery of the cult. It only remains to secure for this effective sharing in salvation certain further psychological effects in the areas of reflection, of the attachment of the heart to God, the *affectus*. Thus one of the Christian realities the monks speak of most readily, even apart from the works consecrated to it, is the world of the sacraments. In them is accomplished the most positive contact of man with God since it is the basis for all other encounters. Attention has been drawn to the great degree of preoccupation with Baptism demonstrated by the Carolingian authors. They also wrote a great deal on the Eucharist, and the latter remained the focal point of interest in monastic circles. We know the importance given it in the work of John of Fécamp. In the twelfth century, Peter of Celle, Peter the Venerable, St. Bernard, Senatus of Worcester, and many others allude to it frequently. Arnaud of Bonneval, William of Saint Thierry, and Baldwin of Ford, wrote treatises on the Sacrament of the Altar. However, they never regard these as opportunities for debating abstract problems. They speak of the Sacrament as a living reality which the Church in its liturgy daily proposes for their adoration, in the words of the Bible.

In the same way, the monastic authors' emphasis on frequent confession followed by absolution comes from an absolute faith in the sacrament which anticipates God's judgment. In the numerous texts where Cistercian and other authors recommend confession and define the requisite conditions for its being followed by pardon, they usually do not mention the simple manifestation of conscience that the religious make to their spiritual father in accordance with a tradition which goes back to ancient monasticism. The confession they are discussing is that sure means given by God to man on earth for doing penance in the fullest sense of the term by admitting he is a sinner and professing his faith in the power given by Christ to the Church to pardon, to purify the conscience, and to prepare it to appear without spot at the Last Judgment. All these attitudes can be understood only in the light of a living conception of the Church. Many authors like Rupert of Deutz have dispersed through their writings the elements of a very rich ecclesiology. But all of them live and write with the same conviction that the meeting between the monk and God, the intimate union which all literature has the mission to prepare, is accomplished in the bosom of the Church. The Spouse who will be revealed in all her glory, the Jerusalem which is the goal of monastic effort is already given by faith to men on this earth; it is only in union with the Church that each of us receives the kiss of the Bridegroom. Devotion to the Church, which is only another aspect of devotion to Heaven, a form of the desire for God, is already a participation in the mystery of God which is celebrated in the liturgy and communicated by the sacraments. Ecclesiology and eschatology unite, consequently, as the two dominating themes of a literature born in the atmosphere of the cult.

Liturgy and Culture

Liturgy has marked with its imprint the whole of monastic culture, first and foremost the language of its writers who abound in reminiscences of liturgical expressions. This conclusion has already been noted with regard to John of Fécamp but it would be no less convincing were it advanced in connection with St. Bernard. The rhythm of the monks' life is also marked by the liturgy and its feasts. A number of their writings have contributed to the introduction of new feasts and the addition of splendor to others recently established; we have only to think of the office of the Transfiguration and the treatise on it, both of which were composed by Peter the Venerable when he instituted this brilliant solemnity at Cluny. Or we may recall the treatise written by William of Saint Jacques on the Trinity as a brief directed against some theologians of his time, and, in reaction to whose rationalistic tendencies, he asked that a feast be inaugurated to proclaim very resoundingly the Church's belief in the Trinity. The whole monastic economy was organized around a life in which leisure for praising God absorbed a great amount of time. Their art, in sum, was the reflection of the whole monastic existence and the habitual thoughts of the monks. Just as the cathedrals of the thirteenth century have been compared to theological summas, monastic writings of the Romanesque period may be likened to the abbey churches of the period: the same simplicity, the same solidity, the same vivacity of biblical imagination. It is known that Rupert of Deutz' treatises influenced Rhenish enamel work and, through the intermediary of St. Denis, the art of many other regions; the Cathedral of Cologne may even, possibly, have been designed after a plan found in Rupert's writings.

No one has better described the bond which unites monastic liturgy and spirituality than Suger in his treatise *On the Consecration of the Church of St. Denis,* where the account of its construction and dedication is inserted in a vast exhortation to peace, the whole of which is climaxed by an allusion to the Most Holy Eucharist: in this mystery, Christ reconciles men here below with each other, with the Angels and with God, and unites in one kingdom this redeemed world which He will offer His Father when He returns. And in the report *On his Abbatial Administration,* Suger defends his having done so much to beautify his basilica. The testimony he gave in his own behalf could be applied to all who represent monastic culture. What Suger did in the field of architecture and the decorative arts, others did in the realm of literature; all tried to use the resources of culture in the service of prayer and Divine praise.

As for me, concludes Suger, I confess that I took great pleasure in devoting all the costliest and most precious things I could find to the service of the administration of the Most Holy Eucharist. If, to fulfill an order from God manifested through the mouth of the Prophets, golden chalices, vases and cups were used to receive the blood of goats, calves and the red cow of the expiation, how much greater is our obligation to use, in order to receive the blood of Jesus Christ, in perpetual service and with the utmost devotion, vases of gold, gems and everything that is considered most precious. Surely neither we nor our worldly goods can suffice to serve such great mysteries. Even if, in a new creation, our substance were changed into that of Seraphim and Cherubim, it would still be unworthy to serve the ineffable Host. We can however offer propitiation for our sins. Some, no doubt, would, in contradiction, tell us that all that is necessary is to bring to the cult a pure heart, a holy soul and true intentions; we also think that these conditions are a prime necessity and have a very special importance. But we likewise affirm that the ornamentation of the sacred vessels used for the Holy Sacrifice should possess an outer magnificence which, so far as is possible, equals our inner purity. We must serve in every way and with the utmost circumspection our Redeemer, Him from whom we receive everything without exception and who has united His nature with ours in a Person who, placing us at His right hand, has promised us that we should truly possess His kingdom, Our Lord who lives and reigns world without end.

Liturgy and the Desire for God

The liturgy is at once the mirror of a culture and its culmination. Just as the office of Corpus Christi, in the composition of which St. Thomas surely participated, crowns his doctrinal work, so the hymns, sequences and innumerable poems written by the monks are the culmination of their theology. The liturgy had been the motive for the renewal of monastic culture in the Carolingian period, and was also its fruit. During the following centuries, it is in the atmosphere of the liturgy and amid the poems composed for it, *in hymnis et canticis,* that the synthesis of all the *artes* was effected, of the literary techniques, religious reflection and all sources of information whether biblical, patristic or classical. In the liturgy, all these resources fully attained their final potentiality; they were restored to God in a homage which recognized that they had come from Him. Thanksgiving, eucharist, theology, *confessio fidei,* all these expressions, in monastic tradition, expressed the only slightly differing aspects of a single reality. In the liturgy, grammar was elevated to the rank of an eschatological fact. It participated in the eternal praise that the monks, in unison with the Angels, began offering God in the abbey choir and which will be perpetuated in Heaven. In the liturgy, love of learning and desire of God find perfect reconciliation.

Bernard Häring
1912-

Bernard Häring was born in Böttingen, Germany. During World War II he spent four years in Russia, first as a member of the German Medical Corps, then as a prisoner of war. Afterwards he received his doctorate in theology from the University of Tübingen and began to teach at the Redemptorist seminary in Gars-am-Inn in 1947. His three-volume work, The Law of Christ, *which appeared in 1954, catapulted him into the front ranks of those who were working toward a renewed moral theology in the Church. He was appointed to the faculty of the Lateran University in Rome in 1955, and was thus in a position to exercise a positive influence both in the time of preparations as well as during Vatican II itself.*

Häring became something of a "cult-hero" in the immediate postconciliar period. Dissatisfaction with the legalism that sometimes plagued earlier exponents of Catholic moral theology led many to breathe a sigh of relief at the appearance of a richer type of thinking. Demand for instruction in the basic concepts of this renewal, especially in the United States, resulted in Häring's visits to this land, lecturing, teaching special institutes, and giving summer courses, so that he was soon one of the best known of the Vatican II periti.

Perhaps the most important aspect of the renewed moral theology was its recovery of the biblical and liturgical dimen-

sions of Christian conduct. As it had developed since the time of Trent, too much of Catholic moral teaching seemed to be but a slightly revised version of Aristotelian ethics. The values undoubtedly present in this heritage were insufficiently rooted in any specifically Christian motivation. Thus this area was a prime target for the "back-to-the-sources" movement in 20th century Catholic theology.

The selection that follows is taken from a book which appeared in 1962, a few months before Vatican II began. In the preface Häring describes its contents as "meditations" expressing the basic ideas that he had been presenting in numerous retreats. "The book's purpose," he explains, "is to encourage the growth of the spiritual life, to help to make liturgical devotion more alive and more profound, to draw meditation and public worship closer together, and to show the organic unity between the realities of faith in the sacraments and the way of life these demand from those upon whom they have been conferred."

The work thus illustrates one important development to which the author was a major contributor: the trend toward integration of liturgy and spirituality by richer use of the Scriptures. It also documents very clearly the oft-repeated observation that Vatican II did not materialize from a vacuum; it brought together and gave institutional sanction to some of the best work that the Catholic pioneers of renewal had been elaborating for some time.

The book is organized into three parts: 1) The Sacramental Basis of Christian Existence, set forth in three chapters, the first two of which are substantially reproduced here; 2) The Saving Mysteries of the Word Incarnate in Each Sacrament, divided into fifteen chapters dealing with all seven sacraments; and 3) The Law of Christ in the Harmony of the Seven Sacraments, treated in two chapters. The final chapter is really a synthesis and summary of Häring's whole approach, so that is also given here to show how he envisions the unity of Christian worship and morality.

A SACRAMENTAL
SPIRITUALITY

PART I

CHAPTER I

THE GOOD NEWS OF THE COMMAND BROUGHT BY GRACE

These words which Mark records as the first words of Jesus' preaching, and which according to the express statement of Matthew (4. 17) formed the introduction to his whole message, show the pattern and the inmost meaning of Jesus' preaching, which is now addressed to us. It is up to us to make those profoundly significant words from the mouth of God the pattern for our lives, too.

They tell us that our life is more than the mere following of the ten commandments of God, as it is often so bleakly described; they tell us that our life is based on the good news of the Gospel, that we live in the age when salvation has been achieved. The standard and the law of our life is now the grace of God given in abundance. Those words also tell us that everything is ruled and governed by the kingdom of God and by his love, and that even the call to repentance is not in the first place a threat, but the joyful news of the fulfilment of salvation at the end of time, of the kingdom of the love of God.

THE GOOD NEWS AND THE SACRAMENTS

The early Church expressed the new and startling experience of the preaching of Jesus with the word *euangèlion,* "joyful news." But this news brings joy not only because of what it has to tell: the main source of joy is the messenger himself, who provides the essential meaning of his message.

"*Jesus* proclaimed the good news." He is not any messenger, he is not one of the great prophets, he is Emmanual, God-with-us, himself. He who brings the news is the meaning and the source of all joy and all happiness. In his words, "blessed are you", which he cries out to the poor, the humble, the oppressed and the despised, we hear the rejoicing of heaven, an echo of the happiness in the heart of God the Three-in-One.

The message does not consist simply of words about great matters; they are the words of the Word himself, in whom the Father expresses from all eternity his fullness, his might and his wisdom. He who speaks to us with power and authority "is not any word, but the word which breathes love"—*verbum non qualecumque, sed verbum spirans amorem* (Thomas Aquinas). Everything that is created came into being in him, the Word of the Father. Wherever this Word is not active in creation, there is simply nothing—and now, in the fullness of time, he is the personal Word of the Father *to us*, the Word who comes to bring us knowledge of the unfathomable and infinite love of the Father, and who, now his earthly task is completed, desires to send us from the Father the Spirit of love. We are chosen and loved by the Father in him and for him.

The words spoken by the Word signify an event, an act that brings salvation, happiness or judgment. When the Word of the Father speaks directly to mankind, the creation is shot through with light, everything is restored to its first glory, and mankind is given a new life. When the incarnate Word of the Father speaks in men's words and brings knowledge of the holiness and love of the Father, the power of God is contained in the humility of his Word. It is no hollow-sounding, empty or powerless word: it creates and renews the face of the earth; it makes the true image of God shine out again in the face of men. Though human words pass away, this Word remains eternally, and so do all words which he speaks.

The first thing that Christ tells us cannot be a commandment, a stern demand or obligation laid upon man. For if that were the case man, through his wretchedness, would still be in the position of one who is trying to set himself up as the centre of his existence. He would be unable to escape from the slavery of his loneliness and his egoism. Man's life does not come from himself; so the most important thing for him is not what he should do with his life: the first thing is the word by which he lives. When the Word of God in person comes to us and encounters our life, we no longer live in the first instance under a commandment which oppresses and threatens us as though from outside. The first thing which the incarnate Word of the Father has to tell us is the good news of the love which makes everything new, of the love which calls us to himself. So Jesus does not come to men first with a demand, but with a message of salvation, with the message of the redeeming kingdom of God. It is this that we must hear and take to our hearts; then we will understand the new voice with which the will of God speaks to us.

Centuries of clarity and confusion lie between the preaching of Jesus and ourselves. But thanks to the inspired writers who have given us a true record of his words, and to the Church which has guarded them faithfully and handed them down to us, we too possess them. To the end of time the Church will proclaim to us the message that Jesus gave in Galilee and Judea. But if we so desire, this message can be more to us than a piece of good news from the distant past. For it is *the word of the Lord to us here and now*. The Church is not only the mouthpiece of Christ. She is the sacrament of his love and of his word. She proclaims his word in his Spirit, whom he himself has given to her. He himself is with her to the end of time.

The proclamation by the Church of the message of salvation reaches its climax in the celebration of the sacraments. In the sacraments, Christ himself speaks his joyful and redeeming word to the Christian community, and with direct personal presence and effect to each individual—*virtue praesens,* in the words of the encyclical *Mediator Dei.* We do not look on the sacraments as something apart from Christ, as simply "holy things"; we look on them above all as powerful "words of the Word"—*verba Verbi.* Because they are the words of the Lord which effectively give something to us, they are no less than the act of salvation made present to us in a dialogue with him who alone possesses "the words of eternal life" (John 6. 68). Everything that the sacraments tell us of the saving acts of Christ, of his love to us, and of our friendly relationship with him, they bring about with a powerful effect, so long as we receive this word with a faithful and willing heart.

The Word that comes to us reveals itself only when we receive it with love and with a readiness to respond. The second person of the Trinity, the eternal Word of the Father, expresses himself in the love in which he gives himself wholly back to the

189

Father. The words of life, which the Lord speaks to us in the sacraments, are the image of his life; we ourselves bear his image in us. That is why our life can bear no fruit unless we respond with love to the words of the Word. The sacraments give us life, joy and love in Christ, and for that reason alone they demand from us the answer of love in return: "What shall I render to the Lord for all his bounty to me?" (Ps. 115. 12). Christ truly speaks to us in the sacraments and our whole life is claimed by the joyful message they contain. He speaks to us and everything is claimed by an inward yet powerful love. So ethical standards find their proper place in a dialogue, which begins with and is always based upon the good news of the Gospel.

It is of immense value deliberately to look at Christian life and the imitation of Christ from the point of view of the gift of God. This prevents us from separating the good news of the Gospel from him who himself is the Word of the Father to us in person; we do not set up the sacraments as some sort of "thing" apart from the Word of God; we do not separate the ethical commandment from the good news. Instead, we see in Christ himself, in his works of grace and in the good news of his Gospel, our salvation and the law of our life.

THE TIME OF THE FULLNESS OF SALVATION

The coming of Christ means "the fullness of time", the time of salvation long awaited but now achieved, which presses us to a decision; the last hour (cf. I Cor. 7. 29; I John 2. 18). The history of mankind is struggling towards its climax, which will be completely fulfilled when Christ the Lord returns with power and glory and delivers everything to the Father, "That God may be all in all" (I Cor. 15. 28).

This final age is the time of abundant grace. However perfect a form may have been given to the law, it no longer operates on the principle of the old law of the letter as a protective barrier of limits and obligations. Now everything must be based on the fullness of Christ's grace, not least the new law.

It has been given to us to live in the time in which the loving purpose that God is resolved to carry out in his creation has been powerfully revealed. It has been shown to all the faithful in the sacrifice of the Son and in the splendour of the resurrection. The sending of the Holy Spirit has made it an inward and joyful reality for us, urging us to make a choice. In him the Father and the Son have given us the personal pledge of the decision they have made for the love of us men.

Each grace—the gift of the love of God which he has resolved to pour out on us—brings us face to face with the mystery of the *eschatological division*, which the old man Simeon prophesied when the Messiah came into the temple: "He is set for the fall and rising of many in Israel" (Luke 2.34). Our decision, and the division God makes between men, is not based on a merely preventive legal system, but is made in the sight of the abundant grace of God, assured and made effective for us in the sacraments.

The last age is the interval between the first and the second coming of Christ; this means that it is the joyful age of grace and at the same time a period of longing for the full revelation of the glory of Christ and the Father. We can also put it this way: the interval between the event at Pentecost and the second coming of Christ is *the age of the sacraments*. They are the signs that the end of time is at hand, but they are given in the interval before the final consummation, so that they reveal both the providence of God at the present time and the division and choice he is already carrying out. In the sacraments Christ comes to us in reality—even though he is hidden—and gives us his Spirit, the pledge of the triumphal conclusion of his work in freedom and glory. The Spirit of Christ is the power in us which through his gifts urges us to make a decisive act of love in answer to the love of God, and so judges us.

The sacraments are not to be thought of principally as a means of salvation, and far less as external aids to help us carry out a law which has already been given. They are themselves an effective and joyous proclamation of the decisive law for Christians, the "law of grace", and they bring all God's commandments into their proper place within this law. The sacraments are signs that "the fullness of time has come"; they are signs of the fullness of grace in this final phase of time. Since Christ himself is present and active in them (*virtute praesens*) they bring us face to face with him, with the promise and claim he makes in the abundance of his grace, with the decisive act of his self-sacrificing love on the cross, and with the glory of his resurrection. The risen Christ, who in the sacraments encounters us truly and effectively, calls us in this way to the joyful and definite expectation of his return: what is to be manifested at the end in the sight of the whole world, "comes to fulfilment" in us now in its fundamental reality through the sacraments. So they are signs which arouse hope in us, signs of the fidelity of God. They arouse in us a longing for the fulfilment of all that is promised to us in them. But they also incline us to order our lives according to the grace we have already received and according to the promise of still greater things to come.

A sacramental man is a man whose heart is set on the next world. That is why he is always awake to the needs of the present time; his heart is set on the world to come not just because he longs for it but because he experiences here and now the effective work of the grace of God. Sacramental piety makes us acutely aware of the needs of the moment. The sacraments are signs of the age of grace and so of the time of decision. We see the great trials of life in the light of the sacraments, and they make us ready to meet them: "At the acceptable time I have listened to you, and helped you on the day of salvation. Behold, now is the acceptable time, now is the day of salvation" (2 Cor. 6.2).

The sacraments assure us that the saving acts of Christ, and even the powers of redemption and judgment that will be his at his return, are at work in every moment of decision in our lives (cf. Heb. 6.5). Everything depends on our being faithful and ready to receive his grace and to make it the law of our lives. Then this brings us "no longer under the law, but under grace" (Rom. 6.14).

THE MESSAGE OF THE KINGDOM OF THE LOVE OF GOD

The basic theme of the Gospel's message of joy, that which brings the fullness of time into being, is the fact that the rule and kingdom of God are approaching. The Word of the Father has become man, not to destroy the world in judgment, but to redeem it (cf. John 12. 47). He brings the world the redeeming kingdom of the love of God. When God speaks all his love in his consubstantial Word, and we receive in faith this

192

powerful message of love, then he sets up his kingdom in our hearts and in our whole lives, and it is a kingdom of love and grace. He wants to rule in us and over us, not by instilling fear of punishment, but through love, through his grace, so that he can let us share in his kingdom.

So the first thing that is demanded of us by the coming of the kingdom of God is that we let God rule within us, in such a way that we make his gift, his grace, the basic rule of our life. The first result of this will be that by the love of God drawing us together we shall all become one, a people of his love. By the power of his grace and through our unity in his love we will then become, for all men and for the whole creation, living tools of the redeeming kingdom of God.

The good news of the kingdom of God and the rule of his love is announced to us here and now, everytime we take part in the sacraments. In his historical ministry Jesus demonstrated the victory of the kingdom of God's love over all the powers of evil. Through the saving acts of his death, his resurrection and ascension he has given an effective demonstration of how total self-giving to the kingdom of the Father's love brings life and victory, for him and for redeemed mankind. These saving actions are brought to us in the sacraments; they enfold us and change us, and make us the people of God, the children and missionaries of his kingdom.

When the grace of the Lord speaks to us personally in the sacraments this always means that his kingdom is claiming us. The sacraments are the mighty acts of God, the joyful news of the almighty Word of the Father in the love and power of the Holy Spirit. So they are bound to be words which take full possession of our beings and make us members of the people of God, gratefully receiving what he gives, but at the same time busy and active in his service. The sacramental words are the saving acts of Christ, at whose feet God has laid all things, and who in his turn orders everything in accordance with his final purpose; to subject all things to the Father, just as he himself has submitted himself completely to the Father's will. Sacramental piety is based first of all on the "kingdom of God".

The kingdom of God means that God's grace comes before the action of men, and that his grace is the final and decisive standard for everything that redeemed man has to do. The primary meaning of the biblical term "the kingdom of God" is not the Church or the people of God. The significant thing about the coming of the kingdom of God in Christ Jesus is that the mystery of the triune love of God is present in the midst of human history: God is establishing the rule of his love. His people are those who open their hearts to his love and let it mould and guide them.

God asks for our loving acknowledgment and thankful adoration of his holiness and of his dominion, when in his grace he makes the free choice to give men a share in the mystery of his life and of his love. God only receives into the majesty of his glory those who renounce all glory in themselves.

The kingdom of God only accepts those who are astonished that God should stoop down to a creature and a sinner. The children of the kingdom know of their nothingness, their weakness, and of how little they can deserve the grace of God: like children they look to their father to give them everything. So the kingdom of God is revealed to the "poor in spirit" (Matt. 5. 3), who bow themselves down before God like beggars. The man who looks for nothing for himself, and consequently sets aside no part of life to be at his own disposal, who hopes entirely in God, yet sets no limits on what God may be pleased to give him—he is the nearest to the kingdom of God.

This is the unceasing message of the sacraments. The doctrine of the primacy of the *opus operatum,* of the work of God to save us, coming before the actions of men; this doctrine, so basic to the nature of Catholic sacramental piety, is in the last analysis no less than the gospel of the rule and the kingdom of God. It is a doctrine which, far from encouraging quietism, demands that we hand ourselves over completely to God's grace. And that, in turn, means a life that is full and active to the utmost degree.

When God gives us such a wonderful gift and renews us inwardly, he also asks that our way of life should be new as well. He asks us for total submission so that he can give himself completely to us. Jesus shows us how each step follows the last; "Repent! Turn round and come home!"

194

Bernard Häring

Jesus' appeal to us to return home is the good news of the kingdom of God. Because repentance is a gift of the kingdom of God which comes to us by his grace, the Lord's call to repentance is the joyful news of the Gospel. Once again it is of decisive importance that we undergo the change with faith and look at our repentance as essentially the result of the word and action of God. Then our exertions and the penance we have to carry out in the end do not cause us to lose sight of the essential fact that it is God who turns to the sinner when he calls him to come home. Everything that man has to do in his turn takes its joyful character and its pressing obligation from the action of God.

The Vulgate translates the Greek word *metanoeîte* in St. Mark's gospel with *poenitemini,* in Matthew 4. 17 with *poenitentiam agite*—"do penance!", but so long as we do not forget the context it is impossible to overlook the joyful character of Jesus' preaching of repentance. In fact the very word itself, let alone its context, is a message of good news, a cry of joy. But the demand made upon men is not the main thing. The first emphasis is not on "worthy fruits of repentance" (cf. Matt. 3. 8; Acts 26. 20). Of course these must be present if the root of the tree is good. A wholehearted and sincere repentance must ultimately be shown in "deeds worthy of repentance". But repentance itself is a directly experienced religious event of immeasurable profundity. The Greek word *metanoeîte* signifies a complete change of heart and mind. This one word recalls the many marvellous promises of God in the Old Testament, that he himself will create a new heart in us. "I will set my eyes upon them for good and I will bring them back to this land. I will build them up and not tear them down; I will plant them and not uproot them. I will give them a heart to know that I am the Lord; and they shall be my people and I will be their God, for they shall return to me with their whole heart" (Jer. 24. 6-7). Fundamentally it is the good news of the action of God to renew us, which speaks to us from outside ourselves, or rather calls to us from within to "be transformed by the renewal of our mind" (From. 12. 2).

There are good reasons for believing that in Aramaic the call to repentance sounded yet another note. Our Lord probably used the word *shub*, "return home". Once again we have a word which echoes the promises of the Old Testament: "I will set my eyes upon them for good and I will bring them back to this land" (Jer. 24. 6). "Then they shall know that I am the Lord their God, because I sent them into exile among the nations and then gathered them into their own land. And I will not hide my face any more from them, when I pour out my Spirit upon the house of Israel, says the Lord God" (Ez. 39. 28 f.). So Jesus' good news follows and forms part of the joyful invitation to celebrate the return from exile. Jesus' preaching of redemption is in its essence the preaching not of a threat, but of consolation, the climax of the joyful proclamation of the kingdom of the love of God.

What Mark records as Jesus' first sermon is developed in everything that Jesus said and did until his final return to the Father. Perhaps the most beautiful explanation of the cry "repent" is found in the story of the great banquet in the parable of the Prodigal Son. The "good-for-nothing" son comes home, and even before he has been able to carry out any positive action at all, his father prepares a great banquet, a deeply affectionate and honourable welcome. The story does not say that the returned prodigal had to show himself worthy of this joyful celebration by his later attitude and behaviour; one might say that this is taken for granted. The most likely person to show "worthy fruits of his return home" is one who has experienced the honour given to a returning prodigal, the happiness in his father's house, the joy and the celebration. Once we have understood this we have before us a pattern for our spiritual life and for our moral striving. It is a pattern for every kind of pastoral care, for priests, for parents, and for lay apostles of every sort.

In the sacraments and through the message of salvation which the sacraments bring us, the joyful news of repentance that Jesus preached is made available to us as an action which brings us salvation here and now; it becomes an invitation: "repent". Through the sacraments we are in effective and direct contact with the good news preached by Christ. Just as he spoke personally to Peter and Andrew, and James and John, so in the sacraments he himself comes to us with his word and in his power and gives us this invitation: "Come, follow me!"

Repentance does not take place without a sacrament or—to express the innermost meaning of the word—without what is given to us in the sacraments. This lays all the emphasis on the fact that when a man repents it is above all the work and the gracious gift of God. Repentance in the religious sense is the joyful event of salvation itself; for when it takes place through the "sacrament of penance" the saving acts of Christ, his death and his resurrection, are brought to us; we receive them and they become reality for us in such manner that the Apostle can say that we have been "incorporated" into the death and resurrection of Christ (Rom. 6. 5). The powerful saving acts of Christ, which in the "sacrament of faith" we experience and receive as a joyful message that sets us free, are the first cause of our repentance. From them comes the power, the invitation, and with it the sacred and binding obligation to make a complete change in our lives and to return to our true home.

Baptism—in the words of the Church Father and apologist Justin "the bath of repentance"—is the sacrament of the "first repentance"; the sacrament of penance is "a second plank to cling to in shipwreck" for those Christians who sin gravely after baptism; it is the sacrament of the "first repentance repeated". All sacraments which build on the foundations of baptism are in themselves "sacraments of the second repentance", that is, of the constant striving for purification and progress in grace, without which the testimony of the words spoken in baptism to the new life which is given us there would never be describing the whole truth. Since God is at work in the sacrament, repentance is a birthright from God. "He saved us, not because of deeds done by us in righteousness but in virtue of his own mercy, by the washing of regeneration and renewal in the Holy Spirit, which he poured out upon us richly through Jesus Christ our Saviour" (Titus 3. 5 f.; cf. I Peter I 3). The gift of God's grace brings with it a commandment: "That we too should walk in newness of life" (Rom. 6. 4), "that we serve in the new life of the Spirit, and no longer under the old written code" (cf. Rom. 7. 6). "Unless one is born of water and the Spirit he cannot enter the kingdom of God" (John 3. 5). Our first repentance, its continuance and its final culmination, and our entry into the kingdom of heaven, are the work of the Holy Spirit, while from the human side they represent a humble and thankful acceptance and affirmation of the redeeming rule of God, and a faithful readiness to be moved and acted on by the grace of the Holy Spirit.

The foundation of repentance, the pattern it follows, and the command it brings with it lie in the "new creation" and "reconciliation" by God in Jesus Christ. "If any one is in Christ he is a new creation; the old has passed away, behold, the new has come. All this is from God, who through Christ reconciled us to himself. . . . We are ambassadors for Christ, God making his appeal through us. We beseech you on behalf of Christ, be reconciled to God" (2 Cor. 5. 17 ff.). Since all this is an undeserved gift of the grace of God, won by the death of Christ, the command brought us by repentance is seen to be based on the new life lived in conformity with Christ: "And he died for all, that those who live might live no longer for themselves but for him who for their sake died and was raised" (2 Cor. 5. 15).

Repentance means that we are rescued from the kingdom of darkness and given a place in the kingdom of the light of Christ (I Peter 2. 9). Christ himself is the light of all who come to him, the light of all who repent and turn to him (cf. Luke 2. 32; John 8. 12). Repentance is a mystical but completely real passage from the death of sin to the life which comes from the death and resurrection of Christ. Thus the deepest meaning of repentance is a mystical dying with Christ and rising with him in his resurrection (Rom. 6).

All these biblical expressions make one fact perfectly clear to us: repentance is the joyful gospel of the *magnalia Dei,* the mighty acts of the love of God towards us, being carried out at the present moment. In Christ Jesus God does great things to us. This gives our response, sustained by God's grace, its true value. The theological doctrine of the primacy of the *opus operatum* of the sacraments teaches us the same. This central doctrine has nothing to do with magic, with impersonal forces of destiny or with an unresponsive acceptance of God's work by men. *Opus operatum Dei* means the powerfully resounding and joyful gospel of the kingdom of God, of the great banquet that celebrates our return home, of the renewal of our hearts, and of the primacy of the love of God.

From the human point of view repentance is a response to the acts of God in his grace. And the central point of this response is *faith* in the good news.

The two interwoven strands of the doctrine of salvation are shown clearly in the New Testament, above all in the Johannine writings: the sacraments and faith. We are saved by the acts of God in the sacraments; at the same time this means that we have our life from faith. St. Thomas has given classical expression to the idea that these two strands are inseparable: "We are saved by faith in Christ who was born and suffered. But the sacraments are signs which profess the faith by which man is justified" (*Summa Theol.* III, q. 61, a. 4). By his word and action in the sacraments God arouses and strengthens in us faith in the love which he has shown us in Jesus Christ. The whole Church, the bride of Christ, bears witness in the sacraments to her faith in the word which he spoke to her once for all and which is constantly renewed and repeated to every gathering of Christians and to each individual member of the Church: "I am your salvation." The sacrament is the meeting-place of the word of salvation and the answer of faith, which is aroused and sustained by the word of salvation. The sacrament of faith is both a gift and the solemn act by which the gift is received. The sacrament is, so to speak, the continuation of that unceasing gift which the Father gave to a world in need of redemption, in his beloved Son, who gave himself for us on the cross. But the word of God which bestows this gift comes to men who are free to choose. To partake of the gift of salvation, men must believe. They must be open to receive the message of salvation with humility and thankfulness; they must respond to God in faith as he brings his gift to them. "By believing in God who justifies him, man submits himself to God's justifying action, and so he receives the fruit of that action" (St. Thomas on Rom. 4. 5). Just as in a chaste marriage the giving and receiving of love becomes a single action, so it is in the sacraments of faith. The saving message, powerful in its effects, and the thankful acceptance which signifies a complete self-giving to God, become one. Through faith and the sacraments of faith we enter into a dialogue; we come into life-giving contact with the Redeemer who is enthroned at the right hand of the Father, and with the saving acts of his death and his resurrection.

In this life-giving dialogue the sacraments have a unique and honoured place because they are wholly, and in a way that nothing else is, the essence of the message of salvation and signs of faith. Yet this dialogue is not restricted to the sacraments; rather they are like sources of light and heat which shed their rays on everything, far beyond their central point. In the light of the sacraments we are able to see among, all that the providence of God has provided for us, his plan of salvation and his love, and so at all times and in every circumstance we become children of God listening faithfully and responding with thanks.

"Believe the good news of the Gospel!" "Yes!" cries the faithful Christian to the kingdom of God's love, when it is brought to him; and this has a deeper effect on his life than all moral striving which has its origin and its purpose in man alone. Without this acceptance in faith man's most noble achievements are never of any consequence, at least as far as his salvation is concerned. But the cheerful and faithful acceptance of the work of God's grace can bring about a complete change in the heart of man and in the whole world; and yet it is a quite personal act of acceptance of a love entirely personal in itself, an act in which man abandons himself to the absolute claims of the love of God. The radical commitment we make when we accept in faith the saving acts of Christ, and let ourselves be seized and changed by him, is described by St. Paul in chapter 6 of the Epistle to the Romans: if we accept that our life has been brought under the rule of grace, which is what is signified by incorporation into the saving death and resurrection of Christ, then a halt is called to our sins much more radically and effectively than by any number of legal commandments coming from outside to threaten us.

Christian repentance begins in faith and grows and is brought to completion by growth in faith, in that faith which works through love (Gal. 5 6). But the power of faith extends also to our moral renewal, for in faith the power of the death and resurrection of Christ, which brings salvation, is present.

Theology speaks of a first and second justification: what God begins when he justifies a sinner, he completes through the unending work of his grace, continually increasing the grace of sanctification as long as man co-operates gratefully. "After you have suffered a little while, the God of all grace, who has called you to his eternal glory in Christ, will himself restore, establish and strengthen you" (I Peter 5. 10). "I am sure that he who began a good work in you will bring it to completion at the day of Jesus Christ" (Phil. I. 6; I Cor. I. 8). This continuous work of God for our sanctification demands from men a ceaseless battle against everything imperfect and a ceaseless striving for true perfection; so just as we speak of a "second justification" we speak also of "continued or second repentance". As we have already emphasized, it means a continuous growth in faith, and that means a continuous and thankful acquiescence in God's desire to bestow his gifts on us.

The Apostles' preaching of repentance to the baptized is not based on the view that perhaps the majority of Christians may be living in mortal sin and need to renew their first repentance. It is not reduced to a list of man's duties or of the human virtues he should practice. The basic and constant theme is the work of God's grace in the sacraments. Again and again the Apostles make the *fact* of the Gospel, that is, the joyful proclamation of what God has done for us, a command for Christian life. God's work of sanctification, which lays down the pattern for our whole life, implies clearly that sin is incompatible with being a Christian, and that we have an obvious duty to increase in joy and faithfulness, basing our lives on God-given holiness. "You were washed, you were sanctified, you were justified in the name of the Lord Jesus Christ and the Spirit of our God" (I Cor. 6. 11)—"Once you were darkness, but now you are light in the Lord; walk as children of light, for the fruit of light is found in all that is good and right and true" (Eph. 5. 8 f.).

"If then you have been raised with Christ, seek the things that are above, where Christ is, seated at the right hand of God" (Col. 3. I). "You have died, and your life is hid with Christ in God. . . . Put to death therefore what is earthly in you. . ." (Col. 3. 3-5). The description of our salvation: "You are unleavened bread; for Christ our paschal lamb has been sacrificed" is followed by an appeal in the same terms: "Cleanse out the old leaven, that you may be fresh dough!" and "Let us celebrate the festival, not with the old leaven, the leaven of malice and evil, but with the unleavened bread of sincerity and truth" (I Cor. 5. 6-8). The following exhortation is based just as clearly on the proclamation of salvation: "Put on then as God's chosen ones, holy and beloved, compassion, kindness, lowliness, meekness and patience . . . above all these put on love, which binds everything together in perfect harmony" (Col. 3. 12-14). In the same way all the exhortations of the Apostle Peter are shot through with the recollection of the saving acts of God and his sanctification: "You were ransomed with the precious blood of Christ. . . . You have been born anew of imperishable seed through the living and abiding word of God. That word is the good news which was preached to you. So put away all malice. . . . Like newborn babes, long for the pure spiritual milk. Come to him, to the living stone" (I Peter I. 18-2.6).

To sum up then, we can say that the preaching of the Apostles has the same basic structure as the first sermon of Jesus: it is the good news of the fullness of salvation in Christ, of the kingdom of the love of God, of the change in men wrought by God. This good news comes forcefully to each individual in the "sacraments of faith". From henceforth the pattern of Christian life is provided by the promise and demand of Christ to sanctify us. This demand is laid upon us for ever and calls for us to hold back nothing from the fatherly love of God. This demand itself expresses the primacy of God's saving acts and the joy of being a child of God. Repentance and the whole Christian life is a life based on the faith that we acknowledge in the celebration and reception of the sacraments, a life based on the sanctification we have received.

O eternal God, infinitely blessed! You have revealed your love to us in Christ; in your love may we be blessed with you forever. Lord, let us accept your good news in joy and thanksgiving, let us keep it faithfully in our hearts and carry it out devotedly in our lives. According to your plan of salvation, help us to draw strength for our struggle to live a good life from the mighty acts of your love, and give us strength from your joy. Through Christ our Lord, who brings all joy. Amen.

Bernard Häring

CHAPTER II

THE SACRAMENTS AND PRAYER

During his last illness the well-known Catholic philosopher Peter Wust (who died in April 1940) wrote a farewell message to his pupils and friends, in answer to their many requests. In this spiritual testament he said: "If you ask me whether I had a magic key that could open the final door of knowledge and truth, I would reply: 'Yes, I have. And this magic key is not that of reflection, as you might expect from a philosopher, but prayer. Prayer, seen as the final act of surrender to God, makes us silent, child-like and objective. . . .' "

"Prayer is the lock to close the evening and the key to open the morning" (Gandhi). It protects us against the powers of evil that prowl about in the darkness; it opens before us the kingdom of light. Not only does it unlock for us the gate of truth and wisdom, as they are found in the greatest philosophy; prayer opens the way to the eternal kingdom of the love of God.

Only the man of prayer can enter into the deepest mysteries of existence. This is above all true of the sacraments of the new covenant: their hidden riches, their glory and their joy are only available to us in so far as we pray. And yet the reverse is even more true: *what Christian prayer is and how we should pray, we learn above all from the sacraments.* They make us partakers of the life of Christ and give us a picture of what it means to be allowed to pray "in the name of Christ."

In one of his sermons, Cardinal Faulhaber, a great man of prayer and a first-class liturgical scholar, gave a golden rule for prayer: "To pray means to go to God; to sidle up to God with the timid steps of a child, to stagger up to God under the burden of care and sin, to hurry towards God with the trusting familiarity of a friend, to fly towards God on the wings of perfect love." If we look at these phrases in the light of the sacraments, this is what they mean:

In the sacraments God comes to us in Christ Jesus: in prayer we go with Christ and in Christ to God our Father.

In the sacraments God gives us the assurance that "according to the purpose of his will he destined us to be his sons through

Jesus Christ" (Eph. I. 5): in prayer we speak to God as children "in the name of Christ", his Son.

In the sacraments we are embraced by the loving kindness and mercy of God "in Christ Jesus": in prayer we bring our trouble and guilt before God the merciful, trusting in our Redeemer Jesus Christ.

In the sacraments God gives us the pledge and surety of the blessings of his love: prayer is the beginning of the endless dialogue of love with God "in Christ Jesus".

TO PRAY MEANS TO GO TO GOD

Dare a creature, dare a sinful man do this? Can he begin to think of going to God? The Preacher in the Old Testament warns us: "Be not rash with your mouth nor let your heart be hasty to utter a word before God, for God is in heaven and you upon earth" (Eccles. 5. I). God is in heaven in unapproachable holiness. He is "quite other" than his creation. Before him we are nothing, powerless and poverty-stricken, men "with unclean lips" (Isa. 6 5). How can we who are sinful men stand before the face of God, before the throne of his holiness, and speak to him? Granted "in him we live and move and have our being" (Acts 17. 28). The heathen already knew that. God is our Creator, he is close to us in his creative power, he holds us in being. And yet—this is a question that sounds again and again in the prayers of the devout pagans: has he even turned his face towards us? Will he condescend to hear me and answer me?

We can go in trust to God and speak to him because he comes to us first and speaks his Word to us.

The almighty Word of God calls every man who comes into the world by his own name. The unimaginable grandeur of the assurance that was given to one of the great prophets for himself alone is true of all to whom God has given breath: "Before I formed you in the womb I knew you, I called you by your name" (cf. Jer. I. 5). Not only were we men created by the word of the Father like other creatures (John I. 3), but besides this we have been *called* in a way which the rest of creation has not, by the Word in whom the Father has expressed from eternity all his love and his glory. And according to our nature as rational individuals, this is a personal call, and we can understand it, and so order our whole lives that they form a response to it; for we are created "in the image and likeness of God". *We are created by the Word and love of God in order to reply to him with love.* Our nature as individuals and the place of each of us in the creation rest on the fact that we are called by God in this way, can understand him, and can answer him. So it is not the case that we exist first of all—that we are existent beings—and then, in addition to this, have been called by God. We are what we are because God has called us. God creates us by the Word in which he speaks to us, and this is what underlies and sustains our existence. That is why the development of our created nature chiefly depends upon how we answer God.

It was the first intention of the Creator that man should be by nature a creature of *prayer.* God walked in the cool of the evening in the Garden of Eden (cf. Gen. 3. 8), and Adam could speak intimately to God. But he barred himself from the Garden where this intimate conversation would be held as soon as he attempted to bring his existence under his own control and reserve for himself a corner of his life.

God, who in his almighty Word, in a wonderful way, created man to pray, in a yet more wonderful way has called him in his Word made man, in Jesus Christ. Not only on the mountains in the cool of the evening, but from the dark night of the Mount of Olives and the burning mid-day heat of Calvary God receives the answer of a perfect and complete prayer "in the name" of all humanity; for Christ is the head of the new humanity. All those whose being is incorporated into him in love are now enabled with him and in him—more than just with his aid—to enter into the dialogue of love with God.

Christ is the original sacrament: he is the great and all-inclusive sign of the Father's love. The Father has given us everything in him; in him he has imparted to us all his love. Through him he gives us his Spirit, the Spirit of Love. In him he has chosen us to be his children, and has called us by a name that cannot be spoken. Christ is not only the word of the Father to us, he is also the original sacrament in which we reply to the Father as his children.

Christ is the original sacrament, which imparts the love of God to the whole world and brings the answer back to the Father's throne, while the seven sacraments bring each individual into this same mystery. In *baptism* God bestows on us the status of a *child,* which no one can fully understand as the Son and his Holy Spirit. In the Holy Spirit, of whose fullness we are made partakers in confirmation, we come to understand the effective word of love and power, which the Father gives us when he puts us in the same place as his Son. In the Holy Spirit we rejoice: "Abba, Father!"

So the individual sacraments lead us into an ever more real and intense share in the great reality of the mission and the life of Christ, into the original sacrament. More than this: through our share in the life of Christ God the Three-in-One draws us into the dialogue of his own life, and lets us take an ever more wonderful part in it.

Through the "sacraments of faith" we have an infallible assurance of the loving words God has spoken to us in faith. In these sacraments Christ speaks to a Christian community who is celebrating them or to any one of his faithful: "I am your salvation, all my love is for you, just as on the cross I offered it for all humanity." In proportion to the liveliness of our faith, the sacrament of faith draws us into the answer given by the bride of Christ, the Church, who unites herself with the answer given by the incarnate Word to the Father.

In the sacraments we are assured of the close presence of God, speaking gently and yet powerfully to us. We know then that for us too he is Emmanuel, God-with-us. In the sacraments heaven is present in a way no less wonderful because it is hidden and accessible only to faith. This truth comes to us most clearly in the holy Eucharist which is at the centre of the whole system of sacraments.

The source and the means of Christian prayer lies above all in the sacraments. Our prayer is quite different from that of the heathen. It is not a cry that goes up from man weighted with the fearful question, "Will God hear me? Will he turn his face towards me?" We can pray. More than this, we are made to pray by our very nature and must pray if we are not to be false to our nature and to our calling.

The sacraments place our whole existence, and every significant task in our life, under the special claims of the grace of God.

They bring us and everything that we are and that we possess into an ever closer and more intense encounter with God. In the sacraments, we can understand and accept in faith the Word by which God created the world, and the gifts and the calling of his divine providence. Those who see themselves as "called" (*kletoi*) —called in the Word of the Father—in every aspect of their lives will see everything as a call to salvation. Everything is resolved and illuminated when we hear God in faith and give him a loving, trusting answer. That we are "called" does not simply mean that we are called to eternal happiness at some time in the future. Even now, while we are on the way to a complete share in the dialogue of love between Father and Son in the Holy Spirit, we are assured of the call of God that redeems us, so sure that we cannot doubt that God will make his word come true for us for all eternity. The only condition is that we should pray: that we should listen to the call of God's grace and order our whole life in answer to it.

TO GO BOLDLY TO GOD LIKE A CHILD TO HIS FATHER

To see a child walk for the first time, however timid its steps, is exciting. And only a mother and father know how wonderful it is when for the first time they are clearly addressed as such. Only they can tell us what it means; it is a great event in their lives. How can we simple and puny men have anything of importance to say to God in our prayers? How awkward we are! And yet it is a great event in heaven when we speak to God as children. It is the answer to his Word, which gave us life, in which he names us as his children and revealed to us that he is called our Father. So our answer shares in the sublimity of God's words to us. When we pray "in the name of Christ," united with him and trusting completely in him and in the power of his Spirit, then we know, "that the Father himself loves us" (cf. John 16. 27).

One might object: "God does not need our words"; did not the Lord himself say: "Your Father knows what you need before you ask him" (Matt. 6. 8)? Certainly God does not need our poor faltering prayers; he does not even need our love, for he is endlessly happy in the eternal rejoicing of his own love, the love of three persons in one. But he has revealed himself to us as the great lover: he wants us to rejoice with him in the love which is the source of his joy. *Love desires to be loved.* All the saving acts of God, and the sacraments which bring them to us at the present moment as nothing else does, assure us that God desires and accepts our love and the childish words in which we express it.

We honour God, our Lord and Father, and the purposes of his love, which he has revealed to us in Christ, by praying to him trustfully for our needs. Our trust is the greater, the more lively our awareness of the loving words which God has vouchsafed to speak to us in the sacraments. How could God deny us anything we need for our salvation, when Christ has offered himself to the Father for us and given us a share in his life! We bear his name and, as we learn especially from the celebration and reception of the Eucharist, we are "flesh of his flesh"; we pray in his name. Our prayer is rooted in the "sacrament of faith", and we can pray "with no doubting" (James I. 6).

The Father has given us everything in Christ Jesus, so that our prayer "in the name of Christ" is the constant praise of our Father's loving kindness.

It is not very long ago since some people believed that a "liturgical Christian" had no room for the prayer of petition, since his whole concern was with worship. That was a great mistake. Just as God glorifies his fatherhood and his fatherly kindness by the many gifts he gives us, so we honour God above all by preparing ourselves to receive his gifts with the humility that never fails to recognize that everything comes from God alone, and by the unshakable trust that is expressed in constant prayer. The prayer of petition, which has its source and finds its substance in the liturgy, is a *Magnificat* sung by the humble bride of Christ, the Church, and all her true children: "He has filled the hungry with good things, and the rich he has sent empty away" (Luke I. 53).

St. Paul's prayers of petition, which proclaim to us with such power the sacramental mystery of our life "in Jesus Christ", are either hymns or end in hymns to "the God and Father of our Lord Jesus Christ, the Father of mercies and God of all comfort" (2 Cor. I. 3).

Bernard Häring

Our hymns, the prayer of adoration and praise, can only be sincere when our petitions keep us constantly aware that we are nothing in ourselves, that we are in fact sinners worthy of punishment, yet God gives us everything in his beloved Son. But the other side of the picture must be made clear as well: the true nature of the Christian prayer of petition is that it arises out of the sacraments and is therefore a prayer of worship and praise, for it is based on the rock-like certainty that the Father himself loves us because we are gathered together "in the name of Jesus" and pray in his name. Such a prayer of petition makes us ready to receive the grace of the sacraments. The prayer of petition and the prayer of thanksgiving constantly overlap.

The Church teaches us that we do not merit the gift of grace that is vital to our eternal destiny, the grace of perseverance, but that we can obtain it by prayer. Just as we can do nothing of ourselves which bears any comparison with the life of grace which we seek from God, so we can only receive the power to continue in grace to the end so long as we always go on praying, in the consciousness that our election by God as a whole is an undeserved gift of his grace. But at the same time the trust we show in our prayer should reflect our faith in the fact that always and in everything God desires our salvation. God desires nothing more than to give us his greatest gift, the grace of perseverance. What he has begun with so powerful an act of love, what he assures us of again and again in every sacrament, he will bring it to perfection, if we ask it of him in trust.

Our child-like and trusting prayer for grace and perseverance in the love and service of God is pre-eminently an act of praise for the undeserved grace by which we are called and are in truth the children of God, and by which there will be revealed to us, in the loving purposes of God, the glory that God has prepared for his children (cf. I John 3. I) ff).

* * * * *

TO CARRY ALL OUR CARES TO GOD

When we care-ridden men go to God and are brave enough to follow the Psalmist's advice to "cast all our care upon the

Lord" (Ps. 54. 23), we do it in the knowledge that our Lord and Master himself "took our infirmities and bore our diseases" (Matt. 8. 17).

He is the good Samaritan who, seized by pity, has taken care of us and entrusted us, the poor and the sick, to his Church and to the intercession of his mother Mary. More than this: he himself is always close to us. In the sacraments power is given to the weak, and means of healing provided for the sickness of our soul, and in them he continually renews his pledge that he is caring for us. We are constantly assured by the sacraments, and especially by the Eucharist, of the truth of those most comforing words of St. Paul: "The Lord is at hand. Have no anxiety about anything but in everything by prayer and supplication with thanksgiving let your requests be made known to God" (Phil. 4. 5 f.).

If anyone is sad or "is suffering, let him pray" (James 5. 13). The worst thing in suffering, in temptation and in grief is often simply the fact of being alone in one's distress. There is no human being to whom one can open one's heart completely and without reserve. So one turns in upon oneself. But anyone who has experienced the nearness of God in the sacraments, who has listened to the mighty words with which God speaks to him in the sacraments, and has joined in that dialogue with God in which nothing is left unmentioned, cannot be overcome by suffering and sadness. He knows that he is "in the protection of the Most High".

Madeleine Sémer, a talented French associate of Nietzsche, brought up her only son in complete unbelief. One day during a long illness, he said reproachfully to his mother, "You know, when you are as bad as this you ought to be able to pray." All the desperate distress of so many people who cannot pray is a pressing reminder to us to do everything we can to pray for them and obtain for them the blessing of prayer. Of course to be able to pray really well and trustingly in distress, we need to have learned beforehand the prayer of trust and love. Then, when we cry to God from the deepest torment and anguish, our words will turn into words of praise and trust. The Psalmist, although he was unable to experience the nearness of God so wonderfully as the man who takes part in the sacraments of the new covenant, prayed at a time of great danger: "The cords of death encompassed me, torrents of perdition assailed me. In my distress I called upon the Lord: to my God I cried for help." But next to this stands a prayer of trust and adoration: "I call upon the Lord, who is worthy to be praised, and I am saved from my enemies" (Ps. 17. 4-7).

Behind the outcry of men in the depths of distress, and behind the wonderful faith of those who pray in spirit and truth and in spite of all tribulations can still trust God, the man of the sacraments, who is "incorporated with Christ in the image of his death" (cf. Rom. 6. 5), can discern the loud cry of him who bore all our sorrow and guilt: "My God, why hast thou forsaken me?" (Matt. 27. 46; Ps. 21. 2), and the answer and solution, the childlike resignation and the childlike trust of: "Father, into thy hands I commend my spirit" (Luke 23. 46).

How could men dare to cry out with absolute trust to God, at the time of this deepest distress and desolation, when he is cut off from God by sin—seeing that he has put himself away from God by his sin—if Christ were not there to restore him, Christ who is the original sacrament, with his sacraments of the forgiveness of sins?

It is true that a man in mortal sin, who has extinguished the life of grace in himself, cannot pray "in the name of Jesus" in the same way as one in whom Christ lives by grace. But when he was on earth Jesus cried out aloud and with unspeakable pain to the Father for these poor sinners. When the sinner sets aside all false reliance on himself and on what he can claim to have done on his own, and trusting only in the suffering, death and resurrection of Christ, begs for forgiveness, he is already praying, in the one way open to him, "in the name of Christ". It is the grace of God which helps and guides him. And the sacraments are still there before him, baptism for the unbaptized, and for the baptized Christian who has fallen into mortal sin the sacrament of mercy and penance. It is the Lord himself who through these sacraments, and through his Church, invites the sinner to listen to the word of God which brings him redemption and new strength.

But we all pray in truth in the name of Jesus, when, moved by the knowledge of our unity with Christ in his work of salvation, we pray trustfully to God, asking for his help for the suffering, the afflicted and for those in temptation, and above all for sinners.

PART III
CHAPTER II
THE SACRAMENTS OF THE NEW COVENANT

THE SACRAMENTS AND THE LOVE OF OUR NEIGHBOUR

"I will put my law within them, and I will write it upon their hearts" (Jer. 31. 33; cf. Heb. 10. 16); so God foretold the new law. The decisive law, "the fulfilling of the law" (Rom. 13. 10), is love, *single and undivided love for God and for our neighbour*. And this love he writes in our hearts through the gift of his own fully personal love, through the gifts of the Holy Spirit.

All the sacraments are demonstrations of the love of God: they all point to the heart of our Saviour, pierced for our sakes. They are all operations of the Holy Spirit, who is love. They all call us to show love, through the gift of God's love. The central point of them all is the sacrament of love in which Christ gives himself as a pledge of his love.

All the sacraments lay in us the foundations of the community of love in which our salvation is found. They are signs of the kingdom of God, the rule of true love amongst all the redeemed. All the sacraments direct us towards our neighbours, in whom Christ seeks to form his image, and upon whom, as on us, the love of the Redeemer and the grace of the Holy Spirit is poured.

All the sacraments bestow the gift of love, and speak of love; but as each brings its own special gift, so each has its own special message. In a chorus of seven voices they chant the Song of Songs of the love of our neighbour.

BAPTISM AND THE LOVE OF OUR NEIGHBOUR

In holy baptism we are all born again into the one great family of God. We become children of God, brothers and sisters of one another, by being conformed to the likeness of Christ.

We become one body with Christ. The love of Christ, which is written into the new existence which the Holy Spirit has created for us, embraces and unites us all. By loving one another, we love each other with the love of Christ; we love Christ in our neighbour. "Anyone who loves the limbs of the body of Christ, the children of God, is bound also to love the Son of God, who is joined with them in unity; but whoever loves the Son of God is bound also to love the Father whose Son he is; and on the other hand whoever loves the Son, loves also the children of God, who are his limbs. And by the very fact that he loves them, he himself becomes a living limb within the body of Christ. Thus Christ loves the limbs, but the limbs love Christ and love one another. It is impossible to love the limbs of Christ, without loving the head; to love the head, without loving the Logos; or to love the Son, without loving the Father . . . , to love the Father and the Son, without loving the body of the Son: *Non potest separari dilectio.* Love cannot be torn apart" (Augustine, *In Epist. Johannis,* tr. 10, n. 3; PL 35, 2055).

Holy baptism, through the inward change it causes in us, brings our life with Christ under the great law of unity with one another in and for the sake of our salvation. Our own salvation lies in love for one another, in concern for one another's salvation. Since by baptism we are limbs of the one body of Christ, St. Paul's words are true of us: "If one member suffers, all suffer together; if one member is honoured, all rejoice together" (I Cor. 12. 26). Because we are baptized we have been incorporated into the saving death of our Lord (Rom. 6. 5), who bore the cross and shed his blood for us all. That is why the law of our lives is that no one should live for himself alone any more. "Let each of us please his neighbour for his good, to edify him. For Christ did not please himself" (Rom. 15. 2f.). Because of our baptism, each of us ought to adopt the same attitude as St. Paul describes: "Give no offence to Jews or to Greeks or to the church of God, just as I try to please all men in everything I do, that they may be saved. Be imitators of me as I am of Christ" (I Cor. 10. 32-II. I).

We are baptized *in the name of Jesus:* the name Jesus means salvation and love. As baptized Christians we bear the name of our Redeemer. But we are only rightly called by his name if we show ourselves to be his disciples through our love and concord. "By this all men will know that you are my disciples, if you have love for one another" (John 13. 35). Through our love and unity we become, "in Christ Jesus", bearers of salvation to all mankind.

We are baptized *in the name of God the Holy Trinity*. "Baptize in the name of the Father and of the Son and of the Holy Spirit" (Matt. 28. 19). Through our baptism we already bear the life of God the Holy Trinity within us, and are destined in the end to join in the celebration of the love with which the Father and the Son love each other in the Holy Spirit, after we have been witnesses, strong in the faith, of this reality through our love and concord. How can we join in the celebration of the love of God with the jubilant choirs of angels and saints, if we have no love between ourselves, if we do not love each other!

In the intermediate period between the coming of the Holy Spirit at Pentecost and the second coming of Christ, the love of baptized Christians for one another is meant to be a revelation of the love between the three persons of the Trinity, and thus an offer of salvation to the whole world. Just as the death and the resurrection of Christ revealed to the faithful the love within the Trinity, so the unity and love of the faithful, who are united in the name of Christ, should be a witness of the love of God bringing salvation to them and to others.

Thus the vocation of the baptized is, in its innermost essence, a vocation of love.

CONFIRMATION AND THE LOVE OF OUR NEIGHBOUR

In holy confirmation, the Holy Spirit, who is the gift of love in person, is given to us in a special way. He is the gift given to us for the apostolate. *A conscious concern and care for the salvation of our neighbour is the very heart of love for our neighbour.*

In order that we can come to meet our neighbour with love, and love him into going with us to God, our capacity for love must be purifed by the Holy Spirit in the fire of the holy *fear of God*. If we have learnt, through the *gift of wisdom*, to have pleasure ourselves in friendship with God, we realize that everything good that we can do for anyone else is futile if it does not help him to grow in the love of God, or to find his way back to the love of God.

A woman who was living in concubinage wanted to return to the sacrament of penance and to holy communion. But she was not ready to leave the man, nor did she want to marry him. Her reason was: "I can't hurt him like that. I am too fond of him." How often do we hear similar assurances of love, or to be more precise, of easy-going good nature of infatuation, of complacence or of passion. It cannot be denied that behind all the perversion and blindness there is still some trace of love. But it is an impure love.

St. Augustine does not hesitate to say that everything in the history of the world has been set in motion by love. But, he says, there are two kinds of love at work: the true and the false. The vital thing is that human love should be purified, and false love driven out by true love. An understanding of true love, and the power to practise it, is given to us by the Holy Spirit. The *fear of God* means that God can look on our love and find it clear and honest. The *gifts of wisdom and counsel give* us a sure feeling for what is genuine, an intuitive delight in true love. Through that gift, we judge everything by the standard of the pure love springing up from God. The *gift of strength* makes our love resolute. It gives us the courage to make sacrifices ourselves, but also the courage to cut off and cauterize, if it is necessary for the healing of the soul. Even love sometimes must be stern.

Our love for our neighbour must be won by a struggle and sustained in suffering. It must be tried in the fire. Its true source is the Spirit, the gift of the risen and victorious Christ who endured the cross and death from love. That is why love is "as strong as death". Many waters cannot quench the flames and ardour of love.

"If I deliver my body to be burned, but have not love, I gain nothing." It is not the greatness or the difficulty of what we do that matters, but that it comes from the same spirit in which Christ died for us on the cross. "Love is patient and kind; love is not jealous, love bears all things, believes all things" (I Cor. 13. 3ff.), because fundamentally it is always the love of Christ, brought to perfection in us by the Holy Spirit.

THE EUCHARIST AND THE LOVE OF OUR NEIGHBOUR

Everything that baptism and confirmation and the other sacraments tell us about the love of our neighbour is summed up in the mystery of the Eucharist. When we are gathered together about one altar, eat of *one* bread and draw life from the love of the one Lord, the love that was ready to suffer death, then the meaning and the urgency of the mystery of our unity and responsibility for each other's salvation, into which we have been brought by baptism and confirmation, become even clearer to us.

The Spirit of Pentecost reveals to us that love is above all zeal for the salvation of our neighbour. It is he also who opens our eyes and our heart to receive the mystery of the love of Christ, in which he was ready to receive death, and which we celebrate in the Eucharist. There it is enacted before our eyes and likewise written in our hearts and in the blood of Christ, that love does not insist on its own way, but bears all things and endures all things.

It was not for nothing that the saints and fathers of the Church based the love of our neighbour, in their sermons and instructions, above all on the mystery of the Eucharist. The Eucharist is the source of grace for the love of our neighbour, the standard we set and the highest motive for carrying it out. In the Eucharist our Lord brings us again and again, every time we celebrate the sacrificial meal, his new commandment: "This is my commandment, that you love one another *as I have loved you*" (John 15. 12). For he showed us his all-surpassing love in the sacrifice of his own life on the cross. The high-priestly prayer Jesus prayed after the Last Supper, before he went out to die for us, is the whole theme of the celebration of the Eucharist, and its words are written on our hearts as we receive his body sacrificed for us: "Father, I made known to them thy name, and I will make it known, that the love with which thou hast loved me may be in them, and I in them" (John 17. 26). By coming to us to give himself in holy communion, the Lord gives us a part in the love that reigns between him and the Father for all eternity. Our life, devoted to love for our neighbour, should

216

be drawn from this stream of living water, and bear witness to the world that is there.

Before all else, the Eucharist teaches us the meaning and gives us the gift of *concord*. The sound of our singing in the liturgy only rings true when our voices and our hearts are in harmony. And another purpose of the Eucharist is to make our common life visible in an outward representation. For the sacraments bring about what they signify, and signify what they bring about. The one table, at which we are fed with the one bread, is meant to create concord amongst us. Acts 2.42: "They devoted themselves to the fellowship, to the breaking of bread and the prayers." "All those who believed were together" (2. 44). "Now the company of those who believed were of one heart and soul" (4. 32). From the time of the Didache we find again and again this symbolic interpretation: the bread which was once many grains of corn has become one, the wine that was in many grapes has become one, and so we become one through the Eucharist. But this ought also to be clearly expressed through the way the whole fellowship shares in the celebration. Yet the most important thing is, that we bear witness to this unity in our lives. Against the immense powers of evil and the mass movements of this world, only a united apostolate, an apostolate carried out in concord, can have any hope of permanent results. And any act carried out without harmony and concord lacks the blessing of Christ.

We can only unite, therefore, our gifts, our lives, and ourselves with the sacrifice of Christ if we approach our neighbour with a love that is ready for sacrifice, and if we all make the sacrifices that are necessary to maintain the bond of peace. Our part in the celebration of the Eucharist is only of value in the sight of God if we are ready to pay the price that has to be paid for love and concord: self-denial and a genuine willingness for sacrifice. "If you are offering your gift at the altar, and there remember that your brother has something against you, leave your gift there before the altar and go; first be reconciled to your brother, and then come and offer your gift" (Matt. 5. 23 f.).

THE SACRAMENT OF PENANCE AND THE LOVE OF OUR NEIGHBOUR

In the sacrament of penance we experience the forgiving love of God our Saviour. He whom we have wounded by our sins prays there for us: "Father, forgive them; for they know not what they do!" If we make a good and full confession, we have an absolute assurance from our Lord himself that he bears no grudge against us.

The sacrament of penance imposes on us the law of merciful love. When we confess our sins we pray: "Forgive us our debt, as we forgive our debtors." As men whose life comes from God's mercy, we have a double obligation to show a compassionate and forgiving love. "Love bears no grudge."

Peter once asked our Lord: "Lord, how often shall my brother sin against me, and I forgive him? As many as seven times?" Jesus answered him: "I do not say to you seven times, but seventy times seven" (Matt. 18. 21 f.). And our Lord illustrated in a parable exactly what he seeks to write upon our hearts in the sacrament of penance: a servant was forgiven a debt of ten thousand talents, which he was not able to pay. He went away and seized by the throat a fellow servant who owed him a hundred pence, and refused to forgive him his debt. All were greatly distressed, including the lord who had forgiven him the debt of ten thousand talents. "In anger his lord delivered him to the jailers, till he should pay all his debt" (Matt. 18. 34).

In the sacrament of penance we meet our Lord as the good shepherd. When we come and kneel before him, it is the sins against the love of our neighbour that should cause us most sorrow. And our confession in the sacrament of penance should make us realize that love is "the fullness of the law". We go on from there to examine our obedience to each individual commandment.

The priest, whose part it is to proclaim the word of peace in the sacrament of penance, has in consequence a very special obligation to present an image of the loving kindness of the Saviour by his understanding and compassion, both within and outside the confessional.

Every sin does damage to the body of Christ, and diminishes the fullness of salvation in the world around us. A true repentance and a genuine thankfulness for the grace of repentance and forgiveness brings with it the resolution to repair the damage done by sin from that moment on, by zeal for the salvation of our neighbour. The best "fruits of repentance" are works carried out for love of our neighbour, and those of the Christian apostolate above all.

THE SACRAMENT OF ORDER AND THE LOVE OF OUR NEIGHBOUR

It is a great mystery that the Son loves us, as the Father loves him. The mystery of the priest, who stands in Christ's place, is to pass the love he has received from Christ humbly on to other men. Through his whole being, and through all that he says and does, he should make the love of Christ visible and comprehensible. "As the Father sent me, so I send you", said Christ to his disciples. The Father gave us his Son out of pure love. In the Son we recognize the love of the Father. Every true disciple of Christ, but especially the priest, has to continue, in the power of the Holy Spirit, the mighty task of Christ, that of showing the Father's love to others. Not only by individual kindly deeds and words ought we to show our love. The priest and everyone who, in our Lord's words, has set his light upon a candlestick—and that ultimately means all the baptized, who together form "the nation of priests"—have a special vocation to be a pattern and witness of the love of Christ in their own person.

On the sacrament of order there is based *a hierarchy of sacred authority*. The priest should give devoted *obedience and love* to the bishop and especially to the Bishop of Rome, to whom the fullness of pastoral authority has been given. The faithful should show to the hierarchy, whom they normally encounter in the priest, love, reverence and thankfulness. But the priest in his turn, with an all-embracing love, should become "all things to all men", as St Paul was able to say of himself.

The bishop says to the newly ordained priest at his ordination: "Receive the priestly garment, which signifies love. For the Lord is powerful to increase love in you and bring it to perfection." Love is the radiant garment in which the priest stands before God on behalf of the faithful, and comes back to them, ready to serve them. The special task set by the sacrament of holy order is that of love, strong in faith, for all the members of the family of God, and especially for those of God's children who have gone astray. The only reason why this powerful command does not terrify and discourage a priest is because before the task was set, and as it is imposed on him, he is given a special grace to carry it out.

THE SACRAMENT OF MARRIAGE AND THE LOVE OF OUR NEIGHBOUR

Through the sacrament of marriage two human beings are drawn so closely into the love of Christ and his Church that they have from then on the ability and the duty to be witnesses and living tools of the love of God. The love of a husband should be such that it is the means of bringing to his wife a deeper and more lively apprehension of the love of Christ that passes all understanding. And the love of the wife should be such that it is the means of helping her husband to become more and more an image of Christ and his Church. Married love, love sanctified by the sacrament, should be an image of the selfless and sacrificial love of Christ on the cross, and the thankful love of the Church for Christ (cf. Eph. 5).

Those who remain unmarried for the kingdom of heaven's sake, especially priests and members of religious orders, should be witnesses to the love of Christ before the whole world, in an even clearer and more radical fashion. For those who remain unmarried for the sake of the kingdom of heaven are drawn more directly into the mystery of the "marriage of the Lamb with the Bride" than those who are married.

Just as the experience of the love of man and wife for each other, and the children's experience of the love of their parents for them, can or at least ought to show them the way to know and accept the love of God, so all the faithful should get an even deeper apprehension of the loving kindness of God from their priest. A farmer said a few years ago of his priest, who had just died: "If I were to imagine that our Lord were to come once again into the world to live amongst us, I would think of him as being exactly like our priest." The priest, who came from a rich family, did not even leave enough to pay for the cost of his burial. He had given everything away. Every Christian, by virtue of the fact that he belongs to the people of God, has the sublime task of showing to his neighbour something of what the love of God is like.

The message of the sacrament of marriage, not only for those who are married but for everyone, is that the deepest mystery of Christ and the Church is love, and that we can only have a share in the riches of this mystery, to the extent that we live together in love for one another.

THE SACRAMENT OF THE ANOINTING OF THE SICK AND THE LOVE OF OUR NEIGHBOUR

The sacrament of holy unction tells us once again, with reference to our last illness and our acceptance of suffering and death, that we have been incorporated into the saving death of Christ (Romans 6). Together with the grace of resignation and patience, this sacrament gives in a special way to the sick man who receives it in faith, a common mind with Christ, so that his suffering and death can become a perfect sacrifice offered for the love of his neighbour.

The spirit of faith, the example of patience, of piety, and of thankfulness for every service carried out by his friends and relations, are outstanding acts of love for his neighbours, a silent but very eloquent apostolate.

Even while we are still in good health the devotions we offer for a good death should be carried out in union with the redeeming love of Jesus, which embraces all men. The sacrament of holy unction should find us ready to be conformed to the ultimate degree to the loving obedience of Jesus, which was also the highest expression of his love for men. But if this is to be so, we have to grow every day in the practice of the love of our neighbour, which directs everything in our lives, our joy and sorrow, and above all the daily carrying of the cross, by which we die to ourselves, towards the salvation of our neighbour.

THE CHURCH – THE SACRAMENT OF LOVE

Each of the seven sacraments is an expression of the original and fundamental sacrament, the love of Christ for his Church. The Church herself, in the fullest sense, is the *sacrament of love*. It is her task to bring the experience of the love of Christ to all men and make it visible to them, just as the well-beloved Son made the love of the heavenly Father visible in human form. The Church is the realm in which love for one's neighbour, which comes from God, and leads to God, has taken on a concrete form, and must continually go on so doing.

In her pastoral office the Church displays her love for immortal souls. All those who take part in any way in the pastoral work of the Church must make it their first concern to see that supernatural love for their neighbour is a powerful force within them, and is clearly expressed in all their words and actions. Anyone who dins the law of the Church into someone else's ears without love is not acting in the name of the Church, but against the deepest intention of the Church. All the laws of the Church are expressions of her pastoral love, and all lead in the end to the great commandment of love. It is therefore of vital importance that this should be visible in the way the laws are put into operation, just as sacramental grace becomes visible in the sacramental signs.

The Church is a *community* of faith and worship. The exercise of the Church's teaching office, like the confession of faith, only takes full effect when it leads to a visible experience of love and unity. Our Lord prayed for his apostles and for all who should come to the faith through them: "That they may become perfectly one, so that the world may know that thou hast sent me and hast loved them even as thou hast loved me" (John 17.23).

Because the Church as a whole, and in every respect, is a sacrament of love, every community that forms part of her, and every individual member, must do their utmost to bear to this mystery a compelling witness, to inspire the faith of others.

The validity of the sacraments carried out in the Catholic Church is guaranteed by the special assistance of God. But it is our unhappy experience that here and there the sacraments are sometimes "administered" so formally and "carried out" by the people in such a purely external way, that it is practically impossible for someone who is not familiar with all this to recognize the mystery of faith and love which they nevertheless still represent. It is the same with the all-embracing sacrament of love, with the Church. There are times when even within the Church "the love of many grows cold" (cf. Matt. 24.12). And this itself increases the power of false prophets to lead men astray.

Just as the essential nature and form of each individual sacrament imposes on us a sacred obligation to make our community of love a living experience in the celebration of the sacraments, so the inner mystery of the Church, as a community in salvation, is an even wider and more compelling motive for bearing before the world a witness of love for our neighbours that arouses faith in others. All of us—as the Church—are effectively "a sacrament", a visible sign, arousing faith, of the love of Christ, if we love each other in thought, word and deed.

THE PROCLAMATION OF THE COMMANDMENT OF LOVE IN EVERYTHING

In the natural creation God has already ordained that we should live together in a community. There is a natural impulse towards altruism. Unless a man's mind is warped, he is sensitive almost as a matter of course to the needs and good qualities of others. He feels the benefit he receives from the community and knows he must commit himself on its behalf. A man only becomes a full individual, a personality realizing all his potential, by serving other people and the community. Only when a man in his heart gives full value to his neighbour, and comes to meet him with a reverent love, does he become completely himself. But if he approaches the other with a disguised selfishness, seeking to use him for his own ends or for the fulfilment of his own personality, he does not even come to maturity himself.

The love of a Christian for his neighbour certainly uses and builds on this natural altruism, but its real foundation and motive lies in the love for us of God, "who loved us first" and who binds us together, through his love, into a supernatural community of love. In the love of Christ the redeemed are joined so closely to one another that St Paul calls them *one* body in Christ. But this truth is more than a reason urged upon us from outside. No less than our natural altruism, in fact to a greater degree, it is *a reality engraved on our own very being.* What Christ lived out for us in his own sublime example he unfolds within us through the sacraments, he writes upon our heart with the flames of his life-giving Spirit. So *the love of Christ is a marvellous and living force of love controlling us from within* (cf. 2 Cor. 5. 14). Just as nothing can separate us from the love of Christ (Rom. 8. 35), if we let him rule us, so likewise no earthly power, no temptation, and not even the "murderer from the beginning", the devil, can shake the love of Christians for one another, or their love for all whom God is seeking to call back to himself through them. God has given us a commandment of love, not only by living a life of love as our example, but also by placing his own power within our hearts.

God proclaims to us the great commandment of love in every way, with the sound of harps, with the bells of Easter Day and with the fanfares of victory, and also with the terrifying trumpets of judgment. Thus are all enabled to hear the words: "Love your neighbour". The divine child, crying in the cold, bare manger, teaches us the humility and self-forgetfulness demanded of us by the love of our neighbour. In words full of the power of love, the divine teacher proclaimed this commandment through the whole land; on the mountain of the Beatitudes, in the Upper Room and on the hill of Calvary he preached his powerful doctrine of a love for our neighbour strong in the spirit of sacrifice. Good Friday and Easter Day tell us of the immense depth, the wonderful triumph and the sacred obligation of this love. And the Spirit whom the glorified Lord sends to us writes it in our heart. The rejoicing of all the angels and saints in heaven shows us the way to this love. The Lord of glory has already let us hear the joyful word that is assured to all who love their neighbours: "Come, O blessed of my Father, inherit the kingdom prepared for you from the foundation of the world!" (Matt. 25. 34). This is none other than the kingdom of rejoicing love in the society of all who love, a kingdom in which none can enter but those who have continued in the love of their neighbours, and have loved Christ in every one of their fellow men.

If there is an ear so deaf and a heart so cold that all this heavenly harmony means nothing to them, then the fearful voice of the judge will start him out of his sleep and his lack of love; for he, the great lover, will say in anger to those who are without love: "Depart from me you accursed, into the eternal fire!" They are accursed by their lack of love. *Love has every blessing: lack of love brings with it every curse.* The promise and the threat of judgment lie in the nature of love itself, for love is so sublime that no one can be admitted to the great feast of love who has not let love come into his heart. After the commandment of love comes judgment; for in love the whole law is contained. The love which God has poured out in our hearts already contains in itself the seeds of every blessedness; for "God is love".

By their gifts of grace, the sacraments write their law of love in our hearts. They bring the most sacred and the most pressing obligation. The more we are ready to follow their urging, the more open we are to receive all their riches. Then they will go on and on making us messengers and witnesses of the love of Christ.

Lord, you have sent the spirit of love into our hearts. In the paschal sacraments you lead us in a wonderful way into the promised land of your love. We beseech you, make us all of one mind, so that the world may know that your love reigns in us, who live and reign with the Father in the unity of the Holy Spirit, God, world without end.

Frederick Richard McManus

1923-

Frederick McManus was born in Lynn, Massachusetts, in 1923. He attended Holy Cross for two years, then went to St. John's Seminary, Brighton, from which he was ordained a priest in 1947. He went to Catholic University for graduate studies receiving his doctorate in Canon Law in 1954. He taught at St. John's from 1954 to 1958, when he received an appointment as professor of canon law at Catholic University, where he has taught ever since.

In the years before Vatican II McManus was a most unusual combination: a canon lawyer who had a keen appreciation for the goals of the liturgical movement. He resolved in his own person (and thereby helped hundreds of others to resolve) the tension between liturgy and rubrics. As editor of The Jurist *and associate editor of* Worship, *he provided the model for a new kind of canonist, one who changed from being part of the problem to being part of the solution in the drive to renew Catholic thought and life. His presence and activity in the Canon Law Society, The Catholic Theological Society, and the Liturgical Conference helped all of those organizations and their members to broaden their horizons to include the fuller picture of a revitalized church.*

The election of Pope John XXIII and the convocation of Vatican II came at the perfect time in McManus' career. His homework had been done and as a *peritus* was able to provide solid input especially for the reform and renewal of the liturgy. The book excerpted here has two principal parts: 1) a commentary on the first three chapters of the Vatican II Constitution on the Sacred Liturgy, and 2) a commentary on the interim directives on the New Rite of the Mass, given in the Instruction Inter Oecumenici *of September 26, 1964.*

In the introduction to this book McManus pays tribute to those who prepared the way for the liturgical reform initiated by the Council. He singles out Jungmann, Bugnini, Wagner, Vagaggini, Schmidt, Bonet, Martimort, Gy, Fischer, Diekmann, Hänggi, Dirks, and Nabuco. Let it simply be noted that his own name deserves a prominent place on that list.

The following selection is his commentary on the second chapter of the Vatican II Constitution, which deals with "The Most Sacred Mystery of the Eucharist." The McManus trademark is evident throughout: attention to detail, while always maintaining the larger picture, the purpose which the entire Council was aiming at. He belongs to a rare breed that might be called "balanced revolutionaries," advocates of change who consistently know the why and how of change without falling prey to extremism. On the one hand, he was convinced that "the Council was indeed only a beginning, but that in 1967 even that beginning is not understood." On the other hand, "the frustrations caused by inaction have inevitably led to clandestine liturgical innovations, sometimes naive, always impatient—but surely a lesser evil than apathy or rejection."

In the period of tension right after the Council, when this book appeared, it was one of the few that looked past the temporary discomforts of change to an enriched future built on the teachings of Vatican II. Proper understanding would solve many of the problems; "the need remains, and grows greater, to explore the meaning of the Council's words and deeds." Few Americans have contributed more to meeting that need than Fr. McManus.

SACRAMENTAL LITURGY

PART I

THE CONSTITUTION ON THE SACRED LITURGY

THE TITLE OF THE CONSTITUTION

To begin, it perhaps should be noted that the title given to this conciliar document—"Constitution on the Sacred Liturgy"—is not entirely accurate. Although it is a Constitution on the Sacred Liturgy in the sense that it contains doctrine, principles and norms applicable to the sacred worship of the whole Church, in its practical norms it deals directly with the Roman rite alone. Since this was done deliberately with an explanation and justification given in the opening paragraphs (Introduction, Article 3), it does not represent any defect in the Constitution itself or in the purpose of the Council.

In fact it is the Roman rite (and especially the Roman rite when it is taken in its broadest sense as embracing all Latin rites related to the Roman) which today stands most in need of renewal and reform. In addition, the facts that the vast majority of Christians in communion with the Bishop of Rome follow the Roman rite, and that it is within the Roman rite that the liturgical movement has attained its present maturity, explain clearly why the Second Vatican Council was able first to undertake the restoration of the liturgy in terms of the Roman rite, and even to employ the broader title "Constitution on the Sacred Liturgy," as it would be most generally understood.

Of greater importance are the words which precede the title of the Constitution. These were prefixed to the document for the first time when it was examined in the public session of December 4, 1963, before its approval and promulgation. In the context of the lengthy debate on the collegiality of the bishops, there is special significance to the heading: "Paul,

Bishop, Servant of the Servants of God, together with the Fathers of the Council."

This expression is in sharp contrast to the practice at certain other general councils, at which or after which conciliar enactments were promulgated in the form of apostolic constitutions, proceeding as it were solely from the authority of the Bishop of Rome.

To appreciate the importance of this deliberate effort to preserve the nature of the Council, with its necessarily collegial character, and not to prejudice the doctrinal or disciplinary expression of collegiality in subsequent documents of the Council, the text of promulgation—coming at the end of the Constitution on the Sacred Liturgy—should also be mentioned.

In accordance with the practice of medieval councils held in Rome and the practice of the First Vatican Council, the *Ordo* of this Council both in its first and in its second edition (by authority of Pope John XXIII and Pope Paul VI, respectively) required the use of the following formula: "and We, the sacred Council approving, decree . . ." In the public session of December 4, however, this formula was suppressed and Pope Paul VI, having heard the results of the vote of the Fathers—2147 in favor, 4 against—proclaimed:

> In the name of the holy and undivided Trinity, the Father and the Son and the Holy Spirit. The decrees which have now been read in this sacred and universal Second Vatican Synod, lawfully assembled, have pleased the Fathers.
>
> And We, by the Apostolic power given to Us by Christ, together with the venerable Fathers, in the Holy Spirit approve, decree and enact these decrees, and command that what has been enacted in the Synod be promulgated for the glory of God.

Since these words, spoken by the Pope and attached to the document, are intended to express the assent of the Pope given after the other Fathers of the Council had manifested their will by vote, the choice of its phraseology depended upon Pope Paul himself. It therefore may be interpreted as representing the clear mind of Pope Paul carefully to respect the collegiality of the bishops assembled in council even before the development of this question in Chapter III of the Constitution on the Church. The manner of promulgation of the Constitution on the Sacred Liturgy thus opened the way to the further deliberations and decisions of the Second Vatican Council concerning the nature of the Church and of the episcopate.

INTRODUCTION

1. Four-point program for the Council. The four aims expressed in this introductory paragraph are the aims of the Council itself, according to the broad scope laid down by Pope John XXIII in calling the Council and in initiating its work in his address of October 11, 1962. The first two aims are pastoral, the other two ecumenical. The first aim is to stimulate the Christian life of the faithful—the inner renewal of the Church. The next is adaptation and accommodation of all the ways and disciplines of the Church that are subject to change and development. The third aim is ecumenical, directed toward the fostering of unity and, rather than speak of "separated brethren," the Council carefully chooses to refer to "all who believe in Christ." Finally and ultimately, the Council turns to all mankind, to those who do not believe in Christ and do not have the name of Christian, and seeks to announce the message of salvation to them.

The point of this paragraph is, of course, that each of the aims of the Council is served directly and immediately by undertaking the reform and promotion of the liturgy in the Constitution which these words introduce. In adopting the expressions "reform" and "promotion" of the liturgy, the Council employs a distinction which runs through the entire Constitution on the Liturgy and especially through the first chapter of general principles.

The Latin term *"instauratio"* is customarily translated as "restoration," but this inevitably suggests a return to earlier practice, without the necessary complementary notions: (a) accommodation to present circumstances and conditions; and (b) the never-ending development of liturgical forms. For this reason the term is best expressed in English by "reform"; it embraces the entire program of reappraisal and revision of rites and prayers which the Constitution commands.

Of equal importance, as will be evident in Chapter I, is the program of "promotion." This latter has reference to what is commonly called the liturgical movement or apostolate—the whole complex of endeavors to teach the meaning of the Eucharist and all the celebrations which depend upon it, to take full advantage of the didactic and formative influences of the liturgy, to develop the fullest active and sincere participation of all the people in the services of worship, to stir up the faith and the holiness of the people of God.

* * * * *

3. *Practical principles and norms.* From the very beginning it should be clear that the entire Constitution on the Sacred Liturgy issued by the Second Vatican Council will include basic principles with regard to the nature of the Liturgy, its present need for revision, and the whole effort to foster a dynamic worship. These principles, called "higher principles," were proposed in a most general way by Pope John XXIII as the scope of the Council's work in the field of sacred liturgy, when he issued the new Code of Rubrics in the summer of 1960.

Some of these principles constitute the doctrine of the liturgy, particularly in the light of recent biblical, catechetical, patristic and liturgical studies. Other principles, of a concrete and disciplinary character, are known from the nature, composition, origin and development of rites and parts of rites—but above all with a view to the pastoral concerns of liturgical celebration.

The general and broad principles are then reduced to practical norms, which have disciplinary and legal force. For the most part, the Council does not descend to particulars; rather it gives a general mandate to be put into execution by organs designated by the chief bishop and by the respective bodies of bishops. Nevertheless, in some instances, such as the extension of concelebration and the concession of the vernacular languages, the Constitution does provide specific detail—because of the intrinsic gravity of the particular matter, because of the long-standing practice now in need of revision, or because of the expectation that without a conciliar decree the desired reform would not in fact be undertaken.

In the first period of the Council, during the fall of 1962, when the draft version of this Constitution was debated by the Fathers of the Council, a serious objection was raised, to the effect that a general council should not undertake to consider the specifics of reforming a single rite, namely, the Roman rite.

On the one hand, this was a valid objection: the preponderance in numbers of the Fathers of the Council belonging to the Roman rite inevitably led to a one-sided treatment of many issues and, for that matter, it is not evident that members of other rites should participate in the particular discussion of the Roman reform. On the other hand, objections of this kind were evidently raised less out of consideration for the Oriental rites than from a desire to delay or defeat the Constitution itself. In any event, the Fathers from the Oriental Churches were the first to declare their willingness to consider this document as a suitable and worthy Constitution to emanate from an ecumenical council, and they readily recognized that its general principles have meaning for the whole Church and for all rites.

This is in fact the sense of the second paragraph of Article 3, that the broad principles and norms may be applied to all rites, while the practical norms are ordinarily directed to the Roman rite alone. What principles are generally applicable and what disciplinary or practical norms refer strictly to the Roman rite must be determined in individual cases.

According to the text of Article 3, the practical norms apply to the Roman rite taken in the strict sense and not to other rites, whether Latin or Oriental, "except for those [norms] which, in the very nature of things, affect other rites as well." Obviously, fewer practical norms given in the Constitution will be applicable to the Oriental rites than to the Latin rites which are derived from or related to the Roman rite in one way or another. With regard to the Latin rites other than the Roman rite, it is possible to invoke the principle employed in the provisional liturgical reform of 1960 (in the motu proprio introducing the new code of rubrics), namely, that they should adopt the reform of the Roman rite only in those matters which are not strictly proper to their own rite.

As is indicated in the next article of the Constitution, the Council desires the reform of all the rites of the Church in accordance with modern pastoral considerations, to the extent that this reform is necessary. Such a liturgical restoration should therefore be considered by the non-Roman Latin rites, as is immediately and directly evident, and by the various Oriental rites. It goes without saying that the practical norms concerning the fostering and promotion of the liturgy, of liturgical understanding and participation, apply equally to all the rites of the Church.

4. *Equal dignity of all rites.* In addition to the matter just mentioned (the reform of all the rites of the Church), over and above the question pertaining to the Roman rite which are directly considered in the present Constitution, this article makes two important points:

(1) The Council most solemnly declares the equality in rank and dignity of all lawfully acknowledged rites, which should be preserved and fostered. This is the first instance of the explicit recognition of the rites, particularly the Oriental rites, which the Church in council must solemnly make. The acknowledgement implies a promise and an undertaking to preserve faithfully all the rites with their spiritual, constitutional, theological, canonical and liturgical traditions. Because similar undertakings, made repeatedly by the popes of recent times, have been contradicted in practice, the Council could not too soon or too often make this point—and, in other contexts, provide realistic guarantees that the Church's will and promise will be fulfilled.

(2) The expression "all lawfully acknowledged rites" has significance because it represents a variation from the draft version of the text. In the original there was recognition of all rites "lawfully in use." The change (in the Latin, from *vigentes* to *agnitos*) indicates the desire of the Council to leave the door open to the development of new rites in the Church.

Later provisions of the Constitution allow for profound and radical adaptations and accommodations of the Roman rite (especially as envisioned in Article 40 of Chapter I) according to the diversity of peoples and traditions. Here, however, there is contemplated at least the possibility of the creation or evolution of an entirely new rite, which would have equal standing with the Roman rite, the other non-Roman Latin rites, and the Oriental rites. This does not preclude, of course, the adoption of rites other than the Roman in accordance with the needs of different regions, nor does it actually propose the establishment of rites distinct from the Roman, but it deliberately opens the door to such developments.

CHAPTER I

GENERAL PRINCIPLES FOR THE RESTORATION AND PROMOTION OF THE SACRED LITURGY

1. The Nature of the Sacred Liturgy and Its Importance in the Church's Life

9. Liturgy and the other activities of the Church. The statement that the liturgy does not exhaust the entire activity of the Church recalls the teaching of Pope Pius XII in his address at the conclusion of the International Congress of Pastoral Liturgy held in Assisi and Rome in September, 1956. The purpose of the late Pope, however, seemed to be to contradict any suggestions that the liturgy absorbs or should absorb all other functions and actions in the life of the Church, from preaching and catechesis to the works of charity. Progress from this position of 1956 is evident in the teaching of the Council.

While the present paragraph maintains the distinction between the liturgy and the other activities of the Church, the question is raised for a different purpose, namely, to emphasize that the liturgy is the summit towards which all the other activities of the Church are directed—as the next article states clearly. Perhaps it should also be noted that the invitation to all the works of charity, piety and the apostolate, of which Article 9 speaks, is extended within the liturgy as well as outside it, since it is in the assembly of the faithful that the individual Christian dedicates and commits himself to the integral Christian life.

* * * * *

235

13. The place of popular devotions. The literal translation of the Latin text here rendered as "popular devotions" is "pious exercises." The latter expression, which is almost unintelligible if not repugnant in English, was employed in the September 3, 1958, Instruction of the Congregation of Rites in order to embrace the whole range of "all religious forms which lay outside the liturgy in the strict sense of that word . . . not only . . . private prayer . . . but all forms of prayer which occur in common, even if held in a church under the direction of an authorized minister, as long as they are not contained in the Roman books," to quote the words of Josef Jungmann.

The Constitution on the Liturgy does not deal directly with the issue of the greater or lesser relationship of devotional practices, both public and private, with the official liturgy—official in the sense, that is, that it can be recognized by its inclusion in the authorized liturgical books. Unfortunately, as Jungmann and others have pointed out, the 1958 Instruction neglected to emphasize the teaching of Pius XII in the encyclicals *Mediator Dei* (1947) and *Musicae Sacrae Disciplina* (1955).

The use of the word "norms" in the proviso that popular devotional practices deserve commendation only if they are in conformity with the "laws" of the Church is not a substantial addition. Nevertheless, if laws are taken in a narrower sense, norms are broad principles, particularly the principles of the Constitution on the Sacred Liturgy, with which the popular devotional practices must be in harmony. An example of such a norm, of the greatest significance, is to be found in the third paragraph of Article 13.

Instances of popular devotions commended by the Apostolic See may be found in the encyclical *Mediator Dei* (nos. 172-185). Similarly, the Code of Canon Law directs the observance of certain such practices on occasion, for example, spiritual retreats by priests and seminarians (canons 126, 1367).

In the second paragraph of this article, the Latin for the phrase "sacred exercise of particular churches" has become clearer in translation. The reference is to devotions celebrated according to the custom of individual places or according to books authorized by the bishop of the individual church (diocese). The fullness of such a development is seen, for example, in the diocesan "song-books" of Germany, according to which forms of public worship are celebrated under the leadership of the bishop or of the priest who takes the bishop's place at the head of the assembly of the faithful.

There is nothing to prevent the development of such forms of sacred worship in the most diverse ways, whether in the individual churches or in the different regions or countries. The important thing is the recognition of their special dignity. This carries with it the recognition of a possible evolution, not unlike that treated in Articles 37-40 of this Chapter, whereby rites related to and parallel to the strict liturgy arise. The Council, moreover, in no way prejudges the controverted question of whether such celebrations of worship are to be considered a truly liturgical observance when they are carried out under the authority of the bishop—that is, as a kind of diocesan liturgy or liturgy of second order.

In virtue of the third paragraph of Article 13, a long, hard look at existing popular devotions, particularly those which are celebrated in common by the faithful led by the priest, is required. This paragraph goes far beyond the statement of Pope Pius XII in the encyclical *Mediator Dei* to the effect that harmony with the sacred liturgy should be considered the criterion of devotional practices (no. 184; see no. 181).

The Council clearly provides norms by which existing devotions (such as evening observances, holy hours, novenas, etc.) should be reappraised: (a) harmony with the liturgical seasons (an easily violated rule); (b) conformity to the liturgy itself and certainly not opposition to its celebration; (c) derivation from the liturgy, that is, at least a broad observance of the liturgical pattern of common worship, its hierarchical, communal, pastoral, didactic shape (see, for example, Articles 24, 26, 30, 34, 35); (d) encouragement by the devotional practices of popular participation in the liturgy itself, for example, frequent reception of the holy Eucharist.

Among current devotional developments, the so-called Bible services are certainly in complete harmony with the sacred liturgy, and for this reason they are specifically commended by the Council in Article 35, § 4.

II. The Promotion of Liturgical Instruction and Active Participation

14. Participation and its prerequisites. Any commentary upon the Constitution on the Sacred Liturgy must early face up to the fact that it is less a disciplinary enactment in the usual understanding than a pastoral document filled with substantial statements of doctrine and inculcating a fresh spirit in the exercise of the pastoral ministry. It is certainly at the same time a true, juridical, legislative enactment emanating from the highest authority in the Church, the general Council constituted by the chief bishop and the other bishops.

The charge of excessive legalism in the practice of the Latin Church has no justification if we look merely to the advantages in clarity and precision of legal statements; these are all to the good. Similarly, the charge of legalism is not justified if the interpretation of law in strict or narrow terms is intended again to give absolute precision to the words of authority and, even better, to relieve consciences from excessive burdens seemingly imposed by inadequately drawn laws or laws which have ceased to have validity in changed circumstances.

Nevertheless, in liturgical matters especially there is the gravest danger of legalism, in the past taking the form of rubricism, now taking the form of a negation of obligation unless a norm is stated as a written canon.

Beginning with Article 14, the Constitution on the Sacred Liturgy contains many doctrinal and pastoral exhortations, but also many norms for pastoral action. In the nature of things, the latter have to be expressed in rather general terms—the Council cannot direct exactly how many minutes or hours of instruction should be given to the faithful in a given parish in a given year, nor can it determine the exact rate or progress in a particular congregation from the minimum of liturgical participation, required everywhere by the nature of public worship, to that measure of full, active and conscious participation which pastoral zeal may achieve.

Thus it is necessary to say, once for all, that the broad directives contained in the Constitution do present a norm for the upright conscience, particularly for pastors and all who have the care of souls. The degree of gravity of this obligation can only be determined from the language solemnly used in the different articles of the Constitution. At the same time, the fulfillment of the expectations of the Council should be prompted by a sincere will to achieve in holier fashion the worship of God by Christ in his members.

These observations have special application, beginning with Article 14, to the directives for the promotion of liturgical understanding and liturgical participation by all the members of the Church, irrespective of the distinct question of liturgical reform of rites.

The formal statement that full and active participation by all the people is the primary and indispensable source from which the faithful are to derive a true Christian spirit is taken, of course, from the text of Pope St. Pius X in *Tra le sollecitudini* (no. 3) of November 22, 1903. As the primary and indispensable source, this active participation, in the view of the Council, is to be considered before all else as the goal: (a) not only of the reform of liturgical rites, (b) but also of the promotion of the sacred liturgy. The latter is the immediate purpose of the section of Chapter I running from Article 14 to Article 20.

In this section, Articles 15 to 18 are immediately directed toward the liturgical education of the clergy, since, as both Article 15 and Article 19 indicate strongly, the promotion of liturgical understanding on the part of the people and their full participation is a chief duty of the pastor of souls.

In the following articles, a successive development can be noted: Article 15 deals with the education of professors of liturgy, who in turn impart instruction to candidates for the clergy; Articles 16 and 17 are devoted to instruction in the liturgy and its celebration in seminaries and houses of religious; Article 18 deals with the post-ordination education of the secular and religious clergy who are already engaged in the pastoral ministry. With Article 19, the Constitution takes up the application of all this in the promotion of the liturgical instruction of the faithful and their active participation.

15. Trained professors for liturgy. Since it is obvious that professors of the science of liturgy in ecclesiastical institutions must have the same technical and scientific background that would be demanded in other disciplines, the Council here provides for and requires the proper education of such professors. Needless to say, such higher education requires the development of a greater number of opportunities in academic institutions. It also requires a period of time for the training of future professors and some interim arrangement for those now teaching liturgy in seminaries and similar institutions to obtain further training.

Obviously, the preparation of professors should be in accordance with the whole intent and purpose of the Constitution, certainly more than an education in the history or law of the liturgy where the intent of the Constitution to promote a pastoral sense of liturgy is so evident. Far from contradicting the pastoral purpose of the document, this requirement of scientific background and training is the only sure foundation for future development. Article 16, dealing with the actual study of the liturgy in seminaries and religious houses of study, indicates the kind of training needed for professors in this field.

The institutions of higher learning to which reference is made in Article 15 may be of different kinds; some, of course, already exist. They may be special institutes formally constituted as such and simply attached to a theological faculty. This relationship or affiliation, which may vary in different cases, prevents the excessive duplication of courses, for example, in sacramental theology, in scripture, etc., and provides a firmer basis for the granting of academic degrees and diplomas. Similarly, an institute of this kind could be established as an autonomous entity, with a broader range of facilities, courses, etc. Finally, a simpler solution, in circumstances which do not permit a more elaborate program, is the constitution of a department or section for liturgical studies within a theological faculty itself.

In all these instances, however, the specialized institute for higher liturgical studies is quite different from the "institute of pastoral liturgy" mentioned in Article 44 of this Chapter. The latter is conceived as a center for pastoral research and promotion, whereas Article 15 is directly concerned with the education of professors in academic institutes devoted to liturgical studies.

16. The place of liturgy in the seminary. This article deals with two distinct questions: (a) the formal teaching of the science of liturgy in seminaries, religious houses of study, and theological faculties; and (b) the relation and integration of other ecclesiastical disciplines and the study of the liturgy.

The broad background of this article is of course the tremendous development that has taken place in the study of the liturgy, reflecting both scholarly research and widespread pastoral experience. In the description given of the kind of course to be taught for the future, the operative words are *theological, spiritual, pastoral* aspects, since in the past there has generally been a more than adequate treatment of the juridical or rubrical aspect of the liturgy and, at least in many seminaries and similar institutions, some attempt to give a historical survey of the matter.

In canon 1365, § 2, of the Code of Canon Law, the study of liturgy is listed as a required subject for the theological course in seminaries. Until recent years, this was felt to refer to the course in the manner of celebration, that is, the study of liturgical legislation and more especially the rubrics.

Not only does the present article of the Constitution change the character of this seminary discipline, it indicates that the course must be considered as "compulsory and major" (in the Latin text, the study of the liturgy is to be counted *"inter disciplinas necessarias et potiores"*). This increased emphasis upon the study of the liturgy does not in itself require that liturgy should be studied for as many class hours as dogmatic theology, for example. Nevertheless, in order to be counted among the more important subjects, it should be required at least for one hour a week throughout the four years of the theological program; this explanation of the meaning of Article 16 was presented to the bishops before their vote.

With regard to theological faculties, that is, schools with courses leading to academic degrees in sacred theology, up until the present time the study of the liturgy has been counted as one of the auxiliary courses, along with such things as biblical Greek and archaeology. This disposition was made in the

Ordinationes issued by the Sacred Congregation of Seminaries on June 12, 1931. The effect of the present article is to remove the study of liturgy from the auxiliary or secondary classification and to rank it with dogmatic theology, sacred scripture, etc. Again, a conciliar constitution is no place to indicate such specific details as credit hours, etc., but the required emphasis upon the study of liturgy, understood in the terms of the Constitution, is now applicable to theological faculties as well as to seminaries.

The second matter treated in this article is of equal importance, namely, the revision of the study of all the other ecclesiastical sciences so that they are adequately related to the study of the liturgy, in order that there may be a unity in the education of the clergy, centered upon the mystery of Christ and the history of salvation, celebrated and made present in the sacred liturgy. While the Council's words refer only to clerical education, the same principles apply to all catechetical instruction.

Since at the time the Constitution on the Liturgy was debated and later amended and enacted, the Council had not yet touched questions of the reorganization of seminary studies, this Constitution goes no further on the matter touched here. Nevertheless, lest the expectation of a future thorough reappraisal of seminary studies and discipline be used as a pretext to put off this important matter, Pope Paul VI on January 25, 1964, indicated that this article had legal force as of February 16, 1964, and that its disposition should be made effective in seminary programs through curricular revision, so that the Council's regulations on this matter would be observed in the next scholastic year.

17. Liturgical life in the formation of priest and religious. The same motu proprio of January 25, 1964, indicated the necessity of putting Article 17 into effect without delay. The description given of the religious and spiritual formation of clerics is radically different from that found in canon 1367. The words of the Code of Canon Law, written in a quite different period, properly enumerate seminary exercises of devotion and worship, but neglect entirely the broad spiritual formation of the seminarian in the celebration of the liturgy. Of equal importance is the requirement by the Council that the other exercises of piety in seminaries, such as retreats, devotional services, etc., should be "imbued with the spirit of the liturgy" (cf. Article 13).

Even more noticeable is the difference in tone and intent between the statement of the Ecumenical Council and the references to spiritual formation in the recent general statutes issued by the Congregation of Religious as an appendix to the apostolic constitution *Sedes Sapientiae* (July 7, 1956; cf. Articles 37, § 1; 40, § 2, no. 1; 40, § 3, of the *statuta*). The norms for spiritual formation in the houses of religious are henceforward to be taken from the Constitution.

18. In-service aid to priests in pastoral work. The primary responsibility for the training of priests who are already engaged in the pastoral ministry rests upon the individual bishop and upon the bodies of bishops, in accordance with the authority of the latter bodies in Article 22, § 2. In addition, a similar responsibility rests upon religious superiors since, in view of the number of religious who are engaged in the pastoral ministry, the Constitution specifies that all priests, both secular and religious, are to receive help in the understanding of the liturgy and in the ways to spread this understanding to the faithful.

The suitable means to instruct the clergy will have to be explored by bishops and bodies of bishops, by national and diocesan liturgical commissions, by the authorities of seminaries and houses of religious, by voluntary agencies and institutes. Already many of the means of providing the so-called in-service training to the parochial clergy have been employed, such as study institutes, seminars, clergy conferences and training sessions, as well as different kinds of published materials, including sermon and instruction outlines, booklets and bibliographies, periodicals, etc.

It perhaps should be pointed out that strong emphasis upon the training of the future priests in the preceding articles may not be used as a reason for neglecting the education of the clergy already ministering to the faithful. Moreover, as Article 19 indicates clearly, while the responsibility of providing assistance to the clergy in this field rests with ecclesiastical superiors, the promotion of the liturgical instruction of the faithful and their active participation is an immediate and direct responsibility of all pastors of souls.

19. Leading the people to participate. The clarity or simplicity of this article on the liturgical instruction and participation of the faithful should not cause it to be passed over lightly. Its purpose is evidently to assert as strongly as possible the primacy of liturgical instruction. However important the revisions and reforms of rites which are taken up in succeeding articles of Chapter I, these are of no avail without the instruction of the faithful. Next to the very celebration of the sacred mysteries, this formation of the people is the principal pastoral duty—directly challenging the zeal and initiative of all engaged in the sacred ministry.

The preoccupation of large sections of the Constitution with liturgical reform may suggest that participation in the existing rites of the liturgy, uncorrected and unrevised, may be put off or is of secondary consideration. The tenor of Article 19 is that the faithful should be instructed without delay and that the kinds of participation, both internal and external, referred to here are to be introduced into sacred celebrations immediately.

This point is vehemently confirmed in the motu proprio of Pope Paul VI, dated January 25, 1964. Without adding anything to the norm given in this place by the Council, Pope Paul urges the fulfillment of Article 19 before touching on either the constitution of a special commission of liturgical reform or upon individual norms of the Constitution which require special mention. In other words, the chief emphasis in Pope Paul's document of execution and implementation of the Constitution was placed upon Article 19.

20. Radio and television. This article differs from the others in the section on the promotion of liturgical instruction and participation. It is an important disciplinary norm affecting all celebrations of worship which are transmitted by radio or television. The text may be compared with the lengthier norm given in the Instruction of the Congregation of Rites of September 3, 1958 (no. 74):

> Express permission of the local ordinary is required for radio or television broadcast of liturgi-

cal services or private devotions, whether these take place inside or outside of the church. The ordinary may not grant such permission unless he previously has assurance:

(a) that the singing and sacred music correspond fully to the laws of both the liturgy and sacred music;

(b) furthermore, if there is a question of televising a sacred service, that all who have a part in it are so well instructed that the celebration may take place in full conformity to the rubrics and with due dignity.

The local ordinary may grant standing permission for a broadcast to originate regularly from a given church if, after due consideration, he is certain that all the necessary requirements will be faithfully met.

75. So far as possible, television cameras should not be brought into the sanctuary. They may never be placed so close to the altar that they interfere with the sacred rites.

The camera men and technicians concerned shall conduct themselves with the gravity due the sacred place and rite, so as not to disturb in any way the devotion of those present, especially at those moments that demand utmost recollection.

The Council does not change the dispositions of the 1958 Instruction but only makes them more emphatic by its brief statement requiring that such transmissions be done with discretion and dignity. The only additional norm is that the bishop should appoint a person, clerical or lay, to lead and direct such transmissions. Since there is question here of the manner in which the sacred liturgy is celebrated on those occasions when it is to be transmitted by radio or television, the bishop who is the local ordinary of the place of transmission is meant.

Just as obviously, in such transmissions the celebration of the liturgy must be done in complete harmony with the teaching of the Council, especially as regards the participation of the people. Thus, it would be the gravest mistake to telecast a celebration of Mass at which the faithful did not respond or did not receive holy Communion. Moreover, the techniques of radio and television may be used either to clarify the nature of the liturgical celebration or to distort it; the latter occurs if the the television camera, for example, is focused on the priest celebrant during the time when attention should be drawn to the singing congregation or to a minister proclaiming a lesson.

Although it may not necessarily be true that the radio or television commentator performs the same liturgical function which is mentioned in Article 29, the importance of the commentary given can hardly be overemphasized. Naturally, since such a commentary is not heard by those who are actually engaged in the act of worship, that is, by the participants in the rite being celebrated within the church or within the place for Mass or other service, the extent of the radio or television commentary may be greater and its didactic or even catechetical development may be broader than in the so-called liturgical commentary.

III. The Reform of the Sacred Liturgy

21. *Clear and authentic signs.* Up to this point, the matters treated in Chapter I of the Constitution are not directly concerned with reform of the Roman liturgy. Consequently, as doctrine to be taught or norms to be observed, these articles need not and must not wait upon the revision of liturgical books and rites.

Beginning with Article 21, however, a very large proportion of the Constitution is concerned with specific reforms, and in many instances its implementation is dependent upon the preparation and publication of liturgical service books, detailed regulations, etc. This is particularly true of the section of Chapter I which runs from Article 21 through Article 40 and which is specifically devoted to the general principles for the restoration of the sacred liturgy. It is also the case with a large proportion of Chapters II, III, and IV—with the obvious exception of the doctrinal introductions to these chapters.

For the most part, it is easy enough to tell from the wording and context what matters have been put off until the missal, ritual, etc., for the Roman rite have been revised. At the same time and with special reference to Articles 21 to 40, it is extremely important to note the following: (a) general principles on the nature of the liturgy, valid irrespective of the forthcoming liturgical reform, are contained in the very articles which give directives for the restoration; (b) the same principles, which are directly intended by the Council as a mandate and as guidelines for the reform commission, are equally significant as indications of the emphasis to be placed in understanding and teaching the liturgy.

In other words, the very matters which the Council proposes as requiring greater stress in the reform of liturgical usages and rites should constitute the subject of teaching and exposition to the faithful. This is especially true because these matters—such as the community and educative force of the liturgy—have received insufficient treatment in the past.

The division within the broad section which begins in Article 21 is indicated in the headings which form a part of the Constitution itself. After the introduction there are: (A) General Norms (Articles 22-25); (B) Norms Drawn from the Hierarchic and Communal Nature of the Liturgy (Articles 26-32); (C) Norms Based upon the Educative and Pastoral Nature of the Liturgy (Articles 33-36); (D) Norms for Adapting the Liturgy to the Culture and Traditions of Peoples (Articles 37-40).

Article 21 itself includes a statement of two fundamental principles basic to all liturgical reform intended by the Council. The first is the so-called sacramental principle, namely, that the rites should express more clearly the holy things which they signify. The second reflects the pastoral purpose, already insisted upon in Article 14, where both liturgical instruction and liturgical restoration are directed, before all else, to the active participation of the community of the faithful.

(A) GENERAL NORMS

22. *Competent authority.* The general norms for liturgical restoration deal in succession with the hierarchical authority over the liturgy, the balance of legitimate tradition and progress

in reform, the biblical orientation of the reform, and the means to reform, namely, the revision of the Roman liturgical books.

Article 22 itself must be taken as the abrogation of canon 1257 of the Code of Canon Law. This canon reads: "It belongs to the Apostolic See alone both to order the sacred liturgy and to approve the liturgical books."

The historical antecedents of this canon are well known, at least in general. Beginning in the sixteenth century with the reservation to the Holy See of the approval of the Roman liturgical books after the Council of Trent, there was a gradual progress in greater centralized control over the texts in "official" service books. In the nineteenth century, for example, this tendency can be seen in the replacement of local French usages with Roman practices and, in a particular instance from the United States, the American use of the Roman Ritual at least from the time of the First Provincial Council of Baltimore (1829).

Canon 1257 of the 1917 Code of Canon Law implies the reservation to the Apostolic See of the right to approve even particular liturgical books, for example, rituals for individual dioceses or provinces, etc. This reservation was made explicit for the first time in the Instruction issued by the Congregation of Rites on September 3, 1958 (no. 12). Since the rites of the sacred liturgy are contained in the text and directions given in the respective service books, the reservation of approval does constitute a centralized control over the liturgical celebrations themselves.

(1) The change in the Canon Law introduced by Article 22 is evident in the first paragraph where the general regulation of the sacred liturgy is said to pertain to the Apostolic See, and, as the law may determine (*ad normam iuris*), to the bishop. It would perhaps have been more logical to have kept the two expressions parallel, either Roman Pontiff and Bishop, or Apostolic See and Episcopal See. The meaning, however, is that authority in the regulation or moderation of the sacred liturgy pertains to the chief bishop, to the Apostolic See itself, and also to the individual bishop.

The qualification placed upon the authority of the bishop is expressed only in the broadest way, that is, in accordance with the norm of law, whether this be a question of divine or human law. The singular noun, bishop, is used to indicate that this regulation of the liturgy refers to its celebration in the individual church or diocese. Thus, it is distinct from the development indicated in the second paragraph, in which the regulation of the liturgy is said to pertain also to the bodies of bishops in the various territories or regions.

(2) Since liturgical adaptations and variations within the substantial uniformity of the Roman rite can hardly be envisioned on a diocesan basis, certainly not in grave matters, the second paragraph of Article 22 determines broadly the corporate or collective authority of bodies of bishops when these are legitimately constituted on a territorial basis. In the preparation of this article, considerable difficulty was encountered because the question was debated in the Council during the fall of 1962, when the schema concerning bishops and the government of dioceses had not yet been laid before the Fathers of the Council for their consideration. This meant, in effect, that the bishops were asked to decide the terms under which the episcopal conferences or assemblies would exercise juridical authority over the sacred liturgy before they had come to the formal and constitutional question of the authority of such bodies.

The reasons for decreeing the legislative authority of these bodies without waiting for the discussion and ultimate approbation of a decree directly concerned with episcopal conferences are apparent. For one thing, the liturgical restoration and certainly the liturgical educational program are envisioned by the Constitution as depending not only on the Bishop of Rome and the individual bishop, but also upon the groups of bishops in the natural territorial divisions, especially by countries or nations. Moreover, the progress of the liturgical renewal, of primary importance to the general *aggiornamento*, could hardly be put off until the precise terms of decentralization should be determined, especially since the will of the Pope and of the vast majority of the other bishops was already certain.

The introductory phrase of Article 22, "in virtue of power conceded by the law," is designed to avoid any prejudice to the theological question of the source of this power. Whether it is something pertaining to the divine constitution of the Church or simply ecclesiastical legislation (that is, an authority conferred upon these bodies by the Ecumenical Council) is not at issue. The definition of the limits of this authority over the liturgy is mostly to be found in the present Constitution, but it is something which may be expanded or contracted in the future either by other ecumenical councils or by the Roman Pontiff.

As the text is written, the territorial bodies are referred to in the broadest terms so that the exercise of this authority would pertain to any lawfully constituted conference or council of bishops. The territorial basis might be provincial, regional in the sense of several provinces or groupings of dioceses, national, or regional in the sense of several nations or parts of nations. Although various possibilities are recognized in the 1917 Code of Canon Law in the case of councils (provincial and plenary or regional), the only such body recognized in a form less solemn than a council is the provincial conference of canon 292. Nevertheless, various episcopal bodies have been constituted in recent decades for different purposes, and such constitution, acknowledged or recognized by the Apostolic See in one way or another, suffices for the purposes of Article 22, § 2.

Even with the promulgation of the Constitution on December 4, 1963, and with the setting of its effective date of February 16, 1964, questions remained with regard to the manner of operation of such bodies, since a juridical and legislative authority had been conferred upon them by the Constitution in a way that had not been true before. In order to solve the difficulty on an interim basis, without prejudicing the exact determinations to be made in the conciliar decree on bishops and the government of dioceses (finally called "The Pastoral Office of Bishops in the Church" and promulgated in 1965), Pope Paul VI in the motu proprio of January 25, 1964, determined that for the present the authority would be possessed by *national* bodies or conferences of bishops.

Since existing national or regional conferences of bishops have been constituted in various ways, with the participation of all the bishops of the territory or of only a limited number, it was equally necessary for Pope Paul to determine the membership in such conferences. This was done by designating that those referred to in canon 292 should take part, with the right to vote, in addition to the residential bishops.

In accordance with what was proposed to the bishops in their debate upon the schema *De Episcopis* during the 1963 session of the Council, Pope Paul also determined that, for the exercise of legislative authority in liturgical matters, a two-thirds majority would be required and that balloting would be secret.

(3) The third paragraph of Article 22 does not in itself require comment. It simply restates what is so emphatically affirmed in the encyclical *Mediator Dei*: ". . . no private person has any authority to regulate external practices of this kind, which are intimately bound up with Church discipline and with the order, unity and concord of the Mystical Body and frequently even with the integrity of Catholic faith itself" (no. 58). The prohibition of Article 22, § 3, was also repeated in the motu proprio of January 25, 1964.

Nevertheless, it would be the gravest misinterpretation of this prohibition to employ it as a pretext to postpone the implementation of the Council's teaching on active congregational participation in the sacred liturgy. The Council places no inhibition whatever upon practices already lawful, and in fact requires the further development of the various forms of participation urged in the past repeatedly by the popes or required, for example, by the encyclical *Mediator Dei* and the Instruction of September 3, 1958.

There are numerous instances throughout the Constitution on the Liturgy where specific matters are committed by the Council to the authority—and to the responsibility—of the territorial bodies of bishops. These include:

(1) determination of the use of the language of the people (Article 36, § 3) and approval of the official translations (Article 36, § 4). To this may be added the specific references to the vernacular languages in the Mass (Article 54), in the other sacraments and sacramentals (Article 63a)—with additional mention of the allocutions at the begin-

ning of the rites of ordination (Article 76)—in the divine office (Article 101);

(2) promotion of studies necessary for adaptations specified in Articles 38 to 40 and the actual introduction or proposal of such adaptations;

(3) establishment of an epicsopal liturgical commission (Article 44);

(4) preparation of a particular or local ritual after the publication of the new version of the Roman Ritual (Article 63b);

(5) introduction of indigenous elements of religious initiation into the liturgy, at least in mission territories (Article 65);

(6) preparation of a rite for the celebration of matrimony (Article 77);

(7) adaptation of funeral rites according to the circumstances and traditions of the region (Article 81);

(8) adaptation of the liturgical year, after the general reform of the calendar (Article 107);

(9) encouragement of the practice of penance in accordance with the penitential elements in the Lenten liturgy (Article 110);

(10) introduction of indigenous musical forms into the liturgy, especially in mission lands (Article 119);

(11) judgment concerning the use of muscial instruments other than the pipe organ in divine worship and permission for this (Article 120);

(12) the adaptation of sacred furnishings and vestments, especially in their material and form, to the needs and customs of the region (Article 128).

In all these instances, the precise authority of the territorial body must be determined from the text and context of the respective articles of the Constitution. Articles 37 to 40 indicate the way in which adaptations are to be introduced, whether on the basis of their inclusion by way of broad direction in the revised liturgical books of the Roman rite or whether, after suitable study and experiment, they are to be introduced only upon the proposal of the territorial authorities, with the consent of the Apostolic See.

23. The relation of tradition to change. With the possession of authority in these matters determined, the Council in the present article gives the first broad norm with regard to revisions of rites. The prior investigation and study which are mentioned oblige not only the commission of reform constituted by the Pope, but also any body or commission engaged in such revisions or adaptations in different regions.

To a certain extent, the limitations set down in Article 23 affect the norm of pastoral usefulness set elsewhere as the chief determining factor in liturgical reform. In other words, the reform does not envision the creation of entirely new rites merely because they seem to satisfy the needs of the present time, but rather an organic development of existing forms. On the one hand, such a rule is justified by respect for the goodness of past developments. On the other hand, it guarantees a better evolution of the liturgy for the future.

The last sentence of Article 23 should not be taken to call into question in any way the legitimate presence in a single territory of different rites, such as the Byzantine, which may exist alongside the Roman rite. The equality of rites is sufficiently asserted in the introduction, Article 4.

In general, what is intended by the present article can be seen in the restoration of the Holy Week services which became effective in 1965. Although the intelligent and active participation of the people was the principal reason and criterion for the reform, each specific change or restoration had some precedent in the Roman or non-Roman rites of the West. It is possible to describe some characteristics of the Roman rite which have proved their worth and should be maintained, for example, the avoidance of repetitions of prayers and verses, the general form of prefaces and collects, etc.

The reference in Article 23 is to recent instances of experimentation, chiefly through the reform of the Roman liturgical books or through indults conceded for particular regions. For the future, the evolution of the rite is to be governed by the norms for adaptation found at the end of this section (Articles 37-40), once the general reform of the Roman books is completed. Needless to say, this is necessarily to be based upon study and experimentation (Article 40, 3).

24. Bible and liturgy. No one could quarrel with the intentions of this article concerning the importance of sacred scripture in the liturgy and in the progressive development of the liturgy. It has, however, a negative application, since whatever is in the liturgical forms at present that may conflict with the biblical spirit should be eliminated. An instance of this may be found in some of the hymns introduced into the divine office in modern times (cf. Article 93).

25. Revision of liturgical books. The norm of this article governs the whole liturgical restoration, since in fact the textual revision of the liturgical books has been the means ordinarily used to bring about official changes in the liturgy. This article may be compared with the decree issued by the Council of Trent (on its very last day, December 4, 1563), in which the revision of the missal and breviary, already underway at that time, was entrusted to the Roman Pontiff.

The liturgical books of the Roman rite include the missal, ritual, pontifical and breviary, together with several subsidiary books. The correction of these books includes a thorough revision of all liturgical laws. Because of the labor involved in this task, it was impossible for the Council to set a time limit, other than to say that the work should be done as quickly as possible. This should not be taken as a reflection upon the Roman Pontiff or a kind of command given to him, but as a clear indication that the Council, that is, the Pope and the other Fathers, agreed on the necessity of prompt action with regard to the reform.

The body envisioned to perform this task should be representative, including not only experts in pastoral practice and liturgical science, but also bishops, at least as consultants. The preparatory commission appointed by Pope John XXIII to prepare the schema of the present Constitution was in fact representative of different regions of the world, with bishops and priests as members, and bishops and priests as consultants. The same diversity of origin and expert knowledge is required in the commission of restoration.

On January 25, 1964, Pope Paul VI established the special commission referred to in this article to implement the Constitution, particularly through the revision of the liturgical books.

(B) NORMS DRAWN FROM THE HIERARCHIC AND COMMUNAL NATURE OF THE LITURGY

26. Ordered roles in the liturgy. Beginning with Article 26, specific norms under different headings are given for the work of the postconciliar commission of reform. Under the heading of the hierarchical and communal nature of the liturgy, the preference to be given to communal celebration, the proper distribution of parts in the liturgical rites, the function of the different special ministers, the kinds of active participation by the faithful, rubrical provision for that participation, and the avoidance of any discrimination in liturgical rites are all taken up successively.

27. Preference for community celebration. It is obvious enough that certain rites, while retaining their nature as public and social worship, will have the appearance of rather private celebrations. This would be the case with the administration of certain sacramental blessings, the sacrament of penance itself, etc. In many cases it is necessary to indicate more clearly in the texts and rites themselves that there is a social aspect to all liturgical observances. This is the import of several references in the chapter on the sacraments other than the Eucharist (cf. Articles 59, 63). In many cases, however, the possibility of community celebration is neglected in favor of individual celebration, and this is the error against which the present article is directed.

Since it appeared to some of the Fathers of the Council that the preference properly indicated for communal celebration might appear to be contrary to the teaching of the Council of Trent on the legitimacy of private Masses, the second paragraph of this article was inserted. In effect, it insists even more strongly than does the first paragraph that this social and communal aspect should be manifested especially in the Mass and in the sacraments.

At the same time the public and social nature of the Mass which is celebrated privately, with perhaps no congregation present other than the server, is insinuated by the espression, "even though every Mass has of itself a public and social nature." Thus the teaching of Trent is safeguarded, but all the emphasis is placed in the other direction, toward a realization both in revision of rites and in practice of the necessarily hierarchical and communal nature of the Christian liturgy.

28. Distribution of roles. This article is intended to correct a mistaken duplication found in many rites, of which the most obvious and unfortunate instance was the requirement that the celebrating priest at sung Mass should recite the parts of the sacred ministers and of the congregation or choir. In the Holy Week restoration and in the new code of rubrics (no. 473), a first step had been taken to correct this error: "in sung Masses, all that is sung or recited by the deacon, subdeacon, or lector, in virtue of his proper office, is omitted by the celebrant."

Although the implementation of this article appears to be simple enough even in the existing rites of the liturgy, its complete application depends upon the appearance of the revised liturgical books or of specific norms.

The basis for determining the actual distribution of roles in the sacred rites should be the "nature of the rite and the principles of liturgy." It may be expected, in accordance with Article 31, that the reformed liturgical books will give definite direction indicating the distribution of roles. Already this has been done to a certain extent in formal written legislation issued by the Congregation of Rites, namely, in the 1958 Instruction (cf. nos. 25, 31-32).

Nevertheless, the more important basis for determining this distribution of parts is not written legislation or rubrical statement, but the very nature of the parts of the rite. Generally, it will be evident from the nature, composition, origin and history of the individual text to whom it properly pertains.

The question may be asked, at least for the future, whether it is suitable for the celebrating priest to sing certain parts of the liturgy which properly are the community's song. In fact, the norm of Article 28 need not be applied so rigidly as to prevent the celebrant from joining with the congregation in its chant or other action. What is contrary to the norm would be any duplication on the part of the celebrant or his taking part, for example, in a response made to his own greeting.

29. Office of servers, lectors, commentators and choir. This article enlarges upon and corrects what had been stated in the Instruction of September 3, 1958 (no. 93). There the enumeration of those who perform a true liturgical ministry (in addition to the ordained ministers) extended only so far as service at the altar and singing in a formally constituted choir, with the apparent exclusion of such other persons as commentators, readers and women who sing in a special choir.

The text of the Constitution extends the concept of "genuine liturgical function" to all these participants. The more important point to be made is this: what objectively constitutes a special liturgical function or ministry is rather to be determined from the nature of the rite than from some juridical enumeration. The rule or principle involved is that, over and above the genuine liturgical function which is the past of the whole body of the faithful, not only the clergy but certain members of the faithful may have particular and specialized roles to play. The principal roles of this kind are enumerated by Article 29.

Perhaps the most important thing to note about this article and the one following is that they pertain much less to the liturgical reform than to the general restoration of liturgical activity. In Article 29, once the declaration has been made with regard to the genuine liturgical function of servers, lectors, commentators and choir members, the responsibility of these persons to perform their office well and the responsibility of pastors of souls, teachers, etc., to train such participants well form the substance of the Council's decree. These injunctions are applicable quite apart from any liturgical reform.

30. Parts proper to the people. Again, what is contained in Article 30 is immediately directed toward the reform of the liturgical rites, to the extent that the parts listed in the article should be attributed to the people for their active participation. At the same time, the article declares authoritatively what parts of the rites, reformed or unreformed, actually do pertain to the people. While this is obvious enough in the case of the simple acclamations and responses, the addition of psalmody, antiphons and songs in general is of the greatest importance.

The terms of the Constitution in no way suppress the role of special choirs of singers, which are in fact referred to in the preceding article as exercising a particular and specialized ministry. The role of the choirs, however, must never be taken to obliterate or minimize the participation of the people in the common song; this is of course assured when the people alternate with the choir even in more difficult chants, or sing with the choir in part music especially composed for congregation and choir.

The concluding sentence of the present article, referring to the silence of the faithful, should be compared with the Instruction of the Congregation of Rites of September 3, 1958, which urges a holy silence on the part of the people (and the choir of singers) after the consecration (no. 27f). Similarly, the people should remain silent (and attentive) during the reading of the lessons of holy Mass, and for the future, other opportunities for silence, without creating any divorce of the individual from the community of worshipers, may be suitably introduced. An instance is the silent period of prayer before the collect and similar prayers.

It should not be necessary to add that everything that is referred to in this article represents the fulfillment of the so-called sacramental principle. All these external actions and sounds are intended to be reflective of the interior piety and devotion of the faithful and intended as well to stir up their faith and holiness.

31. Practical directive. This article simply places in the form of a directive to the new commission of restoration the rule already observed in the revision of liturgical books undertaken by the commission of Pope Pius XII (instituted in 1948). Thus, in the restored Holy Week services, in Part II of the Roman Pontifical, and in the 1962 rite of adult baptism, clear indication of the parts of the faithful is given in the rubrics.

32. No liturgical discrimination. The present article expresses, perhaps more forcefully, what is already found in canon 1263 of the Code of Canon Law and in the Ceremonial of Bishops (Book I, chapter 13, no. 13) with regard to special places for civil authorities and for no others. Perhaps the most blatant instance of distinction or discrimination on the basis of social class or economic condition would be found in the classes of weddings and funerals in vogue in some places.

The extent to which the civil authorities may be shown liturgical privileges depends upon the relationship of the Church to the given civil authority. The liturgical law, elaborated by many decrees, is that special places may be given to the civil authorities, but that these should be outside the presbyterium or sanctuary.

(C) NORMS BASED UPON THE EDUCATIVE AND PASTORAL NATURE OF THE LITURGY

33. Formative role of the liturgy. Some have made the didactic, educative and formative nature of the liturgy so secondary in relationship to the manifestation of cult toward God that the former appears to be incidental. The Council effectively rejects this view in Article 33 by insisting that the entire liturgy, in all its signs and parts, has this formative character. This is also expressed, in relationship to the sacraments and the sacramentals, in the introduction to Chapter III (Articles 59-60).

This does not mean in any way that the liturgy is the sole teaching force in the Church, but rather that it is the principal and central source of Christian formation, to which all other didactic efforts in the Church should be related. Nor does it mean in the least that the liturgy should be turned into any kind of classroom experience or formal instruction; the liturgy teaches through its celebration and through the signs, words, deeds and material things, by which it expresses the worship of God and the sanctification of God's people.

34. Qualities desired in the rites. Precedents for the abbreviation and simplification of sacred rites may be found in the recent restoration of the services of Holy Week and of Part II of the Roman Pontifical. There are many examples of useless repetitions in sacred rites, such as the distinct introduction and conclusion of each of the little hours even when these are said or sung one after the other, or the repetition of the Confiteor in anointing of the sick, Viaticum, and the conferral of the apostolic blessing, when these rites are celebrated together.

It need not be pointed out at any length that in order to be "within the people's powers of comprehension" the revision of rites must always be done in a manner to satisfy the needs of the largest number of the faithful, and can never be completely suited to the extremes of understanding in the body of the faithful. No one would be so unrealistic as to think that the rites can be sufficiently simplified as to require no explanation or study. It is nonetheless quite possible to correct the rites to such an extent that there will never be any deliberately obscure or misleading features in them.

Article 34 does not intend to eliminate the use or usefulness of brief commentaries or promptings during the rites. In fact, as the following article indicates, it is planned that such brief directions would become a more formal part of the rites themselves and would contribute to the clarity which Article 34 requires.

The expression "noble simplicity" has been introduced to make certain that the simplification of rites should not lead to any barrenness or dullness. A greater or lesser degree of nobility of rite (and of length of the services) will always be possible by celebrating on occasion the sung liturgy, the spoken or recited liturgy, or combinations of the two. What is intended is an evangelical simplicity which will carry with it its own excellence and beauty. What should be avoided and corrected, on the other hand, is the complexity and excessive length of many rites, especially of certain sacraments and major sacramentals.

35. Ministry of the word.

(1) The specific application of the first paragraph of Article 35 is found for holy Mass in Article 51 and for the divine office in Article 92a. Over and above this, the use of scripture readings as a part of sacramental rites in general is desirable. Apart from the administration of those sacramentals which are of very minor significance, there is no reason why the reading of the Word of God should not introduce almost every rite. No general rule can be laid down for this and much depends upon circumstances, but even apart from the reforms

contemplated in this article and section of Chapter I, the reading of holy scripture at the beginning of sacramental rites may be encouraged, certainly as much as preliminary exhortations and explanations are recommended (Roman Ritual, tit. I, no. 10).

(2) The second paragraph of this article expands upon efforts made in recent years to integrate the homily or sermon with the liturgical rite, for example, in the Mass of Holy Thursday of the restored Holy Week services, and in the new code of rubrics (no. 474). The application to the celebration of Mass may be found in Article 53. Here the place of preaching in liturgical services in general is emphasized, and the forthcoming reform should indicate specifically the many possible occasions for preaching in the liturgy.

(3) The liturgical catechesis referred to in the third paragraph may be of the most diverse character. It includes the instruction properly given at the beginning of sacred rites by the celebrant or another, any more directly liturgical exposition that might be included in an homily, and the brief directives given in the course of sacred rites in order to guide the attention of the faithful and to prompt them to liturgical participation both internal and external.

The celebrant himself gives such comments or directives in the most formal way, for example, in the invitation to prayer, *Oremus*, which may be elaborated along the lines of the invitation to prayer in the Good Friday rites. The most obvious instance of the "proper minister" is the deacon who dismisses the people, directs them to kneel or stand, tells them to bow their heads in prayer, and according to the example of rites other than the Roman, may frequently intervene as the leader of the people. Finally, such directives and promptings are given by a distinct commentator, whether clerical or lay, whose office is recognized as official and liturgical in Article 29.

It is the intention of the Council that the brief directives should not be confined to the highly formalized ones now allotted to the celebrant or the deacon in the Roman rite, but should be somewhat flexible. Thus the rubrics should be so drawn as to indicate both the appropriate times for such interventions, at least by way of example, and the point to be made, but should allow the precise formulation of such directives to be left free.

This last statement should not be understood as a contradiction of the prudent requirement made by the Congregation of Rites in its Instruction of September 3, 1958, according to which there should be the most careful preparation of any comments to be made: "The explanations and directions to be given by the commentator should be prepared in writing; they should be few and clearly to the point, and spoken at fitting times and in a moderate tone of voice; . . . they should in every respect be a help and not a hindrance to the piety of the faithful" (no. 96c.).

(4) The literal translation of the expression used for bible services is "sacred celebration of the word of God." Although this may be a cumbersome manner of describing such services in English, its full meaning should be considered. The Council deliberately rejected the word "paraliturgical," which has been used in certain countries up until the last few years to describe such services which bear a resemblance to the official liturgy. In fact, if the word has any justification, it should be said that all public devotions are paraliturgical (Article 13). Rather the Council chose to speak of these as full celebrations, obviously celebrations of worship in which there would be a strong biblical orientation.

The form of such bible services is not specified. Ordinarily, they consist of (a) readings from holy scripture; (b) common singing of psalm verses or hymns between the readings; (c) brief homily; (d) prayer. The series of such readings and common song and prayer may be preceded by a kind of entrance rite and concluded by some sacramental action. The relationship of such bible services to the hour of matins in the divine office and to the liturgy of the Word in the eucharistic celebration is obvious.

The fourth paragraph of Article 35 is out of place in the present section of the Constitution, since it does not refer to future reform of the Roman rite but rather to the Council's encouragement of a practice that is already legitimate and already widespread. In the original schema presented for the consideration of the Fathers of the Council, there was no mention of bible services, since in fact they are implied in Article 13. The present reference was added at the proposal of certain Fathers and received almost unanimous approval, as an amendment to Chapter I, in a formal vote of the Council. It thus becomes an instance of a matter, already sufficiently indicated in the Constitution by way of principle, which received this special emphasis and approbation.

Since these services have often been referred to as "bible vigils" or "biblical-liturgical vigils," the encouragement of their celebration is given in the first place for the vigils of solemn feasts. This of course does not in any way suggest a limitation on them, since they are said to be suitable for the weekdays of Advent and Lent, and for Sundays and feast days in the most general way.

A distinction should be made between the general recommendation of such services and the special importance given to them in places where a priest is regularly or temporarily absent. The bible services are everywhere desirable; they are of the greatest importance in the absence of a priest. If a deacon presides over the bible services, they may very well conclude with the administration of holy Communion, according to circumstances. In the absence of a deacon, the bishop should designate a lesser cleric or a lay person to preside and to conduct the service.

36. Language in the liturgy. Perhaps the first thing to be noted about this article, concerned with the greater use of the mother tongues in the liturgy, is that it governs the references to vernacular languages in the subsequent chapters of the Constitution. To understand it fully, it is necessary to compare it with Articles 54 (for the Eucharist), 63a (for the other sacraments and the sacramentals), 101 (for the divine office), 113 (for sacred music).

In general, the purpose of this article may be described as the widespread introduction of the vernacular languages, but in such a way as to respect the liberty of these areas where before the Council there was no broad movement toward the use of the mother tongues. The article appears as a compromise between those who would retain the Latin language in the Roman rite and the other rites of the Western Church, and those who would on principle use the vernacular languages exclusively. It therefore represents a middle course, equally satisfactory: (a) to those bishops who would begin the introduction of the mother tongues in a moderate way but without any ultimate limitation at all; and (b) to those who would respect the regional diversity in this regard while not desiring to introduce the vernacular extensively in their own dioceses.

(1) Although it is not the original language of the Roman rite by any means, the Latin language is here acknowledged to have the first or principal place, and as such it is to be retained. It may be that in some areas the retention will simply mean employing the Latin texts as the basis for translations into the vernacular, at least in the case of those parts of the Roman rite which are themselves original, such as the collects.

The reference to "Latin rites" is deliberate; in this paragraph of Article 36 there is an exception to the rule given in Article 3 that the norms of the Constitution apply directly to the Roman rite alone. And this instance of the retention of the Latin language is applicable to the Ambrosian and Mozarabic, Dominican, Carmelite and other rites.

More important, however, in this first paragraph of Article 36 is the expression, "particular law remaining in force." This refers on the one hand to the special case of the Roman-Slavonic or Glagolitic rite in which the Latin language is not used at all— this is in fact the Roman rite celebrated in Old Slavonic. On the other hand, and of wider interest, this excepting clause refers to all the concessions made by law, custom or indult, according to which languages other than Latin may be used in existing Latin rites. All the bilingual rituals for the sacraments and sacramentals come under this heading, as do the practices in many countries of celebrating high Mass with ordinary chants in the vernacular.

It may not seem that this recognition of the right to maintain existing (or future) concessions is very great in the light of the broader grants to be made later in the Constitution itself. Nevertheless, the specific approval of this expression by a vote of the Council was an important and necessary step; it represented a defeat for those who desired to suppress the concessions already made by the Apostolic See or the usages which were justified by longstanding custom.

(2) Several important expressions in this paragraph need to be mentioned, although its meaning is sufficiently clear. First of all, a distinction is made between the rites in which the vernacular may be introduced (the Mass, administration of the sacraments, or other parts of the liturgy) and those elements within the individual rites where the vernacular may be employed (readings, directives, some of the prayers and chants).

It would of course have been enough simply to mention that the vernacular could be used in different parts of the liturgy, without specifying the Mass and the sacraments. The importance of this reference is the assurance it gives that no limitation on the use of the vernacular may be made simply on the basis that the Mass rite is somehow or other sacrosanct in language. Since the Constitution was considered chapter by chapter and article by article, the present formulation was dealt with, in the first period of the Council (the fall of 1962), long before the actual phrasing of Article 54 concerning the Mass was revised or voted upon. It therefore seemed vital to forestall any future difficulty by indicating from the very beginning that the concession of the vernacular applied equally to the Mass and the Sacraments and to the sacramental rites and the divine office.

The expression "may be extended" (*tribui valeat*) is employed in order to make it evident that the concession of the mother tongue in the liturgy is made contingent upon its regional acceptance, as indicated in the third paragraph of the present article. In other words, there is no question of the Council's suppressing the Latin or making obligatory the introduction of the language of the people. Rather the matter is to be determined on a regional basis and the Council simply says that the concession may be made.

A key expression in the article is "in the first place" (*imprimis*). This means that the lessons and directives, some prayers and chants, are the principal instances where the vernacular may be introduced. No limitation is set and, provided that the terms of the Constitution are observed (especially

Article 54 with regard to the Mass), the concessions may go beyond "lessons and directives, some prayers and chants."

In fact, it will be seen from the text of Articles 63a and 101 that this second paragraph of Article 36 has application only in the case of the Mass. In the case of the other sacraments and the sacramentals and in the case of the divine office, no limitations whatever are set in subsequent chapters on the extent of the vernacular. With regard to the Mass, however, Article 54 does indicate definite limitations in the extent of the vernacular which may be conceded by the territorial bodies of the bishops.

This apparent discrepancy is easily explained by the fact that Article 36, § 2, was agreed upon by the Council before the details of the subsequent chapters had been worked out. The middle course adopted by the Council in Article 36 in order to satisfy the vast majority of the bishops did not appear to be necessary, again apart from the case of the Mass, when in the second period of the Council (the fall of 1963) the use of the language of the people in the sacraments and in the divine office was voted upon.

The reference to "directives" applies in the first place to invitations, instructions, allocutions, "admonitions" (the Latin word is *admonitionibus*), and may be freely applied to various salutations and acclamations as well. "Prayers" refers to the collect-type prayer said by the priest as the president of the assembly; the concession of the vernacular in this instance is not verified, strictly speaking, in the case of the Mass (see Article 54). Finally, the choice of the word "chants" (*cantibus*) is a broad one. The Latin word is intended to cover all types of sacred songs, hymns, canticles, responsories, psalms, etc., and is in no way to be limited to what is understood in English by "chants."

(3) "These norms being observed" has reference to the different regulations found in the subsequent chapters of the Constitution, where specific directions are given for the individual rites of the liturgy and the extent to which the vernacular may be introduced in them. As already noted, the only limitations are found with regard to the Mass, in Article 54.

As was indicated under Article 22 above, on January 25, 1964, Pope Paul VI determined provisionally that the competent territorial authority would be the national body of bishops. Circumstances will determine how much consultation is needed with bishops of neighboring territories which have the same language. In the English-speaking countries of the world, an attempt has already been made—looking to the use of the vernacular in the revised rites—to achieve a common text, and for this purpose an international committee was set up during the second period of the Council. There is, of course, no direct obligation of joint action on the part of bishops of the same language or of neighboring territories.

The concluding words of this paragraph, "their decrees are to be approved, that is, confirmed, by the Apostolic See," were among the most hotly controverted in the entire Constitution on the Liturgy. In the schema presented to the bishops for their consideration, no authority at all to concede the vernacular was acknowledged in the territorial bodies of bishops; the text said simply that the conferences or bodies of bishops could propose to the Holy See the extension of the vernacular language in the liturgy. Such a right to make proposals to the Holy See would differ in no way from the petitions which have been submitted with greater and greater frequency in recent years.

After the matter was debated, the conciliar commission offered as an amendment the present form of the text, which actually corresponds with that presented in the first place by the preparatory commission before the Council. According to this, the territorial authority is competent to enact or decree (*statuere*), its legislative decisions being subject only to the subsequent confirmation of the Apostolic See. (Such a legislative authority in the episcopal conferences had already been acknowledged by the Apostolic See in the decree of April, 1962, on the rite of adult baptism, where similar language was used.)

Because the Council, at the time of the votes upon individual parts of the Constitution on the Liturgy, had not yet reached any decision with regard to the schema *De Episcopis et Dioecesium Regimine*, as already mentioned under Article 22 above, it was not possible to be any more specific in Article 36. A true legislative authority is acknowledged in the bodies of bishops of the respective regions, areas, or countries. (A similar expression, "to enact decrees" [*decreta ferenda*], was employed in the same context by Pope Paul VI in the motu proprio of January 25, 1964.)

The decrees or *acta* of the episcopal bodies must be transmitted to the Apostolic See for what is described as approval or confirmation. This corresponds, at least roughly, to the review or examination of the laws of plenary and provincial councils to which reference is made in canon 291 of the Code of Canon Law. (The schema of the Constitution, in the similar context of Article 63a, made direct reference to this canon of the Code, before it became apparent that such references to the present Code would be inappropriate in a conciliar document.)

Such examination of decrees or legislation of particular councils is termed "recognition" by the canonists. It consists in a simple inspection of the acts by the Apostolic See and their correction if this is necessary, that is, if they should in any way exceed the authority of the body of bishops or council. No additional sanction or authority is thereby conferred upon the acts of a council, whether plenary or provincial.

In some instances, the laws of particular councils have been inspected by the Apostolic See and given a form of confirmation. This is a positive declaration that nothing censurable has been found in the acts of the council and it adds a certain extrinsic authority to the conciliar enactment, but the laws remain those of the council and not papal laws. In more unusual circumstances, the Apostolic See has been known to examine the acts of particular councils and to give them a confirmation that is called "in specific form." This is a positive approval which changes the nature of the conciliar decrees so that they are considered as papal enactments or laws.

In the present case there is nothing more than a question of a simple review of a common confirmation. The Latin expression is *"actis ab Apostolica Sede probatis seu confirmatis."* Before the question was put to a vote, the conciliar commission explained clearly to the Fathers that the word *probatis* (approval) was used in a most generic sense and that the conjunction *seu* (or) was used to show that the following word, *confirmatis*, is the specification or the explanation of the kind of approval to be given. In this case, again as explained formally before the the vote of the Fathers, "confirmation" means that the law enacted by the inferior legislative authority (namely, the territorial body of bishops) is subsequently acknowledged and completed by the higher authority (namely, the Apostolic See).

The subsequent confirmation given by the higher authority confers an additional juridic or moral force, but it does not change the character of the enactment, and the legislative authority involved remains that of the territorial body of bishops. (See Article 63a, where a similar expression is employed; this was interpreted by the conciliar commission to the Fathers of the Council in the same way.)

It should be evident that this question of ecclesiastical authority goes far beyond the precise issue of the introduction of the vernacular languages. The expression approved by the Council makes clear that, in this instance at least, true legislative authority reposes in the territorial bodies of bishops, even apart from the formalities and solemnities of plenary and provincial councils.

In passing, it should be noted that this kind of regional authority has existed in the Church from earliest times. It has taken the form of the authority of the patriarch over other bishops, or of the metropolitan over his suffragans, or—more closely related to the present instance—the authority of plenary and provincial councils to bind all the bishops, clergy and faithful of a given territory. In the Constitution on the Liturgy, such authority over divine worship is acknowledged principally in Article 22, but the present specific reference to the enactment of decrees and their transmission to the Apostolic See for confirmation clarifies the issue.

It is not possible, of course, to deduce from Articles 22 or 36 anything concerning the matters, apart from the sacred liturgy, which the Council itself or the Roman Pontiff may acknowledge as pertaining to the bodies of bishops in their respective territories for the future.

(4) In a broad sense, the proper evolution of the liturgy demands far more than the literal or even free translation of liturgical texts from the Latin language into the vernaculars. The future adaptation of the Roman or other rites demands that new expressions and forms of prayer be composed and created. The immediate question, however, is the pastoral need of the faithful; and this is best satisfied by the translation, although not in any slavishly literal sense, of the existing texts of the Roman rite. With this in mind, the Council directs that the translation of the Latin text into the vernacular, if it is to be employed in the official liturgy, should have the approval of a competent authority, and this authority is specified as the territorial body of bishops mentioned in Article 22.

The purpose of this norm, which was introduced as an amendment to the present article in the course of the first period of the Council, is to avoid an excessive variety of translations, and even faulty translations which would be unbecoming in sacred rites. The effect of this prescription is to require that an official or authentic liturgical text in the vernacular be observed in sacred rites, just as the official Latin text has up to the present time been observed. This in turn corresponds to the prescriptions of such canons of the Code of Canon Law as 733, § 1, and 1148, § 1. In other words, the officially approved text in the language of the people acquires the same authentic status as the Latin text from which it was translated.

This applies primarily of course to those texts of the Roman rite which are Latin in their original composition. It does not apply in the same way to scriptural texts, in which the original is Hebrew or Greek. With regard to them, the translation into the vernacular language to be used in worship should be an accurate reflection of the original. The scriptures should be turned into the modern language so as to convey the values, both spiritual and literary, of the original, as far as possible, and in a way that is suited to liturgical proclamation or praying. In this difficult matter, the authority is the territorial body of bishops.

While nothing in this paragraph of Article 36 should be construed as to impose a greater rigidity upon the use of the liturgical texts than has been imposed in the past with regard to the Latin, it appears evident that the Council's purpose was to have a single official and authentic version in the vernacular approved for the respective parts of the different rites in each territory. Minor modifications necessary for singing, slight transpositions of words, etc., are no more prohibited in the case of the vernacular languages than they have been in the singing of the Latin texts.

At the same time, there is no direct prohibition in the Constitution on the Liturgy of the approval of alternative translations. It thus falls within the competence of the territorial body to permit, for example, the use of two or more versions of the scriptures for the readings at holy Mass.

It was proposed by certain Fathers of the Council that such translations of liturgical texts should be proposed to the Apostolic See, which alone would have the power to approve the version. This suggestion was rejected, with the approval of the Fathers of the Council, by the conciliar commission, since the Council has already indicated its mind in the distinction made between paragraphs 3 and 4: in three, the *acta* or decrees of the territorial body are to be transmitted to the Apostolic See for confirmation; in four, no such confirmation is required.

Subsequent to the promulgation of the Constitution, a new question was raised by article nine of the motu proprio issued on January 25, 1964:

Since according to Article 101 of the Constitution those who are obliged to recite the divine office may in various ways be granted the faculty to use translations in their mother tongue instead of Latin, we deem it opportune to specify that the various versions proposed by the competent territorial ecclesiastical authorities be duly reviewed and approved by the Apostolic See. We prescribe the observance of this practice whenever a liturgical Latin text is translated into the vernacular by the aforesaid legitimate authority.

At first glance, this new requirement appears to be in direct variance with the Constitution, inasmuch as the approval of the document by the territorial authority is described in the motu proprio as a "proposal" of the translation to the Apostolic See. Moreover, the requirement of Article 36, § 3, that the acts of the territorial bodies be "approved, that is confirmed" has been transferred in the motu proprio to the translations themselves, and in stronger terms, requiring both review and approval—"*rite recognoscendas atque probandas.*" Finally, although article nine of the motu proprio appears to be directly concerned with the use of the vernacular languages in the divine office—hence the reference to Article 101 of the Constitution— the second sentence of Article 9 extends this prescription to the case of any translation from the Latin text into the vernacular language made by the territorial authority of bishops.

The motu proprio does not indicate directly whether this submission of vernacular translations to the Apostolic See is a condition for their actual use in the celebration of the liturgy or whether it is simply a question of subsequent review. The latter might be supported by certain precedents, principally the practice of the Congregation for the Propagation of the Faith, which for many years has required the submission of vernacular translations of sacramental rites only after a period of ten years of actual use (cf. letter of the Apostolic Internuncio in India to the Ordinaries, July 8, 1949).

Moreover, even before the celebration of the Council, the Congregation of Sacred Rites, after consultation with the Holy Office and with the Congregation for the Propagation of the Faith, had conceded that the rite of adult baptism could be celebrated, in most of its parts and prayers, in the vernacular language. It was specified that the approval of the vernacular text was to be made by the episcopal conference or even by the individual local ordinary, but without any submission of texts to the Apostolic See (April, 1962).

A partial clarification of this whole question is to be found in the second Latin version of the January 25 motu proprio. In this text, which was issued by the Vatican Press subsequently to the original version which appeared in *L'Osservatore Romano,* article nine is radically changed. The obvious intent of the change is to restore the sense clearly intended by the conciliar Constitution and to acknowledge that the Ecumenical Council had conceded authority in the approval of vernacular translations to the appropriate or competent territorial body of bishops.

The text of the motu proprio, in its second Latin redaction, states that

> the various translations of this kind are to be prepared and approved by the competent territorial ecclesiastical authority, according to the norm of Article 36, paragraphs 3 and 4; but the acts [*acta*] of this authority, according to the norm of the same Article 36, paragraph 3, are to be duly approved, that is, confirmed [*probanda seu confirmanda*] by the Apostolic See.

(The concluding sentence of article nine of the motu proprio has been changed slightly to indicate that its terms are applicable whenever a "liturgical" Latin text is translated into the vernacular language, but this is only a verbal clarification.)

In the first place, it will be evident that the position of the territorial body of bishops is acknowledged (in the new form of the motu proprio) as one of preparing and approving the translations that are to be officially used in the vernacular, whereas the motu proprio suggested originally that these were simply to be "proposed" to the Apostolic See. The reference to the paragraphs of Article 36, moreover, makes it evident that these are the governing law in the matter, and that the motu proprio is intended in no way whatever to contradict the solemn decision of the Eucmenical Council.

The corresponding action of the Apostolic See is described in the new form of the motu proprio precisely in the language of Article 36, § 3, so that it is merely a confirmation added to the decrees (*acta*) of the territorial authority. In the first version of the motu proprio this action was described in the Latin words "*recognoscendas atque probandas*," with reference to the translations themselves. The change makes clear that the approval is to be given not to the translations but rather to the *acta*, and that this approval is to be understood in the same way as the "confirmation" in Article 36, § 4, of the Constitution itself—that is, as described above.

Even the new version of the motu proprio has a further difficulty, at least in the mind of some interpreters. While it is evident enough that it is the decrees of the territorial body that the Apostolic See must confirm and not the vernacular translations, it has been suggested that the *acta* referred to in the Constitution and in the motu proprio include the very translations themselves. If this should be the case, indirectly the Apostolic See would intervene to examine translations into the mother tongues, in spite of the distinction made in the Constitution between paragraphs 3 and 4 of Article 36.

In the practical order, this might seem to be of small consequence. At least in the past, prior to the time when the various congregations of the Apostolic See permitted the use of translations approved regionally without submission to Rome, it was not the actual practice of the Congregation of Sacred Rites, for example, to scrutinize carefully or become deeply involved in the actual wording, style, etc., of the vernacular translations. In such instances the fundamental concern of the Congregation seems to have been to examine bilingual rituals and the like in order to make certain that definite limits were preserved in the extension of the vernacular. In the same practical order, however, the need to submit such translations could easily be a source of great delays, especially for those countries far distant from Rome.

Perhaps only the passage of time and actual usage will indicate how this matter is to be solved. It goes beyond the introduction of the mother tongues into the liturgy and has a profound bearing upon the relationship of the Apostolic See and the other bishops. As will be indicated below, the same question arises with regard to adaptations (Articles 37-40), although it will become evident only upon the publication of the revised Roman liturgical books just which areas or degrees of adaptation lie fully within the authority of the territorial bodies (Articles 38-39), and which require the consent of the Apostolic See upon the petition of the territorial bodies (Article 40).

(D) NORMS FOR ADAPTING THE LITURGY TO THE CULTURE AND TRADITIONS OF PEOPLES

37. A statement of principle. The norms found in Articles 37-40 are in fact an application to the liturgy of the general principles of adaptation which have been recovered or restored in recent decades, especially in the declarations of Benedict XV, Pius XI and Pius XII, with special reference to the so-called missionary lands. The introduction of religious rites and customary usages proper to various cultures, traditions and peoples is an authentic and venerable tradition in the Church. It is only in the modern missionary development and in the modern static condition of the Roman rite that this has been overlooked.

The variety and diversity of rites are already acknowledged in the case of the several Oriental rites, as distinguished from the Roman rite, and indeed in the case of the various Latin rites, again as distinguished from the Roman rite. The following articles, however, have in mind the adaptation of the Roman rite itself, which is the only rite that has been propagated widely in recent centuries. Far from serving the good of the whole community of the Church, this fact has been an obstacle to missionary development, because it has introduced a rigidity and a westernization that have tended to make the Christian message itself unpalatable to those not in the tradition of Latin or Mediterranean culture.

Apart, then, from those elements, indigenous to the religious traditions and culture of peoples, which are inseparably bound up with superstition—and these need not be many—the principle established in Article 37 is that such usages may be introduced into the liturgy itself. A *fortiori*, they may be introduced into public devotions and exercises of worship which are not strictly part of the liturgy.

The provision that rites and forms of worship to be introduced into the liturgy should conform to the true and authentic liturgical spirit has reference to the general principles of the liturgy found in Chapter I, which are based upon the nature of the Church and her worship. They do not necessarily refer to the particular liturgical spirit of an individual rite of the Church, even the Roman rite itself. On the other hand, in addition to those things which pertain to the spirit of the liturgy as such, there should be preserved those characteristics which are found to be possessed in common by all the Christian rites. Many examples of this could be given, such as the ritual unity of the service of the Word with the eucharistic liturgy.

A clear distinction must be drawn between what is found in Articles 38 and 39, and the special provision of Article 40. In Articles 38 and 39, a kind of liturgical accommodation and adaptation is considered which preserves carefully the substantial unity of the Roman rite. It builds upon a core or nucleus of the Roman rite with adaptations. This kind of variation, which may be called minor adaptation, is assumed to be the ordinary course of action of the territorial bodies of bishops. The more fundamental and profound adaptation, which may be called major adaptation, is described in Article 40, where the consent of the Apostolic See is required and where the adaptation may even go so far as the creation of new rites distinct from the Roman rite. In this way, the Council makes certain that no door is closed to future evolution of liturgical services.

Finally, although there is no direct discussion of the desirability of change and diversity in rites simply because of the passage of time, this is just as much understood as is the regional diversity which is immediately considered by the Council. In other words, the Constitution on the Liturgy acknowledges fully the excellence of diversity in the worship of God. This is spoken of directly and immediately from the point of view of regional variations by authority of the territorial bodies of bishops. It opens the way equally to variations, development and adaptations to the needs of peoples of successive generations.

38. Unity in diversity. As already noted, the requirement that the substantial unity of the Roman rite be preserved is applicable in the case of variations upon that rite. In no way does it preclude the spread of other rites now existing or the development of entirely new rites of the Church.

The variations which are spoken of may be by way of additions, subtractions, etc. These may be in accord with the needs of different groups, even bodies within the Church such as religious institutes, different regions small or large, from an individual diocese to a nation or a group of nations, and peoples of differing traditions and cultures.

It is of the greatest importance to note that, while the principle of adaptation of the liturgy, as of other disciplines and practices in the Church, has been invoked most frequently with regard to the younger churches of the so-called mission lands, the Constitution allows the adaptation in any circumstances. This is the intent of the expression, "especially in mission lands." Thus adaptations may be just as necessary in countries where there is a longstanding Christian culture, but where the liturgical forms have not been accommodated to the developments of that culture in recent centuries.

The kind of adaptation intended in Article 38 is possible at any time—in some very limited matters, this was provided for in the instance of the April 1962 rite for the baptism of adults. However, the plan envisioned by the Council in Article 38 is that the Roman liturgical books should first be revised and reformed, and should include "when drawing up the rites and devising rubrics" indications of such possible accommodations and adaptations.

Thus in the Roman Ritual, for example, each of the rites might well include rubrical directions offering alternatives to be chosen by the celebrating priest, or by the authority of the local ordinary, or by the territorial body of bishops. Similarly it should give directions for rites or texts which could simply be omitted by one or other authority, and indicate places into which new rites suitable to the peoples of a given region could be introduced without disturbing the structure or logic of the existing service.

The presence of facultative rubrics in the Roman liturgical books is not something new, but their wide-scale introduction is required by the Council as a part of the reform of the books. And although such possiblities of accommodation do not preclude matters to be left to the decision of the individual celebrant or the individual bishop, the kind of adaptation intended here is such that it would ordinarily pertain to the decision of the whole body of bishops of the given territory.

As a note to this article, some mention should be made of the use of the word "mission" in relation to certain territories of the Church. The term itself is hardly satisfactory, since the mission of the Church is to all mankind and not to some limited territory. In recent years there has been an increasing conscious-ness of the inadequacy of the word. Moreover, those territories which have never been considered as mission lands often ex-perience precisely the same problems of growth and develop-ment which are usually thought of as pertaining to missiological study and endeavor. A prime example of this is found in the churches of Latin America.

At the same time, the various possible substitutes for this term are neither satisfactory nor in widespread use. "Younger churches" would be applicable only to certain areas where the Church has not long been present. In other territories with equal claim for special consideration because of minority status and grave problems, the Church is comparatively venerable, for example, in India. In any event, the use of the term "mis-sions" is generally understood and serves the practical purposes of the Constitution, without prejudicing the hope for develop-ment of better understanding in this matter.

39. Guidelines for adaptation. This article specifies: (a) the authority which is competent with regard to the approbation of adaptations as these will be written into the official editions of the liturgical service books; and (b) the principal matters in which there should be adaptation.

As indicated already in Article 38, the limits of the adapta-tion which would pertain to the episcopal bodies are to be in-cluded in the official liturgical books, and the territorial author-ity would then have the full power to make the adaptations. There is no requirement in this article that the action of the territorial authority should be approved, that is, confirmed by the Apostolic See. Presumably, the adaptations, or places and possibilities of adaptation, which would be included in the liturgical books might themselves fall into different classes of significance. If these would involve considerable changes, then it would be understandable that the rubrics should require the submission of the decree of the territorial authority to the Apostolic See for examination or confirmation.

The schema of the Constitution required that the intro-duction of adaptations along the lines referred to in Article 39 should be done by way of decrees which would then be submitted to the Apostolic See for "recognition"; this provision was eliminated in the text approved by the Council.

The use of the word "especially" (*praesertim*) indicates that the matters enumerated as subject to adaptation are only examples. It is evident that, since the Eucharist is not mentioned directly, adaptations would be less numerous or frequent in this case.

40. Procedures for more radical adaptations.

(1) The more profound accommodation of the liturgy to the needs of various places and circumstances, whether in mission territories or elsewhere, also pertains to the territorial authority, but its power is limited. In this case there is required a formal petition or proposal by the territorial authority to the Apostolic See of adaptations which may appear useful or necessary. The actual introduction of such adaptations requires the consent of the Apostolic See.

According to Article 54 in Chapter II, this procedure must also be followed if the territorial authority wishes to extend the use of the language of the people to those parts of Mass which are not specifically mentioned in that article, namely, the parts of the Mass said alone by the priest, such as the collect and the eucharistic prayer.

This is a discrepancy in the Constitution, inasmuch as the question of the introduction of the vernacular language properly falls under Article 39. In other words, the use of the vernacular is a kind of adaptation which should regularly be considered as minor, as is obvious from the specific reference to liturgical language in Article 39. In effect, Article 54, when it deals with the parts proper to the priest, adopts a greater restrictiveness. This may be attributed to the hesitancy of some of the Fathers of the Council to allow the eucharistic canon in the vernacular languages. Thus the procedure of Article 40—petition or proposal to the Apostolic See, followed by its consent—was invoked in Article 54.

(2) The second paragraph of Article 40 expresses the necessity of prior experimentation where profound adaptations of the liturgy are desired. The Council does not give the faculty directly to the territorial bodies to conduct this kind of experi-

mentation, but where the more profound adaptations seem necessary it is to be conceded by the Apostolic See. In the case of the minor adaptations provided for directly in the revised liturgical books, such experimentation would naturally fall entirely within the authority of the territorial body of bishops.

The faculty to be given by the Apostolic See to the territorial authority may be either general or specific. The bodies of bishops in general might be authorized to experiment along certain lines or in certain services. Or, upon request, an episcopal conference might be conceded the faculty of developing certain new rites by experimentation. The experimentation is to be conducted in suitable places or, more accurately, among certain groups. In almost every case the experimentation should be in parishes, since the pastoral purpose of the liturgical renewal is not satisfied by a liturgy that is adapted to cloistered monastic use or use within religious institutes.

(3) It may appear that the provision of the third paragraph of Article 40 is somewhat out of place, inasmuch as the requirement of expert assistance is sufficiently insisted upon in Article 25, with regard to the general reform, and in Article 44, with regard to all the promotion of liturgical action by national or regional liturgical commissions. Nevertheless its inclusion here indicates that all profound adaptation requires the study of experts, both pastors and scholars, whether this be on behalf of the territorial bodies in proposing such adaptations, or on behalf of the Apostolic See in giving its consent. A particular reason for mentioning this with regard to the missions is the failure in recent centuries to take the particular needs of peoples in mission lands into account.

The entire matter of adaptation places a grave responsibility upon the territorial bodies of bishops, which up to the present have generally been satisfied with the propagation of the Roman rite as found in the official service books. The Constitution gives the territorial bodies the office of scrutinizing the different parts of the Roman rite, so that these may be accommodated to the needs and understanding of the faithful in their particular territories. This matter is again referred to in Article 44.

IV. The Promotion of Liturgical Life in Diocese and Parish

41. Centered in the bishop, liturgy manifests the Church. The two final sections of Chapter I, on the fostering of the liturgical life in the diocese and parish and on the promotion of pastoral-liturgical actions, respectively, may be compared in this way. The first section, consisting of Articles 41 and 42, deals directly with the celebration of the liturgy and its meaning as the expression and manifestation of the Church itself. Articles 43 to 46, in the last section, deal rather with the concrete action to be taken in nation or region and in diocese to promote the liturgical apostolate and movement.

42. Liturgical life in the parish. The parish is not the only community within the Church lesser in scope than the diocese over which the bishop presides. The Council therefore avoids any absolute commitment to the parish community on a local basis. Nevertheless the territorial parish is indicated as the most important community in the Church lesser than the diocese. From this it follows that other public communities in the Church, although lawful manifestations of the Church itself, must not be permitted to rival the parish in the estimation of the faithful.

The reference in the second paragraph of this article to the community worship on Sundays corresponds with the emphasis placed in Chapter V upon the meaning of the Sunday as the Lord's day and the celebration of the Easter mystery of the Lord's passion and resurrection (see Articles 102 and 106).

V. The Promotion of Pastoral-Liturgical Action

43. Liturgical renewal as God's design. The reference in this article is, quite simply, to the liturgical movement of the past five or six decades. The description of the liturgical movement as the sign of the providential dispositions of God in our time is taken from the allocution given by Pope Pius XII at the conclusion of the Assisi-Rome International Congress of Pastoral Liturgy, September 22, 1956. The intent of the Council is to promote this liturgical apostolate further by means of the specific organs described in the next three articles.

44. National commissions and institutes for pastoral liturgy. The question may be raised at once why the Council did not require the establishment of regional or national liturgical commissions. One answer is the general desire of the part of the Fathers of the Council not to impose new obligations without absolute necessity. In most circumstances, however, it would seem that such a commission would in fact be necessary. A second reason for leaving the question rather open is the broad designation of the territorial ecclesiastical authority.

As discussed already under Article 22, the terms of the Constitution in this regard may apply equally to an episcopal conference which includes the bishops of several countries, and the episcopal conference of a province, as envisioned in canon 292 of the Code of Canon Law. It might therefore have been excessive to require a liturgical commission at every possible level. The direct need for such a commission is certainly apparent in the case of the territorial bodies of bishops as defined in the motu proprio of January 25, 1964, namely, the national bodies of bishops.

In this entire article, the example of various episcopal commissions and those who cooperate in their work may be offered as illustrations, without suggesting at all that any one arrangement of commissions, committees, pastoral institutes, etc., is ideal. A clear distinction may be made, simply on the basis of the words of the present article, between: (a) the liturgical commission of the territory, which is made up of bishops; (b) the experts or specialists in pastoral liturgy who assist the episcopal commission; and (c) the institute of pastoral liturgy.

Although the commission on the liturgy is composed of bishops taken from the whole body of bishops and selected according to the constitution or statutes of the episcopal body in question, the Constitution on the Liturgy requires that it have the assistance of experts. These experts may be consulted as individuals or may be constituted in a body or group. If in fact the institute of pastoral liturgy described in the article does exist in a given area, its members in the nature of things would form the body upon which the episcopal liturgical commission would call for expert assistance.

The specialists who are to assist the episcopal liturgical commission, whether they be themselves constituted in a commission (or institute) or not, are to have specialized knowledge in liturgical science, which would embrace the disciplines referred to in Article 16: the theological, historical, spiritual, pastoral and juridical aspects of the liturgy. Properly speaking, they should have the training and background expected of seminary professors of the liturgy in Article 15.

Moreover, the specialists or experts called upon should include some versed in sacred music, that is, according to the spirit of Chapter VI of the Constitution. In effect, this would require knowledge of sacred music in the actual celebration of worship, that is, in its more noble form with the active participation of the people (Article 113). The same can be said of the specialists in sacred art, namely, that their spirit should be that of Chapter VII of the Constitution.

Finally and most importantly, those who assist the episcopal liturgical commission should have expert knowledge in pastoral theology and pastoral liturgy. This kind of specialized knowledge is had by those who have over a period of years experimented with the possible forms of liturgical participation, and who have already been engaged in the promotion of the liturgical apostolate which the Council desires to stimulate even further.

As already noted, the assistance to be given by experts to the episcopal liturgical commission will be more fruitful if they are participants in an institute of pastoral liturgy which the Council recommends according to the circumstances. Obviously, not every nation would be able to establish an institute or center of pastoral liturgy with sufficiently expert members to provide all the assistance needed by the episcopal liturgical commission. Nevertheless, this is proposed as an ideal.

According to the Constitution, the membership of the institute should include laity, men or women, in areas where they are needed. Lay assistance is almost always needed in the fields of sacred music and sacred art, of course, but it is equally necessary in the determination of programs or plans for liturgical participation by the laity.

The nature of the institute of pastoral liturgy referred to here is evident from the the chief existing instances of such organizations, which were the pattern for the statement in Article 44. These are the Center of Pastoral Liturgy in Paris (now the National Center) and the Liturgical Institute of Trier, serving the bishops of France and Germany, respectively. In general the task of such institutes is twofold: first, to engage in the promotion of liturgical knowledge and participation; second, to assist the episcopal liturgical commission and through it the body of bishops. In the first task, the institute of pastoral liturgy acts simply upon its own authority and conducts programs of instruction, publication, meetings and congresses, etc. In its second task, an institute of pastoral liturgy simply serves as a consultative body for the bishops.

In the United States, the function of an institute of pastoral liturgy is fulfilled in large part by the Liturgical Conference, which has been in existence since 1940, and which conducts programs of instruction, holds meetings, and promotes publication. It differs from the German and French institutes inasmuch as it is organized as a society of general membership. In other countries, the corresponding bodies are organized as interdiocesan committees or the like.

The institute of pastoral liturgy that is described here, while it engages in research into pastoral liturgical problems, is distinct from the academic institute mentioned in Article 15. The latter is academic in its nature; it trains teachers and grants degrees or diplomas. Ordinarily it is a part of or affiliated with a theological or other faculty, or with a university.

The last sentence of Article 44 is carefully drawn to indicate that the authority of the episcopal liturgical commission is entirely dependent upon the territorial body of bishops. While it has a responsibility of regulating or promoting liturgical action in the territory or country, the binding force of its decisions depends upon whatever authority is committed to it by the competent territorial body, that is, the entire group of bishops of the region. In any event, the fundamental responsibility of promoting the liturgical apostolate rests with the entire body of bishops of the country or region, over and above the responsibility of the individual bishop for his own diocese.

Frederick Richard McManus

In the United States, the episcopal liturgical commission was established in November, 1958, with the title of "Bishops' Commission on the Liturgical Apostolate"; since January, 1965, it has had a Secretariat in Washington, D.C.

45. Diocesan commissions. The background of the diocesan commission on the sacred liturgy mentioned in this article, as well as the commissions mentioned in Article 46, may be seen in no. 118 of the Instruction issued by the Congregation of Sacred Rites on September 3, 1958. The commission on sacred music has been obligatory since 1903; the commission on sacred art was first mentioned by the secretary of state of Pope Pius XI in September, 1924, and again by the Holy Office in an instruction of June, 1952; the commission on the liturgy was at least strongly urged in the encyclical *Mediator Dei* of November 20, 1947.

The 1958 Instruction made very clear the obligation of the three diocesan commissions, but dealt with the commission on sacred music in the first place. The Constitution on the Liturgy reverses this position and gives primacy to the liturgical commission, with the commissions on music and art in subordinate position. The importance of this article and the following was pointed out by Pope Paul VI in the motu proprio of January 25, 1964, which directs the establishment of such commissions. The text of the motu proprio, however, is no more than a paraphrase of the terms of the Constitution in this regard.

In the past there has been some dispute as to the fundamental purpose of diocesan liturgical commissions, whether they are to be considered as regulatory bodies limiting or restraining the progress of the liturgical apostolate, or whether they are intended to stimulate and foster the liturgy. Any question of this kind is settled definitively by the Constitution, which defines the purpose of the liturgical commission as "promoting the liturgical apostolate."

The expression "under the direction of the bishop" is important, inasmuch as it indicates that any authority possessed by the diocesan liturgical commission depends entirely upon the delegation of the bishop. According to circumstances in different dioceses, it may be desirable that the liturgical commission or its chairman or secretary possess some regulatory

285

authority with regard to the celebration of the liturgy. But this will require some positive decision on the part of the bishop and will be over and above the primary function of the commission, which it possesses by the norm of Article 45, namely, promoting and encouraging the sacred liturgy and the liturgical renewal.

Nothing is said in Article 45 with regard to the membership of the commission. There is no reason why it should be limited to priests, and every reason why lay men and lay women of competence should be included. Since the work of the liturgical commission is largely educational and promotional, it is of the greatest importance that its efforts should be coordinated with other agencies and organizations in the diocese, which in the United States would include the education or school office, the Confraternity of Christian Doctrine, councils of men and women, etc.

The second paragraph of Article 45 is a recognition that in many smaller dioceses it is impossible to set up a liturgical commission composed of those expert in the liturgical apostolate—since in fact both pastoral and scientific experience in the positive promotion of the liturgy should be considered a qualification for membership in the commission. Because of this difficulty, the Council allows for and suggests inter-diocesan liturgical commissions. These would perform substantially the same function for a number of dioceses which the individual commission performs for the single diocese.

In the case of the inter-diocesan commission, however, its efforts to promote the liturgy are to be "by common consultation." This means that the commission of this kind, which serves several dioceses, is perfectly free to stimulate and promote liturgical understanding and participation by every educational and instructional program, but may never issue binding directives or rulings, unless of course the individual bishop deputes the inter-diocesan commission to act on his behalf for his diocese.

46. Commissions on music and art. Fundamentally, Article 46 makes the two other commissions, on sacred music and on sacred art, of equal obligation with the liturgical commission. It recognizes, however, that it is always necessary to have cooperation and collaboration among the three commissions, and that often enough it will be impossible to establish and staff distinct commissions. In the latter case a single liturgical commission may be established, which would then fulfill the functions of the commissions on music and art.

In practice this may work out in different ways. In some dioceses, the liturgical commission has three sections corresponding to the three commissions mentioned in Articles 45 and 46. In other dioceses a satisfactory arrangement is that the single liturgical commission should have two sub-commissions or subcommittees on music and art, respectively.

With regard to sacred music, the appropriate commission should observe in the first place the norms of the Constitution on the Liturgy in regard to the promotion of music. These go beyond and differ from earlier papal directives on music in some ways, for example, in the insistence upon congregational participation as a test of the greater nobility of form in liturgical worship (Article 113), in the stress upon simpler forms of music suitable for small choirs and for the active participation of the entire assembly of the faithful (Article 121), etc.

Since in the United States many dioceses have building commissions which are directly concerned with the design and construction of churches as well as of other buildings, the commission on sacred art should collaborate most closely with any existing building commission. In fact, the norms of the Constitution regarding sacred art and architecture, as found in Chapter VII, should have primacy with the building commission itself.

Again, special account should be taken of those norms or principles of the Constitution which go beyond previous papal directives, for example, the requirement that churches should be suitable "for the celebration of liturgical services and for the active participation of the faithful" (Article 124), the insistence upon moderation in the placing of sacred images in churches (Article 125), and the freedom of the Christian artist (Articles 122-123). Special reference is made to the diocesan commission on sacred art in Article 126, which indicates on the one hand that the local ordinary should hear the opinion of the members of the diocesan commission on art, and on the other hand that its members should include those truly qualified to render judgment.

Edward Schillebeeckx
1914-

Edward Schillebeeckx was born in Antwerp, Belgium, and entered the Flemish Province of the Dominican Fathers in 1935. He studied philosophy and theology at Louvain and received his doctorate in theology from Le Saulchoir. For fourteen years he taught dogmatic theology at the Dominican House of Studies in Louvain, then in 1958 he became professor of theology at the Catholic University of Nijmegen in the Netherlands. Since that time his name has been inseparable from the renewal taking place in the Dutch Catholic Church.

Schillebeeckx as a speculative theologian has few peers on the current scene. He became the principal adviser to the Dutch hierarchy at Vatican II, was a major influence in the production of the popular "Dutch Catechism," and had the full support of Cardinal Alfrink of Utrecht when critics began behind-the-scenes efforts to have his works censured by Rome.

What frightened some of his more conservative colleagues was the seriousness with which Schillebeeckx viewed historical change. He reminds us that "In every generation the Church rereads Holy Scriptures, and she has been doing this for two thousand years, during which time the Bible has gradually been revealing its own meaning, thanks to the light in which the past comes to stand in the present . . . Therefore in examining, in *faith, statements made in the past by the Church, we must take present problems into account."*

In light of this, the fact that a theological interpretation is "new" is no reason for automatically dismissing or condemning it. The "new interpretation" of the Eucharist that Albert, Bonaventure and Thomas put forth in the 13th century became part of the Church's ongoing treasure. To suggest that comparable progress cannot be made in our day reflects a curious understanding of the Church.

As will become obvious in the selection included here, Schillebeeckx began struggling with this area of theology more than twenty years earlier. His book is structured with utmost simplicity: 1) he presents the Tridentine approach to faith, then 2) he describes the "new approach" toward the formulation of faith. Our excerpt begins where he starts to apply his general principles to the Eucharist as such. These pages are a model of clarity and moderation, the work of a man who has a sure touch in a delicate realm. The liturgical movement has not always been blessed with this kind of solid theoretical underpinnings. The strength of Schillebeeckx lies in the fact that, for all the accusations of novelty, he is most firmly grounded in both historical theology and contemporary thought. In attempting to synthesize the two, he is engaging in the richest type of Christian theology, for which future generations will surely acknowledge his contribution.

THE EUCHARIST

PART II

THE NEW POINT OF DEPARTURE FOR THE
INTERPRETATION OF THE EUCHARISTIC PRESENCE

C atholic theology did not proceed at once to follow an anthropological course in approaching the question of the Eucharist when it had forsaken the Aristotelian philosophy of nature. There was a transitional period, in which what we may call simply the "metaphysical" interpretation, without any content of natural philosophy, prevailed. This movement sought the solution to the problem in the distinction berween the *noumenon* and the *phenomenon*—that is, between the reality itself and the form in which it appears. In this way, once more the very essence of the older Thomistic view was touched upon. The unity between the metaphysical and the sacramental aspects was, however, still insufficiently clear here, and the relationship between the phenomenal and the so-called "noumenal" aspects was not closely analysed. The direction in which these theologians were moving did, however, seem to offer good prospects.

When I was studying in France in 1945 and 1946, transubstantiation was a subject of animated discussion among the students. The professor of dogmatic theology, a man well on in years but nevertheless very openminded, observing that the students could no longer find a place for his Thomistic doctrine of transubstantiation (which was itself a reaction against the post-Tridentine theology), allowed them to air their own views in seminars. Even then, words like "transfunctionalisation" and even "transfinalisation" could be heard in these discussions—the idea being that it was not the physical reality of the bread, but its function and meaning that were substantially changed. These discussions were not yet connected with modern phenomenology, which had, at that time, hardly begun to influence Catholic thought, but were prompted by the difficulties experienced in connection with the Aristotelian concept of substance as a result of modern physics and Bergson's criticisms.

The first theologian to rise above both the physical and the purely ontological interpretations and to situate the reality of the eucharistic presence in the sacramental presence was, without doubt, J. de Baciocchi. He accepted an ontological depth in transubstantiation, but placed this on the sacramental level. He did in fact use the terms transfunctionalisation, transfinalisation and transsignification. The ultimate reality of things is not what they are for our senses or for the scientific analysis that is based on this, but what they are for Christ. Christ's power as Lord makes all things be for him. If, therefore, Christ really gives *himself* in bread and wine, God's good gifts, then an objective and fundamental change has taken place, a transubstantiation—bread and wine become *signs* of Christ's real gift of himself. De Baciocchi was reacting here against the concept of a substance situated *behind* the phenomenal world. "The gift of bread and wine is changed by Christ into the gift of his body and blood," and this changes the reality of the bread. This was the first attempt by a Catholic theologian to synthesise "realism" (transubstantiation) and the "sacramental symbolism in its full depth of meaning."

It would seem that, with these views, the interpretation based on the Aristotelian philosophy of nature was completely superseded and the anthropological approach was already recognisable. It is, however, remarkable that this reinterpretation was not worked out until after 1950. This was the year in which the encyclical *Humani Generis* appeared, which denounced the opinion of certain theologians who maintained that transubstantiation was based on an outdated philosophical concept of substance and therefore had to be corrected in such a way that the real presence of Christ was reduced to a kind of symbolism, in which the consecrated hosts were simply efficacious signs of the *spiritual* presence of Christ and of his intimate union with his mystical body and its members. But I have never been able to discover a purely symbolical interpretation of the Eucharist in Catholic theology prior to 1950. Rome's criticism is probably based on a misunderstanding. Together with other theologians of the *Nouvelle Théologie* who favoured the practice of going back to original sources, Henri de Lubac had shown that both the early scholastic theologians and those of the High Middle Ages stressed not Christ's eucharistic presence (*res et sacramentum*), but the unity of all believers on the basis of a eucharistic communion with Christ (*res sacramenti*), the mystical body. Thomas Aquinas also explicitly postulated that the saving power of this sacrament is ultimately situated in the real presence of Christ in the believing community itself. The rediscovery of this datum has in fact supported the new interpretations. Whatever the case may be, De Baciocchi was radically opposed to any purely symbolic interpretation. Post-war Catholic theologians, who had rediscovered the sacrament as a sign, have never again left the path that was first followed by De Baciocchi, the path of synthesis between realism and sacramentality—two poles between which theologians have been trying to find an equilibrium since the ninth century.

In Belgium, A. Vanneste, clearly inspired by De Baciocchi and by Leenhardt's *Ceci est mon corps*, tried to make transubstantiation intelligible, but without appealing either to philosophy or to cosmology or even to phenomenology. His point of departure was the creation, the fact that the ultimate meaning of things comes from God. He made a distinction, not between substance and accidents or between the *noumenon* and the *phenomenon*, but between what things are for God (and for the believer) and what they are for our secular experience as men. Man does not give things their ultimate meaning. If God gives a different destination to this bread, then it *is* metaphysically something different: "philosophically too, the bread is no longer bread."

In Germany, a new approach to transubstantiation was more fully explored in a symposium on the Eucharist held at Passau on the seventh to tenth of October, 1959. In the published account of the lectures and discussions, the papers read by L. Scheffczyk and B. Welte are especially representative. Scheffczyk took as his point of departure the biblical belief in creation, which related the material reality as well as the spiritual to salvation, maintaining that at the deepest level the *being* of things was, in the Bible, a sign and symbol of spiritual and divine realities. This is worked out especially in connection with man and applied in all its depth to the man Jesus, the Son of God, so that the material substance in the Eucharist is fully sign. Although he did not use the word, Scheffczyk, like De Baciocchi, stated that a real transubstantiation must be a transsignification, which is a transfinalisation. B. Welte offered a more fully worked out analysis. His starting-point was that personal and spiritual relationships are more real than physical and material relationships. He therefore viewed bread and wine in the Eucharist in the light of their relationships. Being, being true and being good ("having meaning for") are, in the authentically Thomistic view, interchangeable. In their own *being*, things have a meaning for someone (God, man), an original meaning which belongs to the reality itself, since, without this "having meaning for," something is not what it *is*. This transcendental "having meaning for" is made particular in concrete forms. A chemical substance may be nourishment, but it may also be fuel. If this relationship is changed, the being itself of a thing changes. A Greek temple is something different for its builders, for those who worship in it and for modern tourists. Man himself is essentially involved in this change of relationship, but it is not completely dependent on him—the *being* itself of things changes when the relationship is altered. It is therefore possible to say that the temple has undergone a "historical transubstantiation." There are also relationships which are *brought about* by man. In such cases, *what* the being concerned really *is* is authoritatively determined. A coloured cloth is purely decorative, but if a government decides to raise it to the level of a national flag, then the same cloth is really and objectively no longer the same. Physically, nothing has been changed, but its being is essentially changed. Indeed, a new meaning of this kind is more real and more profound than a physical or chemical change. In the case of the Eucharist too, a new meaning is given to the bread and wine, not by any man, but by the Son of God. The relationship which is brought about by the Son of God is, because it is divine, binding in the absolute sense and determines the being of the Eucharist for the believer. Anyone who does not believe, and consequently does not see it in this way, places himself outside the reality which is *objectively* present—he is outside the order of being.

Welte put forward this idea as a working hypothesis. He was in any case the first to elaborate in some detail a modern interpretation of transubstantiation—a change of the being itself (*conversio entis*) that is much more objective than physical changes, but on the level of giving meaning.

In the Netherlands in 1960, J. Möller, without looking for an ontological basis, put forward an existential and phenomenological interpretation in which the reality of Christ's "giving of himself in the gift" was for the first time painstakingly analyzed phenomenologically. Although these analyses were not closely enough related to the specifically eucharistic context, they are nonetheless worthy of careful consideration by theologians.

The years 1964 and 1965 marked the beginning of a new phase in the reinterpretation of Christ's real presence in the Eucharist. By this, I mean above all that it was then that the new ideas which had been developed in different countries, especially during the ten years following the publication of *Humani Generis* in 1950, became widely known in the Church as a whole. Various theologians presented their views to the Catholic world, in England and the Netherlands especially, in a less academic way and with new shades of meaning.

In England, Charles Davis cautiously suggested a new anthropological interpretation that was in harmony with that of De Baciocchi. In accordance with the general tendency away from the categories of natural philosophy and towards anthropological thinking, he based his argument concerning both grace and the sacramental life not on objective categories, but on interpersonal categories. Davis attempted to define more precisely the distinctive character of the eucharistic presence, which had, in his opinion, also to be interpreted in personal terms—that is, within the category of the interpersonal encounter between Christ and the believer—and to determine in this light what, so to speak, the "real presence" is *in itself* (directed, of course, towards this personal encounter) in the eucharistic bread and wine. It is the first stage of what must become *a reciprocal* presence and of what de facto also makes this reciprocal presence possible. Expressed in scholastic terms, it is the *res et sacramentum*, the first stage of the real presence, of which the *res tantum* is the completion. There is therefore an identification with the *object* and not with an action, although this is certainly assumed. It is a substantial identity and therefore a "substantial presence." "Substantial" here means the manner of being present which has its origin in the identity with an object. This object, the eucharistic bread, is Christ. "As symbolic it embodies the reality it manifests." The reality itself of an object undergoes a change and, for this reason, there is no "consubstantiation," but a real transubstantiation. The identity is, however, not complete. Nothing is changed visibly and empirically, and what we perceive is not a deception. If the reality were changed empirically, there could be no question of sacramentality.

Davis does not, however, explain this by using the Aristotelian twin concept of substance and accidents. The change cannot, in his opinion, be situated at a non-empirical, physical level, separate from the personal and sacramental encounter with Christ, and he therefore proposes that the change concerns the reality the bread has as a "human object." There are objects which only have reality and meaning *for man* and are as such made by him for his needs, plans, self-expression and communication with others. These remain "external" realities (in this sense, an "ontological" reality as bread), but they are no longer "things of nature." Thus, the unity that we call bread is unintelligible without its relationship to man—it is only an agglomeration of diverse constituent parts. To this agglomeration transubstantiation gives a new *human unity*, a new meaning or relationship to man. The real, ontological meaning of the bread, that is, the bread itself, is thus radically changed—it is no longer orientated towards man as bread. A new pattern of unity is brought about, a new relationship to man, even though nothing is changed physically and the elements nourish the body as all bread does. A new object comes into being—the sacrament in which the reality of Christ is the *formally* constitutive element ("the substance as it were") together with the other elements which, subordinated to this new reality of Christ, are the *sign* of this reality and the *medium* by which it becomes accessible to us. The "new object" is thus the sacrament of Christ's body and blood.

Davis insists that the datum of Christ's presence in the Eucharist does not mean that he is, as far as we are concerned, absent outside the Eucharist. He is close to us in an even more intimate manner in the life of grace than he is in the tabernacle. Christ's real presence in the Eucharist therefore only finds its completion in the reciprocal encounter that takes place between Christ and ourselves. Davis' view thus amounts to an *ontological* "transfinalisation" and "transsignification," even though he does not in fact use these words. The basic meaning of the dogma of transubstantiation is guaranteed by Davis, but without the Aristotelian wording.

In the Netherlands, the theologians P. Schoonenberg and L. Smits have moved in rather a different direction, which they prefer to characterise, as equivalent to transubstantiation, as "transsignification" or "transfinalisation." Schoonenberg stresses above all that personal presence, in contrast to spatial presence, is identical with personal communication and is brought about by this. It is a self-communication of a person and a corresponding reception of this communication—in other words, a reciprocal self-communication in which the one person is himself for the other. This is reflected even in spatial presence—it always implies *activity,* the influence of one on the other. Personal presence is corporeally "mediated." It is visibly realised in signs. It is free self-disclosure and spiritual openness in bodiliness. Thus "the material activities of human bodies or things acquire a new dimension—they become *signs* of persons. . . . All making known or perception becomes a sign of revelation and faith, an active sign of human community, the manifestation and cause of personal presence."

This interpretation properly stresses the fact that there are different degrees of personal presence. The two basic forms of personal presence are the presence that is *only offered* and the presence that is *also received* as a gift. "The only complete personal presence is that which is both given and accepted. That which is only offered, but is not (yet) accepted is a secondary presence, which is orientated towards the first as its aim and completion." There is also personal presence which does not come about directly by "mediation" of the human body, but by mediation of even more alien material things, such as a letter, souvenir or a gift. In this context, however, these things become *signs.* "They have a new and deeper being, being as signs, which

297

communicates the personal presence. It is almost possible to say that they are transubstantiated."

Schoonenberg's analysis, of which I have given only a summary of a few main points, may be regarded as generally acceptable to modern existential thought. It is quite possible to say that the contemporary image of man and the world is taken as much for granted in modern theology as the Aristotelian image of man and the world was, broadly speaking, in the theology of the second half of the thirteenth century. This new understanding of man and the world forms, in a less thematised way, the background to all attempts to reinterpret the Tridentine dogma, including, for example, those of Charles Davis and Luchesius Smits.

After having applied this datum to the man Jesus, as God's personal presence among us, Schoonenberg goes on to analyse the eucharistic presence. He correctly presupposes Christ's presence in the community celebrating the Eucharist: "The Eucharist begins with a *praesentia realis* . . . and its aim is to make this presence more intimate." Indeed, anyone who denies this context is bound to misunderstand transubstantiation and make it too "objective." The signs of the eucharistic bread only imply a presence as an offer, emanating from the Lord in his assembled community. The "real presence" that is peculiar to the Eucharist is thus confined to the category of *personal* presence. "It is interpersonal—the host mediates between the Lord (in his Church) and me (in the same Church). I kneel, not before a Christ who is, as it were, condensed in the host, but before the Lord himself who is offering his reality, his body, to me through the host." The host is Christ's gift of himself, and Christ's presence is that of the giver in the gift, as J. Möller and, later, L. Smits have argued. The gift here is food and drink, but these are not a gift from an *ordinary* man, but from Jesus, the Christ, and they are therefore the non-deceptive, but irrevocably authentic gift of Christ himself. It is, of course, true that Christ also gives himself in the other sacraments. But his gift of himself is realised in the most supreme way in the Eucharist—the bread and the wine become fully *signs*. "What takes place in the Eucharist is a change of sign." Transubstantiation is a transfinalisation or a transsignification, but at a depth which only Christ reaches in his most real gift of himself. Bread and wine become (together with the words of consecration) the signs which realise this most deep gift of Christ himself. Schoonenberg concludes: "Those among us who are older rightly regard their faith in Christ's presence under the species as a great treasure. This treasure is not taken away from them when . . . this presence of Christ under the species is situated entirely within his presence in the community."

It is not really necessary to discuss L. Smits' argument separately, as it follows, with a few different shades of meaning, the same basic direction as that of Schoonenberg. He was anxious to find an example which would make it clear that, in our civilisation, a "banquet" tends to develop into a ceremony in which the eating and drinking proper are pushed into the background. His real intentions here were, however, not understood, with the result that he was unjustly regarded, outside the Netherlands especially, as having put forward a kind of "theology of the eucharistic visit." He himself, however, only intended this visit, in which tea and a biscuit were offered, as a suggestive example. His central idea too was the *uniqueness of Christ's* giving of himself in the gift of bread and wine.

THE DISTINCTIVELY EUCHARISTIC MANNER OF THE "REAL PRESENCE"

The authentic context in which the Euchrist should be seen has been very suggestively described by Schoonenberg and Davis especially. I postulate this as well-known—and central—and should like now only to consider *specific* problems more fully.

Biblical Assumptions

As I am not a professional exegete, I must not allow myself to be seduced into agreeing completely with the interpretation of the biblical texts on the Eucharist put forward by the Lutheran exegete Willi Marxsen. I should, however, like to draw attention with some emphasis to certain points contained in his analysis and, in that case, must also mention a study by B. van Iersel which appeared before Marxsen's books and which is in fact complementary to his work. If the arguments which claim that the Pauline tradition is older than that of Mark are accepted, then it is clear that the development of the interpretation of the "celebration of a meal with Jesus" in the primitive Church was parallel to that of a progressive penetration into the mystery of Christ. Originally, the emphasis was not on *interpreting* this meal, but on celebrating and experiencing it. In celebrating this meal, early Christians had the experience of being a Church—an eschatological community on the basis of their personal relationship with Jesus, whom they had come to know explicitly as the Christ in the resurrection. This personal relationship with Jesus—concretely expressed in community with him at table—was experienced then as a *christological* and therefore as an eschatological relationship—as being placed before the living God. The primitive Church had the experience of being an eschatological *community*, the people of the New Covenant, on the way to the kingdom of God, in and by celebrating the fraternal meal, as had happened before when Jesus was still on earth. The deep meaning of this shared Christian meal was indicated by the words that were spoken over the bread at the beginning of the meal and over the wine at the end—this community in Christ determined the relationship towards the kingdom of God. The personal relationship with Christ which was experienced in faith in this Christian fellowship was explicitly pointed at in the liturgical words pronounced over the bread and the wine. They expressed what the personal relationship—the community at table—with Jesus meant to the primitive Church and continued to mean after his departure—namely, his real presence in the assembled community. Jesus had died, but his followers had the visible experience of his continued life and active presence among them, because they, the believers, formed one community by virtue of his death "for our sins" and his resurrection.

This earliest interpretation was further elaborated in the tradition of Mark, in which Christ, united to the eschatological community, was explicitly associated with the food and drink consumed by the community that was united in Christ. The meaning of the community with Christ at table was here preserved only in the words pronounced over the bread and wine and in the partaking of this bread and wine. Christ's real presence in his community was concentrated cultically in his real presence under the forms of bread and wine. This was a legitimate development within the New Testament itself, but it threatened to become one-sided because the eschatological existence of the believing community, in their special relationship with Jesus as realised in their community with him at table, was thus pushed into the background. Even in the New Testament, then, the emphasis was transferred from the ecclesiastical community of grace in Christ (the *res sacramenti*) to the real presence of Christ in the Eucharist under the species of bread and wine (the *res et sacramentum*). The eschatological orientation was now experienced in a cultic event which effectively expressed the deepest meaning of the continuing history.

This progressive interpretation in the primitive Church— safeguarded by the interpretation and the preservation of the Holy Spirit—thus shows that, in the continuing life of the Church, the real presence of Christ in the Eucharist was subordinated to the eschatological personal community with the Lord who had really died, but who continued, on the basis of his real resurrection, as God's saving act, to be effective in his community. It was ultimately a question of the eschatological personal bond with the living Lord, and the celebration of the Eucharist anticipated this as an effective sign. The *soma Christou* was de facto really experienced in this meal.

Like these early Christians, we too must experience this reality within the concrete context of our contemporary lives by constantly making present and reinterpreting here and now, by giving new life to, what these first Christians experienced in contact with the living Christ. The past is also a call to us now, a word that the glorified Christ addresses to *us*, whose situation is equally characterised by his death and resurrection and his sending of the Holy Spirit. It is a call to us to realise a fraternal community by participating in a Christian meal. The living Christ identifies himself with the community at table, he himself becomes the food and drink that is offered at the meal, and we can live in this community from his redeeming death and his being raised to power by the Father.

This is sufficient for Christian *life*. This seems to me to be the meaning of the declaration made by the Dutch bishops, in their pastoral letter on the Eucharist, leaving further interpretation to theologians. This requires a hesitant and reverent approach not only to the original New Testament datum, but also to the elaboration of this datum in the later Church under the guarantee of the Holy Spirit. The witness of the apostles must therefore be our guiding principle in this, and not phenomenology directly. But the basic meaning of this apostolic witness can only be preserved for us in a pure state if it is viewed from our present context of life and thus approached phenomenologically. In this perspective, then, I should like to put forward a few supplementary data which are, in my opinion, necessary if the original inviolable datum of the Catholic confession of faith is to be reinterpreted in a way that is faithful to the tradition of the Church.

The Basic Principle: Reality Is Not Man's Handiwork

The Basis of All Man's Giving of Meaning. In the Eucharist, "the Lord's death is proclaimed" (I Cor. II. 26). This context cannot be overlooked in any existential or phenomenological approach without misrepresenting the mystery of the Eucharist. Christ is present in the Eucharist as the Lord—that is, as the one who gave himself in death "for our sins" and was brought to life for us by God. Our personal relationship with the Lord is also essentially an *anamnesis,* a calling to mind of the historical event of salvation on the cross, not insofar as it is past, but insofar as it endures eternally in its completion. The eternity is, however, not situated behind history, but accomplished in history, and the ultimate completion is the closing of history, not by leaving history behind, but by bestowing a lasting validity on this history itself, namely in its completion. That is why our relationship to the risen Christ is identical with our relationship to the historical Jesus.

Because of the eucharistic context, a "real presence" can never be viewed in isolation. It is clear from the words "Take and eat, this is my body" that *a meal* was constituted a sacrament, not simply food and drink, bread and wine, although these form an inward aspect of the sacrament. The crucified, dead and risen Lord becomes really present in a meal. He gives his death and resurrection as a meal, and this is therefore at the same time an *anamnesis,* a remembrance.

What, then, is the distinctively eucharistic meaning, within this context, of the "real presence"?

Several modern authors correctly regard the creation, the beginning of the covenant of grace, as the background to the eucharistic event as well. For the believer, things are not only what they are in themselves and what man experiences of them in his life within this world. For him, they are, in accordance with their own measure of being, also divine revelation. As a subject standing, because of his own bodiliness, in the midst of the material world, man is the centre of the world and thus, at the same time, the subject in which God's revelation finds a response, is received and interpreted. What is more, this response to and reception and interpretation of revelation takes place in and through what things are themselves. Creation is a divine act which cannot, of its very nature, be directed towards God's completion of himself, but is God's pure and gratuitous communication of himself, his love for his creatures. In concrete terms, it is God's love for man in the world. God's creation thus establishes a personal presence of God in all things (which are there for man—God's gifts to man) and especially in the subject that is called man, to whom these gifts are given out of love. In what they are, things *are,* through God's creative will, really saving values and divine revelation, revealing and veiling at the same time, and they are this both metaphysically and really, and not only in the minds of those who believe, even though someone who does not believe cannot recognise this reality of being, at least in his thematic consciousness. In this sense, it is therefore possible to say that the entire world has a general quasi-sacramental significance. This Christian view of creation does not empty matter of its proper meaning, but renders it intelligible in its deepest meaning. For the believer, the function secular reality has as a *sign* is deeply involved with its *concrete being.*

This has far-reaching consequences for our human knowledge. We confront the world as giving it meaning, certainly, but it is not our handiwork. It is given to us by God as our world. Man, it is true, leads an essentially interpretative existence which to some extent allows light to be thrown on reality—that is, on truth—which presents it precisely as intelligible. But the meanings given by man are governed by a reality which is (not chronologically, but in metaphysical priority) in the first place God's, and only then man's. That is why reality is a *mystery,* the form, disclosing and concealing at the same time, in which God reveals himself. The deepest essence of persons and things therefore always escapes us. Thus our knowledge, which both takes and gives meaning, can only grasp reality insofar as the explicit content of knowledge refers to the mystery which eludes us and is always beyond our grasp. We live in a reality which is given to us as God's gift. We live as strangers in this reality, yet we are at the same time invited to accept it, and we therefore experience it explicitly as a mystery and thus as a gift. But it is in this reality that we are permitted to live and to discover our well-being.

This reality, so difficult to penetrate, in which we live and which we ourselves also are, is the fertile soil of our life of giving meaning. The referential character of our consciousness is therefore essential. As believers, we know that all this is traceable to God's giving, *personal real presence,* which we experience in the shadow that this presence throws on the creaturely reality. Everything that is explicit in our consciousness is therefore only referential, referring to the mystery. We know reality only in signs. Thus, what we consciously experience as bread and wine is also always a sign of the reality which escapes us, even outside the context of the Eucharist. Everything pertaining to things thus always conceals a personal relationship for us. God's personal presence is always the deepest relationship *in everything*—it situates us within the mystery in which we are invited to give a human meaning. The fundamental meaning for me is a gift of the reality itself, which is originally not *my* reality, but is nonetheless given to me for me to give meaning to it.

Because of this fundamental meaning for me, I can go on to establish various meanings which will determine what things signify concretely for me on the basis of what they are themselves. I cannot set about this task arbitrarily, because I am at the same time tied to the reality given to me. Situated within the mystery that is given to me, however, I *establish* a human world, the human meaning of which I am continuously changing. It is only the human meaning of the world that I can change, however, since its deepest, metaphysical meaning is beyond human understanding and intervention.

I propose now gradually to develop this basic idea in connection with the Eucharist. In this, I shall proceed from the more superficial level to greater depth, so that the decisive question—whether transubstantiation and transsignification are identical or not—will be asked and answered last of all.

Human Giving of Meaning—Productive and Symbolic. Man is able to improve certain natural elements by natural processes—he has, for example, in this way obtained wheat, from which he is able, by technical means, to make bread. Wine is similarly the end product of natural and technical processes. In this sense, then, bread and wine are, as products of human cultivation and techniques, the result of a human activity of giving purpose, for the benefit of *man* and for his use. But this giving of purpose by man can and does go further than this.

Bread and wine, already useful to man as nourishing physical life, have a further function in human intercourse. They have a symbolic meaning—bread is the symbol of life and wine is the symbol of the joy of life. Products of human cultivation can therefore be given all kinds of relative meanings at different levels. In the case of men sharing a meal together at table, eating and drinking, already in themselves useful biologically, can be raised to a higher level of human good. They can become the expression of fraternal solidarity, of interpersonal intimacy, of the successful conclusion of an agreement or a treaty or of the sealing of a friendship. Because man in fact lives in a *humanised* world, he is above all concerned with this kind of human giving of meaning—he lives in them and from them, within the mystery of the reality which he cannot himself create, but which has been given to him.

The biological utility of eating and drinking is not denied by this further meaning, but is included in a specifically human event. An animal's eating is *essentially* different from a man's eating, even though the biological process is the same. A thing can become essentially different without being physically or biologically changed. In interpersonal relationships, bread acquires a completely different meaning from that which it has for the physicist or the metaphysician, for example. Remaining physically what it is, bread can be included in a sphere of meaning that is quite different from the purely biological. In that case, the bread *is* different, because the definite relationship to man at the same time defines the reality under discussion. Of course, man lives in fact from continuous "transsignifications"—he humanises the world. And such changes of meaning are more radical than purely physical changes, which are at a lower level and, in this sense, at a less real level. Establishing meaning is more than a psychic intention. There is an essential correlation between the object, the bread, and the subject, the meaning given by man, within the *mystery* of the reality in which the world is given to us and we are given to ourselves. The change of meaning is accomplished precisely in the *humanised* world and in this context it is a substantial change.

It is remarkable how the word "transubstantiation" has seemed to suggest this phenomenon to poets and in the poetic liturgy of the Church. In a letter to this beloved, Goethe, for example, said, "For me, you are transubstantiated into all objects," implying that he experienced her in all the things that surrounded him in everyday life, that plants and trees, flowers and fruit were different for him—the sphere of meaning of an interpersonal communion, the realising sign of the presence of his beloved. This giving of meaning is in contact with a human reality and is not a dream (although it could also be a dream—in human life, "reality" is infinitely varied). Within the sphere of this particular experience of reality, things are different from what they would be in another sphere of experience. It should, however, be remembered that, in this case, it is a question of man's relative attitudes to the world and that the basic assumption that the *being* of reality is *given* and is, in its own being, meaningful to man (*ens et bonum convertuntur*) remains. This preliminary and basic meaning makes man's giving of relative meanings possible and invites it.

In describing the distinctive reality of a definite human datum, it is important not to jump from one level to another. On the basis of these general remarks, it is therefore necessary to say that, even apart from the specifically Christian meaning of the Eucharist, a *positive* answer to the question, "Is the bread still *ordinary bread* after the consecration?" is completely meaningless. This is simply jumping from the cultic level to that of, for example, the physicist. It is, of course, possible to ask about the physical reality, but an answer to this question must not be thought of as an answer to the cultic and, in this case, theological question. Confusion of this kind—it is, of course, much more simply a manner of speaking—has obscured all questions concerning the Eucharist. The answer to a question asked in a eucharistic context ("What is the form of bread *after the consecration?*") can only be eucharistic. The answer given by a physicist or a chemist who is concerned with atoms and molecules may perhaps teach us something indirectly, but it will ultimately be irrelevant to the Eucharist. The Tridentine statement is therefore, apart from its specifically Catholic significance, first and foremost a denial that the bread can still be called bread after the consecration. For the Eucharist as such, it is a question precisely of this. A further analysis of what the bread is, for example, physically or metaphysically, outside this context, is irrelevant.

On the basis of these general principles, it is therefore possible to say that eucharistic transubstantiation cannot be viewed in isolation from the sphere of giving meaning in sacramental signs. Because of the paschal context ("Take and eat, this is my body"), it must moreover be situated within the sphere of reality of Christ's *gifts of himself* that is meaningful and capable of being experienced, a remembrance, both doing and speaking, of Christ's death and resurrection. The level of physics and the philosophy of nature can therefore be disregarded. Transubstantiation is inseparably a "human" *establishment of meaning*. I have, however, not yet said anything about the question of whether transubstantiation and transsignification are identical. I have, on the other hand, ruled out the view that only *our attitude towards* a datum that remains unchanged is changed in the Eucharist.

The Eucharist and "Bread and Wine" in Human Religious Symbolic Activity. When bread and wine were given their place in the Eucharist, their human significance had already been changed. In the first place, they were not simply raw natural elements, but products of human cultivation with an inseparable relationship to man. They were essentially and substantially objects of biological utility, intended as nourishment for man.

They were then included, in a human manner, in the meal and thus acquired a function in human fellowship. The primary sacramental form of the Eucharist is therefore not simply "bread and wine," but the *meal* in which bread and wine are consumed. Sacraments are, after all, never isolated things, but human actions, in which things or gestures are included, for example, *washing with* water, *anointing with* oil, *laying on* of hands and so on. Thus, in the Eucharist, the food, the meal and the community of believers at table all essentially belong to each other— they are the *human* matter which becomes sacrament.

A great deal, however, had preceded the Eucharist. Bread and wine (or equivalent food) had become the symbol of life and had therefore acquired a place in the worship of the natural religions, in which God was experienced as the origin of all life, and especially in the so-called "cosmic liturgy," in which thanks were given to God for his good gifts of life. In Israel, these feasts were given a foundation in history, because Yahweh had not revealed himself primarily as the God of nature, but as the God of history, who had even forced nature to serve the history of his people. Israel's paschal feast was therefore the liturgical remembrance of an event of salvation, an *anamnesis* of the exodus from Egypt, Yahweh's deliverance of his people.

The cosmic cult and Israel's liturgy of Yahweh's history of salvation with his people came together in the Eucharist, achieving their inward but transcendental fulfilment in something that was quite simply entirely new. The primitive Church situated the Eucharist within the context of the Old Testament paschal celebration (with different emphases in the various sources) and also used the paschal bread, but she did this in the perspective of the new Passover, the definitive event of redemption—Christ's sacrificial death and his resurrection. What the gospels say is, This bread—both the symbol of life (*de tuis donis ac datis*—the cosmic liturgy) and the paschal bread (the Old Testament liturgy with its historical significance)—is my body. My body is a paschal sacrifice which I give you here to eat. "I am the Life"—this is what is really experienced in the Eucharist, in *anamnesis* of the Lord who died, but is living.

The transubstantiation that is implied in this context clearly evokes a reality at a very definite level. The level is that of the celebration of a meal, a meal that is celebrated in a religious symbolic activity—that is, in a rite which *asks for life* and which *gives life* and which is a recollection of the living sacrifice or the "death of the Lord." The bread and the wine which are involved in this activity are not simply a hospitable gift at a visit. The idea of a "visit" made by Christ to the elements is alien to the Eucharist. What happens in the Eucharist is that the faithful share in Christ's rising to life and accomplish this with him in faith while giving thanks to God. It is precisely to this that Christ's "real presence" in the Eucharist relates. There is, for example, not directly a presence for the purpose of adoration in the Eucharist. The really sacramental element, the *ratio sacramenti*, is precisely our eucharistic accomplishment with Christ of, and salvific inclusion in, the life-giving death of the Lord. "Into thy hands I commend my spirit"—with, in and through Christ (according to the canon of the Roman rite), we commend our lives into the hands of the Father, in service to man in the world.

The Real Presence of Christ and of His Church in the Eucharist. The specifically eucharistic "real presence" now can also be defined more precisely in the perspective of this specifically eucharistic efficacy of grace. The basis of the entire eucharistic event is Christ's personal gift of himself to his fellow-men and, within this, to the Father. This is quite simply his *essence*— "The man Christ Jesus is the one *giving himself*" (*ho dous heauton,* I Tim. 2.6). The eternal validity of his history on earth resides in this. As I have already said, the personal relationship to the heavenly Christ is at the same time an *anamnesis* of his historical death on the Cross.

The Eucharist is the sacramental form of this event, Christ's giving of himself to the Father and to men. It takes the form of a commemorative meal in which the usual secular significance of the bread and wine is withdrawn and these become bearers of Christ's gift of himself—"Take and eat, this is my body." Christ's gift of himself, however, is not ultimately directed towards the faithful. The real presence is intended for believers, but through the medium of and *in* this gift of bread and wine. In other words, the Lord who gives himself thus is *sacramentally* present. In this commemorative meal, bread and wine become the subject of a new *establishment of meaning,* not by men, but by the living Lord *in* the Church, through which they become the *sign* of the real presence of Christ giving himself to us. This establishment of meaning by Christ is accomplished in the Church and thus presupposes the real presence of the Lord in the Church, in the assembled community of believers and in the one who officiates in the Eucharist.

I should like to place much greater emphasis than most modern authors have done on this essential bond between the real presence of Christ in the Eucharist and his real presence as Lord living in the Church. After all, there is ultimately only one real presence of Christ, although this can come about in various ways. It forms, in my opinion, an essential element in the constitution of the Eucharist. In interpreting the Eucharist, it is not enough simply to consider Christ's presence "in heaven" and "in bread and wine," like the scholastic theologians, who regarded Christ's real presence in the faithful only as the fruit of these two poles, the *res sacramenti*. By virtue of the meaning which is given to them by Christ and to which the Church consents in faith, the bread and wine are really *signs,* a specific sacramental form of the Lord who is already really and personally present for us. If this is denied or overlooked, then the reality of Christ's presence in the Eucharist is in danger of being emptied of meaning. Transubstantiation does not mean that Christ, the Lord living in his Church, gives *something* to us in giving this new meaning, that he, for example, gives us incarnate evidence of love, as in every meaningful present, in which we recognise the hand and indeed the heart of the giver and ultimately therefore experience also the giver himself. No, in transubstantiation, the relationships are at a much deeper level. What is given to us is the giver himself. This gift of the giver himself is quite inadequately rendered by the phenomenological "giving of oneself *in* the gift." "This is my body, this is my blood": this is not a giving of oneself in a gift, not even at a more profound level because the giver here is Christ, the personal revelation of the Father. No, what is given to us in the Eucharist is *nothing other than Christ himself.* What the sacramental forms of bread and wine signify, and at the same time make real, is not a gift that refers to Christ who gives himself in them, but Christ himself in living, personal presence. The signifying function of the sacrament (*sacramentum est in genere signi*) is here at its highest value. It is a making present of himself of the real, living Christ in a pure, meaningful presence which we are able to experience in faith. The phenomenal form of the eucharistic bread and wine is nothing other than the *sign* which makes real Christ's gift of himself with the Church's responding gift of herself involved in this making real to us, a sign inviting every believer to participate personally in this event.

The sacramental bread and wine are therefore not only the sign which makes Christ's presence real to us, but also the sign bringing about the real presence of the Church (and in the Church, of us too) to him. The eucharistic meal thus signifies both Christ's gift of himself and the Church's responding gift of herself, of the Church who is what she is in him and can give what she gives in and through him. The sacramental form thus signifies the *reciprocity* of the "real presence." As the definitive community of salvation, the Church cannot be separated from Christ. If, then, Christ makes himself present in this particular sacrament, the Church also makes herself present at the same time. The presence of both Christ and his Church is meaningfully expressed in this sacramental sign in common surrender to the Father "for the salvation of the whole world" and thus realised in a special way. This is why Augustine was able to say that "we ourselves lie on the paten" and the whole patristic and scholastic tradition was able to call the Eucharist the "sacrament of the unity of the Church with Christ." "This is my body" is "the body of the Lord," the New Covenant, the unity of the Church with Christ. "Because there is one bread, we who are many are one body, for we all partake of the one bread" (I Cor. 10. 17). This does not do away with the real presence of Christ himself, which is, of course, the foundation of the Church. The "body of the Lord" in the christological sense is the source of the "body of the Lord" in the ecclesiological sense. Christ's "eucharistic body" is the community of the two—the reciprocal real presence of Christ and his Church, meaningfully signified sacramentally in the *nourishing* of the "body that is the Church" by Christ's body.

In the Eucharist, then, the new, definitive covenant is celebrated and made present in the community. Priority must be given to Christ in the Eucharist. In the Middle Ages, the really present body of Christ (*res et sacramentum*) was traditionally taken as the point of departure and the really present "body that is the Church" was only considered in the second place. But Christ's real presence to his Church and the Church's real presence to her Lord are really "sacramentalised" in the Eucharist, with the result that this reciprocal real presence becomes deeper and more intimate in and because of the sacramental form and that the *reciprocal* giving of self to the Father in the form of a gift of love to fellow-men becomes, through this celebration, more firmly rooted in the saving event of Christ's death and resurrection. Thus the Eucharist is directed towards the *Father,* "with, in and through Christ," and towards *fellow-men* in fraternal love and service. The Eucharist forms the Church and is the bringing about of herself of the Church which lives from the death and resurrection of Christ.

All this has important consequences for the constitution of the Eucharist and for transubstantiation. The presence offered by Christ in the Eucharist naturally precedes the individual's acceptance of this presence and is not the result of it. It therefore remains an offered *reality,* even if I do not respond to it. My disbelief cannot nullify the reality of Christ's real offer and the reality of the Church's remaining in Christ. But, on the other hand, the eucharistic real presence also includes, in its sacramentality itself, reciprocity and is therefore completely realised only when consent is given in faith to the eucharistic event and when this event is at the same time accomplished personally, that is, when this reciprocity takes place, in accordance with the true meaning of the sign, in the sacramental meal.

The eucharistic presence is therefore not dependent on the faith of the individual, but the sacramental offer cannot be thought of as separate from the community of the Church. It is, after all, a real presence of Christ *and of his Church.* As the scholastic theologians correctly said, the Eucharist was constituted in its sacramentality, not by the faith of the individual, but, thanks to the intention of the celebrating priest as expressed in the rite of consecration, by the "faith of the Church." It is correct to say that the Eucharist is a rite of the Church and the real presence of Christ living in the Church. It implies a "human" giving of meaning which does not, however, come from man, but from the Lord living in the Church or from the Church as living in the Lord. This giving of meaning can therefore only take place within the sphere of the "faith of the Church" in the Lord who really lives and is present in the Church. This does not make transubstantiation any less real or reduce it to a purely subjective or intentional event. It does, however, mean that the eucharistic reality can only be approached from faith and is therefore not valid as a reality for a non-believer because he simply has not reached this level of reality. But this disbelief does not nullify the reality of the Eucharist.

If, however, we try to objectivise the consecrated bread to such a point that it becomes dissociated from the faith of the Church, then it becomes incapable of being experienced and indeed meaningless. Christ's real presence in the Eucharist is, of course, *really* an offer of grace, independent of the individual's faith. But the eucharistic liturgy is also an event which establishes meaning and the significance of the eucharistic bread and wine cannot be determined apart from this. All physical or metaphysical interpretation which takes place outside the sphere of sacramentality is valueless as far as our understanding of the Eucharist is concerned. When anything untoward happens to a consecrated host, but no believer is, or could remotely be, involved in the incident, it does not matter. If, for example, we hear that a mouse has nibbled at it, we need not be alarmed—the level of reality with which the Eucharist is concerned can only be reached by the believer as a *reality* even though its existence is not dependent on the faith of the individual. What then, the "faith of the Church" realises in the coming about of Christ's eucharistic presence as a sacramental offer, the faith of the individual realises in his personal acceptance of this offered presence. The Church's relationship within the Covenant with Christ realises the "sacramental sign," whereas the individual person's attitude in faith within the believing community realises his personal involvement in this Covenant.

Transubstantiation and Transsignification or a New Giving of Meaning

It is only against the background of the whole eucharistic event, as outlined briefly in the foregoing paragraphs, that attention can be focussed on the question, "What *is*, then, that eucharistic bread and wine in the last resort?" The non-Christian cannot see any change whatever, and even the believer cannot see any difference if without his noticing it consecrated hosts are replaced by unconsecrated hosts.

In the very first place, this points clearly to the fact that the bread and wine cannot be dissociated from the rite of the Eucharist. This is why even the reservation of the hosts is so surrounded by marks of reverence that the eucharistic context is clearly preserved. But this poses the question as to whether this reverence is sufficiently explicable on the basis of the Church's transsignification of the meal. And with this, we are approaching the final question—is transsignification identical with transubstantiation, or is it a consequence or an implication of transubstantiation? The question that arises here in its full extent is that of reality.

Reality and Its Phenomenal Appearance. The question we have to ask ourselves is ultimately, What is the *reality* that we experience in our preception of the eucharistic form? We cannot therefore avoid briefly situating the structure of human perception.

Human perception—and I am speaking here only of man— has a very specific unity, that of a spiritual act (that is, of active openness to reality) with what is perceived by the senses. As such, sensory perception (that is, what is perceived by the senses *and* perception) cannot be called either objective or subjective and should not be interpreted either realistically or idealistically. What is perceived cannot be separated from the subject who perceives it. It is not independent of the environment that appeals to man and is therefore not purely a condition of the consciousness. It is also not independent of the reaction of a subject and is therefore not an objective quality of reality. What this naturally implies, then, is that anything that has meaning for sensory perception is bound to lose this meaning if divorced from this perception. This has been clearly illustrated by Merleau-Ponty, who was, however, inclined to apply it to human consciousness in its totality.

Purely sensory perception, however, does not occur in man. He sees, hears, smells, tastes and touches in a *human* manner, and thus humanises both what he perceives and perception. Perception, which, as such, only serves biological unity, is therefore (together with its content) included in the orientation of the human spirit towards reality, the sphere of the specifically human, the *honestum,* what ultimately is—the world as the reality of God which we are permitted to enter. Thus perception (together with its content) is raised above purely sensory relativity and taken in the direction of the spiritual meaning of reality. It therefore refers externally, as in signs, to reality itself which, as such, only has meaning for the human spirit. In this sense, man himself fashions the signifying function that the content of his perception has with regard to reality and makes this content a referential sign. Despite his complexity, man is nonetheless a unity and all his conscious orientation towards reality must therefore be clothed in and borne up by referential sensory perception of this kind. The human spirit cannot approach the mystery of the reality that is constantly escaping him without these references of (humanly qualified) sensory perception. In this sense, our entire human consciousness is situated *in* human perception, and not behind, above or beneath it. The sensory contents which we acquire in vital contact with our environment (in our case, bread and wine) cannot be regarded as an objective qualification of reality. They can therefore neither be called accidents nor objective attributes of a "substance" which is, so to speak, situated at a deeper level. It therefore seems that to make an Aristotelian distinction between substance and accidents cannot help us in interpreting the dogma of transubstantiation.

Partly through sensory perception, man opens himself up to the mystery of reality, to the metaphysical being which is prior to and is offered to man's ontological sense—that is, to his logos, which *makes* being *appear* and thus *establishes meaning.* This previously given reality is not man's handiwork. Reality is never this—it is God's creation. The dogma of creation and the metaphysical realism that is the consequence of this dogma are at the centre of all theological speculation. The reality of creation is necessarily prior to all giving of meaning by man. It is only within this already given mystery, and only if man builds upon the inviolable but mysterious gift which the "world of God" is, that man, giving meaning, can make a *human* world for himself.

Man's condition, however, his life of the senses, his conceptual approach and his concrete association with things—also determines the way in which reality *appears*. A certain difference between reality itself and its phenomenal appearance results from this human condition. The reality does not, of course, situate itself behind its phenomenal appearance—the appearance is the reality itself. But this appearance is, as such, also coloured by the complex way in which man approaches reality, the consequence of his complex mode of being. The human logos, man's own giving of meaning, thus plays a part in the appearance of reality. The inadequacy of man's knowledge of reality accounts for a certain difference between reality and its appearance as a phenomenon. In this sense, the phenomenal is the *sign* of the reality—it signifies reality. In this context, then, the "phenomenal" includes not only the sensory, but also everything that is *expressed* of the reality itself or concretely appears to us, which is, then, inadequate to what is expressed (the reality as a mystery). Explicit knowledge of reality is therefore a complex unity, in which an *active* openness to what communicates itself as reality is accompanied by a *giving of meaning*. What in fact shows itself to me, however, also acts as a norm for the meaning I give to the reality.

The "Body of the Lord" Appearing in Sacramental Form. It is impossible to neglect the general structure of man's knowledge of reality in thematising the Catholic belief in the real presence of Christ in the Eucharist. To do so would be to make a man's faith into a kind of "superstructure," built on top of our human knowledge. Our understanding in faith of a reality of salvation is also a very complex whole. As I have already pointed out, an active openness in faith to what is objectively communicated to us as reality is accompanied by a giving of meaning in faith, as here too the *appearance* of the reality of salvation is coloured by (believing) man's complex mode of being.

If reality (in the potent sense of "what really *is*") is not man's handiwork and cannot be traced back to a human giving of meaning, but only to God's gift of creation, and if it is clear from the entire tradition of faith and from the Tridentine dogma of the Eucharist that the Church, in her consciousness of faith, strongly insists on the *reality* of the presence of Christ in the Eucharist, then it must be clear to the Catholic theologian that eucharistic transsignification is not identical with transubstantiation, but is intimately connected with it.

It is particularly in the case of the Eucharist that we are bound to consider the distinction between the reality itself and this reality as a phenomenal appearance. Normally, of course, we give no attention to this distinction, and the fact that we overlook it does not affect our practical lives at all. But when we reflect about the Eucharist, our noses are, so to speak, pushed into it. *What* appears, in our experience, as bread and wine *is* the "body of the Lord" appearing to us (as sacramental nourishment). The significance of the phenomenal forms of bread and wine changes *because* by the power of the creative Spirit, the reality to which the phenomenal refers is changed—it *is* no longer bread and wine, but nothing less than the "body of the Lord," offered to me as spiritual nourishment. Because what is signified via the phenomenal is changed objectively, the significance of the phenomenal itself is also changed. Believing man is naturally involved in this transsignification of the phenomenal. The new significance of the form of bread and wine means that the believer actively gives the phenomenal a place in his orientation towards, and his openness to, *what* really appears—the "body of the Lord" in the sacramental form of nourishment. In the Eucharist, transubstantiation (*conversio entis*—what *is* the present reality? Christ's body) and transsignification (the giving of a new meaning or new sign) are indissolubly connected, but it is *impossible simply* to identify them. The active giving of meaning in faith by the Church and, with her, by the individual believer takes place within the mystery of grace of the really present "body of the Lord" offered by God and attained by the Christian intention to reach reality. The real presence of Christ in the Eucharist can therefore only be approached by *allowing* the form of bread and wine experienced phenomenally to *refer to* this presence (of Christ and of his Church) in a projective act of faith which is an *element of and in* faith in Christ's eucharistic presence. The event in which Christ, really present in the Eucharist, appears, or rather, offers *himself* as food in which the believer receives him as food therefore also includes a projective act of faith. This act does not bring about the real presence, but presupposes it as a metaphysical priority. Thus the "sacramental form" is really the "body of the Lord" proclaiming itself as food. Christ really gives himself as food for the believer. This "sacramental form" only reaches its fulfilment in the meal in which we nourish ourselves on Christ to become a believing community.

I have struggled with the interpretation of this *mysterium fidei* and, in faithful reverence for what the Catholic *confession* of faith has for centuries allowed Christians to experience in the celebration of the Eucharist, I cannot personally be satisfied with a *purely* phenomenological interpretation without metaphysical density. Reality is not man's handiwork—in this sense, realism is essential to the Christian faith. In my reinterpretation of the Tridentine datum, then, I can never rest content simply with an appeal to a human *giving of meaning alone,* even if this is situated within faith. Of course, a transsignification of this kind has a place in the Eucharist, but it is born up and evoked by the re-creative activity of the Holy Spirit, the Spirit of Christ sent by the Father. God himself *acts* in the sphere of the actively believing, doing and celebrating Church, and the result of this divine saving activity is sacramentally a "new creation" which perpetuates and deepens our eschatological relationship to the kingdom of God. "The Lord left behind a pledge of this hope and strength for life's journey in that sacrament of faith where natural elements refined by man are changed into His glorified Body and Blood, providing a meal of brotherly solidarity and a foretaste of the heavenly banquet."

Yves Marie Joseph Congar
1904-

Yves Congar was born in Sedan, France, in 1904 and joined the Dominicans in 1925. His first major work appeared in 1937 and was translated into English in 1939 as Divided Christendom. In retrospect it stands as the first public expression of a new orientation soon to have great impact on Catholic theology, viz., the ecumenical dimension. The contribution of Père Congar in this domain is simply immeasurable.

Paradoxically it was his 1950 publication on True and False Reform in the Church that brought Congar his most respected status as the foremost ecumenical theologian in Catholicism which also produced the clouds of suspicion under which he was forced to labor for the following decade. In some ways this is thoroughly understandable; it is always the pioneers who are misunderstood and maligned. Catholics and Protestants had a 400-year-old legacy of mutual distortion that virtually guaranteed that they would never understand one another. Thus the first step toward any kind of Christian unity would have to be a conscious effort to set aside prejudice, bad will, and polemical myths in order to try to learn to appreciate the positive factors historically involved.

Congar brought painful attention to the fact that if the separation of Christians was sinful, its continuation is also sinful. The enduring separation, he recalled, "has become a heavy *stone rolled over the mouth of the sepulchre where unity was entombed by the first misunderstandings." But he was too much of a theologian to leave it at that. The new direction in which he began to probe was later to be taken up directly by Pope John XXIII and Vatican II's Decree on Ecumenism, i.e., the implications of baptism. Separate brothers remain brothers despite the separation; they should conduct themselves accordingly and strive desperately to remove the obstacles to unity.*

The selection that follows appeared as an article in Concilium in 1967. It provides a good example of Père Congar at his best. He has ever had a fine knack for deriving insight from history. In a pre-ecumenical era Catholic theologians often felt no need to go further than a compendium of church pronouncements. An argument was settled by appeal to a document, papal or conciliar. Modern biblical studies, however, have called attention to the impropriety of such an approach. Every document has an historical context and stands in need of historical interpretation. If the catechism has made much of the sevenfold number of sacraments, that is all well and good—as long as one does not thereby end up contradicting reality and distorting history. To argue over number without examining the question of the nature of the sacraments in Christian tradition is to do violence to truth.

The principle that Père Congar utilizes in this article found general expression and endorsement in Vatican II. There is a "hierarchy of truths" in Christianity. Some things are more important than other things. Controversies often tend to demolish that realization. An institution is fortunate when it has custodians of history such as Père Congar to restore perspective where balance has been lost. Catholic understanding of liturgy is one among many areas that have benefited from his insight.

THE SACRAMENTS IN GENERAL

THE NOTION OF "MAJOR" OR "PRINCIPAL" SACRAMENTS

I

THE DATA OF TRADITION

The idea that some sacraments are more important than others, particularly baptism and the eucharist, is well supported by traditional theology. In the age of the martyrs we have Ignatius of Antioch, Justin and Irenaeus, who describe these two sacraments as "faith" and "charity". St. Augustine tells us that the people of Carthage called baptism "salvation" and the eucharist "life". He himself wrote in his famous reply to Januarius, so often quoted in the Middle Ages: "Christ bound the community of his new people together by means of sacraments that were very few in number, easy to administer and clear in meaning, such as baptism with its invocation of the Trinity and the communion of his body and blood and some other ones insofar as there is mention of them in the canonical scriptures." In the 11th century Peter Damian added a third one to them, the sacrament of order, to make up the "three most important sacraments". A little later another supporter of Gregory VII wrote: "Holy Church, the mother of all . . . has received several sacraments. There are, however, but a few of them, two given by the Lord himself, others instituted by the apostles." These the Lord officially commanded us to celebrate. The Middle Ages were less exacting than we are about the institution of the sacraments, and easily accepted the idea of an indirectly divine institution. Shortly before 1140 the *Summa Sententiarum* called baptism and the eucharist "the two principal sacraments". Hugh of St. Victor singled out for special treatment the three sacraments of Christian initiation, baptism, confirmation and the eucharist. This was sound tradition. One finds this, for instance, a little earlier in Rupert of

Deutz, and a little later in Hugh of Rouen who says of them that "they establish the city of God". In connection with these three sacraments, Hugh of St. Victor says that there are "certain sacraments in which salvation consists and is received principally", and he adds, "such as the water of baptism and the reception of Christ's body and blood".

It was Thomas Aquinas who molded these data of tradition into a balanced vision, doing justice to the various aspects of the truth. It was universally held that the sacraments which constituted the Church were symbolized by the water and blood that flowed from Christ's side on the cross and that these sacraments were baptism and the eucharist, "the most important sacraments". St. Thomas took up this theme to show that the sacraments draw their power from Christ's passion. Elsewhere, in order to show that the bodily absence of the Lord required the institution of ministers for the administration of the sacraments to the faithful, he started from the institution of baptism and the eucharist, "which are the principal sacraments", by Christ himself. Of course one could consider the order or hierarchy among the sacraments from different points of view. Baptism was the most important "in the order of necessity", but one might say that the sacrament of orders was the most important "in the order of perfection", and that the eucharist is without doubt the most important from the point of view of meaning and contents.

The traditional theology of which I have quoted some texts led the Council of Trent to condemn the proposition that the seven sacraments are equal in every sense. There were two opinions among the theologians that met on January 29, 1547. One section of them held that the proposition could not be condemned without some explanation; the others maintained that it was erroneous and false, and already condemned in various authoritative ways. Apparently the latter won.

Modern theologians broadly accept the idea of principal sacraments, either by reference to the traditional explanation of the water and blood that flowed from the side of Christ on the cross or by reference to that canon of the Council of Trent.

II

REASONS FOR "GRADING" THE SACRAMENTS

The reasons for this grading may be found either in the source of the sacraments, namely, Christ, or in the effect of the sacraments on the faithful and the Church.

1. *The Source of the Sacraments*

Baptism and eucharist are clearly in a position of privilege due to a formal expression of Christ's will, attested by Scripture. The Lord himself determined matter and form, and, essentially, the rite and usage also. Without administering them himself strictly speaking, he directly sanctified the elements, either by his baptism (Mt. 5, 13-7; Mk. 1, 9-11; Lk. 3, 21-2), or by sharing the Passover meal with the apostles and inserting into that meal the new sign of bread and wine (Mt. 26, 26-9; Mk. 14, 22-4; Lk. 22, 19-20; 1 Cor. 11, 23-5). These two sacraments are therefore special from the point of view of being instituted by the Lord: this institution is more direct, explicit and formal than that of the other sacraments.

This priority is probably also due to their more solid relationship with the deed by which Jesus obtained salvation for us. It is true that all the sacraments are related to the Passover of the Lord, his death and resurrection, and this holds equally and absolutely for all of them insofar as that is the only source of their efficacy. But insofar as their content and effective significance are concerned, the other five sacraments are less strictly related, i.e., from a certain angle only or less direct. Baptism and eucharist, on the contrary, are efficacious signs of the Passover by their very sacramental structure: for baptism see Romans 6, 1-11; Colossians 2, 11-3, and for the eucharist Matthew 26, 26-8; Luke 22, 19-20; 1 Corinthians 11, 23-6. Now, the Passover of the Lord lies at the very heart of what he did for us. It is there that Jesus effectively took upon himself our sinful situation and our condemnation, and by the same token it is there that he established himself effectively as our leader, our representative before God. Through this Passover, which embraces his death, resurrection and glorification, Christ became the source of a new, eschatological life for mankind. Because of this he had to die in our flesh and rise again in the Spirit: cf. Rom. 1, 2-4; 4, 23-5; Gal. 2, 19-21; 3, 26-9; 1 Cor. 15, 45-53; 1 Peter 3, 18; 4, 1-2 and 6. On the cross Christ became our second Adam and the effective leader and mediator of that life of reconciliation of the children of God. We must therefore associate and assimilate ourselves to Jesus Christ in his Passover. This is why St. Paul uses the famous verbs with the prefix *syn* to express our association with Christ at the various moments of his Passover. He speaks of "being crucified with, associated in his death, in his resurrection, in his being seated with God in heaven, in glory"; he does not speak of "being associated in the presentation in the temple, or the hidden life at Nazareth". No doubt, we associated with him there, too, but not in the same way or at the same level.

It is obvious that those sacraments, which by their meaning and content are directly and fully linked up with Christ's Passover and "re-present" the reality of this Passover in a certain real way, have a special and outstanding place in the overall sacramental structure.

2. The Effect of the Sacraments

What has just been said explains why a number of texts, quoted above, mention the Johannine symbol of the water and blood that sprang from the side of Christ on the cross. As far as I know, Tertullian is the first to mention this theme. From then on it would be easier and shorter to mention those Christian authors of East and West who do not use it than those that do. This theme is practically always linked to that of Christ as the new Adam who gives himself and unites the Church, the new Eve, to himself: she springs forth from the side of the sleeping Christ. This leads us to consider the special relationship of baptism and eucharist, compared with the other sacraments.

These two sacraments are called *praecipua, principalia, potiora* (more important, principal, more powerful) and this because of the part they play in the very constitution of the Church. This is already clear at the figurative or typical level of the Old Dispensation. For St. Paul, the community of Israel in the desert prefigures the Church, the new Israel: "Our fathers were all under the cloud, and all passed through the sea, and all were baptized into Moses in the cloud and in the sea, and all ate the same supernatural food and all drank the same supernatural drink. For they drank from the supernatural Rock which followed them, and the Rock was Christ" (1 Cor. 10, 1-4). Because he is thinking of Christian baptism and the Christian eucharist, Paul sees them prefigured in the Red Sea and the cloud, in the manna and the water of the rock. He sees there sacraments of unity, turning a multitude of people into the People of God. In the same way Christians are baptized into one single body (cf. 1 Cor. 12, 13; Gal. 3, 27) and constitute only one body (Christ's) because they eat of the same and only bread (1 Cor. 10, 17).

On both these occasions Paul speaks in terms of body and incorporation. When, however, we consider that baptism is traditionally and in reality "the sacrament of *faith*"; that the eucharist, and not baptism, is called the "body of Christ"; that this eucharist contains the very mystery of Christ and not only its power, and that it is clearly more closely related than baptism to the body of the Lord, we shall have no difficulty in seeing in baptism the sacrament that initiates men as "Church", the new People of God, and in the eucharist the sacrament which finally constitutes this people, this "assembly of the faithful", as the *body of Christ*. This is the way Vatican Council II speaks about it in the *Constitution on the Church* (n. 17) and in its *Decree on the Ministry* (nn. 2 and 5).

The Council has also hallowed the description of the Church as the "universal sacrament of salvation". This, together with the concept of People of God, is one of Vatican Council II's richest contributions to ecclesiology. This theme had already been developed in Catholic theology for some ten years. It obviously uses the classical data of the treatise on the sacraments, but puts them into the perspective of salvation-history as set out by Paul in his letter to the Ephesians, under the name of "God's design" and "mystery". Seen in this light, the notion of sacrament assumes dynamic value; it is related to the world and its history. It becomes the concrete historical expression of God's design for salvation in this world, the sign and instrument through which God works out his decision to intervene with his grace in mankind and in creation in order to make them achieve the end for which he had destined them from the beginning: the condition of freedom of the sons of God (cf. Rom. 8, 18-30). Within the world the Church is the sign and instrument (*Constitution on the Church*, n. 1) of that renewal of the world on which God had irrevocably decided and of which the incarnation of his Son inserted the principle into history (*ibid.*, nn. 48, 3). The Church is this both insofar as she contains the means of grace (*Heilsanstalt*) and insofar as she is the People of God among all other peoples, yet owing her existence to a postitive, supernatural act of God's grace.

Every one of the seven sacraments stands in this sign, but it is obvious that baptism is fundamental as constituting the People of God and the eucharist as creating and expressing the unity and communion of Christians in Christ Jesus. The other sacraments sanctify and christianize man in a special situation: sin, illness, marriage, spiritual service, but baptism (confirmation) and the eucharist constitute them as Christian persons pure and simple. They are basic.

Yet, insofar as the Church is constituted as the active sign of God's design for salvation, the sacrament of orders plays a decisive part along with these two: it "structures" the People of God by visibly representing Christ as head and as sanctifier. The Church is not in the world only as a community of the sons of God and of those that are saved, but fully as the sign and instrument of Christ as he actually saves and communicates this quality of "son of God". Therefore, insofar as the Church is the universal sacrament of salvation, the principal sacraments are baptism (completed in confirmation, *orders* and the eucharist.

In itself and educationally we are no doubt right in having a treatise on the sacraments in general. It is less fortunate that we usually place it before the study of each sacrament in particular because it tends to create the impression of a univocal concept that then becomes a rigid framework within which the study of the sacraments in their reality must fit. But the sacraments can only be generalized about in an analogical way. It would therefore be better to treat each one as it is in itself and then to see what they have in common and what can be said about sacraments in general. It is interesting to observe that, historically speaking, baptism and the eucharist served as the starting point and model when a treatise on the sacraments in general was composed in the 12th century. This seems to confirm that these two sacraments were recognized as "principal", "major" or "fundamental".

III

THE IMPORTANCE OF THIS "GRADATION" FOR ECUMENISM

The teaching that I have tried to set out here is common to both East and West. Oriental theology is known to be essentially a theology of the divinization of man. And on this point the Greek Fathers have always given a position of priority to baptism and eucharist. In his *Mystagogia*, Maximus the Confessor deals only with baptism and eucharist in detail. Nicholas Cabasilas only treats of the three sacraments of Christian initiation. Modern Greek Orthodox theologians point out that only baptism and eucharist are expressly reported as instituted by Christ; they call these sacraments the "principal" sacraments, and have stated that on this point they consider the Anglican position acceptable.

Article 25 of the Church of England's Thirty-Nine Articles runs as follows: "There are two Sacraments ordained of Christ our Lord in the Gospel, that is to say, Baptism, and the Supper of the Lord. Those five commonly called Sacraments, that is to say, Confirmation, Penance, Orders, Matrimony, and Extreme Unction, are not to be counted for Sacraments of the Gospel, being such as have grown partly of the corrupt following of the Apostles, partly are states of life allowed in the Scriptures; but yet have not like nature of Sacraments with Baptism, and the Lord's Supper, for that they have not any visible sign or ceremony ordained of God."

There is no doubt that the Anglican position is dependent on that of Luther's Reformation. Luther used to speak of two sacraments as instituted by Christ himself. It should be noted that Luther and also the Augsburg Confession always joined an explanation of confession to their teaching on baptism and eucharist. How far did they refuse a sacramental character to confession? Pressed by the Catholics to say whether he accepted seven sacraments, Melanchthon appealed in his *Apologia of the Augsburg Confession* to the lack of precision and vacillations of the old theology. One could only truly call sacraments those rites for which there was proof that they were instituted by God. In these circumstances he counted as sacraments baptism, the Lord's Supper and absolution or the sacrament of penance, but, without denying their usefulness, he excluded confirmation and extreme unction, and only accepted orders as a sacrament, if one understood by that the ministry of the Word, while he accepted marriage only with many reservations.

Calvin also admitted that one could call sacrament the imposition of hands by which ministers or pastors were received in office, but he maintained, more firmly than Melanchthon, that there were only two sacraments, basing himself on the criterion of a divine institution attested by Scripture, while he distinguished "the five other ceremonies" from these two, as they were "of a lower degree".

I am aware of the fact that to restore in our theology, and therefore afterwards in our catechetics, the traditional idea of "major" sacraments may risk encouraging the Protestant denial of the proper sacramental quality of the other sacraments. But we have seen that this denial is not absolute, but is limited to the aspect of the immediate and explicit institution by Christ. Nevertheless, underneath all this there lies the question of the apostolic tradition, its reality and its proper normative value. All the discussions that are taking place between our Reformed brethren and ourselves show a high degree of closeness and cohesion. We must obviously remain faithful to what a tradition, wholly common to East and West, teaches about the sacraments and their number, since this tradition stems from the undivided Church of the first thousand years. But this should not prevent our accepting the idea that there are principal or major sacraments, as indeed this same tradition prompts us to do. By doing this in the sense of this tradition we shall make the ecumenical dialogue on the sacraments more fruitful.

This is not the only case where the truth, like the concern for a new ecumenical *rapprochement* (as John XXIII would say), encourages us to recognize that there is a grading, a hierarchy, of certain realities which, though going by the same name, are neither heterogeneous or equivocal nor identical. There are major Councils, even among those called "ecumenical". There are major Patriarchates, the five considered such by ancient tradition. The Latin Church venerates twenty-five "Doctors of the Church", and yet, there are four Greek and four Latin ones who are traditionally considered more important than the others. In the same way, the conciliar *Decree on Ecumenism* says that there is a certain hierarchy among the truths to be believed and the teachings to be taught (n. 11). This point is so important that it deserves an article by itself. This is, moreover, also a traditional point. It seems to me, as to several fathers of the Council and a number of observers, that this statement of the *Decree on Ecumenism* is one of the most important made by the Council.

Formally or legally considered, all dogmas, all "ecumenical" Councils, all sacraments are equal. But looking at things from the point of view of their *content*, their place in the saving structure of the Church, and that of "Sacred doctrine", we must accept that there are major dogmas, major "ecumenical" Councils and major sacraments.

Jean Marie Roger Tillard

1927-

Born in St. Pierre, France, Tillard entered the Order of Preachers (Dominican Fathers) in 1950 and was ordained a priest in 1957. He completed a doctorate in philosophy at the Angelicum in Rome and a doctorate in theology at Le Saulchoir in Paris in 1958. Since 1959 he has been on the Faculty of Theology of the University of Ottawa, Ontario, Canada.

The theology of the liturgy and of the religious life are but two aspects of a single interest of Père Tillard. Throughout the 1960s he published a series of books in French which enthusiastically caught the spirit and conveyed the richness of the renewal advocated by the Council. One of the reasons for the success of his writings was certainly to be traced to his familiarity with the varied sources and expressions of the Christian tradition: the Bible, the liturgy, the Fathers, the scholastics.

One of the problems of any tradition is the way in which original insights and breakthroughs are reduced to banality by subsequent generations. What was a dynamic discovery in the beginning is passed on as if it were self-evident and forever fixed. The selection that follows is an article written by Tillard for Concilium in 1971. It is offered here as a fine example of the kind of enrichment that traditional theology can receive when brought into contact with modern biblical studies. Themes that *were separated in the earlier tradition are here brought together in an intriguing way.*

Current concerns about meaningful reform of the sacrament of penance have paved the way for thought such as found here. Just as sin is a pervasive reality in human life, so too reconciliation is an ever-present activity in the redemptive community. The deepened theology of the Eucharist to which Tillard has himself devoted two entire books calls for a different understanding and appreciation of the relationship between it and baptism and penance as well as the other sacraments.

The appeal of Tillard's approach lies especially in its synthetic quality. New interrelationships are perceived and elaborated, resulting in a theology that reflects the unity of experience. All subsequent analysis must not be allowed to take away from this. In this kind of understanding liturgy can never become one compartment of life, nor will it be fragmented into unintelligibility.

SACRAMENTAL RECONCILIATION

PART I

THE BREAD AND THE CUP OF RECONCILIATION

A critical examination of the gospels in search of the very pivot of salvation, the heart of the Christian confession of faith, inevitably ends up at the following words of St. Paul: "Therefore, if any one is in Christ, he is a new creation; the old has passed away, behold, the new has come. All this is from God, who through Christ reconciled us to himself and gave us the ministry of reconciliation; that is, God was in Christ reconciling the world to himself (*kosmon katallasson eautò*), not counting their trespasses against them, and entrusting to us the message of reconciliation. . . . We beseech you on behalf of Christ, be reconciled to God. For our sake he made him to be sin who knew no sin, so that in him we might become the righteousness of God" (2 Cor. 5.17-21).

Although it is difficult to explicate the last verse of this passage, and although exegetes have, especially since the Reformation, offered conflicting interpretations, Christian tradition as a whole is united in the major affirmation (brought out with splendid emphasis by Chrysostom) that the mystery of Christian faith turns on a "reconciliation" arising from the wholly gratuitous love of God and manifest within the world in a humane brotherhood of those who are "reconciled" with one another. The first chapters of Ephesians depend on the same understanding of the essence of revelation: God's mystery opened forth. The grand design hidden from all eternity in the silence of the Father intends not merely communion (*koinonia*), in the same sense of men united in love, but (and here redemption is seen as essentially connected with the purpose of creation) a communion and a human brotherhood of those inescapably characterized by a law of enmity and a fatal flaw setting them against God and against other men, and conducive to division even within the individual's inmost self (Rom. 7. 15-23). This threefold conflict expresses the profound and continually manifest reality of sin. Therefore reconciliation and *koinonia* must go together in God's realistic plan for men. The very essence of the second is primarily related to a transcending of, a victory over, sin. It is a *koinonia* in the reconciliation offered by God; and attains to its proper reality only by means of constant reference to its source and location—Jesus' paschal humanity. And Jesus' humanity was offered on the cross as a "propitiation" for the sins of men (Rom. 3. 25; 1 Jn. 2. 2, 4. 10), and exalted in the resurrection as the first fruits of the new world (1 Cor. 15. 20-23; Col. 1. 18). In the very flesh of the Lord, the Father offers those who will receive him the possibility of new life, open to God and open to other men, thus overcoming the confinement to which man is continually sentenced by sin. The openness of *new life* which, in Jesus, shows forth the dynamics of salvation itself must, by the action of the Holy Spirit, become manifest for the faithful Christian in his actual existence, so that it is opened out in a way wholly conducive to full reconciliation. In this way the Church is born; and St. Paul (aptly, in this perspective) describes the Church as the body of Christ. Day after day, the Church is built up through the action of the Spirit; and, without remission, the Spirit plucks it out of sin in order to lead it towards the truth of actual reconciliation.

I. THE LORD'S SUPPER: SACRAMENT OF "RECONCILIATION"

Understood in the light of the foregoing, the few texts of the New Testament which make explicit reference to what we now call the Eucharist are profoundly homogeneous. They all tend to affirm that when the Church is joined together for the Lord's Supper, it celebrates in thanksgiving and supplication mystery of its own reconciliation. Admittedly, this reconciliation was accomplished once and for all (*ephapax*) in the event of the death-and-resurrection of Christ, but once again it is applied to the Church, *hic et nunc*, in its sinful situation, by virtue of the sacramental character of the celebration and meal. By one and the same action the Church is freed from its sin and enters into a more authentic *koinonia*.

The Lord's Supper is a sacramental memorial. Regardless of whether the Last Supper coincided with an actual passover meal, the accounts of the institution of the sacrament evidently direct us to this interpretation, if only because of the words Paul and Luke attribute to Jesus: "Do this *eis tèn emèn anamnèsin*" (1 Cor. 11. 24-25; Lk. 22. 19): that is, "in remembrance of me". The Greek of the gospel traditions is a translation of the Hebrew *zikkaron*, a term with very precise connotations. In the liturgical context (obviously the case here) it characterizes a cultic act by which a past salvific event is recalled—but in order to relive *hic et nunc* the grace of that event in praise and blessing, which revives hope in the ultimate accomplishment of that salvation at the very moment when God is reminded of his promise and asked to realize it. There is no question of a purely subjective recall—a mere quickening of the believer's memory; what is implied is an objective reality by virtue of which the very effectiveness of the great events of salvation remains present throughout history. In the paschal meal, for example, under the signs of food and the community about the table, the present generation participates in the significant action of the first Easter. The axis of remembrance is this reality, which appears as a pledge from God re-encountered through the mediation of signs. In this way, the everlasting fidelity of God towards his people, and the irrevocable efficacy of the salvific events, continue to enliven those who receive them in faith and hope.

What exactly is the divine action which is thus connected with the Lord's Supper? It is the act of *reconciliation*. According to the words of the gospel narratives themselves, the bread that is broken bears the body given for all (Lk. 22. 19), the cup offers the blood of a covenant (Mt. 26. 28; Mk. 14. 24) which is the new covenant (Lk. 22. 21; 1 Cor. 11. 25), blood poured out for many for the forgiveness (*eis aphesin*) of sins (Mt. 26. 28). All these connotations are entwined in the very reality of the reconciliation that Jesus effected. Jeremiah might be said to have affirmed the characteristics of the new covenant in language based upon the experience of renewed friendship with but one ultimate cause: the fact that God would forgive crimes and forget sins (Jer. 31. 31-34). At the eucharistic meal, the Church is assured that in the signs of remembrance, by the power of the Holy Spirit alone, the body and blood of reconciliation are truly present to it, not merely so that the Church may fittingly praise God but above all so that it may participate once and for all (*ephapax*) in reconciliation. The Church is able to participate in this way by eating the bread and drinking from the cup of salvation. The significance of the latter above all is clear: by joining himself with the blood shed in forgiveness of sins, each believer is made part of the dynamism which we recall, and, reconciled with God, finds in communion through the power of the Lord's *agapé* the necessity and possibility of a life of reconciliation with his brothers, whoever they may be—an existence of due profundity.

This allows a better understanding of 1 Cor. 10. 16-17: "The cup of blessing which we bless, is it not a participation in the blood of Christ? The bread which we break, is it not a participation in the body of Christ? Because there is one bread, we who are many are one body, for we all partake of the bread." The participation—the *communion*—does not come about merely by virtue of the fact that one, unique "body of Christ" is given to all: it originates in the reconciliatory power enclosed in that body. Just as in its paschal meal, generation after generation, Israel entered into communion with the efficacy of the salvific action carried out at the fringe of its history, so in their eucharistic meal the new people of God open themselves to the redemptive and reconciliatory power of the Lord's Passover. Through its major witnesses and in its various liturgical forms, tradition has never ceased to assert that at the Last Supper the Church derived its unity from participation in the nature of the unique event of Jesus' sacrifice of his life "in order to unite the divided and scattered children of God."

Considered thus in the perspective of its foundation, the Eucharist is the sacrament of ecclesial reconciliation. In the tracery, so difficult to arrange appropriately, of scriptural allusions to what one might call the mystery of forgiveness in the Church, baptism and the Lord's Supper stand out clearly as the two most prominent sacraments. Even though a comparative analysis of the documentation on the Eucharist and of the major texts relating to baptism (above all Rom. 6. 2-11; Col. 2.

12-13; Tit. 3. 5-7; 1 Pet. 3. 21-22) shows that these sacraments are both grounded in the same *ephapax* of paschal reconciliation, it also reveals the additional significance or fullness of baptism in the light of the Eucharist. This was, of course, admirably stressed in the primitive form of Christian initiation.

Baptism ratifies the reception of the Word of salvation by introducing the believer to the new life; it is birth into reconciled life, and joins the Christian to the ecclesial body of the Lord. The Eucharist adds its fullness and leaven to this initial reconciliation, so that the ecclesial experience of salvation may, as is needful, be constantly revivified. For, in the strict sense, the table of the Lord is the unique actual (as well as sacramental) form of communication of the community as such, and not only of the individual, with the paschal humanity of the Lord. The ecclesial body to which entry is provided by the new birth in water and the Spirit (Jn. 3. 5) experiences its human mystery in the Lord's Supper by participating in the act of reconciliation. Therefore the reconciliation is no longer merely that of a member of the Church forgiven in the blood of Christ and admitted to the bosom of the Father, and thus called to lead a life in communion with his brothers; it is also the reconciliation, to be re-experienced continually and always progressive in tendency, of the body as such with the Father and in him. For in this reconciliation the local Church celebrates and receives the body and blood of the Passover which, reuniting each Christian to the Father and to his brothers, enables that Church to become—within the world—a "body of reconciliation", a *koinonia* established in a love that is always forgiving.

That is why the baptismal reconciliation itself is oriented to the eucharistic celebration, which is its consummation. But the assertion that the Eucharist is in this way the fulfilment of the dynamism of baptism implies that it is already effective in baptism, in the sense that the end is active in that which tends towards it. When one actuality is wholly oriented to another actuality, the intention of the latter impregnates and conditions the action of the former. It takes effect "primordially" in the very depths of that which is disposed towards it; being, like a call-sign, something in the nature of a trigger for action (because of it, everything is set going), it continually underlies the development of the activity in question, for the one goal is aimed at in every moment of the course. As the sacramental consummation of reconciliation, the Eucharist is already effective in baptism, and dynamically implicit in this initial stage of a mystery which will come to fullness only in that eucharistic consummation. In other words, theologians speak of a kind of objective desire (*votum*), implicit in the very nature of baptism and not only in the believers' intention to be baptized. Aquinas wrote that without the *votum* of the Eucharist there would be no salvation for man, since no one could attain to grace without this aspiration to full eucharistic reconciliation—a form of desire already objectively implied in the structure of baptism and which must pass into the consciousness of the baptized person when mature. The reconciliatory efficacy of baptism depends essentially on the ordination of baptism at the Lord's Supper. The sacramental source and the place of paschal reconciliation are therefore the Eucharist. For reconciliation is not merely a private affair between the believer and the Father, but—at one and the same time—the mystery of man's encounter with his brother, and the mystery of the encounter of the reborn community as such with its God and Father.

Therefore the Eucharist can be conceived as the sacrament of an essentially ecclesial reconciliation. The human experience of the communal meal in which this mystery enjoys sacramental life is in no way incidental. In the very sense of the *zikkaron* of the Last Supper, the Eucharist reveals the nature and the demands of the gift that it bestows only by means of the symbolic texture in which it takes shape. The very experience of eating together, in an atmosphere of celebration, is redolent of a meeting in love, a mutual opening-forth, an advance beyond mere intrinsic individual existence, and therefore (in consideration of what men actually are) a reconciliation: what counts is less the fact of eating than that of eating *together* while sharing the same existential blessing.

Perhaps not enough attention has been paid in this regard to the insistence of the gospel traditions on the rite of the breaking of bread, which constitutes the community of the table in the Jewish meal ritual, and on that of the cup which goes from hand to hand as the sign of being joined together in the same destiny. These two actions, which put the meal symbolically into a context of brotherhood, Jesus made the agents of the Eucharist, i.e., of the bestowal of the reconciliation made possible by his death. The sign that Jesus made the matter of his sacrament is not the bread and the wine in their static existence, or even merely their power to sustain life. It is the bread and the cup already involved in a symbolic act of human encounter and unity. In this way, the reconciliation bestowed is signified in all its fullness: communion with God realized here and now in the communion of human brothers. A sign of human brotherhood encloses the mystery of reconciliation. As the cross before, the eucharistic meal now renders the profound tendency of salvation visible within the Church.

It should now be clear why it would be a serious theological error to separate in the Lord's Supper the reference to the *ephapax* of the cross (the sacrificial dimension) and the reference to the fact of eating the bread and drinking the cup together (the sacramental dimension). It would entail destroying the profound unity of the mystery of reconciliation. The remembrance enacted is not restricted to the act of refreshment: it implies an essential dimension of the action of thanksgiving and entreaty, the fruits of which (being the fruits of salvation) extend beyond both the assembly which celebrates it and the *hic et nunc* of the celebration. This major effect establishes the ecclesial office of intercession which has its proper place and constant resource in the Eucharist; it is intimately connected with the universal extension of the Lord's sacrifice made present in the signs of the Church. Nevertheless, the profound effect of the eucharistic event is fully active on the individual believer's life only in his receiving of the bread and the cup. That reception is the realization of the very tendency of the paschal sacrifice which is being commemorated. When the Church celebrates this memorial, it asks the Father for the gift of participation in the salvation for which it blesses him; the Father answers the prayer of the Church by giving it the body and blood of reconciliation. "Do this in remembrance of me" implies the volition already expressed in "take, eat", "drink all of you." Communion with the efficacy of the paschal event is actualized by receiving the signs in which the Event of salvation is *re*-presented and realized *hic et nunc*. This is one, indivisible sacramental mystery.

Therefore the Church participates in the paschal reconciliation (with its two dimensions opening the Church to the Father and to humankind) by means of the sacramental action of sharing in common the bread and the cup which, in their ultimate depth of significance, have become the body and blood of Christ. This action shows forth the effect desired by the Lord. The eucharistic grace must pierce the brotherhood of the table, which is quite precarious (because of the sin which turns every Christian in upon himself), and always limited. Grace enables the Christian to perceive his ideal image in the transient action of the symbolic rite, and to judge himself; cleansing and revivifying him with paschal virtue and power, it projects him towards a culmination which is nothing less than total reconciliation with God and with men, to be sought for again and again because never encountered in its fullness. Therefore the eucharistic meal has an eschatological reference. It is not restricted to a mere celebration of givenness, and to a ritual ornamentation of a fragment of Christian life that is already wholly fraternal—to the celebration of human friendship already intensely manifest. In the actual inadequacy of our ecclesial *koinonia*, spoiled by our enmities (and therefore our various failures in reconciliation), and by the imperfection of our response to God, incapable of reaching perfection in this world, it sets the body of Christ, which heals this condition and shapes it anew so that it may tend wholly towards the God who will be "everything to every one" (1 Cor. 15. 28).

II. EUCHARIST FOR THE REMISSION OF SINS

In the foregoing I have presented the connection between the eucharistic remembrance and the mystery of reconciliation from the angle of communion, and I have avoided any separation of the positive dimension of entry into the friendship of God and the dimension of the forgiveness of sins within the complex whole of that mystery. In biblical thought, reconciliation is not to be mistaken for the effacement of the past, the forgetting of sins, the extinction of a penalty once incurred. It offers deliverance from enmity and entry into the joy of recovered friendship.

The reconciliation of the prodigal son finds its consummation and full significance in the merrymaking of the banquet (Lk. 15. 11-32). For this reason, the old form of public penance had the reconciliation of the penitents take place on Holy Thursday and culminate in the celebration of the Eucharist.

But Jesus' own words require us not to forget that this joyous celebration of salvation at the eucharistic assembly is grounded in the "remission of sins" made possible by the blood of Christ, and that the action of eating the bread and drinking from the cup bestows the fully redemptive power of his death. The reconciliatory function of the Eucharist necessarily implies its efficacious and direct role in the forgiveness and remission of sins.

Elsewhere, I have given a detailed account of the extent to which tradition has always acknowledged this redemptive character of the Eucharist, which is connected to the totality (inseparable from it, according to the Fathers) of the offering of the memorial and the reception of the sacramental signs in which this is accomplished. In taking the bread and the cup of expiation, the believer participates in the propitiatory power of the cross. His sins also are wiped out. The best scholastic thought did not dispense with this way of conceiving the relation of the Eucharist to the *ephapax* of the death of Christ, even though it distinguished "sacrifice" from "sacrament". Aquinas makes the following categorical assertion in regard to communion: "Considered in itself (*secundum se*), this sacrament has the power to remit all sins, and derives this power from the passion of Christ which is the source and cause of the remission of sins".

In the most realistic sense of the term, the Eucharist is the sacrament of forgiveness, because it is the sacramental presence and communication of the act which remits sins: as the remembrance of the expiation of the cross, it applies that expiation to those who celebrate the memorial by putting them in touch, through the bread and the cup of the meal, with the "once and for all" of the paschal event itself, and calls down on the whole world the infinite mercy of God, the Father of Jesus. Within the Church, it is properly speaking the location of redemption.

The declaration of the Council of Trent on the propitiatory value of the Lord's Supper has to be reconsidered in the light of the foregoing. Without adverting to what I have outlined in another essay, it seems necessary to emphasize the realism of the Tridentine position, which is evident in the perspective of the preceding discussions of 1551-1552 and 1562. Above all in their interventions of December 1551, when the first revision of the text on the sacrifice was being developed, the theologians offered several important qualifications. The reaction of the Reformers made the Tridentine theologians insist on the unique character of Jesus' sacrifice as an adequate expiation of and satisfaction for all the sins of the world: the eucharistic "sacrifice" does not offer another crucifixion but applies the virtue of the cross. But this application relates to all sins, even the most serious, committed after baptism. Admittedly, opinion on this point was not unanimous—a similar situation obtained among the bishops. However, one has to acknowledge that the draft text proposed on 20 January 1552 is an admirable statement, especially in its original form as preserved by Frédéric Nausea, Bishop of Vienna, of both the main line of these discussions and the Council's awareness of the complexity of the question. When, in 1562, the problem recurred in the order of the day (inextricably entwined with controversies as to the sacrificial value of the supper on Holy Thursday), the doctrinal atmosphere was no different. A comparative analysis of the various versions of the text shows that the whole is in fact not perfectly well-knit (probably because the unity of the Eucharist *ut sacramentum* and *ut sacrificium* was not appropriately conceived), but that the ruling idea is the certainty of the power of the Eucharist *as such* to remit *"crimina et peccata etiam ingentia"*.

But how does the Eucharist apply this power? In no mechanical fashion, certainly, for in order to attain to the gift of remission a true heart, an unsullied faith, and above all an *unmistakable* contrition and *unmistakable* penitence are required—for God respects man's freedom. But such is the power of the paschal oblation that, to the man who truly accords with its tendency, God grants the grace of perfect sorrow, which remits crimes and sins however great they are; this remission is made actual in participation in the body and blood of the Lord. The text is not clear. I have shown elsewhere why this is so, and justified my interpretation by reference to the entire conciliar documentation. If my interpretation is correct, one is to a considerable extent referred to the traditional interpretation, which is more flexible than the overly myopic explanations current today.

Of course there has never been any doubt in the Church in regard to conditions of truth of life and of heart required before the eucharistic reconciliation can take effect. Reconciliation is not a divine action effected in violation of human liberty. Even though he always makes the first move, God begins by cultivating man's heart so that a desire for unity with him will eventually blossom there. And, anyway, reconciliation means a mutual desire for reunion in love. When love grows to the desired extent on both sides, reconciliation is effected and ratified. As far as the sinner is concerned, the essential expression of this love is contrition. Through the power of the memorial of the propitiatory sacrifice of the Passover, in the fullness of the communal celebration, God grants the seriously guilty though well-intentioned Christian the grace which allows his contrition to develop and thus permits him *actually* to receive, together with his brothers, the bread and the cup of reconciliation.

Theologians therefore recognize two moments in the indivisible forgiving action of the Eucharist: one is more the moment of opening of the heart (through contrition, God already invites man into the full reception of his love), whereas the other is a moment of consummation in which the new covenant is confirmed. Neither of these moments is external to the Eucharist; neither is without its communal nature: together they make up its ecclesial action of redemptive forgiveness. Through the power of the memorial, God moulds the believer who is well disposed even though culpable of grave sin, and who is taking part in the celebration, in order to make him able *truly* to eat the bread of salvation and *truly* to drink the cup of the covenant. This is evidently much more than a preparatory process of mental purification. It is possible for the two moments to be attained in the same act of sacramental manducation. As is known, this is the Thomist theory: if the insufficiently contrite sinner approaches the Lord's table in quite good faith and reverently, together with the body and blood of the Passover he will receive the charity that inspires his contrition and hence opens him to friendship for God—at the moment when he receives the confirmation of his reconciliation. The Eucharist is a whole in which the various components of the one mystery continually blend and interpenetrate to produce the single indivisible action of grace.

The Eastern tradition is certainly aware of this, as is evident from the inclusion in the anaphora of communal penitential prayers that are virtual petitions for absolution. Just as they ask forgiveness for "involuntary" mistakes, they refer to a certain number of "voluntary", grave sins outside the public confession. This insertion in the Eucharist itself is very significant: the forgiveness which makes the Christian fit to receive the Lord's Supper *truly* is directly produced by the memorial itself; that is, by the Passover, but as commemorated *hic et nunc* by the assembly of the faithful. This is an effect of the Eucharist which is consummated in sacramental contact with the body and blood of redemptive sacrifice given in the meal of brotherhood. This is the basic ecclesial source of all forgiveness in its authentic context of communal reconciliation. The remaining rites serve either to extend or to explain it. In addition, with the introduction of auricular confession the Copts simply drew on these eucharistic penitential formularies in order to construct a private rite, just detaching them from their original setting.

Here the Latin liturgy is less satisfactory in its introductory penitential rite, which is poorly integrated into the whole of the new *Ordo Missae*, where it gives the impression of being a preparation, a preliminary formula, without any indication that the grace requested also derives from the memorial. In this respect the West is noteworthy for its reticence. In the ninth century it allowed only a confession of the ministers at the beginning of the synaxis. Later (no doubt under monastic influence) a general penitential formula was introduced directly before the communion. But this would seem to be no more than a request for mental purification, to allow subsequent reception of the sacrament—hardly conducive to the traditional understanding centering more upon the *truth* of the ensuing action than on the purity required. Nevertheless, in certain instances there appeared between the homily and the offertory an adequate stage of communal prayer, including a general confession, the imposition of a penance, and absolution: a usage that persisted here and there, even after Trent. Of all the Latin customs, this would seem to be the most satisfactory and to conform most appropriately to the Christian understanding of the situation of forgiveness. For the liturgy of the word and the eucharistic liturgy form one whole; the word conveys to each Christian but also to the entire assembly as such the power of conversion deriving from the Passover, and allows them *truly* to enter into the mystery of a reconciliation in which God and man are both involved.

III. EUCHARIST AND SACRAMENTAL PENANCE

This well attested existence of explicit rites of absolution and forgiveness in the main eucharistic liturgy (even though in the present Mass of the Latin rite they serve—alas!—only to open the celebration) leads me to pose a certain question. Understood in the light of the discussions from which they emerged, the Tridentine texts certainly though hesitantly affirm the Eucharist's power of redemptive forgiveness as insisted upon in the rites to which I have just alluded; but these texts insist emphatically on the necessity of reference to the sacrament which for several centuries had been recognized as a sacrament of forgiveness in its own right—sacramental penance. Quite apart from the Tridentine documentation, the entire contemporary discipline of the Church is to be called in witness here. Why, if what I have said is correct, must one hold that "those whose conscience is weighed down with mortal sin must first go to sacramental confession, if they can find a confessor", before they approach the eucharistic table? Does not this improperly diminish the value of full participation in the paschal memorial?

To answer these questions one must distinguish between two categories of sins. According to the medieval tradition of Trent, one would speak of venial sins, wiped out by the Eucharist, and of mortal sins, requiring penance; but these categories are awkward. It would certainly be preferable to have recourse once more to the ideas of Theodore of Mopsuestia, of Ephraem Syrus, and of Augustine, who, writing in the context of an age which was still without our forms of private penance, speak of "major sins" effecting exclusion from the Christian community and demanding public penance, and of sins of weakness (un-reflected or involuntary) the matter of which might well be serious *in se* but which do not imply any formal rejection of God, and are therefore effaced by the Eucharist. If one trans-lated this classification into the present-day context, one would distinguish between sins of real malice in which bad will is evident, and sins which are possibly serious in terms of matter but which imply a capitulation of the will (if, indeed, it has occurred at all) apart from the "pressure of meditated and relished malice". These distinctions, especially the latter, are illuminating: reception of the Eucharist is enough to efface all sins where no real malice is apparent.

Nevertheless, this does not resolve the problem entirely. I have already said that the Oriental liturgies and the penitential rites inserted into the Latin Eucharist after the homily speak of an absolution covering even sins of malice. And, in an inverse sense, Trent was aware that in order to obtain purification of life through the Eucharist, the Christian must have at least a desire (*votum*) for sacramental penance. Trent also remarks that the efficacy of the Eucharist for immediate absolution does not remove the necessity of sacramental penance.

The answer can be found only in a proper understanding of sacramental penance as arising from the Eucharist, inasmuch as it is an expression of an essential dimension of the Eucharist. The ecclesial sacramental source of forgiveness is the Eucharist, which is the celebration of reconciliation in both its private and communal dimensions. All forgiveness bestowed in the Church derives from and is oriented to the Eucharist. I have already noted that baptism itself properly owes its substantive character to the Eucharist. But the paschal memorial stresses above all the intervention of God, who "reconciles men in Christ". Human undertaking is obviously requisite here—an impulse of friendship which, in the case of a sinner, is coloured by contrition. It is enough that this impulse should exist, and one must acknowl-edge the justice of Cajetan's assertion that access to the eucha-ristic table makes obligatory contrition *for* and not confession *of* grave sins. In any case, the eucharistic signs insist above all, in this regard, on the divine action at the Lord's Supper filling to overflowing the brethren whom (if they accept him *in truth*) God's generosity reconciles with him and with one another in the experience of the brotherly meal.

The reconciliation ratified by the Eucharist also implies an important notation of a human action: that of the prodigal son who, with a contrite heart, returns to his father, acknowledges his sin and confesses his suffering to him, and begs him to allow his son once more to enter into friendship with him. The father's love undoubtedly took the initiative, and forgiveness had already been bestowed when the son made his move. But, for the reconciliation to attain to its *full truth*, the son's "attitude" is required; this, even though it does not bring about forgiveness (which can come only from the father), nevertheless expresses the authenticity of the call. This is the action of sacramental penance, which is a sacrament having as its matter the whole of the contrite penitent's actions. It is therefore an expression of the human action included in embryo in the Eucharist, providing it with the full space and development required by the very dynamics of reconciliation. In this sense, sacramental penance extinguishes a tension within the density of the eucharistic experience. If, at the moment when he approaches the bread and the cup of reconciliation, the sinner has not already taken this step before presenting himself at the banquet of friendship (which, in a sacramental perspective in which the laws of grace are one with the rhythms of human psychology, is the usual attitude), he must then have the firm desire (*votum*) and sincere resolution to take it eventually. There can be no true reconciliation without at least this *votum*, which is the manifest expression and guarantee of the existence of authentic contrition, without which no grace of forgiveness can be bestowed upon the man whom God never ceases to consider as his free creature.

In strict theological terms, the presence of this contrition (and of the *votum* guaranteeing it) suffices for the sinner—whatever the gravity of his sin—to be able *in truth* to eat the body and drink the blood of Jesus, and not to his own "damnation" (1 Cor. 11. 27-30). In his own time he will perform the act of sacramental penance which, since the Middle Ages, the Church has officially treated as one, but not the sole or main, step required for the forgiveness of sins. Provided that the *votum* exists, even though he has sinned gravely, the Christian can receive the body of the Lord without previous sacramental confession, and can obtain his reconciliation from that body: one might say that God "anticipates" the confession which will make explicit a reality already essentially present in its eucharistic source. The theologian Ravestein affirmed this in the full assembly of the Council of Trent. Sacramental penance serves only to stress clearly a structural component of the Eucharist within the total mystery of Christian reconciliation.

For reasons of pastoral order which were fully justified at the time of Trent, the present discipline, which relies (if one reads the conciliar texts aright) not on a divine law but on a "custom of the Church", holds that usually (apart from cases of urgent necessity and when a confessor is not available—CIC 856) the Christian guilty of a grave sin must go to confession *before* communion. Surely it would be advantageous in our present situation of rediscovery of the Eucharist and of deep dissatisfaction with the actual forms of sacramental penance (which are felt to be out of tune with the psychology of the present-day Christian) to return to a situation of greater flexibility. Without discarding personal sacramental contact with the Church's minister (but conceiving it as something other than a direct condition of access to communion, and according to a rhythm adapted to individual development), it would be possible, not, certainly, to treat the penitential rite at the beginning of Mass crudely as a general absolution, but at least to see it as an expression of the expiatory power operating in the memorial and applied to those who sincerely regret their sins and are ready to acknowledge them at an opportune moment. This acknowledgment should be made in the exact manner which the Church has the power to lay down, but which is not necessarily tied to the present forms.

This would undoubtedly restore to paschal confession, reconceived in the way I have indicated, its full and proper significance. What is more, the faithful have already sensed this: they have taken the initiative.

Robert Walker Hovda

1920-

Robert Hovda was born in Clear Lake, Wisconsin, in 1920. He attended Hamline University from 1938 to 1941 and, as a conscientious objector, served in a Civilian Public Service Camp during the war. After studies at St. John's in Collegeville, Minnesota, he was ordained a priest for the diocese of Fargo, North Dakota, in 1949. After a decade in parish ministry he became a theology instructor at Catholic University in 1959 till 1962. In 1963 he became chaplain of St. Paul's Student Center at North Dakota State University in Fargo, but in 1965 returned to Washington as editor of Living Worship *and member of the Liturgical Conference's staff.*

Dry Bones, subtitled "Living Worship Guides to Good Liturgy," consists of a selection of the essays that appeared in Living Worship *from 1970 to 1972. The fourteen essays are organized into three section: 1) Approaches, 2) Principles, and 3) Problems. Three of those essays (the first three under "Principles") make up the following selection.*

Modernity—new ways of thinking, acting, experiencing—constitutes the greatest challenge to religion in our age. How can the values of the past be translated into the present and salvaged for the future? Reform, renewal and adaptation in liturgy are all efforts to deal with this problem in a positive way. At stake is the survival of Christian life and faith as we have known them. The problem, however, is so complex, has so many dimensions, and is encountered in so many different ways and forms, that the individual is at a loss in trying to cope with it. Hovda's essays were intended to provide some help in an especially critical time when the basic changes mandated by Vatican II were reaching the grass-roots.

The three essays are "Choosing Quality," "Gaining Experience" and "Letting Symbols Speak." Their purpose was more ephemeral than much contained herein, but they capture something of the atmosphere of a trying time, an important transitional period. They are the kind of writing that has to be redone in every age: pastorally motivated reflections meant to help all to think more clearly and more deeply about what one is doing when one participates in Christian worship and life.

DRY BONES

PRINCIPLES

CHOOSING QUALITY

Facing the question why *Living Worship* chooses month after month to focus on some aspect or facet of public worship (liturgy) is simultaneously to face an inseparable and much broader question that is troubling men and women of faith everywhere. I might put it this way: Why talk about church and liturgy when the world is being torn apart?

So my real concern here is not simply *Living Worship*. It is not even simply The Liturgical Conference. It is really the church and its business in the world. If some of the church's most intelligent members and former members now doubt its relevance . . . if many of the church's most intelligent clergy now question their ministry and their purpose . . . if the rest of the world reveals contempt for church and clergy, sometimes because we seem impervious to its concerns, sometimes because we seem withdrawn—then it would seem that all of us in the churches owe ourselves as well as our sisters and brothers within and without some kind of apologia, an explanation of what we are about as church, a refreshment of our own faith commitment.

Why do we give any kind of priority to questions of the liturgy? Why do we assign so high a place to the seemingly exotic, precious action of a minority of the population on Sabbath or on Sunday? It is news to no one that the participants in these liturgies are not, by and large, the leaders of society. They do not seem to exercise control or even a major influence in the military-industrial complex that governs so much of our lives. They are not evidently the leaders of revolutions which seek to offer new directions and new purposes to the nations.

Judging by the response of the mass of believers to the social questions of the hour, the liturgy is ineffective as a teacher, inept as a force for integration, insipid as a potential dynamic for action. So those who recognize the gravity of the social questions of the hour are damned impatient with the liturgy. There is a plausibility about their claim that we cannot wait for something whose influence is so slow, whose pace is so deliberate as to be practically indiscernible. The crisis, they say, is upon us. All effort, all attention must be focused where it can count against the threats of war, fascism, poverty, racism, the exploitation of resources, excessive population.

Quality and Character

Men and women of faith must agree that the social questions of the hour are so critical, so grave, so urgent as to brook no delays, no stalling actions. With all aware elements in our society, intelligent men and women of faith must be politically involved. Our commitment to radical and thorough attempts to solve our political and economic and broad cultural problems must have the highest priority in our lives, our time, our money, our action.

The tools and agencies we have for these urgent social tasks are those of the political process and political parties. The churches are not immediately useful as tools for these tasks, except in secondary ways that have little to do with their nature and purposes. So if these are our only tasks and if the quality of our lives is an indifferent factor, then the churches are not useful, period. If we have other tasks as well as these, it is possible that the churches are still useful and the liturgy important. Or— and this may be more significant—if our success in undertaking political tasks depends on the quality and integration and dynamism of our own lives as human beings, and if it also depends on our having a vision of politics with transcendental reference, it is possible that the churches are still useful and the liturgy important.

That's why we have to rehearse an answer to the question: Why talk about church and liturgy when the world is being torn apart? Answers to the question are apparently not obvious to many. The faithful wonder why they should stick it out with an institution that seems to have no immediate and practical effect on the problem, e.g., of substandard housing. The clergy wonder why their ministry seems suddenly irrelevant. And we who feel that we should stick it out with institution and with sacramental ministry must give a reason for our sentiments.

For all of us in the communities of faith are tempted sometimes to look at liturgy as at a stubborn tool, an aid (in theory) that balks too much. We are tempted to pass on to other things, to fasten quickly on some deed that bears no ambiguity, no mystery, no paradox. We are tempted to leave liturgy in its agonizing quest for today's contemplatives and turn to sensitivity techniques or political action programs to constitute ourselves as church, to be the center of the church's realization and commitment.

Let me be clear about my meaning. Political action programs are not of the *bene esse* (the well being, the fullest being) of the Christian life—they are of its *esse* (the marrow of its being), because Christians are humans. They are not frosting on the gospel cake—they are the very substance and the dough of Christian life. But liturgy is the leaven, the yeast—in the dough, inseparable from it—without which the dough suffers a fatal diminishment.

Liturgy Constitutes Church

When we speak of liturgy, we are not speaking of an act that adds a certain something to the Christian life and to community. We are not speaking of one of many functions of the church. We are not speaking of a "Godward deed" that nicely "balances" the "manward deed" of meeting the brothers' and sisters' needs. When we speak of liturgy, we are speaking of the act that constitutes the church, that makes it, that identifies it as church. We are speaking of the act in which the church regularly finds itself, finds its meaning and its freedom and its mission. We are speaking of the unique act in which people realize and affirm the Christ-dimension of life, the Christ-orientation and integration of life, of things and deeds. We are speaking of the deed so utterly central to the Christian life that all depends on it . . . and without it there is no covenant people and no church.

So the effort to make liturgy a celebration in every sense, the effort to involve all Christians in the action and to strike sparks in every Christian heart through liturgy's clash of symbols, is no mere facet of ecclesial renewal. It is renewal's heart. It is not an item on the agenda. It is the *sine qua non* of any agenda at all for the community of faith. This is neither understood nor appreciated by large numbers of Christians today. Ancestral ties and bonds of sentiment provide the paste that fastens countless men and women in Sunday pews. And some kind of fleshless dogma—as severely righteous as it is stubbornly narrow—keeps the ecclesiastical wheels spinning higher up. "Why all the fuss?" captures the full intensity of a common reaction (high and low in terms of hierarchical position) to liturgical reform and liturgical concerns.

I wonder, therefore, how accurate we are in assessing the reasons for our failure to communicate, our low popularity rating with youth and with the livelier currents of society. I wonder if some of us have not hurried too quickly to the conclusion that we are not credible or meaningful as church because we do not have the political or economic or cultural answers that our society needs and gropes for. I wonder if our Achilles' heel is really what some of us seem to think it is—our lack of political vision.

Whether we are laymen or clergy or religious, when we play our roles and live our lives as persons in society, are other people dismayed because we have no private political nostrum, no magic program? Do church and liturgy turn them off because we believers, assuming we have a compassionate commitment to justice and equity and peace, have no advantage and no head start in the work of construction or of revolution—whatever is required in concrete circumstances to implement those goals? I don't think so. I don't think that is why some of them are mad at us as church. I don't think that is why many of them are indifferent to us as church.

May it not be, rather, that we are not credible or appealing because we do not seem to know what the church's business is, as such? What our competency as church really is? What our contribution *as church* in society can and should be? Isn't it just possible that a community of faith, a church, cannot get by indefinitely on the image of a comfortable club? Maybe society at large wants to hear something from the church besides our pious platitudes and our oily "thank yous" for the scraps of privilege it tosses us. Perhaps young people would not be horrified to hear the gospel, to feel the impingement of the mystery of God. Why the hell do we have to travel halfway around the world to find a guru?

What Makes Us Tick?

I have been tempted at times to agree with *The Critic's* dictum, "No gurus is good gurus." That is to say, we don't have to import a holy man from India to gain the enrichment of such information as "a penny saved is a penny earned." But Hindu gurus offer more to their own people than they have shared with our television commentators, or they would have become extinct long ago. And the importance of the "spiritual director" in Catholic tradition reminds us that, while it is perfectly true to hold that every Christian should be a guru, it takes both an uncommon combination of personal traits and an uncommon leisure for contemplation to do the job well, to be able to articulate helpfully a way of life that has assurance and meaning and effectiveness.

To articulate helpfully a Christian way of life is only minimally to counsel and exemplify that compassion for a universe of brothers and sisters, especially the suffering, the poor, the oppressed, which is the first step of discipleship (because it is "like" the love of God). If that were all, our gurus could be our sons and daughters. Because surely our land has never seen a generation so compassionate as the present college generation. Yesterday (May 9, 1970) and last November 15 will live forever in my memory and appreciation and admiration as epiphanies of remarkable compassion. A whole middle class generation riding on the crest of a wave of compassion.

It is a great gift they have to offer us, just in their freedom from the cages that our partial answers and our systems and philosophies have become for us. With the vision and awareness offered by contemporary communications and with affluence's freedom, they have become our conscience—a dash of cold water waking us up to all manner of pretense and hypocrisy and inner contradictions in our society.

But they, too, know that riding the crest of a wave—even. of a wave of compassion—can be a brief euphoria, if the insight and motivation are not plugged in to a comprehensive and possible way of life. This is where church and liturgy come in: church, because there is no message, no gospel, without it (and the message is precisely "a comprehensive and possible way of life"); liturgy, because there is no church without the liturgy which constitutes it, in which it is created and recreated, made flesh.

If the community of faith is constituted by and in liturgical celebration, perhaps it is not irrelevant to give that celebration some attention. Like other institutions, the church can suffer a crippling loss of identity, can be diverted from its purpose into stagnant, fetid channels of self-importance, self-service, self-preservation. We believe, for example, that hierarchy and other institutional symbols are important, but we seem to have forgotten why. No one is going to buy our symbols, no one is going to be impressed by what those symbols mean, with that *why*.

Vive la Différence!

Whether we like it or not, our society is not impressed by assertions of abstract truth. It is impressed by processes that work, by deeds that meet the needs of men and women, by affirmations that make a concrete difference. Faith's affirmation is not immune from scrutiny, nor is it safe from claims of rigorous requirement. Its critics may, indeed, be quite uncertain about just what it is that they expect from faith professed. But they are terribly certain about their (vague) expectation. For they, too, are human, and they possess a human instinct that cries out for more than the theoreticians of either political status quo or political revolution can offer them.

For example, one should not expect (we have heard it often, but we have to remind ourselves) a particular political or economic expertise of a man or woman simply because he or she is a Christian. One should not expect a somehow keener grasp of the science of genetics or a greater facility in the mastery of languages. One has no right to expect of a man or woman of faith some kind of immunity from human stupidity or ignorance or even sinfulness. But one has every right to expect *something* from the person of faith, and a collective *something* from the community of faith. Something special. Something even more than the sophistication of advanced sociology and even more than the fervor of the socialist movements. Not only because society offers men and women of faith a place and moderate freedom, but also because the persons of faith possesses a distinctive vision of the world in general as well as of himself in particular.

So one has every right to expect, of people of faith, of the church, a certain quality of life, a certain character, a certain depth and appreciation, a certain serenity in the acceptance of so many reconciliations, a certain hope that is not easily crushed, a certain love that whispers reverence for persons and for things. We call it "grace," because it is in one sense unexpected and unsought. But when we see its visible effects, we thirst and reach and want.

Its effects may impinge upon the world in very simple and ingenuous ways. That is, in fact, the usual case. That's why it is so hard to be articulate and specific about what the presence of a man or woman of faith can mean to other people, what the presence of the church can mean to society as a whole. It is a quality one senses, not an ideology that one can comprehend. Those who have tried to make faith an ideology, whether of the left or of the right or of the middle (the "silent majority" are ideologues, too, and perhaps the most adamant of all in identifying their religious security with their cultural attachments), are serving neither faith nor culture and are depriving themselves of the benefits of both.

A Christian should be distinguished by the fact that he sees the other person as deeply, fatherly-related brother or sister. It is not commitment to human solidarity alone, but to incomparable brotherhood that is the genius of faith. (That is what I mean by "quality" and "character" above.) A Christian should be distinguished by the fact that he pursues the goals of equity and peace as mandates, purposes of the living God. It is not commitment to political and economic revolution alone, but to creation's thrust toward unity and reconciliation that is the genius of faith. A Christian should be distinguished by the fact that he reverences sun and earth and air and water, all things, all beauty, as faint images of one who cares. It is not love of nature alone, but a feeling of kinship with and care for all the universe of things among which we claim a mastery and a responsibility that is the genius of faith.

The difference *(vive la différence!)* is not slight. But it is not dramatic either. It does not touch our senses with the vivid boldness of a political manifesto. It insinuates itself into a culture's warp and woof. Indeed, when the church's presence is relatively strong in history and in culture, many qualities of faith are absorbed by persons to whom faith's affirmation is quite foreign. And the "difference" becomes even less evident. So it is relatively easy for men and women in such a culture to feel that church and faith and liturgy can be dispensed with. They have become unaware of the precious difference.

Celebrate Life in God

The most striking and the most meaningful of the many pieces of literature that fell into my hands during the May 9 student demonstration in Washington was a one-page photograph of human faces with a text by Pierre Teilhard de Chardin (distributed by the Council of Churches of Greater Washington): "If one considers, however briefly, what conditions will make possible the flowering in the human heart of this new universal love, so often vainly dreamed of but now at last leaving the realm of the utopian and declaring itself as both possible and necessary, one notices this: that if men on earth, all over the earth, are ever to love one another it is not enough for them to recognize in one another the elements of a single *something;* they must also, by developing a planetary consciousness, become aware of the fact that without loss of their individual identities they are becoming a single *somebody.* For there is no total love—and this is writ large in the gospel—save that which is in and of the personal. And what does this mean if not that, in the last resort, the planetization of humanity presupposes for its proper development not only the contracting of the earth, not only the organizing and condensing of human thought, but also a third factor: the rising on our inward horizon of some psychic cosmic centre, some supreme pole of consciousness, towards which all the elementary consciousnesses of the world shall converge and in which they shall be able to love one another: in other words, the rising *of a God.*"

"This is writ large in the gospel." It is "writ large" in any Christian liturgical celebration that is faithful to the gospel. It is why the church and the sacramental ministry and the Liturgical Conference and *Living Worship* talk about church and liturgy when the world is being torn apart. It is why we talk about church and liturgy in these and any times with a feeling of mission and of contribution. It is why a great rising up of Christian gurus is so very desirable. It is why, within the church, the sacramental ministry of bishops, priests and deacons cannot find its special relevance in political action (where all of us must find part of our relevance as persons), but must find it in the liturgy and in "the rising of a God."

It is why all Christians—laymen, religious, clergy—fail both their commitment and their possibility when they settle, as the vast majority have settled, for something less than the depths of the church's message and the liturgy's celebration. Most of us, I suppose, have settled for security in one way or another—a tolerable acceptance of a kind of gospel, tamed and colored to fit our culture, affording us a weakly moral stance at little sacrifice. Some of us, rightly and scornfully rejecting this domesticating of Jesus and the living God, have settled for a political or economic messianism—a compassionate service to our neighbor without the complications and the ambiguities of the life-giving word and sacrament. The latter are as appealing as they are still few, because they are compassionate. And compassion is the raw material of discipleship and of the Christian way.

Hanging Loose?

Christians who will not settle for comfortable security, who will not even settle for a radical political stance, but who keep digging into the heart of the church and the liturgy for the qualities of faith, the qualities that make compassion endure and persevere and deepen and expand, the experience of the living God that assures and secures both the importance and the relativity of all else—they are the ones that offer hope. If there is to be any church tomorrow, they are its foundation. They are the gurus of our time. One thinks of a Dorothy Day, a Thomas Merton, a Daniel Berrigan, a Gerard Sloyan.

It is popular for Christians who know that something is terribly, terribly wrong with the churches to pride themselves on "hanging loose." Don't reject the churches altogether because there's vaguely something there. At the same time, don't dig in, don't identify, don't commit yourself. That way you aren't supporting the lousy church leadership. And that way, too, you are "promoting" ecumenical and interfaith developments. After all, you are as close to Buddhism as you are to Christianity. There is a line of reasoning that asserts that this situation somehow must be helpful.

But "hanging loose" is just what we don't need . . . and what the world doesn't need. We've got lots of people—clergy, religious, laymen—hanging loose right now. Lots of them have been hanging loose for a long, long time. Their influence and their contribution to society as Christians is something less than remarkable. To hang loose is to buy the ecclesiology and the liturgiology of present church leadership. It is to join the chorus: "Why all the fuss?" It is to pass by a wounded humanity, ignoring its sharpest cries of pain . . . and of despair.

Nor can hanging loose be considered even mildly helpful to ecumenical and interfaith developments. The latter presuppose individuals of tradition, commitment and faith. To be useful in such enterprises, participants must have reached some depth in their respective traditions and communities of faith. One-man ecumenical "movements" are as useless as they are embarrassingly plentiful at the present time. They foster a grand illusion that walls are being broken down and communication is being established, when all that is really happening is that the depths are being forsaken and the wellsprings are drying up.

Hang loose, indeed, from all the crust, from all of our absolutized formulas and our canonized accommodations. Dredge the river of tradition and dredge it thoroughly and painfully. But treasure the depths—the church, the liturgy that resonate the depths. Stick with them, dig into them, in spite of their apparent friends . . . and you, too, can be a guru.

GAINING EXPERIENCE

In recent weeks I have come upon an uncommonly large number of editorials and columns—in the general as well as the specifically Christian press—devoted to analyses of the utility or lack thereof of what is called the "institutional church." Its sickness and its health, its benign and its malignant aspects, its progressive and its retrogressive effects—disturbingly remote remarks about what are certainly proper subjects of discussion. Generalizations, abstractions, cerebrations, stuffed with the writers' hopes, experiences, convictions until they somehow can stand up, are ready for a fray that lacks only flesh and blood.

The arguments pro are various. From keeping the church alive for posterity to sticking in for the sake of contributing our special gifts to an institution that would otherwise languish. The church needs us, those who think we should stay with the institution tell us. Of course they are right. What I seem to have missed in that pile of paper and print is an indication that the hearts of editorialists and columnists sometimes confess, however secretly, "I need the church." If my brothers and sisters in faith need me, it is possible I also need them.

One of the very many beautiful and encouraging characteristics of the time we live in is the obvious fact that social institutions are being scrutinized, criticized, challenged and reformed on the basis of how they relate to *persons*, how they serve and benefit the individual *person*. This seems to be happening on a scale, both of breadth and depth, heretofore unknown and unattempted. Questions about the "institutional church" are part of this picture. And all of our objective and cerebral answers from the assumed viewpoint of posterity or in terms of some balance of powers, as well as our familiar answers from authority, however true they may be, are less compelling than one voice freely saying, "I need the church."

What I seem to be hearing is: "*I* don't need the church, of course, but my children might . . . or some future generation . . . or civilization . . . or culture." Or, "Why deprive any possibly viable human structure of my talents?" After plowing through so much of this, one searches for distractions. So I started looking at my desk calendar a lot. Someone at Conception Abbey culled some beautiful aphorisms for this year's: "To have been well brought up is a great drawback nowadays. It shuts one out from so much" (Oscar Wilde). "Some things become so completely our own that we forget them" (Antonio Porchia).

"To have been well brought up . . . nowadays" is to have been so trained that whenever one feels like doing or saying something spontaneous a legion of calculations and considerations emerges from the storehouse of one's mind to smother the impulse. It is to be adjusted to the atmosphere of premeditation, to walk easily and breathe easily only under clouds of proprieties. It may be—it seems to be—that many are never moved to a spontaneous expression of gratitude or of need for the church. "Some things become so completely our own that we forget them."

But even if we are so moved . . . even if I want to say, "Thanks, sisters and brothers, for all the church has done and does for me," I am hedged about by fears and cautions. If I say "thanks," I might seem to be making the conservatives even more complacent. If I say "thanks," I might be approving the slow pace of church renewal. If I say "thanks," I might be taking the edge off my no less serious criticisms. If I say "thanks," I might be contributing to the racist and sexist and capitalist caricatures of the gospel which the church has half-contrived. That's the hell of having been "well brought up"! I can't even say "thanks" spontaneously!

Locating the Church

As a matter of fact, they *are* saying a kind of backhanded "thanks"—those editorialists and columnists who are so rightly concerned about the gap between what church leaders are doing and what is expected of and hoped for from the new man in Christ Jesus. Their criticisms, their anger, their railing against the conformism and timidity of church leadership—these are all ways of saying that they care. Those who have ceased to care have also ceased to scream. The pope and many of the bishops and church leaders in all confessions do not seem to appreciate that fact sufficiently.

And they say a kind of "thanks"—again obliquely—in the invention and unfortunately common use of that odious phrase "institutional church." We know that the name "church" refers either to the local community of Christian faith (institutional like all human communities), or to one or all of the networks of communities of faith (tragically divided still—confessional, Orthodox, Catholic—but each of them institutional, like all human societies). That's what "church" means: the institutional unity of believers.

I suppose it is only natural that the person who has grown up dividing himself into a body and a soul and thinking the worst about the former would be inclined to do the same with the church. When he uses the phrase "institutional church," then, he may mean just everything that's "bad" about that indivisible reality. In that case, he's really saying there's something "good" about it, too.

I would like to try to interject into this discussion a loud clear "thanks"—a word of deep appreciation—to the church. Although this necessarily includes thanking myself, it is addressed primarily to my sisters and brothers in my local community of faith and worship (Nova Community in northern Virginia, Diocese of Richmond), and to my sisters and brothers in other communities united to us in belief (Jesus is Lord), in praise, and most completely in the peace of eucharist and common ministry. Here I want to focus my appreciation of and thanks for the church on the *person*, the well-being of the person, the psychological health of the person.

I will go on protesting, criticizing, crying out in anger and in pain about the apparent incapacity or unwillingness of most of the church leadership and membership to respond to the promising times we live in with the gospel rather than with our hangups and our habits. I hope all of us will. But I think it is also important to join to this kind of ferment and challenge the appreciation we feel. Appreciation for the church where it really is to be found, and where it really is. Its liturgy is the actualizations of the church. Liturgy is where one finds the church. This institution is made, formed, created and recreated

363

in the eucharist and other rites of public worship. Christian liturgy is the church's uniqueness and Christian liturgy is the church's nature. To locate the church elsewhere—in one or another of its many related societal functions—is a tragic misunderstanding.

So, if I would thank the church for what it does for me, and for what I think it does for persons generally, in terms of personhood, psychological health and well-being, I must look to its liturgical assembly, its public worship. That's where I find the church. I do this not professionally—not as a doctor or psychologist—but as one who feels his human life would be terribly diminshed without the church. Nor have I any intention of suggesting here that public worship is a cure for mental or emotional illness. My personal experience is quite sufficient to discourage such a thesis. It has taken a half-century and a good bit of psychotherapy to make me free enough of psychic burdens borne since childhood to be able to utter a non-compulsive "thanks," a relatively free and liberated "thanks."

Liturgy Is for People

Like all good things, liturgical celebration can be misused (unconsciously, of course) by people who are sick, and its misuse can contribute to sickness or perpetuate it. The person who lacks a healthy assurance about his own identity and value may lose himself in liturgy or anything else, may participate in public worship in such a way as to use it to fill, or put something in the place of, the emptiness and void he feels . . . or hide it with report cards. For example, I have derived what I consider inestimable values and benefits from regular public worship all my life. But how I regret certain aspects of those years—years in which I could have derived much more had I been a freer person, had I not clung to liturgy, as to a number of good causes and good deeds, trying to make them substitute, as they were never meant to do, for a missing affirmation and acceptance of myself!

Despite all that, my "thanks" is genuine. Paul Tillich (*The Courage to Be*, New Haven: Yale University Press, 1952 and 1971) distinguishes between "existential anxiety," as "an object of priestly help," and "pathological anxiety," "an object of medical healing" (p. 77). My existential anxiety has found the church's liturgy to be an immense source of help and health . . . and this seems to be a fairly common witness of believing mankind. To articulate this help is more difficult than to affirm it. If the liturgy were merely its words and rich intellectual concepts, it would not be so hard. But liturgy is dance and drama, gesture and color, light and music, and the touch and coming together of the assembly. Liturgy is an experience involving so many human faculties and levels: rational, imaginal, emotional, sensuous, that it defies a merely rational analysis.

With regard to its gestures alone, Antoine Vergote writes (*Liturgy in Transition*, Ed. Herman Schmidt, S.J., New York: Herder & Herder, 1971): "Every gesture which is not the manipulation of tools can be called symbolic . . . these are gestures that express an intention and achieve it at the same time. We call them symbolic by analogy with symbolic words and objects, because they unite a bodily attitude with an intended meaning. They become symbolic signs, and rational language will never attain the richness of their communication" (p. 40). But this is an essay and I have to try to express in words what in reality can only be felt and experienced through many concurrent symbols.

Just two more points in this extended introduction. I suspect there may be some Christians, even now, who will resent this whole topic as entirely too "subjective." They will say that one destroys worship when one turns his attention to its human benefits. That objection is a red herring from way back—one that should not have survived Victor White's article on "Modern Psychology and the Function of Symbolism" in *Orate Fratres* (v. 22), forerunner of *Worship* magazine, in the 1940's. In that perceptive little essay, Father White quoted "a European Catholic writer to the effect that: 'It is important that the general principle be borne in mind that the prayers of the church are addressed to God and that the idea of conducting services primarily for the edification of the faithful smacks of Protestantism.' "

Father White comments: "Alas for St. Thomas. Alas for St. Paul's great guiding rubric in 1 Corinthians 14:26. Alas for every theologian who has written on prayer, from Origen and St. Cyprian to St. Thomas and Suarez, who has been at pains to explain that we 'address God' not to 'edify' him, but precisely to 'edify' ourselves" (p. 247).

"God's command to us to worship him is a concession to our needs . . . The worshiper who understands this is far from ego-centricity, and is being cured of the 'false love unto himself' by learning to love his *whole* self with God's own kind of love. He is also proof against the criticism (from within or from without) that our Catholic liturgy—with its lights and colors and dressing-up and fire-making and water-splashing and smoke and music and bodily action—is a childish game, unworthy of a grown-up man and of no appeal to any respectable God. It is play indeed, and that play is needful and good for a child of God . . . " (p. 249).

A Personal Atmosphere

The paradox is clear, but then there is no reason to assume that worship alone among human realities should be free of paradox. Worship is for our good, and yet, if we do it with an eye only to our good, it is no good for us. We need to worship. We need to pray. And yet, if we pray to our own needs and mindful only of our good, the point of the whole deed is lost. In liturgy it is literally true: "The man who loves his life loses it" (John 12:25).

The elements of personal growth and psychological health to which I shall refer are six—six kinds of experience which liturgy affords and which I think are profoundly related to mental health and personal development:

1. Personal Experience of God and Transcendence
2. Personal Experience of Dignity and Worth
3. Personal Experience of Wholeness and Integration
4. Personal Experience of Commonness and Solidarity
5. Personal Experience of Meaning
6. Personal Experience of Hope

Those designations and divisions are somewhat arbitrary, as they must be, but one has to break down this complex reality which is liturgical celebration in order to understand better its elements and benefits.

Robert Walker Hovda

My "thanks" are quite general and not directed only to those sisters and brothers in the church (some of the clergy especially) who have done the most to maximize my liturgical experience. Because I have found all of these elements to be present in some way, and available, even in the most unimaginative, formalistic and rigid liturgical celebrations. That is the advantage of tradition. As experiences, however, they can be heightened to the point of ecstasy or diminished to consciousness zero (although there may be, even then, still something on subconscious levels). The heightening or diminishing depends on the quality and character of the celebration, on the mood and dispositions which the participant brings to the assembly, and on the "at-homeness' and personal atmosphere in which the participants in the liturgical assembly find themselves (and help create).

The quality and character of celebration is the focus of the Liturgical Conference and all of its publications all the time. The problem of the participants' dispositions is at least partly the result of our lousy catechesis and initiation procedures— a different topic, and one to which Christians must give some radical attention very soon. But we can do something—each of us in our communities and parishes—about assuring a feeling of comfortable at-homeness, a feeling of ease and friendliness in the assembly. Maybe (I said *maybe*) we can't do it in quite the same way as the James Joyce Memorial Liquid Theatre is doing it at the Guggenheim Museum these days in New York. (When you come in there, they put you through an experience of loving that has you cooing and really ready for a group activity!) But even with our present precious modesty and our prized inhibitions, we can do something. Making good use of ushers (whose ministry is one of the important elements in effective liturgical renewal), introductions, welcoming of strangers, seating of participants for maximal interaction and confrontation—all are involved in enabling the right personal feelings. In this connection (and in connection with most ordinary problems of liturgical planning and celebrating), I have the temerity to recommend again the Liturgical Conference's recent publication: *Liturgy Committee Handbook*.

A woman in a certain church was asked, after the service, whether she was a stranger there. She responded, "Why yes, I've been a stranger here for forty years" (*Iliff Review*, Vol. XVII, No. 1, Winter, 1960, p. 39). She gained something from that long martyrdom or she wouldn't have undergone it. But her liturgical experience was terribly and unnecessarily diminished by the indifference and lack of hospitality of the group. Some group feeling is fundamental to any liturgical celebration!

1. Personal Experience of God and Transcendence

Christianity is not a temple religion, although the temple temptation is always with us. The God in whom we believe—the power and purpose at the heart of things—is the God not of the forests and the mountains and the seas but of men and women, the God of history, the God whose Spirit is to be sought and found and listened to in the people he forms, one people, a covenant community, formed out of divided, disparate human stock. Christian faith turns us from sacred places to the liturgical assembly of persons, wherever it may be. It is the community gathered to do liturgy that is a special dwelling place of God, for the specific intent of liturgy is to gather our total lives together before God, as a sacrifice of praise, with full consciousness and full awareness, with the kind of advertence that is unlikely or impossible in other—and partial—sectors of our lives.

Public worship, then, offers the person a unique opportunity to experience God and the transcendent. The church gathers explicitly for that purpose, listens for a word the Spirit breathes, prays and gives thanks, celebrates its peace as grace, as given. Every moment has transcendent focus.

Paul Tillich suggests that the most basic and inescapable anxiety of human beings is the anxiety of fate and death, which he defines as "an awareness of being contingent in every respect, of having no ultimate necessity" (*op. cit.*, p. 44). My feelings and my experience correspond to his statement. What he says is news to none of us. But it is not our favorite fact. We are experts at avoiding it, veiling it, and manufacturing idols to distract ourselves from it. Something in us rebels against that fact, and if we do not have the security of faith in an ultimately necessary being, not contingent in any respect, we find security elsewhere, pretending that some creatures are less creatures, less contingent than are we.

All of the other experiences I list subsequently as personal benefits of public worship are, it seems to me, dependent on this one. The strength of the whole worship experience depends on the strength of this aspect of it. And, since this aspect is the experience of the inexpressible, of the one who escapes all our categories and utterly transcends all possibilities of our languages, it in turn depends more on nonverbal than on verbal elements of liturgy.

The manner of ministers particularly and of all participants to some degree, the atmosphere they create, the gestures and processions and other movements, the visual setting, the music and the silence, the symbols and vessels and tools of celebration—all are as critical for this experience as any words that are spoken. Only a person who is himself or herself in awe before the mystery of God can lead in public prayer. Psychologist and priest Eugene Kennedy has pointed out how the mere manner and style of the presiding minister can poison the whole process of ritual: "The church is no stranger to the minister who worships himself rather than God" (*Liturgy in Transition*, p. 55).

In the same volume, liturgiologist Herman Schmidt writes: "Religious ritual is a precious element contributing to man's psychological equilibrium; in the rite he must be able to give expression to his profoundest feelings so that they are not thrust aside and suppressed" (p. 10). On the level of one's "profoundest feelings," actions and gestures of the body communicate more adequately, more richly than words, even when the words are poetry. A bow, the gesture of presenting gifts, the sign of the cross, incensing, drinking from a common cup and sharing pieces from a common bread, the pax embrace—no words can touch these for communicating in a total way to the heart of the person.

Because it is not a rational statement or dogma we are concerned with here, but *feelings*. Feelings of the existential anxiety Tillich talks about. And feelings of assurance and trust in almighty God, in the Other, who is not contingent and who is necessary. Liturgy speaks to those feelings of anxiety, not because its words are rationally convincing or even always right, but because its rhythm and its pulse draw me toward a center and a ground of being to which all my instincts and my needs give assent.

And the same experience of transcendence saves me from the almightiness of the powers that be in my daily life. Society and its mores and its systems and its powers and its ways and habits—all of the offices and institutions that tend to overwhelm me daily are in the liturgical celebration reduced to human size. Everything less than God becomes a creature . . . and contingent like myself. Nothing can enslave me or become my idol as long as I have some experience of the living God.

In the October 1971 issue of *Living Worship*, I referred to anthropologist Victor W. Turner's book, *The Ritual Process* (Chicago: Aldine, 1969). Turner's studies of rituals in a number of societies suggest that the ritual process offers to the human person a precious vantage point and freedom from the status quo which determines so much of one's life. It offers what he calls "liminality"—a *threshold* beyond the structures, free of the structures, outside of the structures of office, class, color, sex, tribe, family, politics, economics, etc.

Christian liturgy, I would say, *par excellence*, offers an experience of God and the transcendent which enables the person to take a position on the threshold of all structures, able to criticize, able to challenge, able to revolt. This is an extremely practical benefit of liturgy and faith. In the wake of Attica, we have been forced to think deeply not just about prison brutality but about the whole system of "crime and punishment." To an alarming extent, crime in any society tends to be defined as what those in power do not like and what the powerless and the poor are, at least in some sense, compelled to do. Another example would be our social definitions of "adjustment" and "mental health," and the extent to which these are conditioned by and overly respectful of the competition and the violence which our society has canonized.

For whatever reason—instinct, evolution, moral training—the person is uneasy with the "absolute" character these structures tend to assume. We might be stuck, for the time being and until we can change them, with such systems and such social definitions, but the personal experience of God and transcendence makes them strangely (and unhappily) vulnerable.

Some of those who are trying to hang on to such superficial elements of the liturgy of former times as its formalism, rigidity, dead language, etc. (as well as to such profound elements of past liturgy as its nonverbal choreography of reverent acknowledgement of mystery and creatureliness) are rightly concerned about this experience. Even in its most sterile and petrified periods, traditional Christian liturgy offered it, afforded it. The polarization can be bridged when every one of us pressing for renewal and vitalization of public worship makes abundantly evident the priority which belongs to this experience.

2. Personal Experience of Dignity and Worth

There is an ancient Jewish saying: "On the Sabbath day, the poorest Jew is a king, his wife a queen, their children royal princes." The very fact of liturgical celebration in a community of faith is a source of tremendous reinforcement for feelings of personal worth.

Liturgy is mystery. In public worship we celebrate our relation to that which is absolutely beyond us, that which we cannot analyze or exhaust. The fact that we celebrate it means that there is also mystery about us—something about ourselves (just as humans, apart from any dazzling achievements) that we cannot fully explain. Otherwise we should not have such a relationship to celebrate.

What enables human beings to pray, and to pray in common, is their humanity and faith, nothing more or less than that. The fact involves an appreciation of what it means to be a man or woman that is dazzling in its own right. The experience of worth in liturgy is dependent on no talent, no vocation, no accomplishment, no status or "place" in life. What admits one to the liturgy of the covenant community is initiation—a member of the human species confesses faith. If one has any special claim to honor, one can leave it at the door. The rational

371

animal, with nothing at all to recommend him except his faith, participates in common prayer.

Here, then, is a quite unique and very quiet personal experience of dignity and worth. All of those social bars we live with all day every day are down. It may be, as anthropologist Turner says, that those social bars, those distinct status roles are what keep our political and economic wheels moving. But it is an experience of basic human value to come upon a situation and a social deed in which they count for nothing. It is *I* who count, and nothing I have done or will do is the source of my worth.

Father James Burtchaell, provost of Notre Dame University, has made the interesting and arresting observation that liturgy is the *only* place where we are *not* "working out our salvation." He proposed that doing liturgy is an *interlude* in the business of "working out our salvation, just as having sex is an *interlude* in the marriage business of making and perfecting love. Self esteem here does not wait upon production. There is no production. It is festivity and celebration.

To listen to the "word of the Lord," and to be called on to respond . . . to speak of sin, in the first place, and then to be accepted in spite of it . . . to assume our needs, our thanks, our sins to be of sufficient note to be petitioned for and offered and confessed . . . the whole experience must seem to an unbeliever a rash and terribly inflated view of woman and of man. To the believer it seems mysterious . . . and very real.

This experience of raw human value, of course, can be greatly heightened or greatly diminished by the quality of the particular celebration. For an example of this, see the poem reprinted on page 31 of our Liturgical Conference membership journal, *Liturgy* (October, 1971 issue), by Saundra Sharp, who is presently acting in the New York production of the superb drama *Black Girl*. It may sound like the warmth of accepting friends, which is in itself no mean thing. But there is even more here than that! There is the warmth of accepting friends in the context of God and transcendence . . . in the context of our deepest (ritual) expression of life's meaning . . . in a context that can make the experience survive the floundering of particular friendships.

3. Personal Experience of Wholeness and Integration

The biblical basis and character of Christian public worship manifests an approach to the human person that is not piecemeal and divisive. Even the wordiest and most rationalized of Christian liturgies, insofar as it is biblical, will not contribute to the tearing apart of man or woman that seems to have been our philosophical bent ever since biblical times. The Bible sees us as one piece.

In the article quoted above, Eugene Kennedy writes: "Prayers and rituals that are based on the notion of a divided man, man the pure spirit hampered by a body pulsing with libido, are counterfeit and cannot possibly contribute to the psychological balance of the worshipers . . . Ritual that comprehends man's unity contributes to his dignity and to the successful achievement of his personl identity" (*op. cit.*, p. 56).

In addition to its biblical words and concepts, liturgy's many levels, its non-verbal elements and rich symbolism—all accept the human body, sex, fantasy, memory, etc., and even glorify them. Good liturgy invites the person to activate his whole being, so good liturgy is an experience of wholeness and integration. There are no detached "souls" at work and at play in liturgy—only people, in all of their fleshly reality.

One hesitates to be very critical in these early stages of liturgical renewal in the church, because we are all feeling our way and we need lots of experimenting, lots of brave willingness to make mistakes, or, rather, to do things which we may discover later are mistakes. But one of the most curious phenomena one observes currently is the tendency among some "experimenters" to try to make the celebration an almost exclusively cerebral affair. In some otherwise progressive places, actions, symbols, gestures, sensuous elements are being done away with or diminished as rapidly as possible, with a consequent dreary emphasis on words, words, words, and more words.

It seems to me that many of us are much too quick and facile about dismissing as irrelevant the traditional, non-verbal elements of Christian liturgy. We have been unimpressed by their half-hearted and mechanical traditional performance, so we conclude with a finality as sweeping as the absence of research or fact that they no longer speak to modern man. It is a pity if reformers in the 20th century make the same mistakes as reformers in previous eras. If we feel compelled to make mistakes, we should be able to invent some new ones.

Christian liturgical tradition is an activation of the whole person and a blessing of the whole person—all the senses, all the feelings, memory and imagination as well as reason. A liturgy which can be *read* (like a book) is a bad liturgy. To the extent that one is able to read a liturgy, that liturgy is terribly defective. In the Catholic tradition, for example, "reading the mass" or "saying mass" or "reading the missal" are phrases (and activities) indissolubly united to periods of liturgical decline and sterility. A time as rich in visual experience as our own, and as sensitive to sound and smell and touch and the body generally, should be encouraging us to use our old ways as well as its new ways to maximize what has always been one of the healthiest elements in our liturgical tradition—the personal experience of wholeness and integration, mostly through non-verbals.

4. Personal Experience of Commonness and Solidarity

Erich Fromm defines the mentally healthy person in this way: "the productive and unalienated person; the person who relates himself to the world lovingly, and who uses his reason to grasp reality objectively; who experiences himself as a unique individual entity, and at the same time feels one with his fellowmen; who is not subject to irrational authority, and who accepts willingly the rational authority of conscience and reason; who is in the process of being born as long as he is alive, and considers the gift of life the most precious chance he has" (*The Sane Society*, New York: Holt, Rinehart & Winston, 1955, p. 275).

Experts generally agree that mental illness very frequently is indicated by a feeling of being "cut off" from other people. While liturgy's function is not medical healing, it does offer us a strong experience of commonness and solidarity. Referring again to Turner's concept of "liminality," we see in liturgy a place, a situation, a deed where all people are radically equal, where financial and political kings are on a level with the handicapped, where the distinctions of daily life which separate people from one another and make them different from one another are transcended. Not only because we are all small potatoes before God, not only because we are accepted in the liturgy for our radical humanity rather than for any accomplishment, talent, or inheritance—but also because the good news we celebrate is news of a coming kingdom of love, equality, solidarity, peace.

This experience of commonness in the church's worship affects time as well as place. History, tradition is a very important part of any ritual. Eugene Kennedy says: "When they are not divorced from their tradition, rituals present a pattern rich with the kind of associations that enlarge a man's sense of relationship with all Christian experience" (*op. cit.*, p. 57). In *The Feast of Fools*, Harvey Cox agrees: "Ritual becomes idiosyncratic when it ceases to be shared by a group or to emerge from historical experience, when it becomes the property of just one, or of just a few people . . . Ritual does for movement what language does for sound, transforms it from the inchoate into the expressive. Therefore an idiosyncratic ritual is ultimately frustrating and self-defeating" (Cambridge: Harvard U. Press, 1969, p. 93).

Liturgy actualizes the church, our commonness and solidarity in the local sisterhood and brotherhood, but it does more than that. It reaches back in history, forward toward the kingdom. And it reaches out around the world. One of our temptations all through history has been for the church to become a community of the saved, a closed "believers' church." Christianity at its best has rejected the temptation and repulsed it, giving potential as well as realized solidarity a clear priority over other ecclesial considerations. Catholic tradition strongly affirms this prority: its worship is open to the man or woman from (or of) the street; and it attaches the greatest importance to unity among the churches and to all the bonds which bind the local communities of faith to one another (including ministry, the episcopal college with Roman primacy and the presbyteral college with the bishop).

In the words of the Second Vatican Council, the church is "a kind of sacrament or sign of intimate union with god, and of the unity of all mankind.. (Dogmatic Constitution on the Church, No. 1). The liturgy which actualizes the church is that sign in its most potent and condensed form. It is all there in sign. It doesn't seem to be there now in our dispositions. That problem of our catechesis and initiation procedures again . . . and of our not-yet-at-all-collegial life as church. We are service station clients with a service station mentality—not a covenant people in covenant community. No liturgical problem is greater than this one, no handicap more frustrating. I don't mind a mission for me, a moral imperative for me. But I resist any real kind of identification with you. I resist the painful collective solidarity of corporate judgment and decision and action. That's the main reason for my conviction that the church should not be "political."

Scripture scholars tell us about the form and content of liturgical prayer in the biblical tradition . . . about how God is described and proclaimed not just as creator but as covenant-maker . . . about how the content of the prayer was the interpretation of the covenant in terms of the here-and-now life of the community exists in the mainstream of liturgical prayer from its biblical roots, then the church is and must be radically political. It is concerned with what our response as a people is—concretely—to God's enduring love and acceptance.

This eschatological experience of commonness and solidarity, then, needs deepening and sharpening and quickening by every possible means. Recently the Guild for Religious Architecture magazine, *Faith & Form*, sponsored a symposium on "shopping center chapels," their legitimacy and usefulness. There is nothing new about shopping center chapels—except the name. A great many urban parishes have been shopping center chapels for generations. That's our problem.

5. Personal Experience of Meaning

Another of the existential anxieties Paul Tillich enumerates is what he calls the "anxiety of emptiness and meaninglessness." He says: "Spiritual self-affirmation occurs in every moment in which man lives creatively in the various spheres of meaning . . . Everyone who lives creatively in meanings affirms himself as a participant in these meanings. He affirms himself as receiving and transforming reality creatively. He loves himself as participating in the spiritual life and as loving its contents . . . The anxiety of meaninglessness is anxiety about the loss of an ultimate concern, of a meaning which gives meaning to all meanings" (*op. cit.*, pp. 46f.).

There is a powerful appeal in liturgy as an experience of meaning, as a "moment in which" the person "lives creatively in meanings" and "affirms himself as a participant in these meanings." I am convinced that it is this appeal, far more than laws or obligations, which accounts for so many "holding on." Liturgy incorporates one into a biblical universe of meaning. The traditional and programmed elements of liturgy perform this extremely valuable service. It is only when liturgy becomes solely tradition, rigid, closed, finished, that it begins to communicate a kind of counter-meaning. Still a universe of meaning but one different from the universe in which we live, separate, enclosed, precious and irrelevant.

For a while we lost the spontaneous, immediate and current elements so necessary in public worship, and it's a terribly difficult job regaining them once they're lost. Our heritage has been a precious paper liturgy. Like its companions, paper orthodoxy and paper morality, it enshrined lots of good things, but with no clear relation to the lives people daily live and the problems people daily face.

In a book related to the Woodstock Center for Religion and Worship's film, "Ritual Makers," Father Lawrence Madden, S.J., writes: "Ritual is a combination of programmed and spontaneous situations, actions, and expressions (both verbal and non-verbal), which mutually complement and at times modify each other, creating a fruitful tension which seems to be a necessary structural element in an effective ritual. *Where either the planned or the spontaneous dimensions are significantly weak, the power of the ritual is diminished"* (*Ritual Makers Guidebook*, Paramus, N.J.: Paulist Press, 1971).

It is largely these spontaneous elements in ritual—current, immediate—that make its experience of meaning an experience of the real world rather than of a paper world, a "sacred world" all by itself. We have seen what happens when that element is lost—how unreal the "sacred" quickly becomes. And perhaps in a few places some of us are seeing now what happens when the programmed, biblical and traditional elements of liturgy are seriously diminished—how thin the "real" quickly becomes.

Through ritual we bring purpose and meaning into our lives, in the sense that ritual is the intense and concentrated expression of the purpose and meaning we believe but cannot (for a number of reasons) put into words. Ritual articulates the inexpressible. And, in terms of cultural context, I wonder whether ritual makers and celebrators in the biblical tradition have ever had the opportunity that is ours today. The history-making thrust of the biblical message is so wholly congenial to this revolutionary age. So many of the movements today are fragments of a vision that, for the believer, is whole in Jesus Christ and the kingdom.

The revolts about us (Black, Spanish-American, Mexican-American, women, American Indians, youth) and the demands of and challenges to so much that has been accepted for so long—these witness to a meaning we profess to see and signal a thirst for meaning we profess to share. Liturgy speaks to this situation, but is not heard except by a few. Until it is heard by the many, ritual needs reform.

6. Personal Experience of Hope

Finally, what liturgy does for the person, and what it can do much, much better than it ordinarily does, is afford an experience of hope. Closely related to the experience of meaning (as well as to the others), hope is an absolutely necessary enabler of Christian—and of all human—life.

"Faith is confident assurance concerning what we hope for, and conviction about things we do not see" (Hebrews 11:1). In his marvelously helpful book, referred to above, Harvey Cox points out that in a work-obsessed and fact-obsessed culture, we tend to think of the person primarily in only two ways: as worker and as thinker. He reminds us that "Western Christian culture, though we rightly speak of it as 'highly developed' in some senses, is woefully underdeveloped in others" (p. 15). "Man's celebrative and imaginative faculties have atrophied" (p. 11). "If festivity enables man to enlarge his experience by reliving events of the past, fantasy is a form of play that extends the frontiers of the future" (p. 8).

To enter into liturgical celebration is to enter into a very necessary and important kind of play and fantasy, eschatological play, play in which person and community insert themselves into a kingdom not yet fully realized or given. A kingdom of promise and of hope, where peace, equality, unity, love are the actual conditions of existence. A vision of the goal given in the midst of our struggle (dare we hope?) for it.

Good ritual, involving both spontaneous and programmed elements, relates our present life to the past events relived in festivity and, no less, to the kingdom future created in fantasy, in hope. Lewis Mumford justifies this kind of play: "Utopia has long been a name for the unreal and the impossible. We have set utopia over against the world. As a matter of fact, it is our utopias that make the world tolerable to us; the cities and mansions that people dream of are those in which they finally live" (*The Story of Utopias*, quoted in Cox, *op. cit.*, p. 82).

So much that passes for independent human enterprise in our culture wears the physiognomy of its ritual progenitor, I find it hard to accept the claims of humanist self-generation. It seems to me that it is to the bowels of faith as they are exposed in ritual that much of the hope which animates our society today can be traced. Whether this is true or not, ritual's kingdom fantasy and service of hope cannot be denied. Theology follows prayer, so it isn't surprising to hear Cox approve Jürgen Moltmann's statement "that theology has interpreted experience for long enough, that the thing to do now is to *change* it. This suggests that the task of theologians is not to come to terms with existing patterns of perception but to explode them, not merely to speak to existing social structures but to undermine them" (*op. cit.*, p. 135).

Leonard Bernstein seems to have perceived this fantasy-hope function of liturgy in his recent work, *Mass*, in which these words are sung to a haunting melody:

You can lock up the bold men
Go and lock up your bold men
and hold them in tow

You can stifle all adventure
for a century or so
Smother hope before it's risen
watch it wizen like a gourd
But you cannot imprison
the Word of the Lord . . .

So we wait in silent treason
until reason is restored
And we wait for the season of
the Word of the Lord.

LETTING SYMBOLS SPEAK

We have to be able to see a problem—we have to be able to identify something *as a problem*—before we can get to work on a solution. To help identify more clearly one of the most practical problems in liturgical renewal at the present time, please try to imagine yourself in this scene:

(1) A musical interlude ending with a crescendo preceded the reading of the word of the Lord. As the crescendo passage began, a minister carried to the celebrant, through the crowd standing around him, a very large (perhaps 26 by 18 inch), handsomely-bound book. He was accompanied by another minister, with smoking censer. The two walked slowly and with measured dignity. When they reached the celebrant, they stood facing him, the celebrant acknowledged them, touched and opened the book with marked deliberateness, found his place and waited calmly. The minister of the book held it in his hands, open toward the celebrant, its top resting on the minister's forehead or chest. The music reached its climax, ceased into a moment of anticipatory silence, and the celebrant began to read.

Now please try to imagine yourself in another scene, this one:

(2) The congregation had barely muttered its "Thanks be to God" after the second reading, when the lector continued rapidly: "Please join in the Alleluia on page ten. Alleluia, Alleluia, Alleluia." After she, like Bob and Ray, had said her song, her verse, the congregation repeated dully, "Alleluia, Alleluia, Alleluia." The lector retired. The presiding priest

shifted forward a foot from his chair, held up one of those little monthly newsprint missalettes, and, without any ceremony at all, read the gospel.

Both are accurate descriptions of recent experiences— fragmentary, but sufficient to make a point. The point is that a great many people who are planning and leading liturgical celebrations these days will spend time choosing a reading, deliberating on the particular translation of the scriptures to be employed, but will not give a thought to the atmosphere created by the action surrounding the reading, the visual and sign value of the way the reading is handled.

The first, of course, was not liturgical. It describes that section of Leonard Bernstein's *Mass: a theatre piece for singers, players and dancers,* as experienced in the audience at the Kennedy Center Opera House last September. The second, of course, was liturgical. It describes that part of a Sunday celebration in a good (in terms of liturgical concern and effort) parish in Washington, D. C., just a few weeks ago.

But what a difference between the audience in the first and the congregation in the second! In the first instance, everything that was done was done in earnest, with a respect and care that were visible in gesture and movement and the quality of all the materials employed. The audience could not help but feel this and sense it. So that, in many psychological ways, that audience became a congregation. We could not help but become involved, because the actors in the theatre piece were so involved, took what they were doing with such obvious seriousness, and did it with concern and care.

In the second, the congregation had to make heroic efforts to prevent itself from becoming a mere audience. And this despite the fact that the parish is not lazy or retrograde, but is widely considered superior for its liturgical celebrations. We suspect that the congregation had a hard time feeling involved, because the leaders didn't *seem* to feel involved, didn't *seem* to take seriously enough the things that they and we were doing. A congregation that takes the trouble to gather for public worship is hungering for an experience of reverence and wonder in the presence of God, of earnestness and seriousness in praise and prayer.

Comparing those two experiences, we get confused. Because, as the curtain had dropped on the very first performance of *Mass*, we had been assured on national television by two outstanding priest professors from the Catholic University of America that Bernstein had failed and that his failure was due to the fact that he simply didn't understand Catholic liturgy. The clear inference was that some people do understand it—namely, Catholics . . . especially clergy.

Symbols Are for Sensing

Now if Catholics, especially clergy, do understand their liturgy, then one would suppose that their celebration of it would come across with at least as much care and respect and reverence as Bernstein's *Mass* revealed and communicated. But it doesn't. Except in rare instances, it simply doesn't. And that's confusing.

One doesn't expect the ordinary parish to celebrate liturgy with Bernstein's musical talent, nor with the resources of an opera house production. One asks of it only a modest attention to the task being done and a modest sensiblity with respect to liturgy's constituent parts and people. You don't have to have money to begin to attend to the things you are doing and to try to become sensitive to them, to employ a minister or at least a fitting stand for the book, to use a large and handsome volume (or impressive cover, for loose-leaf materials) that is itself a visual witness to the importance of the word of God, to accent the reading with an interlude of silence if not of music (Bob and Ray actually thought the idea of saying songs was funny!) and to cultivate some style.

So far we have spoken of only one moment in one particular liturgical action—the eucharist. The same considerations apply to every other moment of significance in that sacrament as well as in every other liturgical service. What we have said so far is only a clue to the amount of work we have to do in rescuing symbol and symbolic gesture from their inhuman neglect.

We tend to be so terribly earnest about many things (mostly abstractions and cerebrations) that one wishes we could be just a little earnest about symbols. Both our commercial, technological culture and our intellectual, rationalist tradition militate against this kind of awakening to *things* and to the symbolic function of things, of which a genuine liturgical renewal stands so desperately in need.

Addressing some of the problems of the current cultural scene, sociologist Robert N. Bellah told the Federation of Diocesan Liturgical Commissions at their meeting in San Francisco last fall: "The intellectual formulas are like gutted empty houses, offering no protection against the cold wind of contemporary reality, not because they are untrue, but because contemporary Americans cannot discern their meaning . . . At the moment we need not so much an overall abstract explanation as to hear what the symbols—the bread and the wine, the fraction and the communion, the stone and the water—are saying. We need to let them speak and we need to listen. In our technological age we have been too concerned with the technique of liturgy, with its manipulation, rather than with listening and contemplation."

It is our feeling that Bellah's appeal is echoed—even if not at all articulated in the same fashion—by large numbers of Christians and former Christians. And by some who think of themselves as traditionalists or extreme conservatives. In our experience, people comment more warmly and respond more openly to a reverent style in celebration—a style that exposes the symbols as fully as possible and lets them speak . . . a style that exposes the symbols with love and care—than they do to advanced techniques of any kind.

The Disease of Iconoclasm

People who take a position with some feeling and emotion do not always articulate with great accuracy their reasons for taking that position. For example, not every Catholic who calls himself or herself a "traditionalist" is all that much in love with Latin, or with the rubrical insanity of the last few centuries. A rigid rubricism and the Latin tongue means something to many of these people that has really nothing at all to do with rubrics or with language. They mean an atmosphere in which people seemed to care, in which conventional signs (no matter how stiff they might have become) of a shared reverence were strong comfort, in which symbols (no matter how shriveled they might have become) seemed to be taken seriously.

And when some object to the symbols being opened up in liturgical renewal—to the waters of baptism becoming a real bath and the bread and wine of the eucharist a real shared meal—they may be misunderstanding and misstating their felt objection to what seems a crudely casual style and manner. When the ministers of public worship set about to try to help us cultivate the hospitable atmosphere that good liturgy requires and a healthier sacramental attitude than the overly-rigid, overly-mechanical one of our recent past, it is not easy to avoid over-reacting. The priest, for example, who becomes aware of the importance of the full symbolism of the shared meal in the eucharist may find himself tempted to turn iconoclast against every traditional gesture of reverence and of care. This is sad and unfortunate, but one can understand the over-reaction just as one can understand the traditionalist's nostalgia.

What prompts these thoughts is the repeated experience of seeing particular liturgical reforms introduced in one community with the generally pleased acceptance and edification of young and old, and in another community (the very same particular reforms) with violent polarization and antipathy. No single explanation is adequate in every instance. Communities have different characters, moods, temperaments, almost as people do. The presence or absence of good continuing catechesis is a significant factor. But another factor, we suspect, is the manner or style in which the reformed rite is celebrated.

Psychiatrists have pointed out something that most of us can recognize. In a faith tradition, a faith community, it is easy for us to identify our attachments and habits with our "devotion." In the course of that renewal, that constant effort at newness, which is a moral obligation of the Christian faith and church, whenever we are urged to separate ourselves from an attachment of the past we tend to regard it as an attack on our devotion. This is our perennial temptation.

We can overcome that temptation if we are persuaded that separation from the attachment, whatever it is, will in fact purify our faith and vivify our prayer. But if the effort to reform, renew, is accompanied by any manifestation of a spirit of iconoclasm, it is self-defeating. In that case, the temptation to retain attachments is strengthened and justified by the untruth apparent in the reformer's efforts. We may know perfectly well that the old practice, the attachment, has elements of superstition in it. But we know there were other things in it, too . . . better things. So when someone comes along to smash it as a false and superstitious practice, our good instincts join original sin, dig in, say "No," and stubbornly resist. When the evil always in us is joined by the unmasking of a lie or an exaggeration, renewal is licked—the combination is unbeatable.

The one who can help us overcome the temptation, achieve renewal steps and preserve the peace is the one who shows, demonstrates, illustrates clearly and convincingly that a reformed practice is not a rejection of what was felt as good in the past, but is indeed its development and its fuller realization. There is little problem, for example, with the administration of the eucharistic bread in the hand, when it is done with obvious reverence and care. There is a problem when the ministers of the sacrament, or those sharing it, feel that insouciance or crudity is the only authentic demonstration of the full extent of their enlightenment.

Sorting Things Out

Our rich (in symbols) ecclesial and liturgical tradition lays two burdens on us who agree heartily with Bellah and are anxious to respond to his appeal. First is the burden of sorting—conciliar times have been called "the time of the great sorting"—so that symbols with deep roots in the human historical experience of Jesus and his message are lifted into sight, above the swamp of cultural accretions. Primary symbols must be identified and distinguished, so that the message of Jesus and reconciliation is not lost in a crowd of peripheral figures. Second is the burden of revealing the symbols fully and handling them well, letting them speak, enabling their peculiar language, never permitting our words to over-explain the symbol itself, or drown it out, or reduce it to a mere occasion for comment.

Sorting is essential activity in any time of renewal. Henri de Lubac, twenty-five years ago, said it as well as anybody: "So that the river of tradition may come down to us, we must continually dredge its bed." Sorting is like dredging the bed of the river, so that the moving currents, the primary symbols, can make their way with some purity and power into the lives of the people. It isn't necessarily for the sake of throwing anything away. It is for the sake of discrimination. So that we can tell—and other people can tell—what we Christians are about.

Our lack of sorting, our lack of discrimination is a terrible handicap in our mission of witness to Jesus and his way. It confuses us, and it confuses our hearers even more. When we seem to assign to the Roman collar the same priority we assign to the bathing waters of baptism, or when we defend mandatory celibacy with the same fervor with which we defend the reconciling office and witness of a collegial ministry (including episcopacy), or . . . (the examples are legion)—then we seem to be inviting people to a cultural melee, not a following of Jesus. In the immortal words of a very good play ("The Basic Training of Pavlo Hummel"): "Ain't that some kind o' world?"

"Ain't that some kind o' world?" When the church, simply by its failure to sort and to discriminate and to get a clearer view of its own priorities, presents a countenance so confused and so confusing that Jesus and the gospel become an object of Ph.D. research? When a person who is searching for meaning, searching for spiritual experience, searching for the freedom of the sons and daughters of God—and who may even suspect that Jesus is relevant to this quest—is turned off by the unsorted features of the very institution which exists to stimulate and aid and offer collaboration and perseverance in that same kind of search?.

We can't be blamed for living in history, and humanly, and for collecting cultural accretions (or enrichment). We *can* be blamed as church for allowing these accretions (or this enrichment) to render the primary realities and the primary symbols indistinguishable.

English artist Eric Gill was a hero of our younger if not better years. In his *Autobiography* (London: Jonathan Cape, 1940, p. 93), he wrote: "It was a long time before I realized that rationalism [editor's note: in those days the word lacked its current connotations] and humility and poverty were all in the same boat and longer still before I realized what that boat was. I do not blame myself for this, for I suppose nothing on earth is more completely camouflaged than Peter's barque, which, from a short distance, looks exactly like the Ritz Palace Hotel."

The sorting has begun, but it's not fast enough, and it does not yet show sufficiently in the symbols of that public worship which is our key activity as church. *We can make it show*—we who are bishops, pastors, liturgy committees, parish priests, planners and ministers in celebrations. This is a practical pastoral problem which all of us can tackle right now.

Letting Primary Things Speak

As we sort, we have to make sure that in our celebrations the primary symbols speak the loudest and the clearest. In the eucharist, for example, there are a great many things we can do (none of them terribly difficult) to emphasize primary symbols and let them speak. We mentioned earlier how Bernstein handled the book and the symbols of the word of the Lord. We can hardly do less. The pax is a climactic eucharistic symbol, of prime importance in the sacrament of unity and the sacrament of peace. But, above all, the bread and the wine and the sharing of all in holy communion are the realities that must tower over everything else at mass.

"It is he who is our peace" (Ephesians 2:14): the real presence of Jesus in sacrament, in symbol, as the agent of our unity in sharing. Bread and wine will be real bread and wine, touched and tasted, seen and felt as bread and wine . . . broken and poured out in the sharing . . . and all with a sense and style of mystery and sacrament.

In the talk quoted above, Bellah, himself a Protestant, pleaded with his Catholic audience: "Guard the real presence! Do not let the eucharist sink into memory and commemoration as the Protestants have done. I do not mean guard theories about the real presence, transubstantiation or whatever, for the real presence is not a theory—it is an experienced, present spiritual reality. That is its power for us . . ."

It is not convenient to reveal the symbols, to let the primary things speak. If convenience is the measure, then little wafers will continue to be used and the cup with continue to be withheld. Any pastor knows that the General Instruction of the New Roman Missal includes contradictory (at least at this time and in this culture) requirements with regard to the bread used in the eucharist: that it be apparent as bread, as "actual food," and capable of being broken and distributed . . . and also that it be unleavened. To let the symbol speak is to give the first requirement a clear priority and opt for it. This necessitates the kind of pastoral decision that liturgical renewal requires frequently, and that Second Vatican recognized in its constitution on the sacred liturgy, No. 11.

In baptism, for another example, bathing waters will be bathing waters, experienced as bathing waters, seen and felt and heard (splash!) as bathing waters. We have seen pages on how to make the celebration of baptism more meaningful which did not even refer to the central and essential symbol in that sacrament—the actual washing with water. Immersion should become normal again. In the rare cases where it is not feasible, then, at least, as Father James Savage of Boston emphasized at the New England Liturgical Week last August, the pouring should be over the whole body—never merely over the head.

In every sacrament, the presence of Jesus, of the Spirit, of grace—God-consciousness—must be communicated more by manner, gesture, style than by words. So opening up the symbols, letting them be themselves, letting them speak, involves not only using the right materials but also using them well, with the care and the conventional reverence of which we spoke above.

Seriousness Is Not Somberness

This seriousness and earnestness about symbols has nothing to do with somberness or lugubriousness. Liturgy is festivity and fantasy and play. Play is to be taken seriously but not somberly. The Christian who would serve liturgical renewal and make public worship serve its purpose must learn how to play—against all of his capitalist and rationalist instincts. This is not as easy as it sounds, and its difficulty accounts for the fact that many priests and liturgical leaders who are trying to be progressive and helpful are really neither. Carelessness is not the same as play. Sloppiness is not the same as festivity. The inability to appreciate and value real things is not the same as fantasy.

When we talk about cultivating some style in celebration, we are not talking about false fronts or phoniness. We are trying to face a fundamental fact: the intimacy and informality of manner appropriate in a group of six people is as phony as a "marbleized" altar in a group of 50 or 500. Yet many of us who are leading liturgical celebrations seem to feel that there is something unreal or unauthentic about working on a discipline of style in the speech, gesture, bearing, clothing, etc., of the larger celebration. All we can think of is the old "pulpit tone," the sacred alias that presiding clergy used to assume whenever they were functioning as such. We don't want *that* at all . . . ever. But boorishness is not the only alternative to that. A patently unreal "intimacy" is not the only alternative to that. Phoniness in the other direction—pretending that every relationship in the liturgical assembly is primary and close—is just as repulsive as the pulpit tone of old.

Primary gestures—of greeting, honoring, blessing—should be broad and fully executed, involving the whole body, and summoning the whole bodies of the others in the assembly. The presider or the leader cannot make any gestures at all if he is clutching papers, books, leaflets, hymnals, and other paraphernalia. The materials he or she needs should be combined—either by looseleaf method or by paper-clipping to the pages of a precious volume (in either case, with a large and impressive cover and binding)—so that one book can be used by the presiding bishop or minister throughout. If a large Bible is used for the readings, then two at the most. In use, the book will be carried by a minister or placed on lectern or altar, freeing gesture.

When the tabernacle of reservation is moved to a proper place, apart from the eucharistic hall, or, at least, apart from the altar area, conventional (bowing) gestures of reverence to the altar, to the congregation and ministers, especially at the entrance and exit and any other strikingly appropriate times, should be carefully maintained. The old habitual tabernacle genuflexion forced a sometimes cursory but nevertheless consistent style, which did more for feeling of reverence than we like to give it credit for. Now that we are concerned about the creation of a truly hospitable atmosphere in the liturgical assembly—with people being welcomed and introduced to each other so that they begin to feel at home and capable of praying in common—such common gestures may be more important than ever.

It is not a remarkable advance if the "old" altar as a shelf for tabernacle, relics, statues, altar cards, candles, crucifix, and the rest, is replaced by the "new" altar as a shelf for programs, music sheets, book, Bibles, utensils, and the rest. If one wants to diminish or destroy the symbolism of the altar, the new method is even more effective than the old. If, however, it should become free of clutter—the holy table of the holy meal of the community of faith—and used only at the proper time and only for the bread and wine and book, then it does not seem odd to bow before it.

Once we have discriminated the symbols that are central and climactic in each rite, relating to Jesus as Savior and to his gospel of reconciliation as the point of it all, then we can assume the burden of fashioning and handling and using those symbols in such a way that they speak with maximal effect. "At the moment we need . . . to hear what the symbols . . . are saying."